300 MORE BEERS TO TRY BEFORE YOU DIE!

D1419775

ROGER PROTZ

CAMPAIGN
FOR
REAL ALE

'Filled with mingled cream and amber, I will drain that glass again

Such hilarious visions clamber through the chamber of my brain

Quaintest thoughts, queerest fancies, come to life and fade away:

What care I how time advances? I am drinking ale today'

Edgar Allan Poe

Published by the Campaign for Real Ale Ltd.
230 Hatfield Road, St Albans, Hertfordshire AL1 4LW

www.camra.org.uk/books

Design and layout © Campaign for Real Ale Ltd. 2013
Text copyright © Roger Protz

ISBN: 978-1-85249-295-3

A CIP catalogue record for this book is available from the British Library

Printed and bound in China by 1010 Printing International Ltd

Head of Publishing: Simon Hall
Project Manager: Katie Hunt
Editorial Assistance: Emma Haines
Design: Stephen Bere
Additional Research: Adam Protz
Marketing Manager: Chris Lewis

ACKNOWLEDGEMENTS
This book was made possible by the support of brewers, suppliers and fellow beer writers in many countries. Thanks are due in the UK to Nigel Stevenson of James Clay and David O'Neill of Morgenrot for supplying samples of imported beer; to Cécile Delorme of the specialist beer shop Brewberry in Paris (brewberry.fr) for recommending French beers; in Ireland Mia Tobin of Brewery Hops (breweryhops.com) and John Duffy of Beior; in Belgium, Ben Vinken of Beer Passion magazine; in the United States Daniel Bradford, Julie Johnson and their colleagues at *All About Beer* magazine; in Australia Matthew Kirkegaard, David Lipman and Kirrily Waldhorn; in New Zealand Neil Miller. My thanks and apologies to all the brewers I emailed, phoned and badgered for information, often at the most inappropriate times of the day and night. To Adam Protz for additional research. Special, heartfelt thanks to Simon Hall and Katie Hunt at CAMRA Books for their support and seeing the long and exhausting project through to completion.

The Publisher would like to thank the breweries for their kind permission in reproducing these photographs. All photographs have been provided by the breweries except:
beergenie.co.uk: p16, p17, p18 (top), p19 (bottom), p23
Cath Harries: p20, p21, p22, p23, p73, p76
Katherine Longley: p258, p259
Bernt Rostad (flickr): p313
U.S. Department of Agriculture: p19 (top)
Warminster Maltings: p18 (bottom)

Contents

Introduction

In the world of beer, the pace of change is breathtaking. New breweries blaze a trail like comets, responding to the demand from drinkers for beers with character and flavour. There's now a dizzying choice available in both established beer-drinking countries and in nations where wine once ruled the roost. Along with the clamour for good beer has come great interest in the styles available. Brewers have dug deep into history books to recreate and revive such great beers as India Pale Ale, porter and stout. But modern brewers are innovators, too, and new types of beer, ranging from intensely fruity golden ales to some infused with herbs, spices, chocolate, and coffee beans, attract people who have never before given beer a second thought.

On my travels I have marvelled not only at the diversity of beers available but also the cross-pollination between brewers in different countries. In the autumn of 2011, I gave seminars on India Pale Ale at a beer festival in Durham, North Carolina, in the sylvan setting of the Durham Bulls baseball ground. IPA was once considered a quintessentially English style. It was brewed principally in Burton-on-Trent as a result of the fine brewing water there, and it was developed originally for export to 'the Raj' in the Indian outpost of the British Empire. IPA was a beer designed to travel and it has lived up to that reputation in recent years. In the United States in particular there has been a veritable explosion of interest in IPA, to such an extent that American brewers, with an unbridled exuberance for the subject, have gone the extra mile and fashioned stronger interpretations dubbed Double and Imperial IPAs. In *300 Beers to Try Before You Die*, first published in 2005, there were just 11 versions of IPA. In this successor volume, there are 34 and only restraints on space stopped me from including more.

Not to be outdone, British brewers have also rekindled an interest in IPA, while the style has found favour in Australia, New Zealand and even Belgium. I have twice visited Australia to take part in a major festival, Beer Expo, in Melbourne. It's a country that epitomises the beer revolution. For decades it was held in the fizzy sway of such lager brands as Castlemaine and Carlton Draught, with the only notable ale, Cooper's, dismissed as a museum piece. Today's Cooper's Sparkling Ale is a growing national brand while dozens of new breweries have sprung up to offer much-needed choice for drinkers. Both Australian and New Zealand brewers are heavily influenced by brewing practice in the northern hemisphere and produce IPAs, Belgian-style wheat beers and fruit beers, porters, stouts and American pale ales. But, in common with their wine-making colleagues, they also bring their own New World verve to brewing and are carving out their distinctive interpretations of classic styles.

North and south of the Equator, Belgium remains the country all others seek to emulate. With its aston-ishing range of beers – abbey, Trappist, sour red, spontaneous fermentation, spiced wheat, pale and golden ales, strong brown ales and saison, to mention a few – Belgium remains an inspiration to brewers through-out the world. Many American, Australian, British, Italian and New Zealand brewers have Belgian-style beers in their portfolios. But beers unique to their countries of origin are not neglected. In Ireland, for example, 20 or more small breweries have emerged from under the giant shadow of Guinness to revive the long-neglected style, red ale. They have also brought back true Cork and Dublin stouts along with plain porter, beers that inspired literary luminaries such as James Joyce, Flann O'Brien and Brendan Behan.

The brewing tidal wave has left the producers of global industrial beers panting in its wake. While they dominate the former Eastern Bloc in Europe and other 'emerging nations' with their industrial brands, in their older, established markets they see sales decline as the demand for handcrafted beers grows. The brewing giants respond in the only way they know: takeover. In Australia, Britain and the U.S., Lion Nathan, Molson Coors, AB InBev and Miller have either bought or taken substantial stakes in successful independent breweries. But the giants have seen the way the whirlwind is blowing. In the 1960s and 70s, takeovers were followed either by brewery closures or dumbing down of products. Today the global producers are bowing to consumer demand. Sharp's in Cornwall, for example, has flourished under Molson Coors and has added a Connoisseur's Choice range of handcrafted ales to its range: it is well-represented in this book. In the U.S., Anheuser-Busch and Miller are happy to act merely as distributors for the craft breweries in which they have an investment. Even the Belgian end of AB InBev has learnt to fear the wrath of beer lovers. With mind-numbing insensitivity, it closed the Hoegaarden brewery in a Dutch-speaking part of the country and transferred the famous spiced wheat beer to the Jupiler factory in Francophone Liège. The resulting uproar forced InBev to scuttle back to Hoegaarden and remove the brewery from its mothballs. It's to be hoped that at the same time it discovered you can't brew a warm-fermented wheat beer in a lager plant.

The producers of handcrafted beer are not challenging the power of the global giants, with their vast marketing muscle and promotional prowess. Independents are offering something distinctively different: the beer equivalent of freshly-ground coffee and slow-fermented bread. They are enjoyed by drinkers who are not frightened by aroma and flavour, and who accept the challenge of beers with profound characters based on rich malt, zingy hops and tart, tantalising fruit.

Flavour is at the heart of the world-wide beer revival. Creative brewers have joined forces with farmers to use a wide variety of pale and dark malts and other grains to make beers with biscuit, coffee, chocolate, smoky and burnt fruit flavours. But beer marches on two feet and hops have become one of the key elements of the revival. Inspired mainly by American brewers, many new hop varieties have appeared in recent years, adding tart, citrus and spicy character to beer. As a result, beer drinkers can now match their wine counterparts by discussing the merits of Amarillo from the U.S. and Nelson Sauvin from New Zealand with as much passion and knowledge as the proponents of Cabernet and Zinfandel grapes.

There has also been an energetic debate in recent years involving how beer is served. Different countries have different traditions. As a British-based beer writer, I believe the finest, freshest and most flavoursome beer is the result of 'cask conditioning', where live beer enjoys a second fermentation in the pub cellar. Other countries store and serve beer from kegs rather than casks, often first filtering and/or pasteurising it and using air, carbon dioxide or mixed gas to deliver the beer to the bar. But older habits survive. If you visit one of the Munich beer gardens in the summer you will see beer being delivered in casks, sometimes made of wood, and served using the natural pressure created by lagering or ageing in the brewery cellars.

This book respects different traditions. It's dedicated to *good* beer rather than industrial beer. You can make a beverage called beer from rice, maize, hop juice and industrial enzymes but they find no favour here. It's a book with a choice of beers I hope will appeal not only to connoisseurs but also to people discovering flavoursome beer for the first time.

Fuller's Bengal Lancer makes reference to the historic origins of IPA

There are many surprises along the way that stress the astonishing changes in the world of brewing and the influences older brewing nations have on younger ones. Arguably the most fascinating of my trips in the course of researching and writing this book was to the Naples region of Italy. This is southern Italy, wine country. But I was invited to take part in 'an evening of handcrafted beer and food' at a specialist bar and restaurant, Ottovonano, in Atripalda. The following day, I was taken to a small brewery, Il Chiostro – the Cloister – close to Monte Cassino, the abbey founded by St Benedict: his strict Trappist followers still make fine beers in Belgium and the Netherlands. Il Chiostro, with Mount Vesuvius glowering ominously in the background, is run by Simone Della Porta who naturally brews a porter and also a Scotch ale. The latter was the result of a visit to Edinburgh and a tour of the Caledonian Brewery there.

Simone Della Porta has been on a voyage of discovery. It's a voyage that knows no boundaries. Just as I was finishing this book, I was asked on Twitter if I had tried 'the new beers from Mexico'. Not yet I replied, but clearly the voyage and the adventure go on.

Thornbridge has established itself as a key player in modern British brewing

A magic carpet ride: the world-wide beer revival

Hyperbole needs to be backed by statistics. The beer revival is underscored by the fast rate of new breweries coming on stream. In 2005, when *300 Beers to Try Before You Die* was published, I recorded 500 independent breweries in Britain. When the book was updated in 2009, the number had grown to more than 700. Today there are over 1,100 independent breweries in Britain. Not to be outdone, the United States, which had 1,200 'craft breweries' in operation in 2009, has seen that number grow to 2,360 by 2013: the term 'craft brewery' in the U.S. means one that produces up to six million barrels a year. In both countries, lower rates of duty for smaller brewers have given their sectors a major fillip that has helped drive their success. Today, it's only beers from the small independent sectors in Britain and the U.S. that show growth in an otherwise declining market dominated by global producers.

But the dramatic increase in the number of brewers, their beers and market share are not due just to lower rates of duty. As I stressed in the introduction, it's also rooted in the fact that an increasing number of drinkers are seeking beers with rich and profound flavours and are not deterred, in particular, by strong hop character. Drinkers are also concerned by the ingredients used to make beer and their places of origin. Such wine terms as 'provenance' and *'terroir'* have spilled over into beer as consumers demand to know the malt and hop varieties used and where beers are made. It's clear from both industry statistics and personal observation in pubs, bars and at beer festivals that young people in particular are ignoring mass marketing hype and are joining the demand for quality beer.

British brewers such as Freedom are now brewing 'real' unpasteurised lager

The British Isles
Great Britain

The transformation of the British brewing scene can be measured most effectively by comparing the first CAMRA *Good Beer Guide*, published in 1974, with the 2013 edition. In 1974, the Guide's brewery section ran to just 124 entries over two pages. The current edition lists more than 1,000 in a section totalling 252 pages, and since it went to press the number has grown to 1,100. In 1974, most brewers produced just two types of beer, Mild and Bitter, with occasionally stronger ale for Christmas. Today, while Mild and Bitter remain important parts of brewers' portfolios, they are joined by a profusion of styles both old and new. The new generation of brewers, many of whom started out brewing at home, have a great passion for beer style and have dug deep into old recipe books. As a result, drinkers are now offered Porters, Stouts, IPAs, old ales and barley wines. But the greatest change has been a new style rather than an old one. Golden ale, first produced as a summer refresher by a handful of brewers, has become a dominant style, to such effect that CAMRA has introduced a new section for it in the annual Champion Beer of Britain competition. Golden ale, made usually with just pale malt, has served a double purpose: it has weaned younger drinkers away from mainstream lager brands; and it has enabled beers to zing with great hop aroma and flavour.

Hops have come in to their own in recent years. As a result of the tireless work of a growing band of beer writers and the willingness of brewers to reveal the ingredients they use, drinkers have been made aware of the myriad of hop varieties and hop flavours available. Many brewers now import hops from around the world, with American and New Zealand varieties especially popular. Several have seized on two new hops, American Citra and New Zealand Nelson Sauvin, to fashion beers with massive notes of citrus fruit and pine. One major brewing group, Marston's of Burton-on-Trent, launched in 2012 and repeated in 2013 a series of seasonal 'single varietal' beers with hops drawn from a number of countries. The base is the

Thistle Whet Your Whistle!

Scotland now has more that 50 independent breweries

same for each brew, made from pale malt only, but hops come from the U.S., Germany, the Czech Republic, Poland, Australia and New Zealand as well as England. The project has been a great success and has helped drinkers to develop a deeper understanding and appreciation of the role of the hop in beer-making.

The pace of change in Britain has been most notable in Scotland. The country has been dominated for decades by two giants, Scottish Brewers (now Heineken) and Tennents, but today there are more than 50 independent breweries bringing much needed choice to drinkers. As well as traditional Scottish styles, such as 70 and 80 Shilling ales, many of the new providers are offering pale and golden ales along with rich-tasting Stouts.

Emboldened by the success of golden ales, British brewers now look abroad for inspiration. Many have added American-style pale ales and IPAs to their repertoires. Honey, spices and real coffee and chocolate are added to beers. Aware of the success of Innis & Gunn's Oak Aged range of beers (see *300 Beers to Try Before You Die!*), a number of brewers are ageing beer in wine and whisky barrels. Even more remarkably, a few brewers are making proper, aged lagers, including Bock, which put to shame the bland apologies for lager from the global brewers based in Britain.

Ireland

Stout is a vital element of Ireland's long struggle for independence, to such an extent that the Irish state and Guinness share the harp as their national symbol. But I was struck when I toured some of the country's new breweries in 2012 by the number of people who told me they view Guinness today as a 'British company', part of Diageo with its head office in London. They feel Guinness has lost its way and its distinctive Irishness. The two other main Irish Stouts, Beamish and Murphy's in Cork, are owned by Heineken. It's this domination of the country by two global giants that has helped fuel the rise of small, independent breweries. The catalyst was Porterhouse in Dublin, which now has three pubs in the capital and a large brewery in the suburbs. It has revived a Dublin speciality, Plain Porter, immortalised by the writer Flann O'Brien, as well as a type of Stout that once found favour with the revolutionary leader Michael Collins. It also brews Ireland's own distinctive interpretation of pale ale, red ale.

There are now some 20 breweries in the north and the Republic. The inspirations are both home-grown and international, with a range of red ales, Porters and Stouts joined by American-inspired hoppy pale ales, golden ales, barley wines and well-made lagers. Irish beer lovers may regret that Guinness has become a British company but brewers are happy to adopt British methods of brewing. A number of the new independents are producing both cask and bottle-conditioned beers.

The Irish beer revival has not gone unnoticed in the board rooms of the beer giants. Early in 2013, Molson Coors, the Canadian-American brewer, swooped on the Franciscan Well brewery in Cork, which has a fine range of Stout, red ale, pale ale, golden ale and even a Belgian-style abbey beer. Molson Coors plans to build a large new brewery outside the city that will be used specifically to make Stout for the American market. It's a development that will be monitored with a degree of trepidation. Will Franciscan Well be allowed to make beers of the highest quality or will dumbing-down follow? And will Guinness, with a long and far-from-noble history of buying and closing smaller Irish breweries, protect its base by going on the takeover trail?

Ireland's new breweries are offering drinkers a
home-grown alternative to mass-produced brands

Western Europe

We have to begin with Belgium, the country that has achieved iconic status among both beer drinkers and brewers in other lands. I am always struck by the fact that when I visit Belgium I come across as many visitors as natives. My most recent visit to the Cantillon lambic brewery and museum coincided with the arrival of a large number of Americans keen to tour the site and sample the beers. At the Bruges beer festival in February 2013, as I queued to enter the magnificent medieval belfry in the main square where the event is staged, I was greeted by many familiar British faces. Many CAMRA members were working at the festival as either stewards or servers. A short walk away, in the Brugs Beertje, one of the world's great beer bars that sells every known Belgian beer – but no lager – it was wall-to-wall Brits.

That is Belgium's problem. As Tim Webb, author of six editions of the *Good Beer Guide Belgium*, points out, 60 per cent of Belgian beer is exported. Drinkers in other countries are more knowledgeable about beer from Belgium than many locals, who are happy to drink uninspired Pils. Brewing is dominated by two giants, AB InBev (Belle-Vue, Hoegaarden, Jupiler and Stella Artois) and Heineken (Affligem, Alken-Maes and Morte Subite).

The onslaught of Pils brewing throughout the 20th century led to a tragic diminution in the number of producers of the country's greatest and singular contribution to the world of beer: lambic and gueuze. Now only a handful are left and the style is often traduced by the giant brewers with easy-drinking interpretations, the fruit versions of which are sickly sweet as the result of the use of syrups rather than whole fruit.

The same criticism can be aimed at some – but not all – brewers of abbey beers. Many abbeys ceased to brew or lost their beer-making equipment as a result of wars stretching back to Napoleonic times. It seems perfectly reasonable for the monks to work with commercial brewers to make beer using the monasteries' names in return for royalties that help maintain the churches. But many abbey beers, despite images of cheery monks and stained glass windows, have no ecclesiastical connections and the products are not even bottle-conditioned in the true Trappist fashion.

But great beers can still be found. Cafés and bars often have beer lists that indicate the brews available. Using both this book and Tim Webb's guide you will never be far from a good Belgian beer. That holds true in other countries, too, as a result of the substantial amount of beer that's exported. And Belgium has a long reach. In Britain, the U.S. and as far away as Australia and New Zealand you will find local beers inspired by the Belgian experience. There is a new Trappist brewery operating in a remote apart of Austria while the monks at Chimay have helped an abbey in northern France to return to the Trappist fold. In England the monks of Ampleforth Abbey, with more than a little help from their Belgian brothers, have restored a tradition lost at the time of Henry VIII.

The Netherlands, despite its proximity to Dutch-speaking Belgium, offers a fraction of the choice available across the nominal border. The country is dominated to such an awesome extent by Heineken that 'ubiquitous' fails to do its control justice. What isn't run by Heineken is mainly in the hands of Grolsch, a proud family brewery until the early 21st century when it sold its soul in return for a large cheque from SABMiller. There are a handful of small independents, with Brand, Gulpener and St Christophel featured in *300 Beers to Try Before You Die!*, along with the Trappist beers from Koninghoeven. Beers from the independents range from good Pils-type lagers to warm-fermenting ales that include pale ale, blond, brown, Dutch versions of Bock and even a few lambic-style beers. Among brewpubs, Ij in Amsterdam is one of the longest-serving and its bar beneath a windmill is worth a visit to taste its idiosyncratic ales.

France is so revered as the home of the world's finest wines that many people find it hard to believe the country also has a brewing tradition. But if you dine in a *brasserie* you are using the services of what is, strictly speaking, a brewery. Few French bars brew on the premises these days though Les Trois Brasseurs, a brewpub founded in Lille, now has 20 similar outlets throughout the country. Le Frog and Rosbif, a Paris brewpub inspired by the former Firkin chain in England, has seven outlets. Beer-drinking and the appreciation

TOP: **Veltins Pilsener, Germany**

BOTTOM: **Liefmans, Belgium**

of the subject are growing. The country is dominated by Kronenbourg lager, based in the Alsace region with its powerful Germanic history and traditions. Kronenbourg is owned by Carlsberg of Denmark while another large Alsace lager group, Fischer, is controlled by Heineken. But in French Flanders in the far north a quite different tradition of warm-fermented ales known as *bières de garde* – keeping beers – survives and flourishes. Ale brewing is spreading. There are several new breweries in Normandy, the traditional home of cider, with one run with considerable chutzpah by a British ex-pat. And brewing has made the journey as far south as the Ardèche while beer with the addition of the finest brandy can be found in Cognac itself.

Italian acquaintances once told me they looked on beer as a quick summer refresher. But younger drinkers are ignoring their elders and are turning to beer in growing numbers. The interest in beer can be seen by the arrival of global breweries in Italy. The main Italian group, Peroni, has been bought by SABMiller while its main rival, Moretti, is now part of Heineken. But there is a counter-culture. A specialist course at the University of Udine teaches brewing skills to a new generation while the University of Gastronomie, which is linked to the influential Slow Food movement, also holds seminars on brewing and world beer styles. The pace of change has been faster in Italy than most other countries. There are now some 300 breweries. They are small and include a number of brewpubs, run by people with a great passion for American, British and, in particular, Belgian styles. Love of good beer and brewing are spreading as far south as the Naples region.

Germany is far and away the biggest brewing nation in Europe, world-famous for the quality of both its lager and wheat beers. It has around 1,250 breweries, a figure that includes brewpubs. That is roughly the same number as in Britain but German drinkers consume far greater volumes of beer. While a number of new brewpubs have opened in recent years, the market is so crowded that it's difficult for new entrants to set up in business. But the once-cosy German beer scene, rooted in the universal production of Pils, with wheat beers in Bavaria and such ales as Kölsch in Cologne and Alt in Düsseldorf, is undergoing change. It's a change that once seemed unthinkable in such a bastion of brewing. Foreign intervention was considered impossible as a result of the *Reinheitsgebot*, the 16th-century purity law that permits only malted barley or wheat, hops and yeast and water to be used in brewing. But the European Union, egged on by the lager brewers of Alsace who were keen to cross the Rhine with their products, declared the *Reinheitsgebot* to be a restrictive practice.

Most German brewers claim they still adhere to the *Reinheitsgebot* for domestic production but may use cheaper ingredients for export. Relaxation of the brewing disciplines has encouraged global brewers to enter the once closed shop. In Hamburg, mighty Holsten is now owned by Carlsberg of Denmark, fitting retribution some may feel for the loss of Schleswig-Holstein to the Prussians in the 19th century. Also in the north, Beck's is owned by AB InBev, while in the far south, such titans of Munich brewing as Löwenbräu and Spaten have also fallen into the hands of AB InBev. Paulaner, creator of the classic Bock style, is owned by Heineken, which also controls another large Munich group, Hacker-Pschorr.

There has been considerable concentration of ownership from within Germany, too. The Dr Oetker group, best known for cakes and pizza, owns Binding, Henninger and Jever and has reduced Dortmund, once called the Burton-on-Trent of Germany, to just one producer. But visitors need not fear. The tart wheat beers of Bavaria along with black Dunkel lagers, and the ales of Cologne and Düsseldorf are still superb, while to drink the smoked Rauchbier of Bamberg is to enter beer paradise.

Central and Eastern Europe

Following the fall of communism, breweries in the former Soviet bloc have been energetically vacuumed up by global brewers from the west. Carlsberg, Heineken and SABMiller have been especially active in the vast region. The Czech Republic, which emerged from former Czechoslovakia, maintained both a large number of breweries and a deeply-rooted beer culture under communism: the state did not interfere with breweries that could boast the world's first golden lager from Pilsen and the original Budweiser beers. But with the exception of Budweiser Budvar, still owned by the government, such famous names as Pilsner Urquell, Staropramen, Gambrinus and Kozel are all in such global hands as SABMiller and AB InBev. Spurred by the interest created by Budvar's Yeast Beer – an unfiltered and unpasteurised lager – Pilsner Urquell is now offering a similar beer. Dark lagers remain popular and a number of new breweries, mainly brewpubs, have emerged to offer greater choice. One welcome arrival has been Konrad in the far north, close to the German border in the former Sudetenland. The brewery was owned and closed by the British group Bass, which also ran Staropramen (now AB InBev) in Prague. The substantial Konrad plant has been reopened by a local businessman who is vigorously exporting his beers.

Gambrinus and Pilsner Urquell can both lay claim to the name Pilsner – a beer 'from Pilsen'

Poland has followed a similar course to the Czech Republic. There are some 70 breweries in the country but the vast majority of beer produced comes from groups owned by global giants: Carlsberg with Okocim, Heineken with Žwyiec and SABMiller with Tyskie. Their brands tend to be ubiquitous. But small independents and brewpubs have emerged and the Gdansk region is becoming a good place to drink. Even the beer giants have retained their faith in Polish Porters, originally based on the English style exported to the Baltic but which have morphed into strong and full-bodied black lagers.

During the Soviet period, beer for Russians meant thin lagers sold in bottles and made by state-controlled breweries. There were 700 breweries scattered throughout the vast country, most producing beer under the Zhigulevskoye name. Not surprisingly, most Russians stuck with vodka. Following the collapse of the regime, Zhigulevskoye was briefly exported but without success. In Britain it was labelled Zhiguli with the grotesque tag line 'The beer that grabs you by Zhigulis'. It sank without trace – or failed to drop. Back in the USSR, the global brewers moved in. Carlsberg is now far and away the biggest player in Russia, owning the Baltika brands that are brewed in large plants strategically scattered throughout the country. The main independent, Tinkoff, offered a chain of brewpubs that were sufficiently successful for the owner to build a stand-alone brewery. The brewery was eventually bought and closed by Heineken while Mint Capital bought the pubs and the main brand, Tinkoff Gold, has disappeared. Imperial Stouts and Porters, once a great feature of pre-Soviet Russia, have made a comeback as small independents emerge. But they have a major battle on their hands in a country where young drinkers think canned beer is cool.

Nøgne ø brewery, Norway

Nordic countries

For more than a century, beer in Denmark meant Carlsberg or Tuborg, two breweries that eventually merged into one. If you didn't like bland lager, then you didn't drink in Denmark. But now it's a dynamic and exciting place, with scores of new small breweries opening and offering a wide variety of styles. They are influenced in the main by the American experience, though not all consumers appreciate 'extreme beers'. But dark beers and Belgian-style beers are appearing. The pace setter for change and for interest in both a diversity of styles and the use of unusual ingredients is Mikkeler, which is dubbed a 'gypsy brewery' as it owns no plant of its own but produces collaboration brews with other companies as far flung as in Alaska.

Norway has also been in the grip of beer giants, with such main brands as Hansa and Ringes owned by Heineken and Carlsberg. Choice came from the independent Aass brewery, which fortunately is pronounced 'Oss' and means a low hill. It's the country's oldest brewery and makes a highly regarded Bock style lager. The range of beer is improving with the emergence of several micro-breweries, of which Nøgne is the pace-setter with a substantial portfolio that include an imperial stout.

Sweden has the dubious distinction of offering the most heavily taxed beers on the planet, with brands for take home sold only through the state-owned Systembolaget stores. In such a regimented market, it's not surprising that production is dominated by one giant, Carlsberg, which owns Falcon and Pripps. Spendrups is a long-standing independent that makes some good lager beers, including Old Gold (see *300 Beers to Try Before You Die!*). A handful of small independents have emerged in recent years, of which Nils Oscar is the best-known as it has a vigorous export policy. Drinkers can now enjoy a choice that includes barley wine, Porter, Stout, an Irish-style red ale and some single hop pale ales such as Amarillo from a number of micros and brewpubs.

Finland is living proof of that fact that, as with American Prohibition in the 1920s, severe restrictions on alcohol are counter-productive. Finnish beer is massively taxed and take-home sales are restricted to state stores known by the risible name of Alko. The scheme is undermined by the vast amounts of cheap alcohol that pour into the country on the ferries from Estonia, accounting for twice as much beer as Alko sells. More than 90 per cent of home-brewed beer is controlled by Heineken – Hartwall and Lapin Kulta – and Carlsberg – Sinebrychoff. Remarkably, a small number of micros and brewpubs have opened in recent years, with the Tempere brewery establishing itself as a serious presence. Drinkers long starved of choice can now find pale ale, Baltic Porter, Stout, properly-brewed lager and even a Finnish version of lambic.

Iceland's beer scene has been enlivened by the Einstök brewery, which is well represented in this book and offers pale ale, toasted Porter and Doppelbock.

China and Japan

In brewing terms, China is a far-away country of which we know little. Consumption of beer is low but, as a result of its vast population, the country is the biggest producer in the world, with production running at 400 million hectolitres or 340 million barrels a year. With the exception of exported Tsingtao lager, little Chinese beer is seen outside of the country. But the brewing industry is likely to undergo substantial change in the next few years as the rising middle class and increasing wealth will lead to increased consumption and a demand for better beers. While the government controls the industry, it has allowed Western brewers to enter and work with local producers. Change is already under way with the development of brewpubs: the German Paulaner company, owned by Heineken, has opened around a dozen brewpubs, with the brewing equipment visible to customers. The beers produced are Helles (light lager), Dunkel (dark) and wheat beer. A number of other companies have emerged to copy the Paulaner model.

In Japan, beer was unknown until it was introduced in 1853 by the American navy whose gunboats encouraged the locals to open their country to 'free trade'. In return, the Americans taught the Japanese how to brew beer. In 1908 the government introduced a law that stipulated that no new brewery would be licensed unless it could produce 1,800 hectolitres in its first year, an impossible target in a country where most people were poor peasants and beer was drunk mainly by the urban middle class. As a result of these restrictions, Japan became dominated in the 20th century by four large breweries: Asahi, Kirin, Sapporo and Suntory. But as a result of the severe economic depression of the 1990s, the government relaxed the law, allowing small brewers and brewpubs to emerge. Almost in the blink of an eye, some 250 new small brewer-ies and brewpubs appeared. Many of them make what they called *jibiiru* or 'local beer' made with the finest quality grains and hops. Today, in a still fast-changing beer scene, drinkers can enjoy IPAs, pale ales, wheat beers and Stouts.

The Americas
United States

The impossible has happened: the giants that dominate American brewing to an awesome and frightening extent now look on in puzzlement as their sales decline while craft brewers take an ever bigger share of the market. It's been a long, slow haul. When Prohibition was lifted 1933, only a handful of brewers had survived the shut down. With the vast country under their sway, they could swamp it with increasingly bland apologies for lager, made with large amounts of rice or corn. Their domination grew during the Depression, followed by World War Two when large numbers of potential beer drinkers were shipped abroad for the duration. As late as the 1980s, the U.S. had just 50 breweries. Then all hell let loose. Tired of drinking industrial near-beer, an army of disgruntled drinkers and home-brewers set up shop and started to produce beer with something unheard of for 50 years: *flavour*.

From small beginnings – New Albion and Anchor Steam in California and Yakima Brewing in Washington State – both the number of breweries and the styles have mushroomed. At first, craft brewers were content to copy the great European styles – pale ale and IPA from Britain, proper German-style lager and Czech Pilsners, and a variety of Belgian-inspired brews – but with success has come a rugged determination to break the mould and develop distinctive home-grown styles. American craft brewers like to go the extra mile or, in modern terms, push the envelope. So IPAs have to become Double or Imperial with strengths as high as 12 per cent. American interpretations of Pilsners and lager are equally of a strength rare to Europe, while Belgian Tripels and Double Stouts cry out to be made in the U.S.. Sometimes sheer exuberance can get out of hand, as with Black IPAs. As the American beer writer and Brooklyn brewmaster Garrett Oliver said on the subject: 'Don't get me started!'

With strength has come aggressive bitterness. Many craft beers are heavily hopped, with units of bitterness in the 60s or 70s. To meet with the clamour for hops with great depth of bitterness and flavour, hop growers have developed a spate of new varieties such as Amarillo and Citra that boom with tart citrus and tropical fruit character.

The craft beer revolution shows no sign of slowing down and some of the breweries, including Sam Adams in Boston and Sierra Nevada in California, enjoy national status, producing one million barrels each a year. Bemused by their success, the national giants have bought a few independents or invested in others. The purchase of Goose Island by Anheuser-Busch caused ripples of concern but to date there has been no diminution in the quality of the Chicago beers. Restless for innovation, craft brewers are now ageing beer in whisky barrels, blending beer and wine, and are developing their own sour beer interpretation of Belgian lambic.

TOP: **Brooklyn brewery, New York**

BOTTOM: **Flying Dog's brewery tap in Frederick, Maryland**

Canada

Canada, in common with its southern neighbour, has also suffered from Prohibition and restrictions on beer being exported from one province to another. As a result, a few large companies such as Carling, Molson and Labatt dominated Canadian brewing for decades with thin lagers. The logjam started to move with breweries in the English-speaking regions developing the likes of pale ale, Bitter and Scotch ale while in the Francophone areas there was a rising demand for good beer to match fine cuisine. In Québec, tax breaks for small breweries enabled new independents to develop. The most successful has been Unibroue with a range of beers inspired by Belgium rather than France. Such beers as Maudite, Blanche de Chambly and La Fin du Monde created such a furore that several other brewers, including Dieu de Ciel and Le Trou Diable, rushed to emulate Unibroue's success. Unibroue has been taken over by Sapporo of Japan but continues to produce full-tasting and idiosyncratic beers.

In the English-speaking provinces, choice is now abundant with a host of new small breweries offering nut-brown ale, Porter, Stout, IPA and, with a deep bow to the Old Country, Bitter.

Latin America

The problem that faces micro-brewers in Latin America is the sheer scale of the domination of such giants as AB InBev. This group in particular controls brewing in large swathes of the region, from north to south. The group was formed as a merger between Ambev of Brazil, Anheuser-Busch of the U.S. and InBev of Belgium. Ambev itself was the result of an earlier merger between Brahma and Antartica and it's difficult for smaller brewers to break the armlock it has on Latin America.

One country largely free from its grip is Mexico, where Grupo Modelo is a national company, though its main rival Sol is now owned by Heineken. Mexico has a fascinating brewing history. The country was briefly and incongruously part of the Austrian Empire and arguably the only benefit it derived from the occupation was the habit of brewing Vienna lager, a deep bronze beer quite different to Pilsner. The style survives in such beers as Negro Modelo and Dos Equis, though the two main groups behind the beers concentrate most of their efforts on astonishingly thin lagers such as Corona and Sol. A few small breweries are attempting to enter the market, with Cerverceria Primus in Mexico City the most prominent, producing among others an Alt Bier.

The country most likely to change is Brazil. In spite of the presence of AB InBev, Heineken and Kirin, the rapid growth of the economy and an expanding middle-class bodes well for better beer. There are now an estimated 100 small breweries in the country and they offer beers that indicate considerable knowledge of European brewing styles. Beers that can be found include a Belgian-style Tripel, a Dortmunder Export, German-style Weisse, a Bamberg-style Rauch and even – for homesick Scots – a Wee Heavy.

Argentina is showing a welcome growth in the number of small breweries and brewpubs that challenge the hegemony of the purveyors of ice-cold near-beer. The country has a sizable hop-growing industry, which bodes well for brewers seeking aroma and flavour in their products. Much-needed choice comes from Antares, which runs a dozen brewpubs. Argentina is also home to the world's most southernmost brewery in Tierra del Fuego, Cerveza Beagle, which presumably is a reference to Charles Darwin's ship. Stouts, IPAs and brown ale can now be found.

There's a new micro-brewery on the Falkland Islands. It's run by real ale fan Jeff Halliday, who picked up the necessary skills on a course at the Brewers' Laboratory in Britain. He brews Maiden Bitter, which has proved popular in the islands' pubs and hotels. His only problem is the time it takes to get ingredients from Britain. Hops from Argentina? Don't ask...

Australia and New Zealand

There's far more than Carlton Draught and XXXX in Australia today. Around 154 breweries bring much-needed quality beer to parched drinkers. In spite of the searing temperatures for most of the year, drinkers are demanding – and getting – beers packed with flavour rather than fizz. Cooper's of Adelaide, for decades the lonely flag-bearer for ale in the country, remains the brewery revered by beer lovers. But many others have picked up the torch and choice is abundant.

In such a vast country, brewing is not confined to the big cities. Small breweries have appeared in coastal resorts and deep in wine country. But Sydney, Melbourne, Perth and Fremantle have become major areas for small independent brewers, some of which are no longer small and have achieved national reach. In the spring of 2013, Lion Nathan, Australia's brewing giant, bought Little Creatures, one of the leading independents and a multi-award winner for its beers. Will this be a benign partnership? Lion already owns the Sydney-based Malt Shovel brewery run by pioneering brewer Chuck Hahn and has given Hahn the funds to launch a chain of brewpubs in major cities under the James Squire name, so Little Creatures may be free from interference.

The beer range and choice in Australia is remarkable. Brewers look to the northern hemisphere for inspiration. From the Old Country they have brought IPA, Porter and Stout to the New World. They have witnessed the brewing revival in the United States and have followed in those giant footsteps with American-style pale ales and properly-brewed Pilsners. And, of course, they make a deep bow in the direction of Belgium with abbey ales, Dubbels and Tripels. There's far move to Aussie beer these days than a cold tinnie.

A similar situation exists in New Zealand with some 65 to 70 breweries. The Kiwis claim that they edge ahead of Great Britain with the number of breweries per head of population. In common with Australia, New Zealand is in the grip of Lion Nathan, part of the Japanese Kirin group. But thin lager is under attack from a new breed of small brewers who offer drinkers a growing choice of pale ale, IPA, Porter, Stout and Belgian-style beers. Kiwi brewers enjoy the advantage of having fine hops grown on their doorsteps. So good is the quality that brewers in the northern hemisphere queue to buy them. The new Nelson Sauvin, so-called because its fruity character is reminiscent of Sauvignon wine, is in great demand.

There's a gritty determination that drives New Zealand brewing. When one small brewery was badly damaged by the Christchurch earthquake of 2011, the owners moved to new premises and started again. Fire, pestilence and plague can't stand in the way of good beer.

Good beer has spread to the Deep South in the U.S., including French-influenced Louisiana

Barley is the essential building block of beer

The magic of brewing

Beer may be a drink that lurks in the giant shadow cast by wine, but it should never be dismissed as a simple refresher. Beer can be as complex as wine: capable of myriad flavours, styles and tastes. In appearance it ranges from pale gold to deepest black. In common with most wines it can be drunk young, but it can also be aged for months or even years to allow flavour and character to develop.

It's also the world's oldest form of alcohol. It dates back to the dawn of history, to 3000 years BC or possibly earlier. In the Old World of Babylonia, Egypt and Mesopotamia, where fruit rotted quickly, people learnt to make a life-sustaining drink from grain at a time when water was dangerous and insanitary. Civilisation and beer go hand in hand. The hunter-gatherers of antiquity stopped roaming and created settled communities in order to grow grain for the production of the essential staples of life: bread and beer.

Beer's unique flavours come about as a result of the complex way in which it's produced. To make wine, you crush grapes. With cider, you crush apples. Distilled spirits are either made from grain (gin, whisky and vodka), or fruit (Cognac, Armagnac and Calvados). Beer is the result of the blending and interaction of two quite different ingredients: grain and hops. The grain – malted barley – delivers a toasted biscuit character while hops add aroma and flavour along with essential bitterness.

Gin and some vodkas have flavourings added, while Dutch genevas have many different flavour additions. The flavourings in gin and vodka come late in the production process or are even added in the bottle. Beer stands out from the crowd as the flavourings used – hops – are vital to the character of the end product and are added comparatively early in the brewing cycle. Hops are more than just flavouring. The complex mix of oils, tannins and acids contained within the plant not only add aroma and bitterness but also stabilise the beer and keep bacteria at bay. The hop plant has had a long struggle for acceptance but today it's universally recognised as a vital component of all beer styles – for the only exception to this, see p301. The brewers of 'spontaneously fermented' lambic and gueuze beers in Belgium avoid bitterness but need hops for their antiseptic qualities. The rapid growth of the craft beer movement in the U.S. has created great interest in hops and the introduction of new varieties with even more pronounced fruity, piny and spicy characteristics.

It's not my aim to make beer precious or to cloak it in language and terms that divorce it from everyday experience. But it's a drink worthy of respect, as are the awesome skills of the craftsmen and women who make it.

Two-row barley

Ingredients
Grain

Brewers call malted barley 'the soul of beer'. It's the essential building block of brewing, providing the starches and enzymes that make beer-making possible. Barley is the preferred grain because it has a husk that acts as a natural filter during the mashing stage, and it delivers a clean, juicy and biscuit character to the finished product. Even wheat beers are made with a blend of barley and wheat. Oats and rye are also occasionally used but in small amounts as their oily, creamy and bready notes can overwhelm the gentler notes of barley malt.

Grains of ripe barley ready for malting

Most modern maltings are mechanised and automated, the cereal grain hidden from view in large steel drums. There are a few traditional 'floor maltings', where the grain is spread across large floors and turned by hand: some brewers consider that floor-malted barley gives the finest flavour to beer. The curious aspect of malting is that a grain of barley looks scarcely different to a grain of malt. Yet the steps taken to change barley into malt trigger natural chemical reactions that lead to the creation of fermentable sugar.

Most barley grown worldwide is fit only for animal feed or for making malted drinks. Barley suitable for brewing can be either 'two row' or 'six-row', so-called as a result of the number of grains contained within each ear. Maritime two row, grown, as the name suggests, close to the sea, is considered the finest of all varieties for brewing. Six-row, widely grown in the United States, produces coarser malt but as it contains a high level of enzymes it can be blended with rice or corn as it also converts their starches to sugar. Many American light lagers are made in this fashion – the makers of American Budweiser list rice before barley malt on the label – but craft brewers in the U.S. will use two-row wherever possible and will even import it from Britain.

Barley varieties suitable for brewing fall into two categories: spring and winter. Winter barleys, despite the name, are sown in the autumn and have to be hardy to withstand cold, frost and snow. Ale brewers favour winter barleys, such as Maris Otter and Pipkin, for their robust nutty and biscuit flavours. Lager brewers consider that spring barleys, such as Alexis, grown in the spring when the weather is kinder, have a gentler, sweeter character. New varieties of barley, especially 'high yielding' ones that produce more grain per acre, are regularly developed. A new British barley, Tipple, has proved popular with brewers.

When barley arrives at the maltings it's dried to reduce the water content and nitrogen: nitrogen can lead to beer with a haze. The grain is thoroughly cleaned by large sieves to remove soil and stones and is transferred to 'steeping tanks' and soaked with water for 60 hours: the water is changed regularly. This stage not only cleans the grain and removes bacteria and wild yeasts but also increases the water content to encourage germination. The serious business begins when the grain is spread across the germination floors in a floor maltings where it's raked several times a day as it starts to germinate, or when it's transferred to

TYPES OF MALT

Pilsner or lager malt is the palest of all types, and is used to make golden beers.

Pale malt is used predominantly in such styles as pale ale and IPA and is slightly darker than Pilsner malt.

Mild Ale malt, as the name implies, is used for the production of English Mild and bottled brown ales. It's darker than pale malt and a higher kilning temperature is required. Many modern Mild ales are made with pale malt and coloured with caramel.

Vienna malt is similar in colour to Mild Ale malt and was used in the 19th century by the great Viennese brewer Anton Dreher for his 'Vienna Red' style of lager that was halfway in colour between the darker lagers of Munich and the golden style from Pilsen.

Munich malt is the classic style used for the bronze-coloured lagers of the Bavarian capital. A further kilning produces Munich Dark malt, used for Dunkel or dark lagers.

Amber malt is a British variety that is little used today but gives a deep bronze or copper colour to beer. It's well kilned and has low enzymic power.

Chocolate malt is kilned at a high temperature until the grains resemble coffee beans. It's used sparingly to give a luscious chocolate/coffee note to beer.

Pilsner malt is lightly kilned

Black malt is heavily roasted

Black malt is heavily roasted and gives a slightly astringent character to dark beers, and an acrid bitterness. It imparts a flavour similar to that of espresso coffee.

Wheat malt is used in Bavarian wheat beer as, due to the stricture of the Reinheitsgebot or Purity Law, all grain used in brewing has to be malted. It's almost as pale as Pilsner malt. Many ale brewers use a touch of wheat, either malted or raw, as the grain gives a good frothy head to beer.

Stewed malts are made in a similar fashion to toffee. They have no enzymic power and are used solely for colour and flavour. Following germination, the green malt is loaded into a sealed kiln so the moisture cannot escape. The temperature is raised to 45°C/113°F, which matches the mashing temperature in a brewery. The enzymes inside each kernel of grain convert some of the starch to sugar. Vents in the kiln are opened and the temperature is increased so that the sugar crystallises. Some sugar in the form of dextrin is not crystallised and as dextrin cannot be fermented by brewers' yeast it leaves a fullness of palate and a nutty flavour in the beer. The main type of stewed malt used in British ale brewing is crystal, called caramel malt in the United States. Carapils or cara malt is the type produced in continental Europe.

---

the malting beds in an automated factory. Amazing biochemical changes take place inside the grain. The starch becomes soluble, enabling the journey that ends with sugar to begin. The clear sign that germination is underway is when the rootlet breaks through the husk. Hidden from view, the plant's embryo or acrospire starts to grow, leading to a change that turns protein into enzymes. Only partial germination takes place in the maltings: if full germination was allowed, the grain would start to consume its own sugars. The great skill of the maltster is to judge when partial germination has gone far enough. He does this by the simple process of chewing some of the grain. If it's soft or 'friable' in the mouth then 'modification' – the growth of the embryo and the solubility of the starch – has progressed successfully.

Germination is stopped by loading the grain into a kiln. The floor of the kiln has a slotted wire or metal base. Heat from gas fires comes blasting up from below. The damp or 'green malt' stays in the kiln for 48 hours. Pale malt, the basis of all beer, is heated at a temperature that rises from 65° to 75°C (149° to 167°F) and then to 90°C (194°F) for the final eight hours. Darker malts are kilned at higher temperatures to create the colours and flavours the brewer requires. They have lower levels of enzymes or 'diastatic power', which is why pale malt is so crucial to the brewing process. Some heavily roasted malts, as well as unmalted roasted barley – frequently used in stout – are said to have no 'diastatic power' and are used solely for colour and flavour.

Barley being malted by hand at a traditional floor maltings

Adjuncts

Cereal adjuncts and brewing sugars are controversial. In Germany they are outlawed under the terms of the Purity Law. But the protracted double decoction mashing and long lagering method used there and in other countries, such as the Czech Republic, that produce classic lagers remove such problems as protein haze and off-flavours. Ale brewers, who use a system based on simple infusion mashing and seven days of fermentation and short conditioning, feel that adjuncts used sparingly not only tackle haze but give added flavour to beer: 'It allows me to play tunes,' one leading British ale brewer told me.

The main adjuncts used are wheat flour, flaked (gelatinised) grains or torrefied (scorched) grain – torrefied grain is similar to popcorn. Brewing sugar, either in the form of candy sugar (sucrose), which is popular with Belgian ale brewers, or invert sugar (glucose and fructose) encourages fermentation, reduces haze and adds subtle flavours. As sugar is highly fermentable it – contrary to expectation – counters sweetness in beer and encourages a dry finish. The levels of adjuncts and sugars used in ale brewing are low.

Hops

The main function of the hop is to add bitterness to beer but this amazing plant contributes far more than that. The hop delivers aromas and flavours that are spicy, herbal, grassy, perfumy, fruity (citrus in particular), peppery, woody/piny and resinous. It gives added dimension and depth to beer. It balances the biscuit sweetness of the malt's juices. An English Fuggle or Golding, a Czech Žatec (Saaz in German), a German Hersbrucker or Perle, a Slovenian Golding, an American Cascade or Citra, and a New Zealand Nelson Sauvin will give taste prints to beer as distinctive as the world's great grape varieties.

The cultivated hop plant is called Humulus lupulus, the 'wolf plant', so-called because of its voracious growing and climbing abilities. It's a member of the same plant family as cannabis and nettles. The hop is dioecious, meaning the male and female plants grow separately. With the exception of English and some American and Belgian varieties, hops are not fertilised. Only the female hop is used in brewing and most lager brewers want seedless hops as they feel the more pungent and resinous character of fertilised hops does not marry well with the delicate flavours of lager beer. Ale brewers, on the other hand, consider that the qualities of seeded hops better balance the more robust and fruity nature of their beers.

The hop thrives in well-drained loamy or sandy soil. In some regions, such as the American Pacific North-west, the soil has to be irrigated. The plants need warmth as well as moisture and long hours of sunlight. They are trained to climb tall trellises in order to attract the sun. They grow at spectacular speed, as much as 35 centimetres or 12 inches in a single day. By early July, the hops will reach the tops of their trellises (4.8 metres or 16 feet in height) and will start to flower for three to four weeks, allowing the cones to form and mature. The cones will be ready for picking in late August and September in the Northern Hemisphere.

The hops go through a picking machine that removes stalks, leaves and earth. They must be dried quickly or they will rot within a few hours. The plants are laid out on perforated floors in buildings known as hop houses in Germany or oast houses in England. Underfloor heating from kilns dries the hops, with the temperature held at 60°C/140°F for around 10 hours.

The hop cones contain a fine yellow powder called lupulin that has the essential oils and bitter compounds needed by the brewer. The compounds break down in to humulone and lupulone: the former creates the alpha acids that give bitterness to beer, while lupulone helps stabilise the wort during brewing. The oils in the cone give distinctive flavours to beer. Tannins also play a part, adding flavour and helping to prevent infection during the brewing process.

Hops divide into two main groups: bittering and aroma. Bittering hops are high in alpha acids while aroma hops have low rates of acid and are used mainly for the delightful bouquet they give to beer. When hops reach the brewery they are added in stages during the boil in the copper. A proportion is added to the wort at the

Hop bines grow to some 16 feet (4.8 metres) in height

Challenger hops

Phoenix hops

Hop pellets

Different varieties of hops in storage

Many of the beers in this book record their IBUs – Units of Bitterness. The level of bitterness gives drinkers some indication of the bitterness level they can expect from a particular beer. There's an obvious difference between Pilsner Urquell (40 IBUs) and the Texan Shiner Bock (13 IBUs). IBUs are the result of co-operation between the American Society of Brewing Chemists and the European Brewery Convention in the 1960s.

To calculate IBUs, iso-alpha acids in the wort or finished beer are measured in a laboratory by HPLC – high-pressure liquid chromatography. For further information on the formulas used to determine IBUs go to the websites www.realbeer.com/hops or www.probrewer.com.

No two people have the same taste buds or reactions to bitterness and 'a bitter beer' is a subjective assessment. In the case of Pilsner Urquell and other Czech lager beers, the desire to create a strong 'mouthfeel' means that some of the hop bitterness is masked by a rich malt character. This means that more fully-attenuated lagers – i.e. with fewer malt notes – may taste more bitter that Czech lager when the IBUs are actually lower.

start of the boil in order to extract the oils and bittering compounds. But most of the aroma evaporates during the boil and there are further additions midway through the boil and a few minutes before it ends. Ale brewers often add a handful of hops to casks before they leave the brewery to intensify aroma and minimise the risk of infection. Brewers with traditional coppers, which have slotted bases to separate hopped wort from spent hops, use the plant in its whole flower form. Modern plants that use two vessels for the boiling stage – a brew kettle followed by a whirlpool or separator – use pelletised hops. Pellets are made by crushing the hops into small tablets. Hop oil, a green juice extracted from the plant, is used by large, industrial breweries but is frowned on by many smaller producers who feel the oil gives a harsh backtaste.

Starting in England, a new type of hop called a dwarf or hedgerow variety has been developed. Hedgerow hops climb to only half the height of conventional varieties and are easier to pick. They are also less prone to the pests and diseases that plague hop farms and which can, in extremis, wipe out an entire harvest. The First Gold variety in England has been especially popular. The unstoppable demand for new and exciting hop aromas and flavours, in the U.S. in particular, has led to new varieties being developed such as Amarillo and Citra that give even more pronounced citrus/grapefruit character to beer.

For a full list of all known hop varieties see *For the Love of Hops* by Stan Hieronymus, Brewers Publications, published in the United States and available online.

Esters

As well as aromas and flavours derived from malt and hops there is a third type of flavour known as esters. These are flavour compounds created naturally during fermentation and they are reminiscent of banana, butterscotch, pear drop, apple, roses, honey, sultana, raisin and fresh tobacco. Brewers will use yeast strains to either avoid powerful esters or encourage them. Lager brewers in particular want clean aromas and flavours and will use yeast cultures that create low levels of esters. They are especially keen to avoid a compound called diacetyl that gives a buttery or butterscotch character to beer. Some ale brewers, on the other hand, positively welcome diacetyl.

Water

Even the strongest beer is made up of 93% water. The quality of water is therefore crucial to brewing. For centuries, long before brewers were able to adjust water to suit their recipes, breweries developed around wells or springs. River water was also used before such sources were ruined by pollution.

In a brewery, water is always known as liquor. Its formulation will depend on the minerals present in the rocks and soil of a particular area. Soft water is the result of rain falling on insoluble rock such as slate or granite. Where soluble rock is present, water will pick up such sulphates as calcium and magnesium, also known as gypsum and Epsom salts. It is these salts – present in the waters of the Trent valley – that made Burton-on-Trent a key town in the development of brewing. The hard waters help acidify the mash, encourage enzymes to work, ensure the best extraction of aromas and flavours from malt and hops, and discourage astringency. Yeast thrives on magnesium. On the other hand, the soft waters of such famous lager brewing towns as Pilsen emphasise the soft malty character of the beer. The total salts in the waters of Burton amount to 1,226 parts per million. In Pilsen, on the other hand, the figure is just 30.8. Brewers can now adjust their liquor to suit their purposes: many ale brewers 'Burtonise' their waters by adding gypsum and magnesium salts. All brewers thoroughly cleanse their liquor to remove impurities and such agricultural chemicals as nitrates, which can create a haze in beer.

Water used in brewing is known as liquor

Yeast

It was not until the 18th and 19th centuries that scientists, including Louis Pasteur, were able to explain yeast's role in brewing. Until then, fermentation was looked on as some kind of witchcraft. The foam produced by this strange alchemy was known as 'God-is-good'. Pasteur demonstrated with the aid of a microscope that the production of alcohol was the result of a natural chemical reaction in which yeast cells multiplied as they turned sugars into alcohol and carbon dioxide.

Yeast is a fungus, a single cell plant that can turn a sugary liquid into alcohol and CO2. There are two basic types of brewer's yeasts: ale and lager. Ale yeast is classified as Saccharomyces [sugar fungus] cerevisiae, while lager yeast is labelled Saccharomyces carlsbergensis, as the first pure strain of lager yeast was isolated at the Carlsberg breweries in Denmark. It is also known today as Saccharomyces uvarum. The two types are often referred to as 'top fermenting' and 'bottom fermenting' strains. This is because ale yeast creates a thick collar of foam on top of the fermenting beer, while lager yeast produces a smaller head and sinks to the bottom of the vessel. The terms are misleading, as both yeasts must work at all levels of the liquid to convert malt sugars into alcohol. I prefer the terms warm fermenting and cold fermenting yeasts, for ale yeast will only work at 12°C (55°F) and above, while lager yeast is tolerant of cold and will happily work at temperatures as low as 5°C (40°F).

Yeast is not a neutral substance. It does more than produce alcohol. As the same strain reproduces itself many times over during fermentation, it does not die out and can be used to start the next brew. A brewery's yeast culture picks up, retains and passes on vital flavour characteristics from one brew to the next. Breweries not only safeguard their cultures but lodge samples in yeast banks – if a brewery has the misfortune to get a yeast infection, fresh supplies can be obtained from the bank.

For the role of wild yeast strains in the production of Belgian lambic and gueuze beers, see p257.

Brewing
Ale brewing

To describe the brewing process for this book I visited the brewers at the Aylesbury Brewhouse in Buckinghamshire, England, to make a special beer. I chose an India Pale Ale as it's a style of great historic significance that is being revived with great passion and fervour in many countries. The brewhouse is a small, specialist plant attached to the Hop Pole pub, both of which are owned by Vale Brewery.

At 7.30 in the morning I joined brewers Simon Smith and David Renton to rinse out the mash tun with hot water or liquor in order to start the day's brew. We were using a recipe with the blessing of the Durden Park Beer Club, a group of dedicated home brewers who recreate classic English beer styles from the 18th, 19th and 20th centuries. The original Victorian recipe was high in malt, hops and alcohol. We reduced the quantities slightly as there were limits on how much malt could placed in the Aylesbury mash tun, while we knew

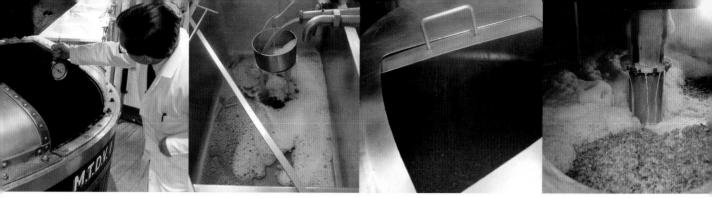

Checking mash temperature   **Running off the wort**   **Sparging the mash**   **Hops added to the copper boil**

that modern hops are much higher in bitterness than those grown a century or more earlier, so fewer would be needed to achieve the same hop bitterness. We were aiming to brew a beer of 7% alcohol and with 80 units of bitterness – that's twice as bitter as most premium beers.

We underscored the traditional nature of the beer by plumping for all English ingredients: Maris Otter pale malting barley and Fuggles and Goldings hops. To make seven barrels of beer, Smith and Renton used 13 bags of malt, each one containing 25 kilos of grain. They heaved the grain into a hopper, from where it was fed to the mash tun alongside. By 7.45 all the grain had been transferred to the tun, where it was thoroughly mixed with water at a temperature of 74°C. The brewers 'Burtonised' the water: adding such mineral salts as gypsum and magnesium to reproduce the salty waters of Burton-on-Trent, the historic home of IPA in the 19th century. The mash would stay in the tun for 90 minutes. During that time the temperature would fall to 65.5°C – the mash temperature – and enzymes in the malt would begin to convert starch into fermentable sugar.

We stopped for brewers' breakfast. The staff of the Hop Pole provided a gargantuan fry-up with lashings of hot tea to keep us fully operational for the rest of the day. At 9am we returned to the brewhouse to prepare for the run-off – the transfer of the sugary extract known as wort from the mash tun to the copper. The large, spacious room, with its wood-jacketed brewing vessels, was filled with the inviting aroma of fresh, warm bread – the result of the creation of malt sugar in the mash tun. Smith and Renton turned a tap at the base of the tun and the aroma of fresh bread intensified as the wort flowed into a receiving vessel called the underback, where it's transferred to the copper for the boil with hops. Rotating arms in the roof of the mash tun revolved, sprinkling the thick bed of grain with more hot water to flush out any remaining sugar, a system known as 'sparging'

By 10.15, the run-off was finished and the wort frothed as it poured into the copper. It was time for the worst part of brewing – digging the spent grain from the mash tun. The brewers bent their backs and filled sacks with the warm grain, which would go to local farms as cattle feed.

At 11.10 the first batch of hops – a 50:50 blend of Fuggles and Goldings – was poured in to the top of the copper. The warm bread aroma now blended with the herbal, piny, resinous character of the hops. More hops would be added five minutes before the end of the boil, with further additions in the fermenting vessels and in the casks where the beer would mature. The boil lasted for 85 minutes. The hopped wort stood for 10 minutes and was then re-circulated in the copper on the bed of hops to pick up maximum aroma.

The piping hot liquid passed through a heat exchange unit that lowered the temperature in preparation for fermentation. Fifty minutes later, the hopped wort, with a temperature of 21°C, reached the fermenters, where it was vigorously mixed with yeast. Now nature would run its course. Fermentation lasts for seven days and the beer would then be stored for five months: we chose that period to replicate the time a cask of Victorian IPA would have taken to travel from England to India by fast clipper. The long brewing day ended at 5.45pm.

The IPA was called Sink or Swim, an allusion to the famous Aylesbury Duck, which is the symbol of the town, and the arduous sea journey to India in the 19th century. The beer that emerged from the long ageing process was 6.8% – a tad less than planned – but with the aimed-for 80 bitterness units. It had a pale bronze colour with 'lemon jelly' fruit on the nose, powerful hop resins, a rich malt loaf grain character and a hint of butterscotch and fresh tobacco. Tart and tangy orange and lemon fruit built in the mouth, with chewy malt,

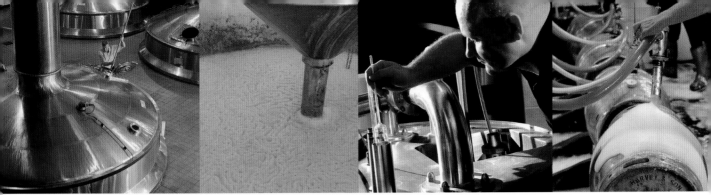

| Checking the copper boil | Head of yeast on fermenting beer | Measuring gravity of conditioning beer | Filling casks of ale |

intensely bitter hops and a continuing hint of butterscotch. The finish was bittersweet to start but became dry, with solid contributions from tart fruit, butterscotch/toffee, malt loaf and a quinine-like bitterness.

It's a wonderfully refreshing beer and the hint of sweetness from the malt chimed with my belief that the 19th-century IPAs would have had some sweetness to satisfy members of the Raj in India, who were also great consumers of Hock and other sweetish wines.

Lager brewing

Traditional lager, as opposed to global brands, is made in a quite different manner to ale. In ale brewing, mashing is a simple infusion system using 'well modified' malt. Lager brewers uses a decoction system that reflects the fact that when modern commercial lager brewing developed in the 19th century, the quality of barley malt in Continental Europe was of poor quality. A long and more exhaustive mashing regime was needed to counter the high levels of nitrogen in the grain that would cause the finished beer to have a haze. Lager malt is also less modified: this means the conversion of starch to sugar has not progressed as far during the malting stage as is the case with malt prepared for ale brewing.

In a traditional lager brewery, the malt grist is mixed with soft brewing liquor in a mash kettle at 32°C/90°F. The temperature is then raised to 52°C/125°F, at which point the protein in the cereal starts to break down. A third of the mash is pumped to a second vessel where the temperature is raised to 65°C/149°F. This is the temperature, in both infusion and decoction mashing, at which saccharification takes place – the final conversion of starch to sugar. The temperature is held while conversion takes place and is then raised to 70°C/158°F, which is too high for the enzymes to work and saccharification stops. This portion of the mash is then boiled and returned to the original vessel, where it raises the temperature of the whole mash to 65°C/149°F. A further third of the mash is pumped to the second vessel and goes through the same process until returned to the first one.

The whole mashing process lasts for four hours. The sugary extract, wort, is then pumped to yet another vessel, the lauter tun. This has a slotted base and revolving rakes in the roof. The thick bed of grain is sprinkled with hot liquor to wash out any remaining malt sugars as the wort percolates through the base of the tun. The wort is pumped to the brew kettle where it's boiled with hops for two hours. Hops are usually added in three stages: at the start of the boil, half way through and at the end. The hopped wort is cooled by passing through heat exchangers and pumped to fermenting vessels for primary fermentation.

Depending on the brewery, fermentation may be in open or closed vessels. Yeast is pitched or mixed in the wort when the temperature is measured at 8°C/46°F. Fermentation causes the temperature to rise as yeast begins to turn sugar into alcohol and carbon dioxide. To prevent off flavours developing, the fermenting liquid is cooled and maintained at 4°C/39°F for seven days and is then pumped to the lager cellar. The beer matures and enjoys a slow second fermentation at a temperature just above freezing. Lagering can be in horizontal tanks or upright conical vessels. Some brewers believe that yeast acts more slowly in horizontal vessels and a cleaner beer is created. The length of lagering will depend on each individual brewery but the professional view is that the longer a beer is aged, the better it will be. The classic Czech golden lager Budweiser Budvar is lagered for 90 days.

Tasting beer

A little care, skill, and understanding of the art of the brewer is required to appreciate beer at home. First: the glass. You can use a conventional pint or half-pint beer glass, or similar measures in metric countries. You may be lucky enough to have one of the glasses designed to accompany a particular beer. Or you may use any suitable glass container in your home. Whatever you use, it must be scrupulously clean and, above all, it should contain no residue from cleaning agents. If you take a glass from a dishwasher, rinse it thoroughly under running cold water. Washing-up liquids and detergents will not only leave a vile taste in the glass, but will also kill the head on the beer. Avoid pouring and drinking beer in a kitchen area. Oil or fats used in cooking infiltrate a beer glass, leave unpleasant flavours and also kill the head.

BELOW AND TO p26:
Examples of some of common beer glassware. Beer glasses are often specifically designed to enhance the particular qualities of different beer styles.

There is more to pouring beer into a glass than merely emptying the liquid from one container into the next. Hold the glass and bottle at eye level. Slowly pour the beer into the glass, raising the glass from the horizontal to the vertical as it fills. Let the beer trickle down the side of the glass. When the glass is two-thirds full, raise it to the vertical and pour more quickly: this should give the required healthy head of foam. Don't pour too slowly or the head will fail to materialise. Pouring at eye level is important when a beer contains yeast sediment. You can monitor the passage of the yeast, which will rise from the bottom of the bottle towards the neck, and stop pouring just before it leaves the bottle. If some of the yeast does get into the glass, don't worry: it will do you no harm and is full of healthy nutrients.

| Pokal | Tulip | Goblet | Wine glass | Weizen glass |

If you are pouring a German wheat beer, you cannot avoid the yeast sediment getting into the glass. It's meant to be served that way. A German beer waiter will deliberately rotate the bottle as he or she pours, and will give a final dramatic roll of the bottle to ensure all the yeast enters the glass.

If you are giving a beer tasting at home, you may find that large stemmed glasses intended for red wine are the most suitable containers, as they allow the aroma of the beer to develop, while the stem on the glass enables drinkers to swirl the beer to release the aroma to the full.

Whether you are drinking for pleasure or taking part in a tasting, begin by appreciating the aroma. Depending on the style, you will detect malty and hoppy aromas plus a fruitiness from either the hops or as the result of natural chemical esters created during fermentation.

As the beer passes over the tongue, you will detect more malt, hop and fruit notes. The tongue spots sweetness, bitterness and saltiness. Finally, let the beer slip down the back of the tongue and throat to appreciate the aftertaste or finish. This is an important part of the tasting process, as a beer that starts malty on the aroma may finish with a pronounced degree of hop bitterness, or vice versa.

BEER FLAVOUR CHART

Alcohol, Fullness, Grainy, Sweet, Worty, Metallic, Malty, Sour, Caramel, Medicinal, Roast, Meaty, Bitter, Sulphur, Astringent, Spicy, Hoppy, Vegetable, Fruity, Diacetyl, Apple

——— **Example beer flavour profile**

This flavour chart is used by CAMRA tasting panels and others in order to produce distinct flavour profiles for individual beers. The chart indicates the aromas and flavours produced by different types of malt along with hop characteristics and beer faults. It is a useful tool not only for identifying the key elements of a beer's flavour but also for comparing the flavours of different beers. The flavour elements on the chart are some of the most commonly found, although they are by no means exhaustive. The blue 'spider' trace shows the flavour profile for an example beer with the most dominant flavour elements plotted towards the outer edge of the chart.

Mug

Pilsner glass

Stange

Flute

If you are organising a beer tasting, you will need a good supply of glasses. If you reuse glasses, rinse them thoroughly between beers. You should also have a good supply of uncarbonated mineral water to drink between beers, plus plates with crackers or other kinds of dry biscuits to cleanse the palate further. Many tasters like to have small squares of cheese as well, but these should be of the mild variety, as the likes of blue Stilton or mature Cheddar are too overpowering, especially if you are tasting delicately flavoured beers.

You should involve only one style of beer in a tasting: there is little point in attempting to match, say, pale Pilsners with English barley wines. Using the beers mentioned in this book, you could arrange tastings of Bocks, wheat beers, Belgian ales or English pale ales.

Draught beer can be difficult to handle for a tasting at home. If you know a pub or bar with a friendly land-lord and an upstairs room, you could arrange a tasting there. In Britain, many brewers of cask-conditioned beer supply their products for home drinking in polypins containing 18 or 36 pints. Follow the simple instruc-tions on the box to set up the beer, which must be allowed to settle for 24 hours. It is crucial that cask beer is kept in a cool place with a temperature of 11–12°C (52–55°F). Several British brewers now supply cask beer in a take-home can containing eight pints. The cans are easy to set up and serve from, and other brew-ers may follow the example.

Bottled beers should be kept in a cool place prior to serving. Many brewers will suggest a serving tempera-ture on the bottle label. A simple rule of thumb is that lager beers should be served cold (8–9°C/46–48°F), ales served cool (11–12°C/52–55°F). You will have to experiment with your refrigerator and a thermometer to see how long beers should be stored. Beers containing sediment should be stored upright unless the bottles have corks, in which case they should be laid down to keep the corks moist. Sedimented bottles should be opened and left to stand for five or 10 minutes to vent off some of the carbonation created by bottle conditioning and to stop the beer 'fobbing' or gushing out of the container. Strong ales such as barley wines can be served at a slightly higher temperature of around 13–14°C (55–57°F) to allow the full aroma and palate to develop.

You will need tasting sheets with the names of each beer and with columns that allow the tasters to give marks out of 10 for appearance (clarity), aroma, palate, finish, and adherence to style. With some styles, you may wish to add marks for colour. Many beers called India Pale Ale, for example, are too dark, while a true Irish Dry Stout should be jet-black but with just a tiny hint of ruby around the edge when held against the light.

Above all… enjoy!

Becker

Tumbler

Nonic

Straight pint

India Pale Ales

Historic beer styles have a habit of emerging, fighting fit, from the grave. India Pale Ale was first brewed at the close of the 18th century and continued to be produced with great vigour for most of the following hundred years. But its lifespan was brief. As the name suggests, it was brewed in England for export to India. Its success led to the beer travelling further afield to other British colonies, including daunting voyages to Australia and New Zealand. It was even popular for a while in the United States.

Flying Dog IPA

In spite of initial success, the development of golden lager (which, ironically, was prompted by Austrian and German brewers studying the way English pale ale was made) led to the rapid demise of IPA. When American brewers exported to Africa and India they sent not only beer but ice as well. The invention of ice-making machines further boosted the fortunes of lager beer in countries with hot climates. For example, when the Foster brothers arrived in Australia from the United States in the 1880s, they came armed with a refrigeration unit as well as a determination to convert the locals from ale to lager.

Undeterred, the British brewers of India Pale Ale retreated back to their homeland and launched, with the aid of the new railway system, a lower-strength version of IPA called simply pale ale. It had less alcohol and hops for the good reason that a beer designed for the domestic market didn't have to withstand a three or four-month journey by sailing ship to Bombay or Calcutta.

But IPA was not forgotten. It was embedded deep in British brewing folklore, mainly as a result of the way it had transformed the fortunes of a small town in the English Midlands: Burton upon Trent. Export beer for India was first produced by a brewer in East London called Hodgson, conveniently located at Bow Bridge close to the East India Docks. However, brewers in Burton were able to make a superior version of pale ale as a result of their access to the remarkable spring waters of the Trent Valley, rich in such natural minerals as gypsum and magnesium. The sulphates act as flavour enhancers, drawing out the full, rich flavours of malts and hops. The Burton brewers were further aided by the new technologies of the Industrial

Revolution. Coke fuel, for example, was invented in neighbouring Derby and enabled maltsters to produce grain much paler in colour than versions heated over wood-fuelled fires. Cast-iron brewing vessels held heat better than wood, while improvements in malting, hop growing and yeast cultivation all enabled the Burton brewers to produce beer of a quality that astonished and captivated the beer-drinking world.

Fuller's Bengal Lancer

Within a few years, leading Burton brewers such as Allsopp, Bass and Worthington had eclipsed Hodgson and went on to dominate trade with the rest of the colonies. Burton was, for a while, the most important brewing town in the world, with Bass the biggest brewer, producing one million barrels a year.

The decline of Burton as a major brewing town in the 20th century, as takeovers, mergers and closures took their toll, makes the revival of IPA all the more welcome. In recent years scores of new brewers on both sides of the Atlantic have dug deep into history and old recipe books to recreate new interpretations of the style. The beauty of IPA is that brewers need not be shy of using substantial amounts of hops. In the 19th century, the hop was used in abundance in exported pale ales to keep them free from infection. Today hops balance the oatcake, biscuit and cracker-like character of malt with piny, spicy, peppery and citrus aroma and flavours.

Brooklyn Brewery

With their renowned exuberance, many American brewers have gone the extra mile with 'imperial' and 'double' IPAs. While there is no historic justification for these labels, there's no doubt that stronger IPAs add to our pleasure as a result of even greater depth of aroma and character. I have, however, drawn the line at beers called 'black IPAs'. Just which part of India *Pale* Ale do these brewers not understand?

Acorn IPA

Source: Acorn Brewery of Barnsley, Barnsley, South Yorkshire, England

Strength: 5%

Website: www.acorn-brewery.co.uk

If you want to choose one brewer who exemplifies the re-kindled passion for IPA, then it has to be Dave Hughes. He opened his brewery in 2003 and since then he has produced no fewer than 50 versions of the style. At the same time, he has restored a much-loved name to South Yorkshire.

The original Barnsley Brewery was founded in the 1850s and built up a loyal following for its ales, Barnsley Bitter in particular. In the early 1960s it was taken over by John Smith's of Tadcaster for no other reason than to acquire Barnsley's pubs and snuff out the competition. The Tadcaster company said it would close the Barnsley Brewery and supply its own Bitter to the pubs. In 1970, John Smith's in turn was taken over by the major London group, Courage, which underscored the decision to close the Barnsley site. To rub salt into the wound, Courage not only closed Barnsley, but transformed John Smith's into a keg-only plant, which meant drinkers in Barnsley were given pressurised beer instead of the cask-conditioned variety.

When Dave Hughes – a former chef, and Head Brewer at Barnsley Brewery – and his wife Judi, opened Acorn in the Wombwell area of Barnsley, they were determined to restore the good name of the long-lost local Bitter. Dave was able to get a

supply of the original Barnsley Bitter yeast culture and started to brew in July 2003 using a 10-barrel plant from a former brewpub. As a result of the success of Barnsley Bitter, Dave and Judi were able to move to a new site and install a 20-barrel kit that enables them to produce 100 barrels a week. They have extended their portfolio and the capacity of the new plant has enabled Dave to indulge his passion for IPA to the fullest.

He produces a new interpretation on a monthly basis. He uses the same grain recipe for each brew – Maris Otter pale malt and a touch of crystal – but builds on that solid malt backbone with a different hop variety each time. Bedazzled by American versions of IPA, he uses many hop varieties from the United States: recent brews have been hopped with Gladiator and Warrior.

In January 2012 he launched three new American-style IPAs: Delta, Glacier and Northern Brewer, named after the hop varieties used in each brew. All three beers are gold in colour. The version that used Northern Brewer had 55 bitterness units, and a big tangy fruit nose reminiscent of plum jam with earthy hops and nutty malt. Sweet juicy malt built in the mouth, balancing tart fruit and bitter hops. The finish was bittersweet with cracker-like malt, plum jam and earthy, spicy hops.

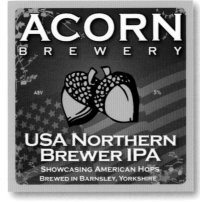

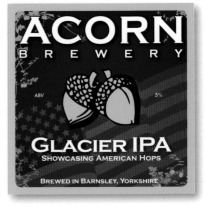

Samuel Adams Latitude 48 IPA

Source: Boston Beer Company, Boston, Massachusetts, USA

Strength: 6%

Website: www.samueladams.com

The Boston Beer Company's commitment to using the finest hops in its beers is underscored by the name of its IPA, for the 48th Latitude marks the 'hop belt' – the region of the northern hemisphere where most of the major hop-growing nations are clustered. The beer uses varieties from America, England and Germany, and they leave their imprint throughout the brewing process. As well as being used during the copper boil, they are also added as 'dry hops' to the finished beer for additional aroma.

The Boston Beer Company is better known as Sam Adams, and the resolute face of one of the leading American rebels during the War of Independence stares from the labels of the brewery's beers, clutching a foaming tankard of ale. Samuel Adams was a brewer and maltster in Boston. He helped organise the Boston Tea Party in 1773, which signalled the start of the rebellion against Britain and its tax impost, and he was also a signatory to the Declaration of Independence.

Jim Koch (pronounced 'Cook') is also something of a rebel. He's descended from German immigrants who became brewers but whose breweries were wiped out as a result of takeovers. Louis Koch, for example, had the misfortune to run a brewery in St Louis, Missouri, which is the home town of America's biggest brewer, Anheuser-Busch, producer of Budweiser. A-B put him out of business while Jim Koch's father similarly lost his brewery in Ohio to takeover in the 1950s. Jim was a successful management consultant but brewing was in his blood and he was determined to avenge his relatives. In 1985 he launched Samuel Adams Boston Lager, brewed under licence, but the immediate success of the beer encouraged him to open his own plant three years later in Boston. He now has a wide portfolio of ales

and lagers and is the biggest independent craft brewer in the U.S., producing one million barrels a year. As well as Boston, Jim brews in other plants strategically placed around the country. His many airport bars include one at St Louis: what Anheuser Busch thinks of this is best left to the imagination.

Latitude 48, introduced in 2009, is brewed with three pale malts, Copeland, Harrington and Metcalfe, with caramel malt and Gambrinus honey malt. No fewer than five hop varieties are used: Ahtanum, Hallertau Mittelfrûh, East Kent Goldings, Simcoe and Zeus. Ahtanum, Goldings and Simcoe are additionally used for dry hopping. The massive infusion of hops creates 60 units of bitterness. The beer has a burnished copper colour and a luscious aroma of floral, earthy and piny hops, raisin and sultana fruit, 'Barleycup' malt and a rich waft of honey. Bitter hops and tangy fruit build in the mouth but they are finely balanced by crisp malt and a continuing honey note. The finish is long and with enormous depth, piny and grassy hops vying for attention with sappy malt, citrus fruit and the smooth honey note.

TASTING NOTES

APPEARANCE:

AROMA:

TASTE:

OVERALL SCORE:

TASTING NOTES

APPEARANCE:

AROMA:

TASTE:

OVERALL SCORE:

Brooklyn East India Pale Ale

Source: Brooklyn Brewery, Brooklyn, New York, USA

Strength: 6.8%

Website: www.brooklynbrewery.com

Garrett Oliver, the celebrated brewmaster at Brooklyn, has a sharp eye for history. He knows, from his regular visits to Britain, that IPA is virtually synonymous with Burton upon Trent but he is anxious to pay due respect to George Hodgson from East London who is believed to be the first brewer to develop beer for the India trade. Garrett calls his interpretation East India Pale Ale as it marks Hodgson's use of the East India Docks in London where the beer was packed into the holds of sailing clippers, its arrival in the eastern cities of India, and the critical role of the East India Company that controlled trade to the subcontinent.

Along with founder Steve Hindy, Garrett Oliver has restored the brewing tradition to a suburb of New York City that lost its producers during a long war of attrition that began with Prohibition and was followed by takeovers and mergers in the 1950s. The new Brooklyn Brewery built its success on Brooklyn Lager, which is based on a pre-Prohibition style known as Vienna lager. The demand for the beer enabled a new and much bigger plant to be installed: the ribbon was cut by Mayor Rudy Giuliani in 1996. In 2011 further expansion was underway that will enable Garrett and his brewing team to introduce more regular and seasonal beers.

Garrett uses only imported English pale ale malts for his IPA and he blends American and English hops: East Kent Goldings and Northdown from England with Centennial and Willamette from the U.S. (East Kent adds a further touch of eastern magic: it's considered the finest region of the county for hop growing. The area of Kent where the soil is too poor to grow hops is known as 'bastard Kent'.) The hop character of the Brooklyn East India Pale Ale is heightened by dry hopping.

The beer has a deep bronze colour and an entrancing aroma of lemon grass, citrus fruit, piny hops and cracker-like malt. Bitter hop resins, accompanied by tart citrus fruit, build in the mouth, with a rich, sappy malt backbone. The finish has a superb balance of tangy fruit, juicy malt and persistent and lingering piny hop bitterness.

The beer has a deep bronze colour and an entrancing aroma of lemon grass

Chimera IPA

Source: Downton Brewery Company, Downton, Wiltshire, England
Strength: 6.8% cask; 7% bottle
Website: www.downtonbrewery.com

It's an odd name for a beer. Chimera (ki-meera) is a wild and unrealistic dream, an organism made of DNA from different sources, and also a fire-breathing monster in Greek mythology, with a lion's head, a goat's body and a serpent's tail. Downton clearly had the mythology in mind when naming the beer, though you won't find any trace of goat when drinking it. The brewery was launched in 2003 by Martin Strawbridge who had had worked for Fuller's in London and then trained with near-neighbour Hop Back in Downton, on the outskirts of Salisbury: the original brewing equipment was leased from Hop Back. Martin now makes six regular beers along with monthly, seasonal and speciality brews and in total produces 1,500 barrels a year using 20-barrel brewing kit and three fermenters.

Chimera is brewed with pale malt, a touch of maize, and Goldings and Pioneer hops. The straw-coloured beer has a pronounced aroma of the confectionery known as sherbet lemons. I have often wondered why some pale ales – Deuchars IPA is a good example – have this delicious character-istic and I sought advice from two revered brewers, Stuart Howe at Sharp's and Fergus Fitzgerald at Adnams. Their opinion was that the lemon note undoubtedly comes from the hops. While such

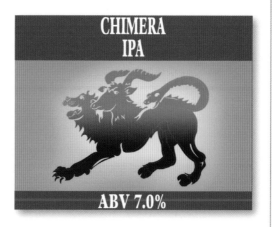

English varieties as the Golding are better known for their peppery and resinous character, fermenta-tion temperature and the interaction with yeast can produce esters – organic compounds – that are similar to fruit: banana and pineapple are often found in English-style ales while Belgian ales offer apricot, peach and mango notes.

Along with sherbet lemons, Chimera has a 'fresh bread' malt note. The palate is bittersweet, a fine balance of juicy malt, bitter hop and tangy lemon fruit. The finish is long with a solid backbone of malt balancing bitter hops and tart fruit.

TASTING NOTES

APPEARANCE:

AROMA:

TASTE:

OVERALL SCORE:

> *Downton clearly had the mythology in mind when naming the beer, though you won't find any trace of goat*

Curious IPA

**Source: English Wines, Tenterden,
Kent, England**
Strength: 5.6%
Website: www.englishwinesgroup.com

A curious brew, indeed! English Wines is based at the Tenterden Vineyard in Kent, in the heart of one of the major hop-growing areas. It sells wine under the Chapel Down name and, in 2005, decided to add beer to its portfolio but to adapt wine-making techniques to the brewing process. The company produces three beers, two of which are bottle-conditioned: IPA and Porter (featured in the Porters & Stouts section). The third beer is a lager. The beers are brewed by Andy Hepworth of Hepworth & Co in Horsham, West Sussex. The beer used to be called Cobb IPA, the name coming from Canterbury Cobb, an early-cropping version of the Golding hop. Andy suspects other brewers may use the Cobb variety but call it a Golding.

The beer is produced in the traditional manner of warm fermentation using ale yeast but is then conditioned for a long six weeks using champagne yeast supplied by English Wines. Andy says he tried fermenting the beer with champagne yeast but that was 'a nightmare' as the wine yeast normally works with fructose – fruit sugar – and struggles with maltose. The beer needs the long conditioning period for the yeast to slowly tackle the remaining malt sugars and convert them to alcohol. The result, Andy says, is a peach fruit note in the finished beer.

Curious IPA is brewed with Maris Otter pale malt, with hops added four times for aroma and bitterness. It's a copper-coloured beer with a distinctive aroma of fruit – peach and lemon – and a firm biscuit malt note underscored by floral hops. The palate is bittersweet, with the rich fruit notes building on the tongue but balanced by bitter, resinous hops and juicy malt. The long finish offers a fine balance of tangy fruit, bitter and peppery hops, and mellow malt.

Deschutes Hop Henge Experimental IPA

Source: Deschutes Brewery, Bend, Oregon, USA

Strength: 9%

Website: www.deschutesbrewery.com

Deschutes is one of the remarkable American Dream, rags-to-riches stories. The brewery was founded in 1988 by Gary Fish and brewed just 300 barrels in its first year. By 1993 a move to new premises was necessary and new equipment enabled more than 3,000 barrels a year to be produced. Expansion and additional kit the following year meant 50 barrels a time could be made, but still demand grew and in 2011 a new 100,000 plant was added, bringing total production capacity to over 400,000 barrels. There are now two brewpubs, in Bend and Portland, and the beers are widely exported within the U.S.

Deschutes is now the fifth largest craft brewery in the country and the eleventh in total sales – a remarkable achievement when you consider that ahead of them stand the likes of Budweiser, Coors and Miller. In spite of its success, the company remains committed to using only the finest raw materials, including hops that grow in abundance in Oregon and neighbouring Washington State. Hops have a deep imprint in the region: the Cascade Mountains that overlook the brewery in Bend give their name to one variety while Willamette National Forest has also given its name to a popular hop. Deschutes has a water recycling system that saves on water use, and also employs a capture system for carbon dioxide to avoid the gas created by fermentation leaching into the atmosphere.

With the Deschutes River running by the door and surrounded by such stunning scenery, it's a shock to find the Stonehenge prehistoric circles in Wiltshire, southern England, on the label of the IPA. As Stonehenge is thought to have been built between 2800 and 1500 BC, the site is a mite earlier than the first India Pale Ales of the late 18th and 19th centuries. But no doubt the elders at Stonehenge would have made some life-enhancing alcohol from grain.

The Deschutes IPA makes unstinting use of hops – a plant not available when Stonehenge was a working temple. Cascade and Centennial hops create a mighty 90 units of bitterness: this is one of the bitterest beers in the world and drinkers can expect an explosion of citrus fruit, with grapefruit to the fore. The grains are pale, crystal and carastan malts – the last two are stewed malts used for colour and flavour as they cannot be fermented by conventional brewers' yeast. The deep copper-coloured beer has a booming aroma of sweet toasted malt, ripe bittersweet fruits including grapefruit, mango and orange, along with piny and floral hops. Intense hop bitterness builds in the mouth with rich tart fruits and chewy malt. The finish is long and complex with a quinine-like hop bitterness mellowed by nutty malt and bittersweet fruit notes.

TASTING NOTES

APPEARANCE:

AROMA:

TASTE:

OVERALL SCORE:

Devil Dog Imperial IPA

Source: Laughing Dog Brewing, Ponderay, Idaho, USA

Strength: 10%

Website: www.laughingdogbrewing.com

A yellow Labrador called Ben calls the shots at the brewery. According to owners and founders Fred Colby and Michelle Douglass, Ben – like Emperor Nero – gives the thumbs-up or thumbs-down to each new brew. In Ben's case, it's one bark for 'yes' or two barks for 'no'. I think his owners' Imperial IPA is worth more than one bark but clearly canine beer tasters are a restrained breed.

Fred and Michelle launched their brewery in 2005 surrounded by the Selkirk Mountains in Idaho, which gives them access to pure mountain water ideal for brewing. They brew with the finest natural ingredients – malt, hops and yeast as well as pure water – and avoid cheaper grains and adjuncts. They have a 15-barrel plant and produce 4,500 barrels a year, with their beers now widely exported throughout the United States.

Their Imperial IPA is brewed with pale, caramalt and Munich malts and has no fewer than five hop varieties – Ahtanum, Cascade, Columbus, Northern Brewer and Simcoe – that create a shattering 98 units of bitterness. To achieve this level of bitterness, Fred and Michelle add 5.6 pounds of hops to each barrel they brew. The finished beer is copper coloured and the aroma has a massive assault of tangy citrus fruits with blood oranges to the fore and powerful hints of lemon and grapefruit in the background. There's a big peppery hop note and an underpinning of rich grain that's reminiscent of newly-mown barley fields. The powerful fruit notes dominate the palate but spicy hops and toasted caramel malt add to the pleasures. The finish has some malt sweetness from the darker grains but the balance of hops and tart fruit avoid any tendency to cloy.

A memorable beer: if I had a tail, I'd wag it. Ben, at the time of writing, is well into middle age. But he has a son called Ruger who will take over tasting duties in due course. Every dog has its day...

The powerful fruit notes dominate the palate but spicy hops and toasted caramel malt add to the pleasures. The finish has some malt sweetness from the darker grains but the balance of hops and tart fruit avoid any tendency to cloy. A memorable beer: if I had a tail, I'd wag it.

Epic Armageddon IPA

Source: Epic Brewery Company, Otahuhu, Auckland, New Zealand

Strength: 6.6%

Website: www.epicbeer.com

The beer is described as 'American-style IPA' and won a gold medal at the New Zealand beer awards in that category in 2011. But brewers Luke Nicholas and Kelly Ryan have adopted a 19th-century English technique to produce a fascinating variant of the main beer.

Luke founded the brewery in 2008 after living for several years in California where he fell in love with beer, Sierra Nevada IPA in particular. When he eventually returned home he launched Epic and developed his own interpretation of IPA with Armageddon. He doesn't stint on hops, with the equivalent of 42 hops in each bottle of beer. Kelly had earned his brewing spurs at the pioneering Thornbridge Brewery in Derbyshire before returning home to link up with Luke.

Armageddon won plaudits from drinkers and beer judges but Luke and Kelly, delving deep into the history of the first IPAs, were inspired to mature a batch of the beer in oak casks and to send them on the equivalent of a sea journey from England to India. In 2010, they filled two medium toast oak barrels imported from the United States with IPA and lashed them firmly on board the Cook Strait ferries that link New Zealand's North and South Islands. The casks endured six weeks on the ferries and 126 crossings. When the beer was tasted it was deemed to

be 'magnificent', with new aromas and flavours of oak and vanilla. The beer had also – intriguingly – increased from 6.6% to 7.2% in strength as a result of wild yeasts in the oak turning remaining malt sugars to alcohol.

The following year, Luke and Kelly filled 125 casks with IPA and repeated the experiment. But this time, when the beer had aged in wood, they blended it with fresh Armageddon at the rate of two-thirds wood aged and one-third fresh beer. They are likely to repeat this exercise on an annual basis, producing the blended aged beer as a seasonal offering. The beer is brewed with English pale ale malt with a touch of caramalt. Four American hops are used: Cascade, Centennial, Columbus and Simcoe, which create 60 units of bitterness. The pale copper-coloured beer has an enormous blast of lemon and grapefruit on the nose from the hops along with hop resins and slightly toasted/oatmeal malt. Bittersweet fruit, oatcakes and massive, iodine-like hop bitterness coat the mouth while the finish is long and complex, with tangy fruit, bitter hops and biscuit malt vying for attention.

With the aged beer, there are further contributions from oak and vanilla and a hint of sourness from wild yeast activity.

TASTING NOTES

APPEARANCE:

AROMA:

TASTE:

OVERALL SCORE:

TASTING NOTES

APPEARANCE:

AROMA:

TASTE:

OVERALL SCORE:

Fire Island Red Wagon IPA

Source: Fire Island Beer Company, Fire Island, New York, USA

Strength: 7%

Website: www.fireislandbeer.com

There's a touch of the Great Gatsby about this beer and brewery. Fire Island is known as 'the other New York' – a small island off Long Island and Manhattan Island, approximately 31 miles long and just 400 metres wide. It's accessible only by ferry and a tall red-and-white lighthouse guides boats to safe harbour. Wild deer roam free. Two brothers, Tom and Bert Fernandez, with their cousin Jeff Glassman, spent summers on the island and eventually took over a bar called The Shack on Atlantique Beach. They were keen home brewers and when they served their own lager in the bar they were encouraged to brew commercially. In 2007, they launched Fire Island Beer Co with Lighthouse Ale and followed that with Red Wagon IPA: the name commemorates an older genera-tion of islanders who moved goods around with red wagons. Indeed the island is still almost entirely motor traffic-free. Their beers, in bottle and on draught, are now available in New York City and other urban areas.

Tom, Bert and Jeff plan to build their own brewery on the island. At present they make small amounts of beer but the bulk is produced for them by the Olde Saratoga Brewery at Saratoga Springs, New York State. In spite of the name, it's a comparatively recent brewery, established in 1997 and owned by the Mendocino Brewery in California. It was set up to brew Mendocino beers for the east coast and it also produces beers for other companies.

Red Wagon IPA is brewed with two-row pale malt, caramunich, Canadian Munich and amber malts. The hop varieties are Cascade, Crystal and Warrior, which create 45 bitterness units. The darker malts are used sparingly, for the beer has a pale bronze colour with a su-perb spicy and peppery hop aroma balanced by resins, cracker wheat malt and tangy citrus fruit. Bitter and spicy hops kick in powerfully in the mouth, with gooseberry fruit and honeyed malts. Some malt sweetness comes through in the finish, balancing the shat-teringly bitter hops and tart fruit.

Florida Beer Swamp Ape IPA

Source: **Florida Beer Company, Melbourne, Florida, USA**

Strength: **10%**

Website: **www.floridabeer.com**

On trips to the U.S. and Canada, when the weather has been good and the surroundings inviting, I have often said: 'I'm just going for a walk in the woods.' To which I always get the response: 'Don't – bears!' Having learned my lesson, I would hesitate to enter Florida's swamps and Everglades for fear of meeting a Swamp Ape, described as 'a beast with a potent aroma and bite'. The beer named in its dubious honour certainly has a potent aroma and bite but they come from generous hop rates rather than the rancid teeth of a wild animal.

The Florida Beer Company is the state's biggest craft brewery, now run by Jeff Roberts and Thomas Barris. It started life as Indian River Brewing Company in 1996 and grew to its present size by merging with the Ybor City and Key West breweries. It has an impressively large portfolio which includes pale ale, porter, wheat beer and lager and the beers are sold as far north as New York City and Illinois. The standout beer is described as an imperial IPA: a number of American brewers produce beers with this designation. There's no historical justification for such a style but it does give brewers free range to indulge in even greater hop character in these big, bold and brassy interpretations. Swamp Ape uses a blend of Amarillo, Cascade, Centennial and Chinook American varieties along with Bavarian Tettnanger. They combine to produce a stunning 85 units of bitterness. The malt grist is equally complex: two-row pale malt, Europ and cherrywood smoked malt. The beer is deceptively pale – gold with a hint of bronze – and it has an enormous aroma of over-ripe pears and equally squashy strawberries, balanced by an explosion of spicy, floral and grassy hops and a smoky note from the malt. The ripe fruit overwhelms the palate at first, but smoky and oatcake malt, and bitter hop resins break through. The finish also starts with an intense ripe fruit note but ends with a blast of pungent hops and rich malt. It's a monster of a beer.

TASTING NOTES

APPEARANCE:

AROMA:

TASTE:

OVERALL SCORE:

TASTING NOTES

APPEARANCE:

AROMA:

TASTE:

OVERALL SCORE:

Flying Dog Imperial IPA

Source: Flying Dog Brewery, Frederick, Maryland, USA

Strength: 10%

Website: www.flyingdogales.com

This is more than a remarkable beer. If IPA is a well-travelled beer style, then Flying Dog is also a fascinating journey that weaves literature and art with brewing. The company started life as a humble brewpub in Aspen, Colorado, run by George Stranahan, a wealthy entrepreneur, philanthropist and rebel who became known as the godfather of 'Gonzo journalism'. In 1983, Stranahan climbed K2 in the Himalayas and, to celebrate, drank beer with his team in a bar in Pakistan. He noticed a painting on the wall of a flying dog, a Pakistani artist's interpretation of an English bird dog. It inspired Stranahan to return to the U.S. and open a brewpub in Aspen, Colorado, which he called Flying Dog. His neighbour was the writer Hunter S. Thompson and Stranahan encouraged him to develop Gonzo journalism, a gritty style of writing, often in the first person, with no attempt at objectivity. Thompson toured the U.S. on a motorcycle to search for the American dream, a journey fuelled by drugs and alcohol. His best-known book is *Fear and Loathing in Las Vegas*. Thompson introduced Stranahan to Ralph Steadman, a British artist famous for his savage political and social caricatures, who had illustrated some of Thompson's journalism. Encouraged by Thompson, Steadman agreed to design labels for Stranahan's beers.

There was a furore in 1995 when Flying Dog launched Road Dog Porter in 1995 with a label by Steadman that bore the slogan 'Good Beer, No Shit'. The beer was banned from shelves by the Colorado Liquor Board. Stranahan responded by changing the words on the label to 'Good Beer, No Censorship' and launched an ultimately successful appeal against the ban. The original slogan is still used on Road Dog Porter. The dispute didn't harm Flying Dog. The brewpub became a fully-fledged brewery in Denver and then moved east and south to a state-of-the-art plant in Franklin, Maryland, capable of producing 100,000 barrels a year.

The strong IPA is a further example of the American imperial style. As well as the strength of 10 per cent, it uses just one hop, the Simcoe, which creates 70 bitterness units. According to Steadman's label, Simcoe was the Greek god of beer and relaxation who developed tools for people to grow grain and hops. Most American craft brewers prefer to combine several hop varieties in their brews but Simcoe is a new variety, a hybrid bred for both aroma and bitterness. The beer has a pale bronze colour with a big grassy hop, mango fruit and cracker wheat aroma. Bitter hops, tart fruit and juicy malt fill the mouth while the finish is long and complex, with succulent tropical fruit, intensely bitter hops and lightly toasted grain. Steadman's drawing shows a bat with a face like a cartoon film producer: I leave you to work that out. If the 10 per cent beer is not to your liking, Flying Dog produces a 7 per cent Snake Dog IPA.

Flying Dog Brewery

Fuller's Bengal Lancer

Source: Fuller, Smith & Turner, Griffin Brewery, Chiswick, London, England
Strength: 5% cask; 5.3% bottle
Website: www.fullers.co.uk

Fuller's produced an excellent 4.8% IPA as a seasonal beer from the mid-1990s but this was replaced in 2010 by an up-rated version called Bengal Lancer that was an immediate success due to both its superb taste and clever branding that made it stand out from the crowded IPA sector. The beer is named for a cavalry regiment formed in the 18th century by the Nawab of Awadh in northern India. By the 19th century, the regiment was under the control of the British Army in India and the name symbolised the bamboo lances carried by the cavalry men. The officers of the regiment were either British or Anglo-Indian and the regiment served not only in India but also in Egypt, the Sudan and China. In China they helped put down the Boxer Uprising of 1900, a revolt against foreign presence in the country and the role of Christian missionaries. The Lancers fought alongside Japanese troops to defeat Chinese forces.

Fuller's development of a wide range of bottle-conditioned beers in recent years has underscored the company's commitment to both quality and to restoring forgotten or neglected English beer styles. Bengal Lancer is brewed with pale and crystal malts, hopped with Fuggles and Goldings and then dry hopped with Goldings and Target. The units of bitterness are 47. It has a deep gold colour and a rich and inviting aroma of nose-tingling hop resins, sherbet lemon fruit and a caramel note from the crystal malt. Passion fruit and lemon jelly dominate the palate but they are firmly balanced by a peppery and spicy Goldings hop presence. The finish is long and deep, with a bittersweet character from malt and fruit but with a massive hop presence – piny, spicy and peppery – from the English varieties.

The cask-conditioned version of the beer is available from October to January: check the brewery website for dates.

> The beer is named for a cavalry regiment formed in the 18th century by the Nawab of Awadh in northern India.

TASTING NOTES

APPEARANCE:

AROMA:

TASTE:

OVERALL SCORE:

TASTING NOTES

APPEARANCE:

AROMA:

TASTE:

OVERALL SCORE:

Greene King IPA Reserve

Source: Greene King Westgate Brewery, Bury St Edmunds, Suffolk, England

Strength: 5.4%

Website: www.greeneking.co.uk

Big brewers, in common with giant oil tankers, take a long time to turn round. Greene King is one of England's oldest breweries, dating from 1799 and based in the historic town of Bury St Edmunds, with its ruined abbey and handsome Georgian buildings. It's a major brewer of cask beer, with national brands that include the famous and redoubtable strong beer, Abbot Ale (see *300 Beers to Try Before You Die!*). But there's also been lingering controversy surrounding its biggest-selling beer, IPA. It's a highly successful beer, the biggest-selling standard Bitter in Britain, and it won a gold award in the 2004 Champion Beer of Britain competition. But at just 3.6% many people feel it should not be labelled IPA. For years, the brewery ignored the complaints but in 2012 changed course with startling speed, launching two new beers labelled IPA: Gold and Reserve.

The abrupt change was the result of extended market research by Greene King that showed that while cask beer was consumed mainly by drinkers of 35 years and above, a growing number of younger consumers were also switching to ale from lager. The research revealed that younger males drinking cask beer in the 25-34 age group had grown by 19 per cent. As a result of the research, backed by the simple fact that real ale was the only sector of the brewing industry showing any growth, the brewery expanded its range and in particular met its critics head-on with a new IPA that met the criteria of the style. I played a small, walk-on part in this bibulous drama. For several years I had lobbied Greene King's genial head brewer, John Bexon, to produce a stronger, genuine IPA. To this end, I gave him some 19th-century recipes for the style. The result was a delicious bottled beer called Very Special India Pale Ale but, sadly, sales were disappointing and it was discontinued. Then in 2012, Greene King announced a major promotion for two new draught and bottled IPAs, Gold and Reserve, as well as its mainstream IPA. The company spent £4 million on the launch, including a TV commercial that features casks of beer being tapped in a pub cellar and then enjoyed by happy revellers one floor above.

Reserve is brewed with Tipple pale malt, a comparatively new variety of barley grown by farmers just a few miles from the Westgate brewery. Only one hop is used, Styrian Goldings from Slovenia, which create 36 units of bitterness. The beer has a deep bronze/pale copper colour with grapefruit and orange notes on the aroma, slightly toasted malt and fresh pine hop resins. In the mouth, biscuit malt, citrus fruit and tart hops combine and lead to a long, dry and hoppy finish with continuing tart fruit and toasted malt. It was worth waiting for...

Holgate Hopinator

Source: Holgate Brewhouse, Woodend, Victoria, Australia
Strength: 7%
Website: www.holgatebrewhouse.com

Australia is a country with a fascinating mix of influences where food and drink are concerned. The first immigrants, of course, were British (not all of them there on a voluntary basis). But, as visitors find today, the northern hemisphere's traditions have been joined by those brought by more recent arrivals from Asia and the Pacific. This melding of cultures can be seen at first hand at Holgate. Paul Holgate is from Manchester, an English city steeped in brewing traditions, while Natasha Holgate is from Sri Lanka and she has a great passion for good food and cooking. They toured the United States and Europe in the 1990s and were bowled over by the beers they discovered on the trip. They were inspired in particular by the American craft brewing revolution and were determined on their return home to offer distinctive beer and food from their rural base in the Macedon Ranges in Victoria.

Paul was a pastry cook and in 1999 he put his knowledge of working with grain to good effect by switching to brewing. He and Natasha built their brewery alongside Keatings Hotel in Woodend, which had once acted as a stopover for prospectors making the journey from Melbourne to the Bendigo gold fields in the 19th century. In 2002 they bought the hotel and renovated it, allowing Natasha to use her skills to offer top-quality meals in the restaurant and bar. Paul has brought an Old Country touch the bar, where some of his beers are cask conditioned and served with imported British handpumps and beer engines.

His interpretation of IPA is amber-red in colour. Alongside pale malt, Paul uses an Australian version of Vienna Red malt that originally gave the characteristic colour to Viennese lagers and the Oktoberfest beers of Munich. He blends in 'a good whack' of English pale crystal malt and German CaraRed. He adds hops no fewer than six times during the brewing process. The varieties are Australian aromatic and resinous Topaz with American Chinook and Citra. Paul then adds Australian-grown Cascade whole flower hops in the fermenting tank. This, he says, gives an effect similar to 'first wort hopping', which means adding hops at the start of the copper boil. The hops combine to produce an impressive 65 to 66 units of bitterness.

This is not a beer for the faint-hearted. The aroma and palate are assaulted – in the best possible way – by a massive blast of fruit from the hops: grapefruit, orange, lemon and passion fruit, balanced by a solid backbone of rich malt with a powerful hint of caramel and butterscotch. The long finish is hoppy and bitter with a continuing influence of wholemeal malt and caramel notes. It ends dry and shatteringly hoppy.

In the restaurant the beers play more than a walk-on part. Natasha recommends beers to match with her dishes and also cooks with Paul's brews, which feature in such signature dishes as beef and ale pie. As well as serving beer on handpump, the British tradition is underscored by such good old offerings as fish and chips and sausage and mash.

Hopshackle Double Momentum

Source: Hopshackle Brewery, Market Deeping, Lincolnshire, England

Strength: 7%

Website: www.hopshacklebrewery.co.uk

Nigel Wright's mission in life is to recreate old English beer styles, and he naturally turned his attention to IPA. His first interpretation of the style was called Momentum as the flavours seemed 'to go on and on'. He then moved up a notch with Double Momentum, which, at 7 per cent, is true to the IPAs brewed in the 19th century. Nigel says Double Momentum is based on an 18th-century recipe, which is early for the style, but we do know that George Hodgson was brewing beer for export to India in East London towards the end of that century.

Nigel has had a peripatetic journey since he started brewing commercially in 2006. His kit was made for him by engineers at the Charles Wells' brewery in Bedford, using converted Grundy tanks, vessels used in the food and drinks industries. The kit was installed at the Saracen's Head pub in Cambridge and from there moved to the Cox's Yard leisure complex overlooking the River Avon in Stratford-upon-Avon. At this stage, Nigel was using malt extract in the manner of home brewers but when he moved yet again, to the ancient market town of Market Deeping, on the banks of the River Welland, he added a mash tun in order to use malted grain rather than syrup. The town has had an open-air

market since the 13th century but is better known for its stone buildings, including several coaching inns from the 18th century.

Double Momentum is something of a hybrid, a cross between a true English IPA and the more aggressively hopped modern American versions. Nigel uses double the amount of hops – English Challenger and Goldings – than in Momentum. They are added three times drring the copper boil, with the final addition 15 minutes before the end of the boil. The massive hop addition creates 100 units of bitterness – be warned, this beer will leave crease marks in your tongue! The grains are Maris Otter pale malt and wheat malt with the addition of invert sugar.

The beer has a pale bronze colour and a pungent nose of hop resins, toasted malt and tart orange and lemon fruit. There's ripe, bittersweet fruit – now more peach and mango than citrus – biscuit malt and bitter hop resins. The long finish offers a late burst of grapefruit – the competing fruits in this beer are stunning – with juicy malt, and tangy and bitter hop resins; it's finally dry and intensely bitter. When I queried the 100 units of bitterness with Nigel, he confirmed the rating but pointed out that the bitterness would soften over time and my sample was two years' old. It's clearly a beer to be laid down.

Houblon Chouffe Dobbelen IPA Tripel

Source: Brasserie d'Achouffe, Achouffe, Belgium

Strength: 9%

Website: www.achouffe.be

The name, in common with the beer, is quite a mouthful. It's also a conundrum: Belgium had colonies but they were in Africa and Belgian brewers were not involved in the India trade. It's a measure of the rekindled interest in IPA that this idiosyncratic brewer has added its version of the style to the burgeoning list. Beers from Achouffe all bear on the label the image of the bearded and red-hatted gnome that inhabits the dense forests of the Ardennes region. The brewery has grown from its humble beginnings in a tiny building in the remote village of Achouffe in the Luxembourg region. It was founded by brothers-in-law Pierre Gobron and Kris Bauweraerts, passionate home brewers who went the extra kilometre and quickly found a ready market for their strong bottled-conditioned beers (the keg versions also have small amounts of live yeast). They moved to bigger premises in old farm buildings in 1986 and finally opened a new complex of modern brewhouse, bistro and visitor centre as a result of the success of the beers in French-speaking Canada. Today, Achouffe is a celebrated name, with the village on the tourist map and an annual beer festival in August, while the beers are exported widely.

On the label of the IPA, the Chouffe gnome is surrounded by hop bines growing on their frames, an indication of the bitterness to come in the beer. Tripel in the name reflects the fact that three hop varieties are used: Amarillo, Saaz and Tomahawk. The last two are used as bittering hops during the copper boil while Amarillo is added as a 'dry hop' to the finished beer. All three combine to create 59 units of bitterness. The malts used are pale and Pilsner while the brewing water is 'Burtonised', which means sulphates are added to intensify malt and hop character.

The beer has a hazy gold colour and a rich fruit aroma of blood oranges, lemon and peaches, backed by creamy malt and peppery and spicy hops. Hops with an iodine-like intensity burst across the tongue with tangy lemon fruit and creamy malt. The finish has enormous length with a quinine-like bitterness, oatcake maltiness and tart fruit. As a result of the strength, this would be a good beer to lay down for a few years to monitor its development.

In 2006, the brewery was acquired by the major Belgian independent Duvel Moortgat, famous for its strong golden ale, Duvel. There has been no diminution in the character of the Chouffe beers and it seems that Duvel – the Devil – and the Chouffe gnome make good companions.

TASTING NOTES

APPEARANCE:

AROMA:

TASTE:

OVERALL SCORE:

TASTING NOTES

APPEARANCE:

Golden
Cloudy
3

AROMA:

Strong Hoppy
5

TASTE:

Fruity/G'fruit
Biscuity
Pepper. 5

OVERALL SCORE:

13.

The Kernel India Pale Ale

Source: The Kernel Brewery, London, England
Strength: 6.1%/7.2%/7.3% (but varies)
Website: www.thekernelbrewery.com

The Kernel wears its heart on its sleeve: founder Evin O'Riordain has named his brewery for the seeds and the husk of a grain of barley that provide the motive force to produce malt and fermentable sugar. Evin, as his name suggests, is not a London Cockney but an Irishman with a passion for beer styles from the British Isles, including Ireland. He worked for Neal's Yard Dairy in Covent Garden and Borough Market where he gained a useful knowledge of restaurants and bars in London. In 2009, he opened his brewery under railway arches in Bermondsey, where the rumble of trains overhead drowns the quieter noises of making beer. Evin taught himself to brew and made beer at home for more than two years. He never went on a specialised brewing course for, as he frankly admits, there's a lot of information available on the internet.

He works with his partners Chrigl Luthy and Toby Munn and the three quickly established a reputation for fine-tasting beer on draught and in bottle. Evin supplies a number of top London restaurants, including Chez Bruce, Hawksmoor and Pied à Terre as well as a growing number of bars and pubs. Kernel's beers use complex mixes of grains and hops: to date the brewery has used 18 different malts and 25 hop varieties.

Evin's interpretation of IPA is based on a malt base of Maris Otter pale malt with cara and cara gold malts for colour and flavour. But the hop regime varies. Two tasted for this book included one made with American Centennial and Chinook hops. The beer, 7.3%, is bronze coloured with a big aroma of spicy and peppery hops, mango, peach and raspberry fruit and an oatcake malt note. There are tart and intensely bitter hops in the mouth, bittersweet fruit and a ripe, biscuit malt note. The finish has an iodine-like bitterness with creamy malt and ripe melon and peach fruit.

The second version, 7.2%, is a 'single hop' beer brewed with just the American Citra variety. Again, the beer is bronze coloured but the nose is met by an explosion of bittersweet grapefruit with hints of grass and a sweet Ovaltine malt character. Tart fruit builds in the mouth, balanced by creamy malt and earthy, herbal hop notes. The finish has pepper and spice from the hops, continuing ripe fruit and biscuit malt.

The finish has pepper and spice from the hops, continuing ripe fruit and biscuit malt.

THE KERNEL BREWERY LONDON

INDIA PALE ALE

CITRA

6.1% ABV

Lagonda IPA

Source: Marble Beers, Manchester, England

Strength: 5%

Website: www.marblebeers.co.uk

The Marble brewery has a mission: to brew beers that are organic and vegan. Ingredients are sourced from chemical-free agricultural suppliers and the beers are cleared without the use of finings made from fish bladders. The original five-barrel plant was installed in 1997 in the Marble Arch Inn on Rochdale Road. As a result of growing demand for the beers in both cask and bottle, a second, 12-barrel unit was built in 2009 in the Newton Heath area. Brewing continues at the Mable Arch, one of the finest pubs in the country. It's Grade II-listed, with a red granite exterior and, inside, ceramic tiled walls, a glazed ceiling, an elaborate frieze that lists a vast range of alcohols and a floor that slopes alarmingly from the entrance towards the back of the pub, which houses the brewery. It's possible to think you've had too much to drink before a drop has passed your lips. The Laurel & Hardy Appreciation Society meets in the pub on the third Wednesday of every month to watch the duo's films and the comic possibilities of the sloping mosaic floor wouldn't have been lost on Stan Laurel. He was born in Lancashire, though it's not known if he ever visited the pub.

The two breweries produce a vast range of beers: 33 are listed but they are not all available at any one time. Lagonda IPA is a regular and is named for the famous Aston Martin luxury limousine, one of which was owned by the father of the current licensee of the pub, Jan Rogers. The beer is brewed with lager malt, wheat malt and caramalt, while the complex hop recipe includes Admiral, Boadicea, Goldings, Hallertau Aroma and Motueka. The last two hops both come from New Zealand: the Hallertau variety is an offshoot of a hop from the Bavarian Hallertau while the Motueka is similar to a Czech Saaz. If lager malt seems an odd grain to use in an IPA, there's historic justification for its use. In the 19th century, English brewers often imported lager malt from mainland Europe as its pale colour gave their IPAs the pallor expected by drinkers.

Lagonda has a golden colour and an entrancing aroma of citrus fruits from the hops, with lemon and grapefruit to the fore. There's also a piny note from the New Zealand varieties and creamy malt. Pine is also evident in the mouth, with sappy malt, citrus fruits and firm hop bitterness. The finish is bitter and hoppy with a good balance of grapefruit and creamy malt. Lagonda is also used in the pub kitchen as a marinade for steak and ale pie; several of the other house beers are also used in the preparation of meals.

Organic hops have come a long way in a few years. I was a judge in an organic beer competition held at the Marble Arch some years ago. It was a difficult task for the judges, as just about every beer used New Zealand hops. Mercifully free from hop pests and disease, New Zealand for years was the major supplier of organic hop varieties. But now many more are available from other countries, including England, and they are given free rein in the Marble Arch.

ORGANIC

LAGONDA
IPA

a deceptively robust classic

TASTING NOTES

APPEARANCE:

AROMA:

TASTE:

OVERALL SCORE:

Little Creatures Stimulus IPA

Source: Little Creatures Brewing, Fremantle, Western Australia, Australia

Strength: 5.4%

Website: www.littlecreatures.com.au

In 2009 and 2010, when I was a guest at the Australian International Beer Awards in Melbourne, a glittering occasion in a large hotel on the waterside, I could have been forgiven for thinking there was only one brewery in the country. Time and time again, representatives of Little Creatures trudged almost wearily to the stage to pick up yet another prize. Their awards include Best International Brewery and Best Australasian Brewery. They are fitting tributes, for the Perth and Fremantle areas of Western Australia are recognised as the cities were Australian craft brewing was born, bringing relief to throats parched by sweet and fizzy brands. If you've ever sampled Swan Lager you'll appreciate why Western Australians needed something more stimulating.

It comes as something of a surprise, therefore, to learn that Little Creatures was founded in 2000 by two wine makers, Janice McDonald of the acclaimed Stella Bella winery, and Phil Bexton. But I've found on my visits Down Under that many wine makers head for the nearest bar for a cool beer at the end of the working day. Janice and Phil, with their experience of wine-making, were fascinated by the profound citrus character imparted to beer by American hop varieties, which led to a long love affair between Little Creatures and American Cascades, which come fresh off the boat in the harbour.

They built their first small brewhouse by the waterside of the Fishing Boat Harbour in a shed that had once been part of a crocodile farm: no jokes, please, about their beers having a good hop bite. The success of the first beer, an American-style Pale

Ale, saw rapid growth of the company. In 2008, a new brewery was installed along with a Loft Bar and a Burger Bar. The candlelit restaurant has become a major attraction for both locals in 'Freo' – Fremantle – and visitors. Little Creatures prides itself on having a hop back in the brewery, thought to be the first in Australia, where the hopped wort circulates over fresh hops following the copper boil, picking up additional aroma and flavour.

Stimulus IPA is brewed with pale, dark crystal and Munich malts and just one hop, Cascade, which is added in the copper, the hop back and the fermenter. The Cascades create 55 bitterness units. The beer is copper coloured, perhaps a tad dark for the style. It has a mighty waft of grapefruit and passion fruit on the nose, balanced by hop resins and rich toasted/caramelised malt. Bittersweet fruit coats the tongue but there's a solid backbone of rich, chewy malt and bitter hops. The finish is long, with continuing ripe and tangy fruit, bitter hop resins and nutty malt.

The nationwide demand for Little Creatures' beer has led to the company opening a bar and restaurant in Melbourne: the Dining Hall, 222 Brunswick Street, Fitzroy, where the beers can be enjoyed alongside pizzas, burgers, and fish and chips.

In 2013 the company was bought by Australia's biggest brewing group, Lion Nathan. Fingers crossed...

 Their awards include Best International Brewery and Best Australasian Brewery.

Little Valley Python IPA

Source: Little Valley Brewery, Cragg Vale, Hebden Bridge, West Yorkshire, England

Strength: 6%

Website: www.littlevalleybrewery.co.uk

Little Valley is based in the upper Calder Valley, with superb views of hills and dales, high above Hebden Bridge. Brewer Wim van der Spek is in an ideal location for using fresh Pennine water for his beer. Along with his wife, Sue Cooper, Wim is dedicated to using only organic malt and hops, with pure water as an added bonus. His beers have the seal of approval of both the Soil Association and the Vegan Society. Isinglass, made from fish bladders, is used in most breweries to clear finished beer but Wim won't use it. The brewery is based on a former chicken and pig farm: the site is being redeveloped as a rural business park with power supplied by a wind turbine.

Wim is from the Netherlands and grew up close to Rotterdam. At the age of 18 he created a beer called De Gustibus est Disputandum, which translates roughly as either 'taste and discuss' or 'get pissed and fight'. He went on to study at Wageningen University where he obtained an MSc in food science. As a student, he did a placement with the leading Dutch brewery, Gulpener, and then studied to become a master brewer in Munich. He settled in Britain in 2000 after meeting Sue Cooper while they were cycling to Tibet. Wim was searching for the world's highest brewery. Sue, in contrast, was working for Voluntary Service Overseas in Nepal. She grew up in Jarrow in North-east England and worked for 20 years in community and economic regeneration in Yorkshire, Lancashire and the North-east before joining VSO.

Wim set up Little Valley with a ten-barrel plant in 2005 after working for two years with Black Isle Brewery in Inverness in Scotland. Sue joined him at Cragg Vale in 2008 and is in charge of sales and marketing. They produce 3,000 barrels a year and Python IPA is their premium product. It's named after both the Indian snake and the water-cooled pipes in pub cellars that keep cask beer at the correct temperature as it travels from cask to bar. There are no known Monty Python connections, though the beer would appeal to Terry Jones of that clan: he's a beer lover who, in the 1970s, helped fund the Penhros Brewery in Herefordshire.

Python IPA is brewed with pale, Munich and wheat malts and is hopped with First Gold, Fuggles and Pacific Gem varieties. It has a bright gold colour with sulphur on the nose, spicy hop resins, orange fruit, freshly harvested grain and a hint of butterscotch. Butterscotch comes from diacetyl, a compound created by yeast during fermentation. Tart citrus fruit and bitter hops dominate the palate while the finish is long and complex with spicy hops, tart fruit, toasted malt and the continuing hint of butterscotch. The beer is available both cask conditioned and bottle conditioned.

TASTING NOTES

APPEARANCE:

AROMA:

TASTE:

OVERALL SCORE:

Murray's Icon 2IPA

Source: Murray's Craft Brewing, Port Stephens, New South Wales, Australia

Strength: 7.5%

Website: www.murraysbrewingco.com.au

At Murray's Brewing scant attention is paid to that old warning that one shouldn't mix the grape and the grain, for the brewery shares its site with the Port Stephens Winery, the major wine maker in New South Wales, on 35 acres of land with vineyards and eucalyptus trees. The complex shares a shop, the Cellar Door, and also a restaurant where fine beer and wine are matched with food.

Murray's has the good fortune to be in an area of outstanding natural beauty in the Hunter Valley area of North South Wales. The bay at Port Stephens is more than twice the size of Sydney Harbour and has the biggest stretch of sand dunes in Australia, with bottlenose dolphins and whales populating the sea.

The brewery started life in 2005 in Taylor's Arm on the north coast of NSW. In 2009 it relocated to Bob's Farm in Port Stephens where it now has the capacity to produce 30 beers with a bottling line that can fill 2,000 bottles an hour.

Head brewer Shawn Sherlock has a passion for hops, so much so that for his IPA he adds hops not only to his boiling copper but also in the mash tun and during the 'run off' – when the sweet wort leaves the tun. This is a rare, if not unique, practice. In total he adds one kilo of hops per 100 litres of beer. While the beer makes a bow in the direction of 19th-century English IPAs, Shawn's version is heavily influenced by modern American pale ales. His pale malt is imported Maris Otter from England, with German Vienna malt and crystal malt for colour and flavour. The hops,

used in pellet form, are New Zealand Nelson Sauvin and Pacifica, which create a literally stunning 80 units of bitterness.

The finished beer has a deep copper colour with an aroma of passion fruit and tangerine, peppery hops, and caramel from the stewed malts. There's sweet biscuit malt in the mouth balanced by bitter and peppery hops and tart fruit. The finish is shatteringly dry and hoppy with a quinine-like bitterness but balanced by rich malt and tangy, bittersweet fruit.

Murray's has added a bar and restaurant in the Manly district of Sydney that has 18 beer taps plus two handpumps for cask-conditioned versions of the brewery's beers.

North Cotswold Monarch IPA

Source: North Cotswold Brewery, Stretton-on-Fosse, Warwickshire, England

Strength: 10%

Website: www.northcotswoldbrewery.co.uk

TASTING NOTES

APPEARANCE:

AROMA:

TASTE:

OVERALL SCORE:

Jon Pilling is a man in a hurry to brew good beer and to delve deep into brewing archives to recreate old English styles. His Arctic Global Warmer, an interpretation of a 19th-century style developed for Arctic explorers, was listed in *300 Beers to Try Before You Die!* He has added an IPA with great hop character and a strength that puts the beer in line with modern American imperial and double versions.

Jon brewed on a 10-barrel plant. He's a chef but he was always fascinated by beer and brewing. He worked in Loughborough next to a pub called the Phantom & Firkin, part of a nationwide chain of brewpubs. He offered to help in the brewery and was soon taken on as second brewer. When the entire Firkin group closed, Jon worked for a number of artisan breweries, including Alcazar, Cox's Yard, Exe Valley, Grainstore and Wicked Hathern. I first met him at Cox's Yard in Stratford-upon-Avon where I was impressed by his passion for brewing.

He proved his commitment to the cause in 2005, when he sold his house in order to buy North Cotswold. The brewery dated from 1999 and when the founder moved on, Jon was keen to run his own show. The site now has a visitor centre and shop where Jon brewed a wide range of regular and seasonal beers in both cask and bottle-conditioned form.

Monarch is brewed with an eye to both detail and history. Jon gave up his Christmas holiday to start the mash and the finished beer is then stored in cask until August to mimic the journey of a 19th-century IPA from England to India. It's brewed with Maris Otter pale malt, light crystal malt and wheat malt. The hops are four American varieties: Columbus, Tomahawk, Simcoe and Warrior. Tomahawk lives up to its name: it brandishes a powerful cutting-edge of bitterness, while the other three pile in with massive hop resins and citrus fruit.

The beer has a hazy bronze colour with a massive blast of peppery hop resins on the nose, a fresh bread and buttery malt note, and bitter orange fruit. Fruit builds in the mouth and now takes on a passion fruit and even marmalade character; fruit is balanced by ripe, sweet malt and bitter hops. The luscious, long finish has buttery malt, spicy hops and bitter-sweet fruit, but finally ends dry and intensely bitter.

The bottle-conditioned version of the beer can be extremely lively. I would recommend easing the cap off at one edge to allow excess carbon dioxide to vent; leaving the bottle to stand for several minutes before removing the cap. This should avoid gushing.

John Piling moved on again late in 2012, but his beers continue to be brewed.

Odell Myrcenary

Source: Odell Brewing, Fort Collins, Colorado, USA

Strength: 9.3%

Website: www.odellbrewing.com

Doug Odell is a master brewer, a leading light in the American craft brewing movement, and an ambassador for good beer. Regular presentations for American beer held in London always feature Doug, who talks quietly yet passionately about his love of beer. In the autumn

of 2011, when I lectured on IPA at the World Beer Festival in Durham, North Carolina, who should pop up but Doug Odell, charming, worldly-wise and still full of enthusiasm even though he's reached that time of life when he should be hanging up his mashing fork.

TASTING NOTES

APPEARANCE:

AROMA:

TASTE:

OVERALL SCORE:

Along with family members Wynne and Corkie Odell, Doug launched his brewery in 1989 in a converted grain store in Fort Collins. It was only the second microbrewery in the state of Colorado. Doug had been planning his commercial venture for years. He was a long-standing home brewer and had researched and refined brewing recipes that he then created in his kitchen in Seattle. Finally, he settled on two beers, 90 Shilling – based on a Scottish style – and Easy Street Wheat. He launched them by selling them door to door in Seattle, using an old pick-up truck. He was sufficiently successful to move to the grain store in Fort Collins. By 1994 he was selling 8,300 barrels of draught beer a year. He added bottled beer two years later. Today the substantial company produces 45,000 barrels a year and its beer is sold throughout the U.S.

It's typical of Doug's attention to detail that his double IPA takes its name from myrcene, one of the essential oils in the hop plant. The grains used are pale, Pilsner, crystal and Vienna malt while the hop varieties are all-American: Cascade, Centennial and Chinook, which create 80 units of bitterness. The beer has a powerful aroma of sherbet lemons, piny and resinous hops and cookie-like malt. The palate is a fine balance of citrus fruit, juicy malt and earthy hop resins. The finish becomes dry at the end but along the way offers bittersweet fruit, piny hops and a malt note reminiscent of Polish rye bread.

TASTING NOTES

APPEARANCE:

AROMA:

TASTE:

OVERALL SCORE:

Peerless Full Whack

Source: Peerless Brewing Company, Birkenhead, Merseyside, England

Strength: 6%

Website: www.peerlessbrewing.co.uk

Full Whack is a 'Scouse IPA', according to brewery owner Steve Briscoe. Terms such as 'whack' or 'wack' and Scouse are unique to Merseyside. Liverpudlians are known as Scousers, from a type of stew eaten in the area, while Wack is a form of greeting similar to London Cockneys' 'mate'. Sailors from Liverpool used to demand their 'full whack' of food when manning ships.

Steve is from Cumbria and worked first in telecoms before turning his hand to brewing. He was a dedicated home brewer and a visit to the Bass breweries in Burton upon Trent made him a keen drinker of cask beer. He built his brewery in Birkenhead, across the Mersey from Liverpool, in 2009, using equipment originally made for a restaurant-cum-brewery in Manchester called Mash & Air, owned by restaurateur Oliver Peyton: Alastair Hook, now at Meantime in Greenwich, brewed at Mash & Air. When the restaurant closed, the brewing kit moved to the Grand Union brewery in Hayes, Middlesex, and finally to Birkenhead.

The name Peerless comes from the trademark of the former Birkenhead Brewery, which closed in the 1960s. The distinctive tangerine-coloured brewing vessels, including small conical fermenters, can produce 33 barrels of beer a week. Steve has been joined by Mark Powell and Alex Morley, young men with a passion for good beer and recreating authentic styles. Full Whack uses Maris Otter pale malt and a touch of crystal and is hopped with First Gold and Fuggles. The pale amber beer has a powerful aroma of spicy and floral hops, tart fruit and a 'fresh bread' malt note. Hop bitterness builds in the mouth but is well balanced by juicy malt and tangy fruit. The finish is long and ends dry and bitter but there are continuing contributions from honeyed malt and tart fruit.

Pitfield 1837 India Pale Ale

Source: Pitfield Brewery, Epping, Essex, England

Strength: 7%

Website: www.pitfieldbeershop.co.uk

Pitfield has, for 30 years, been a pacesetter among Britain's artisan breweries. It was created in 1982 by Rob Jones and Martin Kemp who ran the small brewery in North London alongside the Pitfield Beer Shop that specialised in selling beer from other small producers. The brewhouse was so cramped that the equipment was designed along the lines of a Russian doll, with each piece of kit – mash tun, copper and hop back – slotted inside one another. In 1985 Martin and Rob launched Dark Star, a dark 5% beer that just two years later won the prestigious Champion Beer of Britain award from CAMRA at the Great British Beer Festival.

When the partners decided to go their separate ways, Rob took the brand name Dark Star to Brighton in Sussex, where he set up a brewery of the same name. Martin takes a keen interest in the environment and – inspired by a group of environmental campaigners led by a character called Swampy – launched a range of beers called Eco Warrior, which use only organic materials. He later added a series of beers that recreated old English styles, including Porter, imperial Stout and IPA. In 2006, he moved Pitfield to Essex where he now brews on a farm with 25 acres of organic barley for his use. All his beers are now organic, they have the seal of approval of the Soil Association and are suitable for vegans. The beers are sold at farmers' markets, the brewery's own shop, which sells online, and in selected pubs in Essex and London.

While Martin concentrates on sales and deliveries, back on the farm beer is brewed by

Andy Skene. Andy is a Canadian whose parents came from Aberdeen and Norwich. When he left college, he toured Britain and mainland Europe, where he was startled to find that beer could be packed with aroma and flavour, unlike the mass market bland lagers back home (the beer scene in Canada has changed dramatically since his voyage of discovery 25 years ago). He was keen to learn to brew, met members of SIBA, the Society of Independent Brewers, and heard there was a vacancy at Pitfield. He meant to stay for three months and is still there 25 years later.

Pitfield's IPA is based, as the name suggests, on an 1837 recipe. Organic materials are not always easy to source but, at the time of writing, Andy was using an English organic malting barley variety called Westminster, which is grown in East Anglia. The hops are English First Gold and Rakau from New Zealand: Rakau is a Maori name. The hops create 42 units of bitterness. Andy also uses organic cane sugar from Cuba, which is added during the copper boil: he explained that his mash tun is not big enough to hold sufficient malt to achieve 7 per cent alcohol. He also blends in a small amount of chocolate malt to give the copper colour he believes is true to the 19th century style.

The copper/amber beer has a deep aroma of peppery hops, citrus and mango fruit and a faint hint of chocolate. In the mouth, 'barley-cup' malt is balanced by bitter and peppery hops with a continuing ripe fruit note. The finish becomes dry and bitter but there are powerful contributions from lemon, mango and passion fruit as well as oat-cake notes from the grain and a hint of chocolate.

TASTING NOTES

APPEARANCE:

AROMA:

TASTE:

OVERALL SCORE:

Ridgeway IPA

Source: Ridgeway Brewing, South Stoke, Oxfordshire, England

Strength: 5.5%

Website: None

Peter Scholey is a brewer who understands the importance of yeast. He was the head brewer at the revered Brakspear brewery in Henley-on-Thames and, when it closed in 2002, Peter was determined to carry on brewing and to create beers with a distinctive Thames Valley character. The Brakspear yeast is especially interesting as it was used at Henley in a 'double drop' fermentation system: two storeys of fermenters were ranged one row above the other. When fermentation was underway in the top storey, the unfinished beer was dropped down to the vessels below where a more vigorous fermentation continued. Unwanted protein and dead yeast cells were left in the top vessels. One of the signatures of Brakspear beer was a butterscotch note from diacetyl created during fermentation.

Peter Scholey's Ridgeway operation takes its name from the Ridgeway, England's oldest road – no more than a broad path these days – that was created by druids centuries ago. It crosses five counties as it cuts across the Wessex Downs and Chiltern Hills. Peter doesn't brew in these sylvan surroundings as he uses the plant at the Cotswold Brewery in another beautiful area of the English countryside at Bourton-on-the-Water in Gloucestershire. Peter has his own fermenters at Cotswold, which is predominantly a lager producer and uses American-built equipment based on a mash mixer and lauter tun system. Peter produces beers in both cask- conditioned and bottle-conditioned formats and he vigorously exports bottled beer to the United States.

Ridgeway IPA is brewed with Maris Otter pale malt and is hopped with Cascade, Challenger, Styrian Goldings and Target. Peter stresses that the Cascades are an English version of the famous

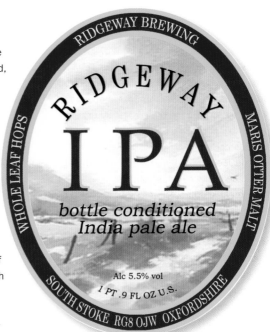

American hop. They are grown on just one farm in Kent and have a more restrained citrus note than the American version. The pale gold beer has a rich fruit aroma of tart lemons with fresh, earthy hop resins and a 'wholemeal bread' malt note. Lemons join forces with bitter oranges on the palate but there's a solid backbone of chewy malt and bitter and spicy hops. The long finish is bitter and hoppy but has continuing contributions from juicy malt and citrus fruit, with just the faintest hint of butterscotch from that good old yeast culture. The beer has won several awards including Champion South-East Bottled Beer in 2005 and 2006 in the Society of Independent Brewers' annual awards and Southern region champion in the Tesco Drinks Awards in 2009.

Rogue Brutal IPA

Source: Rogue Brewing Company, Newport, Oregon, USA

Strength: 7.1%

Website: www.rogue.com

From my experience, accountants tend to be a conservative bunch, but Rogue Brewing owes its existence to a passion for good beer from a member of the noble order of number crunchers. Jeff Schultz was the accountant in question. He was a keen home brewer and he urged one of his clients, Bob Woodell, to launch a small commercial brewery along with his friends Jack Joyce and Rob Strasser. The first brew pub was in Ashland in breathtaking Oregon countryside alongside a creek. The founders' mission was to brew hand-crafted ethical beers made without additives or preservatives and to use ingredients grown with the minimum use of fertilisers. Their creed is a simple one: 'We prefer to be David rather than Goliath.'

The Ashland site was launched in 1988 and the first beers were met with acclaim by drinkers. As a result, a year later Jack Joyce went in search of a new site in Newport and was offered a substantial part of the original restaurant in the Mo's Clam Chowder chain. Later that year the Bay Front Brew Pub opened and the founders had the good fortune to be joined by master brewer John Maier, who had cut his teeth at Alaskan Brewing. Since then, John has built a large portfolio of award-winning beers, including brilliant stouts that featured in *300 Beers to Try Before You Die!* For all his beers, he uses pale malt made from a blend of two-row Harrington and Klages barleys grown on volcanic-rich land in the Pacific Northwest where only a limited amount of fertiliser is permitted. He also imports small amounts of grain from selected European maltsters for specific beers: for example, he uses some English pale malt in Brutal IPA.

There's a touch of carawheat in the beer for head retention and flavour, while the only hop is the American Crystal, which creates 59 units of bitterness. Crystal is known as a 'triploid' variety, cloned from German Hallertau with American Cascade, Brewers Gold and Early Green. John Maier uses a Pacman yeast culture that he says is ideal for bottle conditioning and produces little diacetyl or butterscotch notes. Brutal IPA has a pungent aroma of citrus fruit, with lemon and grapefruit to the fore, with cracker wheat malt and spicy hop resins. Bittersweet citrus fruit builds in the mouth but there's a solid backbone of biscuit malt and bitter hops. The finish is long and complex, finishing dry and bitter, but with continuing notes of tart fruit and ripe malt.

Rogue now has a third brewpub in California.

TASTING NOTES

APPEARANCE:
COPPER CLEAR - THIN HEAD 4.

AROMA:
FRUITY BISCUITY 4

TASTE:
CITRUS LONG AFTER TASTE 4 STRONG

OVERALL SCORE:
12

ROUNDED SMOOTH

RISK

ROGUE

1 PT. 6 FL.OZ. 650 ML.

Brutal IPA — INDIA PALE ALE

TASTING NOTES

APPEARANCE:

AROMA:

TASTE:

OVERALL SCORE:

St Austell Proper Job

Source: St Austell Brewery, St Austell, Cornwall, England
Strength: 4.5% cask; 5.5% bottle
Website: www.staustellbrewery.co.uk

Roger Ryman, head brewer at St Austell, blends the old and the new in his IPA, a beer that so impressed judges at the annual Champion Beer of Britain awards that it won the bottled beer gold trophy in both 2010 and 2011. Roger goes to the hop fields of the Yakima Valley in Washington State in the U.S. every year to select the finest hops and he brings the pungent, fruity character of American varieties to meet the traditional oatcake malt notes of England's finest barley, Maris Otter. He likes the flavours of Maris Otter so much and the harmony it strikes with his yeast culture that he has encouraged six farmers in Cornwall to grow the barley for him on long-term contracts. Cornish Maris Otter now accounts for two-thirds of St Austell's barley supply.

Following the mash, Roger and his brewing team add Chinook and Willamette hop pellets to the copper boil. The hopped wort then rests on a bed of Cascade, Chinook and Willamette whole hops. Fermentation temperature is low in order to allow malt and hop flavours to dominate: too high a temperature and fruit would overwhelm the raw materials. The finished beer is conditioned in the brewery for 10 to 14 days. It's then filtered and re-seeded with a fresh batch of the same yeast used for primary fermentation. Roger says the yeast works well in bottle as it sticks to the bottom of the glass.

The beer takes its name from Cornish dialect: a 'proper job' means a task well done and refers to the role of the 32nd Cornwall Regiment in protecting the British residency in Lucknow during the Indian Mutiny of 1857. The regiment was raised to the status of a Light Infantry detachment by a grateful Queen Victoria. Proper Job has a powerful fruit aroma of grapefruit, orange and mango, with strong contributions from oatcake malt and tangy hop resins. Bittersweet fruit, chewy malt and bitter hops combine in the mouth while grapefruit comes to the fore in the finish but is beautifully balanced by biscuit malt and tangy, bitter hops.

St Austell is a family-owned brewery in Cornwall, founded by Walter Hicks in 1851 and still run by his descendants. His great-great-grandson James Staughton is now in charge and, working with Roger Ryman, has boosted the fortunes of the company with such striking new beers as Proper Job and Tribute. The brewery has traditional wooden and copper brewing vessels housed in buildings made of mellow Cornish stone. The site has a fine visitor centre, packed with fascinating brewery memorabilia, while an annual Celtic Beer Festival is held every winter in the brewery cellars.

BOTTLE CONDITIONED

PROPER JOB

POWERFULLY HOPPED

INDIA PALE ALE

Sebago Frye's Leap IPA

Source: Sebago Brewing Company, Gorham, Maine, USA

Strength: 6.2%

Website: www.sebagobrewing.com

New England meets old England in this vibrant version of IPA. The beer was first brewed in 1998 by a craft brewery with an acclaimed restaurant where beer and food are matched. The IPA has become so popular that it's brewed all-year-round and is distributed throughout the eastern seaboard of the U.S. The IPA takes its name from the cliffs that tower over Sebago Lake on Frye Island in Cumberland County. The island is in remote countryside and is accessible only by ferry or private boat. It's a popular summer retreat for people throughout New England and New York State but the island is uninhabited from November to April when the lake is covered in thick ice and the ferries stop running.

The brewery, wisely, is based on the mainland. Its beers are all-malt and use American two-row barley malted by the Briess Malting Company. The IPA is made with pale malt and two caramel or stewed malts. Cascade and Centennial hops are added three times during the boil in the kettle: at the start of the boil, halfway through and finally five minutes from the end. Following fermentation, the beer is matured for two to five days, during which time the equivalent of one pound of hops per barrel are added to the conditioning tanks. Finally the beer is dry hopped with a further addition of Cascade and Centennial. In total, this big insertion of hops creates 55 units of bitterness.

The beer that finally makes it to the glass has a bright bronze colour and an aroma of spicy, herbal hops, cracker wheat grain, tart citrus fruit and a hint of fresh tobacco from the stewed malts. Bitter hop resins and tangy orange fruit dominate the palate, underpinned by slightly toasted malt with a hint of toffee from the caramalts. The long finish has massive hop bitterness with hints of quinine and iodine, complemented by citrus fruits and nutty, sappy malt. In Sebago's restaurant that adjoins the brewery, the chef recommends lobster and shrimp risotto, spicy BBQ tenderloins, swordfish, chicken cordon bleu or oven-roasted prime ribs to accompany the IPA.

Bitter hop resins and tangy orange fruit dominate the palate

TASTING NOTES

APPEARANCE:

AROMA:

TASTE:

OVERALL SCORE:

Shepherd Neame India Pale Ale

Source: Shepherd Neame Brewery, Faversham, Kent, England

Strength: 4.5%

Website: www.shepherdneame.co.uk

In the autumn of 2012, Shepherd Neame launched two beers, India Pale Ale and Double Stout, which were faithful recreations of two beers brewed in the 19th century. Master Brewer Stewart Main and brewery archivist John Owen had discovered brewers' logs from the Victorian period with beer recipes written in code. The code was felt necessary to avoid rival breweries stealing the recipes. Such clandestine activity was not unusual: the founder of the Brakspear brewery in Henley-on-Thames, Oxfordshire, invented his own form of shorthand to stop his recipes being copied. In the case of Shepherd Neame, it stood opposite another brewery, Fremlins, in Faversham and the rivalry between the two companies was intense.

Shepherd Neame is England's oldest brewery. It formally dates from 1698 but it's believed that brewing was carried out on the same site many years earlier. The brewery is still run by the Neame family and today it's a major presence in the brewing industry. It produces 200,000 barrels a year and owns 360 pubs. As well as the main ale and lager brands, Shepherd Neame has installed a micro-plant where Stewart Main is encouraged to develop special and historic beers. When he and John Owen had cracked the code in the brewers' logs, they set about creating an IPA that had first been brewed in 1870 at the height of the craze for strong pale ales. The beer is brewed with pale and crystal malts and is hopped with classic Fuggles and Goldings varieties, which create 40 units of bitterness: the hops are added three times during the copper boil. Brewing started in oak mash tuns still in use at the brewery.

The beer has a bright orange/bronze colour and has massive tart fruit on the aroma reminiscent of that old confectionery known as orange and lemon slices, along with spicy hop resins and cracker bread malt. Bittersweet citrus fruit, juicy malt and bitter hops combine in the mouth while the long finish is dominated by bitter hops and citrus fruit but with a solid underpinning of sappy malt. It's a wonderfully quenching beer that also comes in a stronger 6.1% ABV bottled, although non bottle-conditioned, version complete with labels and crown cap that carry the brewery's logo from the 19th century. The beer is part of the brewery's Classic Collection and is available online from the brewery shop.

Sierra Nevada Torpedo Extra IPA

Source: Sierra Nevada Brewing Company, Chico, California, USA

Strength: 7.2%

Website: www.sierranevada.com

It's impossible to avoid the clichés: Torpedo blows you away. This is an impressive interpretation of IPA, but you would expect nothing less from one of America's most revered craft breweries. The company was launched in 1981 by two passionate home brewers, Paul Camusi and Ken Grossman, who wanted to offer drinkers beer with aroma and flavour in place of bland national brands. Using converted tanks from the dairy industry, they opened their modest brewery in the university town of Chico where thirsty students rapidly spread the word about the wonders of the new beers on offer. By 1989, Paul and Ken were able to invest in a custom-built copper brewhouse made in Germany. Eight years later, the German manufacturer had to make additional vessels in order that Sierra Nevada could grow production to 800,000 barrels a year.

The brewery's reputation was built on its Pale Ale and its Bigfoot barley wine, both listed in *300 Beers to Try Before You Die!* The brewers use pure water from the snow-topped Sierra Mountains with only the finest grains and hops. Torpedo has created enormous interest both inside and outside the U.S. as the brewery has developed a new vessel shaped like a torpedo where the beer rests on a deep bed of hops before it's packaged for draught and bottled consumption. The hop regime, which results in 65 bitterness units, is complex. In the brew kettle, the bittering hop is Magnum, with Crystal and Magnum added at the end of the boil. In the torpedo, Crystal and Magnum are joined by Citra, which lives up to its name by delivering stunning aromas and flavours of citrus fruit. The grains used are two-row pale malt and crystal malt.

The beer has a burnished bronze colour with a great waft of grapefruit and lemon jelly on the nose, with spicy hop resins and a 'fresh bread' malt character. The palate is shatteringly bitter, with touches of iodine and quinine, but the bitterness is softened by the rich bittersweet fruit and chewy, sappy malt.

Grapefruit, lemon, passion fruit and even lime marmalade pack the finish with spicy hop resins and rich, slightly toasted malt. Sublime.

TASTING NOTES

APPEARANCE:
DK GOLDON-
RICH HEAD
4

AROMA:
STRONG
CITRUS FRUIT
HOPPY
3

TASTE:
DEEP STRONG
TASTE -
GRAPEFRUIT
ROLLS ON 5
TONGUE

OVERALL SCORE:
12

VERY CLOSE
TO OUR
S/N

Teignworthy Edwin Tucker's East India Pale Ale

Source: Teignworthy Brewery, Newton Abbot, Devon, England

Strength: 6.5%

Website: www.teignworthybrewery.com

The Teignworthy Brewery is based in the ideal place for making good beer: a maltings. The brewery shares the Victorian stone buildings that make up Tucker's Maltings, the last producer of barley malt in the West Country. John and Rachel Lawton launched their small brewery in 1994, naming it for the local river, the Teign, while 'worthy' comes from the Viking *wortha*, meaning homestead: the Vikings had a settlement in the area. The brewery, which has won many prizes for its beers, now has a 20-barrel plant and produces 100 barrels a week. As well as their own cask and bottled beers, John, Rachel and their brew crew also produce a range of bottle-conditioned beers for Tucker's, which are available in the maltings shop and online (www. tuckersmaltings.com).

Tucker's was founded by Edwin of that clan in 1831 and an IPA brewed in his honour is fitting, as he supplied malt to brewers at the height of the first wave of India Pale Ales in the 19th century. As well as being the only producer of malt in the region, Tucker's is a traditional 'floor maltings'. Most modern companies produce malt in rotating drums but Tucker's remains true to the older style of spreading grain on heated floors, turning it by hand to encourage germination and finally loading it in to a kiln. The kiln is a type of oven where the grain is spread on a mesh frame and heat blasts up from below: the temperature used determines whether pale or darker malts are produced. Tucker's now has gas heaters but for many years it used coke: the maltings stands alongside the main railway line from the West Country to London and wagons used to unload coke direct into the maltings from the tracks. Tours of the site, including the brewery, are available: see the website above.

Teignworthy's IPA is brewed with lager malt, which may come as a surprise. But in the 19th century a number of English brewers imported lager malt from mainland Europe in order to give their pale ales a genuine light, golden hue. The brewery blends in a touch of wheat malt to give the beer a good collar of foam. The hops are Bramling Cross and Goldings. The bright, golden beer has an inviting aroma of lightly toasted malt with lemon citrus and peppery hop notes. Creamy malt, spicy hops and tangy fruit fill the mouth while the finish becomes increasingly bitter, with earthy and peppery hop resins, tart fruit and a lingering 'fresh bread' malt note.

> *Teignworthy's IPA is brewed with lager malt, which may come as a surprise. But in the 19th century a number of English brewers imported lager malt from mainland Europe in order to give their pale ales a genuine light, golden hue.*

Uinta Hop Notch IPA

Source: Uninta Brewing Company, Salt Lake City, Utah, USA

Strength: 7.3%

Website: www.uintabrewing.com

When you consider the importance of mineral-rich brewing water to the production of India Pale Ale, Salt Lake City sounds the ideal place to brew a modern version of the style. The Salt Lake is saltier than the ocean but Uinta prefers to use the pure waters of the mountain ranges in the state and then to add salts as required for individual brews: the brewery takes its name from the Uinta Mountains. The brewery began in the most humble way in 1993, in the shed of a former garage mechanic. Beer was sold to local bars, restaurants and liquor stores. A bottling line was added in 1996 and increasing demand led to a major move in 2001 to a custom-built complex measuring 26,000 square feet. The buildings were put together at remarkable speed, in sharp contrast to Salt Lake City's most famous building, the Mormon Temple that took 40 years to finish: the city is home to the Church of Latter Day Saints, with its followers known as Mormons.

The brewery is modern in every respect and uses wind power to drive the brewing process: the company slogan is Earth, Wind and Beer.

IPA is part of a series called Classic Line. It's brewed with pale malt and small amounts of Munich and cara malts. The complex hop regime includes Apollo, Cascade, Chinook, Bravo and Zythus; bitterness units are a mighty 82. The beer has an entrancing gold colour and a dense, fluffy head of foam. There's a big aroma of peaches and mangoes, with creamy oatmeal malt and tangy hop resins. Bitter hops and ripe fruit dominate the palate with a strong backbone of clean, juicy malt. The finish has some pleasing malty sweetness but it's balanced by earthy hop resins and a continuing mellow fruitiness.

TASTING NOTES

APPEARANCE:

AROMA:

TASTE:

OVERALL SCORE:

59

TASTING NOTES

APPEARANCE:

AROMA:

TASTE:

OVERALL SCORE:

Westerham National Trust Viceroy India Pale Ale

Source: Westerham Brewery Company, Crockham Hill, Kent, England

Strength: 5%

Website: www.westerhambrewery.co.uk

Robert Wicks opened his brewery in 2004 at Westerham, which is close to Chartwell, the country home of Sir Winston Churchill. Churchill, in common with members of the Royal Air Force who were stationed at Biggin Hill airfield during World War Two, enjoyed the beers brewed by the local Black Eagle Brewery. Black Eagle was taken over in 1959 by the giant Ind Coope Brewery based in Romford and in Burton upon Trent, which closed Black Eagle in 1965. Robert has restored the brewing traditions of the area, down to using the same water supply as Black Eagle and two of its yeast strains stored in the National Collection of Yeast Cultures in Norwich.

Robert, who uses custom-built brewing equipment made in Canada and shipped to England, has rapidly built a strong base for his cask ales. He has seven regular beers, along with seasonal ales and several bottle-conditioned beers, including Viceroy IPA. He brews at Grange Farm on land owned by the National Trust and the Trust approached him to make a beer in honour of Lord Curzon, who was the Viceroy of India from 1899 to 1905. He was also a great supporter of historic buildings. In India, he restored the Taj Mahal to its former glory. When he returned to England, he bought Tattershall Castle in Lincolnshire in 1911 and Bodiam Castle in Sussex in 1916. He also set about restoring the family home at Kedleston Hall, Derbyshire, which eventually passed to the National Trust in 1986.

Curzon was a controversial figure both in India and at home, but he was known to enjoy good beer. In his memoirs, *Leaves from a Viceroy's Notebook*, he tells of the time he was trekking from Afghanistan to India on horseback

and he was hallucinating about beer. 'As I rode down the grassy slopes, I saw coming towards me in the distance the figure of a solitary horseman... at that moment I would have given a kingdom, not for champagne or hock and soda, or hot coffee, but for a glass of beer!' When the horseman drew level with Curzon, he pulled open his coat and handed the viceroy a bottle of Bass Ale.

The Westerham beer that carries Curzon's name and image on the label is brewed with Maris Otter pale malt and hopped with Target and Progress varieties that are grown in Scotney Castle's hop garden. The units of bitterness are 50. It has a honey colour with spicy hops, wholemeal biscuits and plum fruit on the nose. Tart and peppery hops, chewy malt and ripe plum fruit fill the mouth while the finish is bitter and spicy but with a good balance of juicy malt and tangy fruit. The beer is available in National Trust shops that are licensed to sell alcohol (www.nationaltrust. org.uk), from independent retailers in South East England and from the brewery online.

There's a connection between Curzon and Churchill. A piece of doggerel about the viceroy went as follows: My name is George Nathaniel Curzon/I am a most superior person/My cheeks are pink, my hair is sleek/I dine at Blenheim twice a week. Blenheim Palace near Oxford is the ancestral home of the dukes of Marlborough. Winston Churchill was the grandson of the seventh duke and frequently stayed at the palace. In common with Curzon, Churchill enjoyed a glass of beer (among other liquids) and famously said: 'I have taken more out of alcohol than alcohol has taken out of me.'

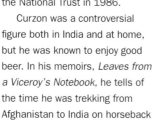

Pilsners

When drinkers throughout the world call for a Pilsner or a Pils they expect to receive a golden beer that is stronger than a standard lager but that may have only a fraction more flavour or character. Brewers can be careless with terminology and Pilsner – often spelt Pilsener – is a case in point.

Freedom Pilsner

The first golden lager appeared in the Bohemian city of Pilsen in 1842 and the term Pilsner meant, in German, a beer 'from Pilsen'. As the rest of the world rushed to copy a beer style that transformed lager brewing, the Pilsen brewery belatedly labelled its beer Pilsner Urquell in 1898, meaning the Original Source of Pilsner. The registration document referred to the 'absurdity and illogicality of using the word "Pilsner" for beers brewed in towns outside of Pilsen'. It hoped the title would act as an appellation and prevent passing-off. But as the Czech lands became embroiled in a struggle for independence from the Austro-Hungarian Empire, followed by Nazi invasion and then 50 years of dictatorship, Pilsner Urquell was reduced to a beer produced mainly for countries within the Soviet bloc. Brewers in the West took the opportunity to use, misuse and often bowdlerise the term Pilsner.

In some cases, the term was rendered meaningless. When the giant American brewer Miller launched its Miller Lite brand in Britain in the 1990s, it found British drinkers were concerned more with flavour than low levels of carbohydrates. As a result the beer was renamed Miller Pilsner, an insult to both history and taste buds. The name Pilsner was soon dropped from the British product, but Miller had the last laugh. The global company is now called SABMiller, following a merger with South African Breweries, and its portfolio includes none other than Pilsner Urquell (featured in *300 Beers to Try Before You Die!*).

The greater availability of the Czech beer – which, after more than a decade of indifferent quality, has now returned to something of its old character – has reawakened public attention to the style. Drinkers are more aware of its origins, and the rich and complex aromas and flavours that a true Pilsner should offer.

The style is a product of the Industrial Revolution. It was the ability to produce pale malt in kilns fired by coke – a relatively clean-burning fuel, and to keep storage cellars cold with the aid of ice-making machines that made golden lager possible on a mass scale. But lager beer is far older than 19th century Pilsner. *Lager* is a German word meaning storage place. For centuries, brewers in central Europe had struggled with the problem of keeping beer free from infection during long, hot summers. As early as the 11th century, monks at the monastery of Weihenstephan – Holy Stephen – in Freising near Munich had matured their beer in caves deep below the church. During the course of the following centuries, brewers matured their beer in icy caves in the Alps and they noticed that yeast worked more slowly at a low temperature, while wild yeasts and bacterial infection were held at bay. The yeast strains used were developed into a culture that became the norm for producing beer by cold or 'bottom' fermentation, so-called because the yeast dropped to the bottom of fermentation vessels but continued to turn malt sugars into alcohol.

The early lager beers were brown in colour as their malts were prepared by roasting them in kilns using wood fuel. The breakthrough came in Pilsen in Bohemia when disgruntled tavern owners poured an entire batch of the local brewery's beer down the city's drains when it was found to be sour and undrinkable. The tavern owners demanded a switch to the 'Bavarian' beers being made in Munich. As a result, local businessmen invested in a new company, the Burghers' or Citizens' Brewery. A brewer from Bavaria, Josef Grolle, skilled in the art

LEFT: **Veltins Pilsner, Germany**   CENTRE: **Gambrinus brewery, Czech Republic**   RIGHT: **Freedom Pilsner pump, England**

of lager beer, was hired, while Martin Stelzer, the architect who designed the plant, returned from England, where pale ale was in vogue, with a malt kiln that was fuelled by coke.

When the first golden lager appeared in Pilsen in 1842 it was embraced with fervour not only in the Czech lands but throughout the Austro-Hungarian Empire. It quickly conquered Germany and Scandinavia while brewers from Central Europe took the knowledge and skill to make golden lager to the United States and Latin America. But in the 20th century, while Czech beer disappeared from western sight during the Soviet period, golden lager suffered an arguably worse fate in the United States, the world's biggest brewing country. Prohibition, which lasted from 1920 to 1933, led to the closure of most breweries. Those that remained, including such giants as Anheuser-Busch, Coors and Miller, had a vast market to themselves and they refashioned lager as a thin, bland and over-carbonated parody of the European style.

> *Brewers in the United States and, more recently, Australia and New Zealand, have restored the good name of Pilsner.*

The brewing world has now moved on. The Soviet bloc is no more and drinkers who now visit the Czech Republic and other central European countries have discovered the fine beers that survived the dead hand of bureaucracy for half a century. In the West, craft brewers in the United States and, more recently, Australia and New Zealand, have restored the good name of Pilsner.

Independent German brewers, keeping faith with the *Reinheitsgebot*, the 15th-century purity law that permits only malted grain, hops, yeast and water to be used in brewing beer, continue to make their drier and more hop-accented versions of the style.

While the Czechs may wish that only the beers from Pilsen were labelled Pilsner, they can rest easy in the knowledge that both brewers and drinkers are now more aware of an important difference in the manner of making a Pilsner – or for that matter a Prague beer or a Budweiser – to the versions produced in other countries. In February 2012, Josef Tolar, the retired but still revered brew master at Budweiser Budvar in the Czech Republic, explained in a talk in London that Czech beers, including Pilsner, are brewed with some unfermented 'extract' or malt sugar remaining in order to give fullness of palate to the finished product. This is why Pilsner Urquell, with 40 units of bitterness, nevertheless has a rich, rounded flavour, in which creamy and toasted malt balances the floral, piny character of Czech Saaz hops. German Pilseners or Pils on the other hand (the difference in spelling or the contraction are deliberate to avoid confusion with the original) are fully fermented out and are drier and more bitter as a result.

I have chosen for this section versions of the style from Germany, the U.S. and Australasia. With respect and deference to the Czechs, the only interpretation from the republic comes from Pilsen where the Gambrinus Brewery shares the same site as the illustrious Original.

Samuel Adams Noble Pils

Source: Boston Beer Company,
Boston, Massachusetts, USA

Strength: 4.9%

Website: www.samueladams.com

The Boston Beer Company may be best known for its pale ale and IPA but founder Jim Koch started his brewing career with a lager. It stressed his family's German roots and restored the lager-brewing traditions of five generations of Kochs that made beer. A Koch-owned brewery in St Louis, Missouri, was taken over by Anheuser-Busch so, decades later, Jim was delighted to win the beer concession at St Louis Airport and prove that beer called lager could have a rich flavour even in the home town of American Budweiser.

Noble Pils is a recent addition to Boston's portfolio and is a blend of the Bavarian and Bohemian interpretations of the style. The term 'noble' comes from the German use of the word to describe hops from Bavaria and Franconia that have a delicate, floral and spicy character. Five hop varieties are used to make Noble Pils and they are added at three stages of the copper boil to give the correct balance of aroma and flavour. The hops are Hallertau Mittelfrüh, Hersbrucker, Spalt and Tettnanger from Bavaria and Franconia, with Saaz from the Czech Republic. The beer has 34 units of bitterness.

The malts have been chosen with equal care. They are all 'floor malted', which means the malt slowly germinates on heated floors rather than in rotating drums. Jim Koch and his brewers believe floor malt gives the richest biscuit character to the finished beer. The barley varieties used are Copeland, Harrington and Metcalfe pale malt from America, while Czech Pilsner malt adds a dash of authenticity as well as a touch of bronze colour to the beer.

The beer has spicy and floral hops on the nose, along with toasted malt and a hint of citrus. Bitter hops dominate the palate, with tart lemon fruit and juicy malt adding their own distinctive character. Lemon fruit and spicy hops dominate the long finish but there's a solid underpinning of toasted malt. It's a complex, rewarding and refreshing beer.

TASTING NOTES

APPEARANCE:

AROMA:

TASTE:

OVERALL SCORE:

63

TASTING NOTES

APPEARANCE:

AROMA:

TASTE:

OVERALL SCORE:

Croucher Pilsner

Source: Croucher Brewing Company, Rotorua, New Zealand
Strength: 5%
Website: www.croucherbrewing.co.nz

Paul Croucher and his partner Nigel Gregory have won plaudits and prizes for their Czech-style Pilsner since launching their brewery in 2005. They work in the 'thermal wonderland' of Rotorua, on the shores of a lake of the same name, in an area famed for its constant eruptions of steam, hot water and even mud as a result of volcanic activity. The town is a three-hour drive from Auckland on North Island. Paul was a student at Dunedin University where his ambition was the noble one of making great beer.

He began brewing at home, then went into business with Nigel. They started to build their brewing plant in 2004 and were rewarded with the top prize in the Bohemian Pilsner class of Brew NZ that year, even though the brewery was not officially open. Demand for their beers, which includes another much-praised Pale Ale, forced the partners to move to a bigger site in 2008 and they were boosted by winning the championship award in the international lager class at Brew NZ in 2010.

The beer is brewed with all New Zealand ingredients: Pilsner malt and Motueka and Riwaka hops, with 10 per cent wheat malt for a good head.

The finished beer has a burnished gold colour with a thick collar of foam. The aroma offers toasted malt with tropical fruit and spicy hops. The palate is dominated by a full-bodied toasted malt character with a good balance of citrus and hops. Hints of caramel make an appearance in the long finish alongside tart orange fruit and spicy hops. The beer finally becomes dry and quenching.

The aroma offers toasted malt with tropical fruit and spicy hops.

Emerson's Pilsner

Source: Emerson's Brewing Company, Dunedin, New Zealand

Strength: 4.9%

Website: www.emersons.co.nz

In 1983 Richard Emerson, aged 18, travelled with his parents from Dunedin in New Zealand to Scotland, a trip made by many Kiwis of Scottish descent keen to see the original Dùn Èideann, the Gaelic name for Edinburgh. It turned out to be a rite of passage journey for Richard, for he had his first taste of British and European beers during the trip and he was entranced by both the flavours and variety of styles he came across. They were in sharp contrast to the standard bland lagers available back home and he returned determined to improve the diversity of beer on offer.

He launched his small brewery in 1992 and immediately attracted attention with his first beer, London Porter. A year later he had to expand his plant and by 2005 he had outgrown that and moved yet again. His current brewery has two kettles (coppers), one with a 1,200 litre capacity and the second with 5,000 litres, which gives him great flexibility in producing short-run as well as regular beers. With a full-time staff of nine, Richard currently produces one million litres of beer a year.

His Pilsner, in common with all his beers, is unfiltered and is brewed with organic Gladfield lager malt grown locally, plus a touch of Carapils. Just one New Zealand hop variety is used, the Riwaka. Richard says the fruitiness of the hop compares with the celebrated Marlborough Sauvignon Blanc grapes grown in New Zealand. The beer has 33 units of bitterness and is lagered for three weeks. It's one of the most popular in the country and in 2009 won the overall championship in Brew NZ, following with a bronze medal the following year. The beer has a toasted malt and citrus hop aroma, with ripe orange and passion fruit on the palate, balanced by a 'corn-on-the-cob' note from the malt and a fresh-mown-grass hop note. The finish is long, with a fine balance of juicy malt, bitter hops and tangy fruit.

TASTING NOTES

APPEARANCE:

AROMA:

TASTE:

OVERALL SCORE:

Flensburger Pilsener

Source: Flensburger Brauerei, Flensburg, Schleswig-Holstein, Germany

Strength: 4.8%

Website: www.flensburger.de

The German brewing industry used to pride itself on the fact that it was made up of a large number of small, independent and often family-owned companies that offered great choice to drinkers. But in recent years many of them have fallen into the hands of global groups. Two famous names in Munich brewing, Spaten and Löwenbräu, are now part of the world's biggest brewing group, AB InBev, while the Dr Oetker pizza empire has taken control of a number of major breweries and has reduced the great brewing city of Dortmund to just one producer. In Hamburg, Holsten is now owned by Carlsberg of Denmark, belated retribution perhaps for the annexation of Schleswig-Holstein by Prussia in the 19th century.

It's therefore comforting to find that the Flensburger brewery in the Bundesland region of Schleswig-Holstein remains firmly independent. In the manner of the Pilsen brewery, it was founded by citizens of the town in 1888 and is still controlled by two families, Petersen and Dethleffsen. In the early days of the brewery, before the development of ice-making machines, the citizens would cut ice from local lakes and pack it into the brewery cellars to keep the lager rooms cold while the beer matured. The brewery uses brewing 'liquor' from a well that is fed by pure, soft Ice Age water that flows down from Scandinavia.

The beer is labelled 'Pilsener' to mark an agreement between German brewers and Pilsner Urquell made just before World War One that avoids the use of the Czech spelling of the style. But locals in the town and surrounding area merely call the beer 'Flens', which should satisfy the Czechs. The brewery was a pioneer of swing-top bottles, which are still used today and give an important signature to all the Flensburger brands. The company highlights the 'plop' as a bottle is flipped open but keeps quiet about the fact its bottles are popular with home brewers.

The beer is brewed with pale malt and is hopped with varieties from the Hallertau region; bitterness units are 38, reflecting the fact that drinkers in the far north of Germany demand beers with a pronounced hop bitterness. Flensburger Pilsener is lagered for around one month and has an aroma of herbal and floral hops, a light hint of lemon fruit and toasted malt. Hop bitterness builds in the mouth but is balanced by rich malt and a touch of lemon fruit, followed by a dry, hoppy and juicy malt finish.

Freedom Pilsner

Source: Freedom Lager Company, Abbots Bromley, Staffordshire, England

Strength: 5%

Website: www.freedomlager.com

Whisper it quietly, but genuine lager is being brewed in England. Freedom is a different beer to the mainstream global lager brands brewed under licence, which are not stored or conditioned in the correct lager fashion and are moved through their breweries with a speed that would leave most ale brewers gasping in astonishment. Freedom was founded in Fulham, London, in 1995, moved for a while to the Covent Garden area of the capital but in 2004 made a major change of location to Staffordshire. A cheeky move, you might say, as Abbots Bromley is not far from that renowned capital of ale brewing, Burton upon Trent. The brewery uses water that has percolated through limestone and as a result gives a very English twist to the Pilsner model.

In its new rural retreat, Freedom supplemented its 10 hectolitre maturation tanks with additional vessels bought from China and, as demand grew, five new fermenters were added. In London, Freedom was seen as a boutique brewery supplying a few bars and restaurants, but now it has carved a unique presence in the beer market. In 2008, the company was bought by Ed and Susan Mayman, who have built sales throughout the country and now produce more than 2,500 barrels a year. Sales are divided equally between draught and packaged, with most draught going to pubs. Ed Mayman says he is not attempting to compete with mass lager brands: 'We can't match the global brewers. Customers have to buy into what Freedom is about. If people want something cold, yellow and fizzy, then that's not an outlet for us.' As well as Pilsner, Freedom brews an Organic Lager and – digging into European brewing heritage – a Dark Lager, too.

Brew Master Ian Ward has brought years of well-honed experience to the company. He was awarded an MSc from Birmingham Brewing School, then worked for Wilson's Brewery in Manchester and Allied Breweries before travelling the world to advise new small craft breweries. For his Pilsner, he uses lager malt developed for him by Warminster Maltings in Wiltshire. Four hops are added in stages to the copper boil: Challenger and First Gold – two English varieties – are used for bitterness, with American Liberty and Czech Saaz for aroma. The finished beer has 18 units of bitterness. This is low by Pilsner standards but it says a lot about brewing water or 'liquor' in Staffordshire. Most European Pilsner brewers use water so soft that it's almost free of mineral salts. But the water of the East Midlands and the Trent Valley in particular are rich in such minerals as gypsum and magnesium and they draw out the full flavours of malt and hops. As a result, Freedom is an very bitter Pilsner even though the bitterness levels are comparatively low.

The beer is lagered for 40 days – Ian Ward will mature the beer for as long as demand allows. It has a toasted malt and spicy hops aroma with a strong tang of citrus. Malt, hops and fruit combine to give a full palate, while the finish becomes dry and hoppy but with continuing contributions from biscuit malt and tart fruit.

TASTING NOTES

APPEARANCE:

AROMA:

TASTE:

OVERALL SCORE:

> ❛ *Whisper it quietly, but genuine lager is being brewed in England* ❜

TASTING NOTES

APPEARANCE:

AROMA:

TASTE:

OVERALL SCORE:

Gambrinus

Source: Pivovar Gambrinus, Pilsen, Czech Republic

Strength: 4.5%

Website: www.sabmiller.com

Gambrinus lives in the shadow of its illustrious neighbour, Pilsner Urquell. In common with Urquell, it's now part of the global empire run by SABMiller, a merger of South African Breweries and Miller of Milwaukee. But in the Czech Republic, Gambrinus beers are among the most popular and it's rightly considered to be a true Pilsner – 'from Pilsen'.

The brewery was founded in 1869 by a group of businessmen in Pilsen who were keen to follow the remarkable success of Pilsner Urquell. Among the investors was Emil Škoda, the car manufacturer, but most of the investors were German speakers and they called the company Erste Pilsner Actienbrauerei: *Actien* means a company controlled by shareholders. They were keen to challenge the hegemony of the Czech-run brewery next door. The new brewery called its main product Pilsner Kaiserquell – King's Original Pilsner – but references to the Kaiser became unpopular during World War One and the brewery was renamed Gambrinus after a famous boozy medieval prince in the Low Countries, who has given his name to several beers and breweries.

The two Pilsen breweries, separated only by a wall, and using the same soft water supply from artesian wells, fought each other with great vigour for market share. But following World War Two they were merged by the communist regime into one nationalised conglomerate called West Bohemian Breweries. They continued as one company, Pilsner Urquell Corporation, following privatisation, and became part of SABMiller as global giants

snapped up the breweries of the old Soviet bloc. The combined output of the two breweries is around 3.5 million hectolitres, with Gambrinus accounting for half of that production. Czech brewing has such a proud heritage that new Western owners have not traduced it by drastically speeding up production times or using cheap ingredients. In *300 Beers to Try Before You Die!*, I was critical of brewing methods at Pilsner Urquell that I believed had led to a diminution in the character of the beer. But that happened when the brewery was part of a Czech-owned company following privatisation. They stopped fermenting and lagering in wood and switched to modern stainless steel conical vessels. Although the beer will never regain the complexity of its wood-aged past, it has improved demonstrably in recent years.

Gambrinus beers were never brewed in wood: the original vessels were made of cast-iron and they were replaced by stainless steel in the 1990s. The original tiled brewhouse remains. In common with most Czech breweries, it uses Moravian malt and hops from the Žatec region north of Prague, famous for its floral and spicy varieties. The beer has 33 units of bitterness and has a fine aroma of fresh-mown grass and spicy hops, with juicy malt and grassy hops on the palate, and a finish in which malt and hops are beautifully balanced.

Visitors to the Gambrinus/Pilsner Urquell complex can tour both breweries and sample the beers in on-site restaurants. In the Czech Republic Gambrinus comes in two forms: a 10 degree beer is made with sucrose as well as malt. The 4.5% beer is known as a 12 degree beer and you should specify that when ordering in bars.

Kaiserdom Pilsener

Source: Kaiserdom Privatbrauerei, Bamberg, Germany

Strength: 4.8%

Website: www.kaiserdom.de

Kaiserdom is the biggest brewery in one of the world's greatest and certainly most fascinating brewing towns. Bamberg is in the Franconia region of Bavaria. The area is heavy with beech wood forests and for centuries wood from the forests has been used to help the Bamberg brewers produce their speciality: *Rauch* or smoked beer. Beech wood logs are used as the fuel in the kilns where malt is dried and gently toasted prior to being used in the brewing process.

Bamberg once had dozens of tiny house breweries, with walk-in caves – still visible from the street – where beer was lagered, using ice cut from the local Regnitz river. There are still 11 breweries operating in Bamberg, which has a population of just 70,000. Several produce mainstream lager beers as well as a Rauchbier and a Pilsener. Pilsener is the main product

from Kaiserdom, which has a total annual production of 200,000 hectolitres. The brewery was founded in 1718 and until 1983 it was known as the Bürgerbräu or Citizens' Brewery. It is still independently owned by the Wörner family. A new greenfield site was built in the 1960s to cope with increasing demand for the beer.

The Pilsener is brewed with pale malt and hops from the Hallertau. The label of the beer carries the terms *Herb* and *Würtzig*, meaning dry and spicy, a good description of the beer in the glass. It has a rich toasted malt aroma balanced by spicy hops, with the spicy hop note building on the palate and finish but balanced throughout by rich toasted malt with a gentle hint of citrus. The brewery doesn't reveal the length of the lagering period but in the Bamberg tradition it will enjoy a long, slow maturation in the cellars.

TASTING NOTES

APPEARANCE:

AROMA:

TASTE:

OVERALL SCORE:

Lindeboom Pilsener

Source: Lindeboom Bierbrouwerij, Neer, Limburg, Netherlands

Strength: 5%

Website: www.lindeboom.nl

The Netherlands is dominated by the global colossus Heineken, with the large Grolsch group – now part of SAB Miller – panting in its wake. Independent brewers are thin on the ground, but Lindeboom remains firmly and proudly in family hands. It makes much of the fact that it's not so much a Dutch as a Limburg brewery, a region with a long history of brewing distinctive beers. Lindeboom's slogan: *'t Bier van Hier* (the beer from here) is deliberately parochial.

The brewery was founded in Neer in 1870 by Willem Geenen on a site where a linden tree – *lindeboom* – had been planted by his German ancestors. The tree still stands in the brewery yard and descendants of the founder, Ben and Willem Geenen, run the company today. The Geenens introduced Pilsener in 1912 and,

aware of a court case between Pilsner Urquell and German brewers, carefully used the Germanic spelling of the style rather than the Czech version.

Lindeboom has its own on-site well that provides high-quality, soft water for brewing. Their beer is brewed with Pilsener malt and it has 3.5 colour units. German hops – Magnum, Northern Brewer and Tettnanger – create 24 units of bitterness.

The beer is lagered for between six and eight weeks. It has a delicate aroma of fresh corn, herbal and grassy hops and a gentle hint of lemon fruit. Hop bitterness builds in the mouth but there's a firm underpinning of sappy malt and tart fruit. The finish starts bittersweet but hops dominate towards the end, which is bitter and dry.

TASTING NOTES

APPEARANCE:

AROMA:

TASTE:

OVERALL SCORE:

TASTING NOTES

APPEARANCE:

AROMA:

TASTE:

OVERALL SCORE:

Matilda Bay Bohemian Pilsner

Source: Matilda Bay Brewing Company,
Port Melbourne, Victoria, Australia
Strength: 4.7%
Website: www.matildabay.com.au

When Matilda Bay was launched in Fremantle in 1984 it was the first new brewery to open in the vast continent since World War Two. It marked the start of the independent brewing movement in Australia that has not so much challenged the hegemony of the likes of Castlemaine and Foster's but has brought distinctive beer to a more discriminating audience. The brewery came about as a result of a group of passionate beer lovers meeting in the Sail & Anchor hotel in Fremantle who decided – on a wing and a prayer – to open their own brewery.

One of the guiding lights of the Matilda Bay Brewing Company was Janice McDonald, who formulated the recipe for Bohemian Pilsner and was the first-known modern brewster – woman brewer – in what was then an extremely macho culture. Her lager beer came after the company had launched a wheat beer, Redback, named after an Australian spider, and Dogbolter strong ale. Dogbolter took its name from an ale of the same name that was made famous by the London group of Firkin brewpubs. The first two beers were followed by a honey beer, Beez Neez, and then Bohemian Pilsner.

As demand for the brewery's beers grew, it opened a second facility in Port Melbourne that gave it a presence on both sides of the continent.

In the 1990s, Matilda Bay was bought by Carlton and United Breweries, later renamed the Foster's Group. The original Fremantle plant was closed and Philip Sexton, a former brewer with Swan in Western Australia, was brought in to build a new brewery in Port Melbourne and was given a substantial investment by Foster's. In Australia, unlike Britain, big brewers are relaxed about smaller companies they take over and allow them to pursue an independent course. Lion Nathan, for example, owns the Malt Shovel brewery and James Squire brew pubs but gives them almost complete autonomy.

The long, lingering finish has a fine balance of juicy malt, bitter, spicy hops and light citrus.

In 2012, Matilda Bay moved to a bigger site in Melbourne where the original kit with a brew length of 2,500 litres has been extended with additional vessels. A restaurant and bar are on-site attractions for visitors. The brewery has again changed ownership, as the Foster's Group was bought by the international giant SABMiller in 2011. It's unlikely to interfere with Matilda Bay, as Bohemian Pilsner was crowned Grand Champion Beer in the 2011 International Beer Awards in Melbourne. It's brewed with pale malt and Saaz hops from the Czech Republic, which are added to the kettle boil in two additions. Units of bitterness are 35. The yeast culture came from Berlin. The beer has an aroma of spicy and floral hops, backing a rich toasted malt note. There are some tangy citrus notes in the mouth, with hop bitterness building on the palate. The long, lingering finish has a fine balance of juicy malt, bitter, spicy hops and light citrus. The brewery says the beer is a good companion for pork and duck dishes, chilli and Thai curries.

Red Hill Bohemian Pilsner

Source: Red Hill Brewery, Red Hill South, Victoria, Australia

Strength: 5.9%

Website: www.redhillbrewery.com.au

Red Hill is in the rolling, fertile plains of the Mornington Peninsula, Victoria's wine country. Australians, surprisingly, can be snobbish and the wine growers objected strongly to such a proletarian concept as a brewery in their elegant midst. David and Karen Golding had a long battle to get planning permission to build their brewery and restaurant but today the wine makers often drop in for a beer after a hard day tending their vines. With a name like Golding, David and Karen just had to grow hops and visitors to the brewery are greeted by a small hop plantation where such varieties as Tettnang, Willamette and – naturally – Goldings are grown. You may spot a quizzical kangaroo wondering whether the hops are edible: not a sight you come across in the hop fields of Kent or the Bavarian Hallertau.

The Goldings lived in England for a while, in Hertfordshire and then London, where they were close to Fuller's brewery and acquired a taste for beer with flavour and character.

They certainly pack great flavour in to the wide range of beers – ale, wheat beer and lager – produced at Red Hill. The brewery is based in a barn and, as a result of constricted space, David's mash tun doubles as the copper: the mash is filtered in a lauter tun before returning to the mash tun for the boil with hops. In a region long on heat and short on water, rain is collected in tanks on the roof. The water is soft and David hardens it for some of his brews. For his Pilsner, he uses Pils, light Munich and Carapils malts. The hops are Tettnang for bitterness and they are added three times during the boil. The finished beer is dry hopped with Hallertau. The hops create 35 units of bitterness. The beer is lagered for six weeks and David adds further hop flowers in the lager tank.

The beer has a luscious golden colour with a big aroma of toasted malt, floral and spicy hops, and a touch of citrus fruit. Juicy malt and tart, bitter and floral hops fill the mouth, followed by a long, lingering finish packed with rich, creamy malt, spicy hops and lemon fruit flavours. Along with the other beers, Bohemian Pilsner can be enjoyed in the restaurant where Karen produces sensational food. This is Australia and her version of a ploughman's lunch would keep most Brits going for a week.

TASTING NOTES

APPEARANCE:

AROMA:

TASTE:

OVERALL SCORE:

APPEARANCE:
CLEAN/CRISP
LIGHT & THIN
HEAD - FIZZY
4

AROMA:
MALTY - DRY

2.

TASTE:
LIGHT, CLEAN
LIVELY PALATE
SWEET AFTER
TASTE 3

OVERALL SCORE:

9/15

Veltins Pilsener

Source: Brauerei C&A Veltins, Grevenstein,
North Rhine-Westphalia, Germany
Strength: 4.8%
Website: www.veltins.de

Veltins proves that big brewers can make good beer. It produces 2.4 million hectolitres a year and is one of the top ten breweries in Germany in terms of production – and it concentrates on using the finest raw materials and slow, thoughtful production methods. It's based in the same region as such big-ticket brewers as Krombach and Warsteiner but its Pilsener is one of the top five brands in the whole of Germany. The company dates from 1824 and is still family-owned: leading members of the family live in a handsome chateau alongside the brewery. It dominates the small village of Grevenstein, which stands in an attractive area of hills, mountains and forests. From this rural retreat, Veltins can satisfy the thirsts of industrial workers in the Ruhr, Dortmund and Düsseldorf as well as tourists who visit the region for walking, climbing and skiing.

The company produces soft drinks but its only beer is Pilsener. In 1926, Carl Veltins took the decision to concentrate on the style when a report from the College of Brewing Technology in Berlin said the soft water from the mountains surrounding Grevenstein was ideal for brewing Pilsener.

The beer is not pasteurised, which demands a fast turnover, but means it has a fresh, hoppy character, with hops from the Hallertau region, which create between 25 and 28 bitterness units. Malt comes from summer barley. The brewing regime is unusual for a number of reasons. The modern, 1980s Steinecker brewhouse is based on a mash mixer and lauter tun system and uses an infusion mash. This is rare in lager breweries where most use a decoction system in which parts of the mash – the mix of malt and water – are pumped from one vessel to a second, where the temperature is raised, and the mash then returns to the first vessel. Lager brewers believe this leads to a better extraction of malt sugars. Infusion mash is used principally by ale brewers, with the mash taking place in just one vessel, the mash tun.

At Veltins, following the boil with hops in four brew kettles, the hopped wort undergoes a system of fermentation that I've not encountered before. The liquid is run into upright 'floater tanks' where it's mixed with yeast, which begins to convert malt sugars into alcohol and also creates natural carbon dioxide. After 24 hours, 80 per cent of the fermenting liquid is run off while the remaining 20 per cent is mixed with fresh hopped wort. This is repeated for four days, after which the tanks are emptied and cleaned. The system ensures consistency of flavour and quality: the brewers claim that one bottle of Pilsener will be made up of 200 different brews.

Following the floater tanks, the beer has a rapid primary fermentation that lasts for just two days, and is then held for a minimum of four weeks in the lager cellar. The beer that emerges from this lengthy production cycle has a rich toasted malt aroma balanced by robust spicy and floral hops, and a touch of lemon fruit. Bitter hops dominate the palate and finish but there are solid contributions from juicy malt and tart fruit. The beer is exported to 30 countries and sales are growing in Germany, where Veltins enjoys a high profile as a sponsor of the Porsche racing team and also FC Schalke, which plays in the top football division, the Bundesliga.

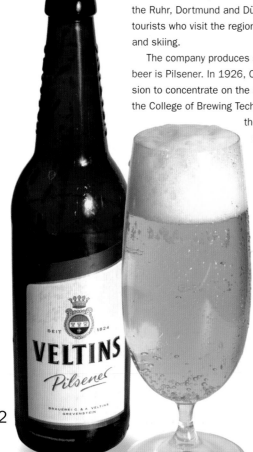

Brown & Mild Ales

The spotlight has been turned with full force in recent years on the revival of such historic styles as Porter, Stout and India Pale Ale, leaving a beer type of equal historic importance, brown ale, lurking in the shadows. Yet, quietly, this beer is reviving too. In England, where draught brown beers are called Mild, there has been a remarkable resurgence, with dozens of artisan breweries offering their interpretations of the style.

Brunswick Inn brewery

The Mild revival has been marked by several brewers of the style winning major awards in the annual Champion Beer of Britain competition. A beer that was listed in *300 Beers to Try Before You Die!*, Mighty Oak's Oscar Wilde, won the overall championship in 2011.

In Belgium, a country where great reverence is given to beer and style, stronger versions of brown ale, often called *Oud Bruin* – Old Brown – remain a potent part of the brewing scene. Belgian brewers weave history as well as flavour into their brown beers. The history reflects the tangled past of a country where, depending whether a brewery was based in French, Dutch or German-speaking areas, laws determined whether beers could be brewed with or without hops.

In North America a growing number of brown ales are produced, some of them dauntingly strong by European standards. Low-strength Milds don't exist there: American craft brewers look askance at the very name.

In England, Mild suffered for several decades from a bad image. It was seen as old fashioned, 'cloth cap' – an old man's drink. As Milds tend to be dark in colour, unscrupulous publicans would top up casks of Mild with 'the slops' – spilt beer. The result was stale, vinegary beer that people avoided like the plague. The problem was compounded by the fact that brewers drastically reduced the strength of Mild during the course of the 20th century until it was seen as a weak substitute for more robust pale ales and bitters. The decline of Mild was a tragedy, for it was once the dominant beer style. It was a beer fashioned to suit the demands of both agricultural and industrial workers in the 19th century, who wanted a sweeter and cheaper beer than the prevailing Porters

and Stouts. The style was first brewed with brown malt but this was replaced by pale malt when it became more widely available as a result of improved malting technology. Pale malt was blended with darker grains, caramel and brewing sugar to give the beer both the colour and sweetness demanded by drinkers: the saccharine nature of the beer was important to drinkers who needed to restore lost energy after long hours in field or foundry. But the Mild ales of the 19th and early 20th century were not weak. In 1871 the typical strength of Mild was given as 1070 degrees original gravity – 7% alcohol in modern measurement. At the turn of the 20th century, the average strength of beer was 5.5% at a time when Mild was the main type available. It was called Mild not because it was weak but as a result of being less heavily hopped than Porter, Stout and pale ale.

Research into the origins of Mild and a greater understanding of how it was brewed, the raw materials used and the typical strengths of the 19th and early 20th centuries have all helped fuel the revival of the style. As a result, the British beers listed in this section can stand proudly alongside the brown ales of other countries and match them in aroma and flavour.

Nøgne ø brewery

Banks & Taylor Black Dragon Mild

Source: B&T Brewery, Shefford, Bedfordshire, England

Strength: 4.3%

Website: www.banksandtaylor.com

B&T is one of Britain's longest-running artisan brewers, formed in 1982 by Martin Ayres and Mike Desquesnes, who were aided in the early days by the advice of Bill Urquart, one of the pioneers of small independent brewing with the Litchborough Brewery in Northamptonshire. The company was first called Banks & Taylor as Martin and Mike felt their names didn't fit the bill, especially Desquesnes, which many people struggle to pronounce (it's 'De-cain). Their wives' maiden names – Plum and Smith – were also deemed unfit for purpose, so the partners settled on their mothers' maiden names, Banks and Taylor.

With the help of national brewing giant Whitbread, where Martin had worked, the new brewery was able to sell its beers in a number of Whitbread pubs and even leased one from the group in Luton. Banks & Taylor expanded into London and at one stage had seven pubs in the capital. But the company over-stretched itself financially and in 1994 it was re-structured as B&T, though the original name lives on in the email and website addresses.

Building more judicially, B&T today runs five pubs while 60 other outlets take their beer. The brewery has a substantial portfolio of 12 regular beers along with monthly seasonal offerings. A map pinpointing the brewery should, perhaps, include the ancient ritual of adding the words of warning 'Here be dragons' as Martin and Mike are keen on the mythical beast – a fondness that can be seen in their beer names. As well as Black Dragon Mild, they also brew a stronger golden beer called Dragonslayer.

The Mild, which won the Strong Mild category of CAMRA's Champion Winter Beer competition in 2007, is a beer full of dark malt character but with a solid underpinning of Goldings hops, the only variety used. The grains are Pearl pale malt, with black and crystal malts, roast barley and a touch of wheat malt. The dark ruby-coloured beer has coffee and liquorice on the nose, with a smoky note from the roasted grain and a light peppery hop note. Espresso coffee, liquorice, smoked malt, burnt fruit and spicy hops fill the mouth while the finish is long and complex, with dark fruit, coffee, liquorice, smoked malt and bitter hops.

Beckstones Black Gun Dog Freddy Mild

Source: Beckstones Brewery, Millom, Cumbria, England

Strength: 3.8%

Website: www.beckstonesbrewery.co.uk

Dave Taylor, whose Black Gun Dog Freddy won the Mild category in the 2008 Champion Beer of Britain competition and a Silver in the overall competition, is a small brewer happy to stay that way. His building and mechanical skills helped him construct a brewery on a shoestring budget. He was a motor mechanic and keen home brewer. When he was made redundant, he turned his knowledge of beer making into a commercial venture by buying the five-barrel kit from the closed High Force brewery in Co Durham. He installed it in a former corn mill in a hamlet between Millom and Broughton-in-Furness, an area that once had a substantial iron works industry. The mill provided solid foundations with a slate stone floor from a local quarry and Dave was able to draw good quality brewing water from a 200 feet-deep well on the site.

The Mild, named after his dog, is brewed with Maris Otter pale, crystal and chocolate malts, flaked barley and wheat. The single hop is Bramling Cross.

The beer has a robust aroma and palate, with burnt fruit, roasted grain, dark chocolate and spicy hops. The dark malt character builds in the mouth, with roasted grain, bitter chocolate, raisin and sultana fruit, hints of liquorice and vanilla, and a good underpinning of peppery hops. The finish is long, with a solid dark malt note, chocolate and roast flavours, and a lingering note of fruity and spicy hops.

Beowulf Dark Raven

Source: Beowulf Brewing Company, Brownhills, Staffordshire, England
Strength: 4.5%
Website: www.beowulfbrewery.co.uk

The Beowulf brewery dates from 1997 but it has a lot of history surrounding its name, beers and location. It was founded by Phil Bennett, who had won many awards in the West Midlands for his home-brewed ale. He decided to use his skills commercially in order to bring greater choice to Birmingham and its drinkers. His first site was in a former Co-op in Yardley in Birmingham. He named the brewery after the famous 8th-century Old English epic poem *Beowulf*, which told of the exploits of its titular hero in slaying such monsters as Grendel and its mother. By sheer good fortune, in 1999 the Irish poet Seamus Heaney won the Whitbread Prize for his modern translation of the poem. Whitbread at the time was a national brewery and the happy coincidence of *Beowulf*, beer and prizes helped put Phil Bennett's modest company on the map.

His first beer was called Heroes and he went on to give most of his ales names linked to heroism and gallantry. In 2003 he moved to bigger premises in Chasewater Country Park alongside a reservoir in the Forest of Mercia. The forest is in the former ancient kingdom of

Mercia, ruled by, among others, King Offa, who built the dyke that separated Mercia from Wales and also created a shrine to England's first Christian martyr, Alban. In keeping with the history of the area, the units that contain Phil's brewery are designed in the wattle-and-daub medieval style, with green oak beams. He brews 360 gallons a week.

Phil rapidly built a strong reputation for his beers, especially the darker varieties. They are sold widely throughout the West Midlands and further afield via wholesalers. His beers have won many prizes in CAMRA competitions, and Dark Raven picked up Silver awards in 2009 and 2010 in the Champion Winter Beer of Britain competition and Bronze in 2011 and 2012.

Dark Raven is brewed with Maris Otter pale, black and crystal malts and is hopped with Fuggles. It has a big smoked malt aroma with liquorice, espresso coffee, dark chocolate and burnt fruit. Bitter hops break through on the palate with coffee, dark fruit and roasted grain. The finish has creamy malt alongside hop resins, bitter coffee, dark fruit flavours and liquorice.

TASTING NOTES
APPEARANCE:

AROMA:

TASTE:

OVERALL SCORE:

Brunswick Father Mike's Dark Rich Ruby

Source: Brunswick Brewery, Derby, England

Strength: 5.8%

Website: none

Brunswick brewery is attached to the Brunswick Inn, one of England's classic Victorian ale houses. It was built in 1842 at the end of a row of cottages constructed by a grateful railway company for its workforce: Derby station is just a few yards away and the city was once the main manufacturer of locomotives in the country. The inn is a red-brick, wedge-shaped building with impressive chimneys and a large pub sign promising 'a true ale house and brewery'. The interior layout is unusual, with a large serving area dominating a long corridor from which a number of small rooms radiate. The rooms have open fires, old station furniture and lamps, with a plethora of fascinating steam-age railway memorabilia. At the far end of the corridor, the small brewery churns out a large range of house beers, including three dark Mild ales, among them Father Mike's.

The Brunswick Inn was in danger of being demolished in the 1980s but a campaign led by the Civic Trust, the Derbyshire Railway Trust and CAMRA saved it. The pub was taken on by Trevor Harris in 1987, who added the brewery four years later. When pub and brewery were bought by Everards, a large Leicester brewery, Trevor moved on and launched the Derby Brewing Company. Everards installed Graham Yates as brewer and publican and he expanded trade in the pub by taking on two chefs who match the brewery's beer with food for special events, including Burns Night and Valentine's night. Father Mike's is used as a companion to a selection of English cheeses. Graham retired in 2013.

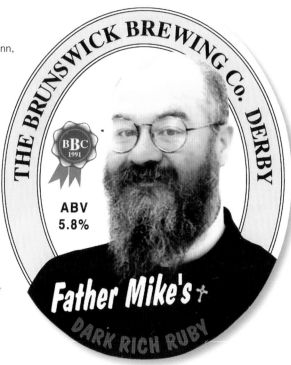

The Brunswick Inn

The beer is named for a local priest who likes dark, strong ales. It's brewed with Maris Otter pale malt, black and crystal malts and is hopped with Challenger and Goldings varieties. It has 22 units of bitterness. The colour is black with hints of red and the beer offers a rich aroma of espresso coffee, liquorice, burnt fruit and dark grain. Spicy and peppery hops make a powerful entry in the mouth, balancing creamy malt, dark fruit and coffee flavours. The finish is long and lingering, with a dry note from hops and malts, underscored by burnt fruit, coffee and liquorice.

Cigar City Maduro Brown Ale

Source: Cigar City Brewing, Tampa, Florida, United States
Strength: 5.5%
Website: www.cigarcitybrewing.com

It's a long way from Florida to Newcastle-on-Tyne and Sunderland but the American brewers have done their research well and describe their beer as a 'North England-style brown ale with the addition of flaked oats'. They've also added a big punch of alcohol, as the classic Geordie and Wearside brown ales are lower in strength. But there is a powerful link between the working economies of Tampa and the English North East, as this style of beer was first brewed to refresh industrial workers after long hours digging coal, building ships or – in the case of Tampa – making hand-rolled Cuban cigars.

Tampa is called Cigar City as it was the centre of the cigar trade for many years. Tobacco was imported from Cuba and Cuban workers followed the jobs. They worked long hours and they needed beer as well as better pay and conditions. Not surprisingly, a major brewery in the area, the Florida Brewery Company, was founded by cigar industrialists in 1896. It survived until 1961 and brewed ale as well as La Tropicana lagers, based on beers made in Cuba. It was followed by the Ybor City Brewery – Ybor is a district of Tampa – which brewed brown ale, Porter and wheat beer between 1994 and 2003. But the tradition of brewing brown ales in Florida disappeared when Ybor City closed. It's been restored by Cigar City, thanks to the determination of founders Wayne Wambles and Joey Redner. They described Tampa as a 'beer wasteland' and they set out restore the city's 'beer culture and heritage'. They opened their brewery in 2008 and its success can be measured by the fact that the 15-barrel plant now has a visitor shop and a tasting room where regular beer-and-food events are staged.

Brown Ale is brewed with pale, crystal and chocolate malts, special roast, flaked oats and Victory – a toasted malt. The hops are Northern Brewer and Willamette, which create 25 units of bitterness. The beer has a fine claret colour and a pronounced chocolate note on the nose, with roasted grain, a hint of vanilla, freshly-baked bread and floral, spicy hops. The palate is delightfully clean and quenching, the rich dark grain and chocolate beautifully balanced by increasing hop bitterness. Roasted and toasted grain, vanilla notes, chocolate and spicy hops combine in the long and refreshing finish.

> ❜ It's a long way from Florida to Newcastle-on-Tyne and Sunderland but the American brewers have done their research well and describe their beer as a 'North England-style brown ale with the addition of flaked oats'. They've also added a big punch of alcohol ❜

TASTING NOTES

APPEARANCE:

AROMA:

TASTE:

OVERALL SCORE:

TASTING NOTES

APPEARANCE:

AROMA:

TASTE:

OVERALL SCORE:

Dupont Moinette Brune

Source: Brasserie Dupont, Tourpes-Leuze, Hainaut, Belgium

Strength: 8.5%

Website: www.brasserie-dupont.com

Dupont is a famous Belgian brewer of the style known as Saison, originally brewed by farmers as seasonal beers to refresh their labour force during the long summer months. In common with several other brewers in the French-speaking region of Belgium, Dupont now produces its Saisons on a regular rather than seasonal basis: its main Saison Dupont appeared in *300 Beers to Try Before You Die!* But it has added to its range with both organic beers and pale and brown bottle-conditioned ales under the Moinette label.

The brewery was founded in the 18th century when it was based on a farm run by the Rimaux-Deridder family. Farming no longer takes place, but the low-slung buildings, cobbled courtyard and flat, windswept land alongside the Tourpes road still have a farming aspect. The brewery underscores the rustic air by selling cheese, including one spiced with hops, from an adjoining farm. The brewery was bought in 1920 by Louis Dupont who gave it to his son to dissuade him from emigrating to Canada. Marc Roisier, the grandson of Louis Dupont, now runs the brewery with his sisters. The success of the company, which produces around 6,500 hectolitres or 143,000 gallons a year and exports to North America, throughout Europe and the Far East, has forced Marc to hand over brewing to Olivier Dedeycker.

Hard brewing water from an on-site well is ideally suited to ale brewing. Some of the brewing equipment dates from the 1920s, with mashing and boiling carried out in the same open vessel – a Belgian farm-brewing tradition. The entire brewery fills with steam when boiling is underway. The complexity and richness of all the Dupont beers is due to the yeast culture used, which is composed of several different strains. It's thought that one of the strains may originally have been a wine strain, which would account for the fact that the yeast is tolerant to high fermentation temperatures: the temperature in the fermenting tanks at Dupont can reach 32 degrees Celsius, some 10 degrees higher than the norm.

The russet beer has a complex bouquet of roasted malt, spicy hops, dark fruit and vanilla.

For some years the Moinette brands were labelled 'abbey': *moine* is the French for monk and it was thought that an abbey once stood close to the farm and brewery. But Dupont now says moinette is based on an old French word *moene*, which means swamp. This accurately describes the terrain surrounding the brewery, though swamp has less marketing appeal than little monk. Abbey has been dropped from the branding.

Brune is brewed with Pilsner malt and three darker malts and is hopped with East Kent Goldings and Styrian Goldings. The russet beer has a complex bouquet of roasted malt, spicy hops, dark fruit and vanilla. On the palate, rich roasted malt, burnt fruit and peppery hops are underscored by the continuing vanilla note, while the long finish is bittersweet, with vanilla, dark fruit, spicy hops and a lingering, subtle hint of chocolate. Brune has a five-day primary fermentation, one to two weeks secondary fermentation and is then warm conditioned for six to eight weeks at 23°C before it's bottled with a fresh dosage of yeast.

Grainstore Rutland Panther

Source: Grainstore Brewery, Oakham, Rutland, England

Strength: 3.4%

Website: www.grainstorebrewery.com

Grainstore brewery was founded in 1995 by two beer lovers called Davis and Davies: the legal name of the company is Davis'es Brewing Co. Tony Davis was head brewer at Ruddles, which made much of the fact that it was based in England's smallest county: its slogan was 'Much in Little'. It had the misfortune to be taken over by a giant drinks group, Grand Metropolitan, which prompted Tony to leave. He was great friends with Mike Davies, whose expertise as an engineer meant they could pool their skills to open a new brewery.

They now claim to be the 'biggest brewer in England's smallest county', following the closure of Ruddles in 1999. Messrs Davis and Davies found a former derelict Victorian grain store at Oakham railway station, which they thought would be the ideal location for a brewery. It's on three storeys, which means the 15-barrel plant is designed along the lines of a 19th-century tower brewery, with the production process flowing from floor to floor without the use of pumps or hydraulics.

The brewery has a tap room on site where beers can be tasted: as the old saying goes, it's worth missing a few trains for. Rutland Panther is a fine example of a true English Mild, low in alcohol but rich in taste. It found sufficient favour with judges in the Champion Beer of Britain competition in 2005 that it won Gold in the Mild category. It's brewed with Maris Otter and Pearl malts (50:50 blend), with brown and chocolate malts, caramel and a small amount of No 3 treacle, which is molasses by another name. The hops are Fuggles and Goldings, which create 30 units of bitterness, a respectable level for the style.

The beer has a fine ruby/black colour with an enticing aroma of dark grain, chocolate, burnt fruit, peppery hops and treacle. The palate is a complex blend of creamy malt, treacle, dark fruit and spicy hop resins. The finish is bittersweet, with rich treacle and nutty malt notes balanced by dark chocolate and bitter, peppery hops.

Ruddles, before its demise, was granted a PGI – Protected Geographical Indicator – for the use of Rutland in its beer names. This status has now passed to Grainstore and means Rutland Panther can truly claim to be Much in Little.

Hobson's Mild

Source: Hobson's Brewery, Cleobury Mortimer, Worcestershire, England

Strength: 3.2%

Website: www.hobsons-brewery.co.uk

Hobson's is a proud Shropshire brewery – despite a quirk of the postal system that puts it in Worcestershire. It was founded in 1993 by yet another Davis family – but no relation to Grainstore – and was based in an old saw mill before relocating to a former granary on a farm. The brewers are passionate about protecting the environment. Rainwater is collected from tanks on the roofs of the farm buildings and is used for washing brewing vessels, casks and vehicles. A wind turbine provides around one third of the brewery's power while a ground-source pump heats the bottle store. Cask beer supplies are confined to pubs within 30 miles of Cleobury Mortimer to save on carbon. Local cricket clubs are supported to help maintain village greens. Equally important, local ingredients are used wherever possible, including acclaimed Fuggles hops from Worcestershire.

> *Equally important, local ingredients are used wherever possible, including acclaimed Fuggles hops from Worcestershire.*

Hobson's Mild, at 3.2 per cent, is a fine example of the traditional Mild ales that refreshed country labourers after long hours in fields and farms. It has won many awards, including the supreme accolade of Champion Beer of Britain in 2007. It has also been honoured in several championships run by the Society of Independent Brewers and was named CAMRA'S Champion West Midlands beer in 2011.

It's brewed with Maris Otter pale malt with chocolate and dark crystal malts for colour and flavour. The hops are Fuggles and Goldings. The ruby red/black beer has toasted and roasted grain on the nose, backed by rich chocolate and gentle spicy hops. Chocolate, dark toasted grain, toffee and gentle hop resins build in the mouth while the long, lingering finish is a fine balance of toffee, chocolate, creamy malt and spicy hops.

Mild

3.2%

HOBSONS

DARK CHAMPION BEER

Liefmans Goudenband

Source: Liefmans Brouwerij, Oudenaarde, East Flanders, Belgium

Strength: 8%

Website: www.liefmans.be

Liefmans has a long brewing history, both ancient and more modern. It's world famous as the renowned producer of *Oud Bruin* or Old Brown, a style that's a powerful link to the blended brown ales that dominated brewing before Europe's Industrial Revolution. These are beers with a lactic sourness, and the style was not confined to Belgium: Greene King's Strong Suffolk Ale (see *300 Beers to Try Before You Die!*), for example, is a living reminder that England, too, once produced strong country beers, blended with ale matured in wood for long periods.

To understand brewing in Oudenaarde and the distinctive beers from Liefmans and neighbouring Roman brewery (see p85), you have to begin with the history of the town. It's famous for its tapestries, silverware and a striking Gothic town hall that dominates the market place. Beer is part of the tapestry of the town. A fountain in the market place was donated by the French king Louis XIV and during an annual beer festival the fountain foams with beer, not water.

Oudenaarde is divided by the River Schelde and it's the river that has determined the course of brewing in the town. At one time, it marked the dividing line between the French and German empires. In the 14th century, breweries on the German side of the river, in the Duchy of Brabant, were forced to use hops. Producers on the left bank controlled by the French, however, were banned from using hops and had to employ a mixture of herbs and spices, known as *gruut* in Dutch.

Despite this, all the breweries in the area had one thing in common: the local water from many small springs. The water has a high level of sodium bicarbonate that makes it ideal for producing brown beer. Oudenaarde was once packed with breweries. Eight survived until the 1950s but today only Liefmans and Roman remain. Cnudde, a tiny family-owned company, brews part time and has financial support from Roman.

I included Liefmans Oud Bruin in *300 Beers to Try Before You Die!* I returned to the town to attempt to untangle the recent history of a company founded in 1679, at the dawn of modern brewing. Liefmans was based in the centre of Oudenaarde until it moved to its present site on the banks of the Schelde in 1933. In the 1970s and 80s, the brewery achieved a greater public profile thanks to the tireless work of its manager, Rose Blancquaert-Merckx. Her retirement prompted a takeover of Liefmans by the Riva group based in Dentergem, just across the border in West Flanders. Riva began what seems a curious practice of producing wort, the sugary extract that starts the brewing process, which was then trucked to Liefmans for fermenting, conditioning, bottling and storage. In 2007, Riva was declared bankrupt and Liefmans closed. Gasps of horror were heard from beer lovers world-wide. It seemed we would lose an iconic producer of a style on the verge of extinction. But, a year later, Liefmans was re-opened by Duvel Moortgat in Breendonk, best known for the strong golden ale, Duvel.

The company has maintained the practice of producing wort at its own plant and transporting it to Oudenaarde. The reason is twofold. Liefmans has small mash tuns that are insufficient to feed its two enormous open fermenters, one of which can hold 450 hectolitres of beer. And the mash tuns and kettles themselves were old and creaking at the seams – costing a lot of Euros to replace. Moortgat's plant can produce 30 brews a week while Liefmans could manage only one. It therefore makes economic if not aesthetic sense to start the brewing process at Breendonk.

But Moortgat is adamant on one point: it will not ferment Liefmans' beer in its main brewery as it won't run the risk of the Oudenaarde yeast culture infecting its own beers. It's the Liefmans' yeast strain

TASTING NOTES

APPEARANCE:

AROMA:

TASTE:

OVERALL SCORE:

that gives the beers their unique character and lactic sourness. The character has developed over the centuries and has many contributors: the local water, extremely low ceilings in the fermenting room that impact on temperature, and help from wild yeasts and other flora in the atmosphere.

Goudenband, which means gold ribbon, is a blend of young and mature beers in the manner of 'country beers' of the 17th and 18th centuries. The malts are Pilsner, caramalt and roasted grain. The hops are all Belgian varieties that contribute 20 units of bitterness. The beer is a blend of Oud Bruin and a stronger beer that has matured for between six and eight months. Both beers are centrifuged to remove the yeast and the blend is then re-seeded with fresh yeast and priming sugar to encourage fermentation in the bottle. The bottles are matured for a further three months in the brewery cellars before being released. A young Goudenband has little sourness on the nose, which is dominated by woody and vanilla notes. But sour fruit, rich malt and light hops build in the mouth. The finish is bittersweet, with burnt grain and sour fruit. A year-old version has more sweetness on the aroma with rich fruit on nose and palate, with sourness developing and spices, smoky malt and tobacco in the finish.

The high point of my visit was a tour of the cave or cellar where hundreds of bottles of vintage Goudenband are stored. The bottles are corked and laid down horizontally. Acidity plays a major role in the ageing process, along with the same microbiological changes that take place in fine wine. The dust was wiped from a bottle dated 1989 and cradle and cork were gently eased from the neck. The beer gushed and foamed in the glass, then settled down to the familiar russet/brown colour. But the aroma and palate were markedly different to a young Goudenband. The nose had a butterscotch note followed by smooth malt, toffee, and raisin and sultana fruit in the mouth with a gentle hop note. The finish offered more butterscotch balanced by dark, roasted grain, light hops and only a hint of sourness. It was a fascinating example of how a strong beer can age and change over the years.

The brewery is open to visitors and there are also facilities for banquets and beer-and-food matching events.

Nøgne ø Brown Ale/Imperial Brown Ale

Source: Nøgne ø Bryggeri AS, Grimstad, Norway
Strength: 4.5%/7.5%
Website: www.nogne-o.com

The name of the brewery means 'Naked Island', a description used by playwright Henrik Ibsen for the stark, rocky outcrops off the southern coast of Norway. The founders of the brewery think it sums them up well, as they stand out like a sore thumb in a country where 98 per cent of beer is pale lager. The brewery was founded in 2003 by two keen home-brewers who wanted to share their passion for beer with aroma and flavour with other drinkers starved of taste. They call their beers 'real ale' in the British fashion. The beers are all bottle-conditioned, which, the founders believe, leads to complexity and a full-bodied, fruity character: they call themselves 'craft brewers of uncompromising ales'.

I met head brewer Kjetil Jikiun in 2012 in the unlikely setting of a large hall near the Gare du Nord in Paris. We were both attending a food and drink festival, and I was bowled over by the two interpretations of brown ale he exhibited. He told me the company is run by people who love beer and work long and hard to brew and sell their products. For the first few years nobody was paid a salary, and today all the employees are shareholders. In

Nøgne ø's modern brewplant

Brown Ale

TASTING NOTES

APPEARANCE:

AROMA:

TASTE:

OVERALL SCORE:

TASTING NOTES

APPEARANCE:

AROMA:

TASTE:

OVERALL SCORE:

2003 the brewery produced just 300 hectolitres, but volumes have grown to 3,500 hectolitres a year. Kjetil buys Maris Otter malting barley from England as he believes it gives the best biscuit flavour to his beers and works in harmony with his yeast culture. He imports hops from England, mainland Europe and the U.S. He uses pellet hops as his modern plant is based on a mash filter, lauter tun, brew kettle and hop whirlpool system.

All his beers are re-seeded following fermentation with fresh yeast and wort, and warm conditioned to encourage a second fermentation in the bottle. Kjetil is proud of the fact that he doesn't own a filter: he believes in living beer. The two versions of brown ale have identical recipes: Maris Otter pale malt with amber, brown, chocolate and Munich malts and a touch of wheat. The hops are Aurora, Bobek and Columbus. The Brown Ale has 27 units of bitterness, the Imperial 30.

The Brown Ale has smoky malt, chocolate and roasted grain on the nose with peppery hop resins. Roasted grain, dark fruits and bitter hops fill the mouth, followed by a bittersweet finish with spicy hops, dark fruit, chocolate and roast. The Imperial, as the name suggests, has the same characteristics but magnified. Chocolate, liquorice, tobacco, old leather and a powerful peppery hop note attack the nose, while roasted grain, bitter hop resins, chocolate and dark fruits fill the mouth and the finish. Kjetil says his brown ales are good companions for red meat, barbeques, strong cheese and fruit. He advises people to consider beer next time they automatically reach for wine as a companion for food.

Nøgne ø's conical fermenters

Chocolate, liquorice, tobacco, old leather and a powerful peppery hop note attack the nose

Imperial Brown Ale

Roman Adriaen Brouwer/Adriaen Brouwer Dark Gold

Source: Brouwerij Roman, Mater-Oudenaarde, East Flanders, Belgium

Strength: 5%/8.5%

Website: www.roman.be

My visit to Liefmans (see p81) was organised by Anneliese Mertens of the East Flanders Tourist Agency. When we left the brewery, she said she would drive back to Brussels along the old Roman road that links Cologne and Dunkirk. We had gone just a short distance from Liefmans when we entered the village of Mater and I spotted ahead of us a tall, imposing, castle-like building topped with the words Roman Brouwerij. It was late afternoon but, without an appointment, we were greeted with great courtesy and given a tour of the brewery and a beer tasting.

Roman is a company of great antiquity. It was founded in 1545 as a tavern called the Bell by Justitius Roman. Both the family name and that of Mater (mother in Latin) may go back to Roman times. The current brewery buildings date from the early 20th century. They are set round a large court-yard with stables and a hall that houses a museum of brewing, with old brewing equipment, including a steam engine. The impressive 1930s brew house has copper vessels in Dutch tiled surrounds, standing on a multi-coloured tiled floor.

The company is still owned by the Roman family. The 17th generation is now in charge and it must surely be one of the oldest family breweries in the world. Its main product is a Pils lager and it is best known for a strong ale called Sloeber and the Ename range of Abbey beers. But it has built its reputation on its own interpretation of *Oud Bruin*, which was its only style until the 1950s: in common with many Belgian breweries, Roman only began brewing its Pils to meet demand following World War Two.

In 2003, Roman renamed its Oudenaards Bruin beer Adriaen Brouwer and introduced a stronger version of the beer called Adriaen Brouwer Dark Gold. The face of Adriaen Brouwer glowers from the labels of both beers. Brouwer, which, fortuitously, is the Dutch word for brewer, was a 17th-century painter from Oudenaarde who died aged just 32 as a result of over-consumption of both alcohol and tobacco. He studied under Frans Hals, had his portrait painted by Van Dyck and developed a style of miniature paintings depicting the seamy side of life. Examples of his work hang in Oudenaarde town hall.

TASTING NOTES

APPEARANCE:

AROMA:

TASTE:

OVERALL SCORE:

TASTING NOTES

APPEARANCE:

AROMA:

TASTE:

OVERALL SCORE:

Both beers are brewed with Pils malt and darker roasted malts and hopped with Belgian varieties. The 5% beer is russet brown with a hint of chocolate, burnt fruit and hop resins on the nose. Bitter hops build in the mouth with notes of dark fruit and chocolate. The finish is dry with roasted grain, dark fruit, chocolate and bitter hop resins. Dark Gold has a candy sugar aroma with burnt fruit and light floral hops. Hop resins, candied fruit and creamy malt dominate the palate, followed by a bittersweet finish with warming alcohol, hop resins, dark fruit and rich malt.

Critics who say Roman's versions of *Oud Bruin* are inferior to Liefmans' are missing the historical point. The Roman brewery was once in the German-controlled area of Oudenaarde and had to use hops rather than *gruut* in its beers. As a result, its beers have developed in a different manner to Liefmans and are noticeably hoppier. They should be equally revered as fine examples of a style that deserves encouragement if it's to survive. In 2010, Dark Gold won a gold medal in the European Beer Awards, judged by professional brewers, which gave greater recognition to the beers of Oudenaarde.

Rudgate Ruby Mild

Source: Rudgate Brewery, Tockwith, York, England

Strength: 4.4%

Website: www.rudgatebrewery.co.uk

Rudgate brewery is based in old armoury buildings on a disused World War Two airfield and it's tempting to say its success has been explosive since it won the title of Champion Beer of Britain in 2009 at the Great British Beer Festival. The beer has also won a fistful of awards at both CAMRA and SIBA – Society of Independent Brewers – regional competitions. The original 15-barrel plant has been replaced by a 30-barrel kit. Craig Lee and his team brew twice daily and they supply around 350 outlets in the region. Based close to the historic city of York, which was founded by invaders from Scandinavia, most of the beers have Nordic names, including Viking and Battleaxe.

The site for the brewery was chosen as a result of the high quality of the water that brings out the full flavours of malt and hops. Craig brews in the Yorkshire tradition, using whole hops and fermenting in open vessels. His Ruby Mild is strong by modern standards and is more in line with the Mild Ales brewed a century ago. The recipe is complex, with Pearl pale malt augmented by brown, pale and dark chocolate and crystal malts along with roasted barley. Challenger hops are used in the copper for bitterness, with a late addition of Challenger and Bobek from Slovenia for aroma. Units of bitterness are 32, high for the style, and they give a welcome balance of aroma and bitterness to the solid backbone of malt. The beer has a rich aroma of roasted grain, creamy chocolate, burnt fruit and tangy hop resins. Chocolate, fruit and roast flavours build in the mouth but hops add a firm, piny and bitter balance. The long and lingering finish is bittersweet with a delicious creamy and wholemeal malt character, with contributions from chocolate, dark fruit and tangy hops.

TASTING NOTES

APPEARANCE:

AROMA:

TASTE:

OVERALL SCORE:

Surrey Hills Hammer Mild

Source: Surrey Hills Brewery, Dorking, Surrey, England

Strength: 3.8%

Website: www.surreyhills.co.uk

Ross Hunter's ambition to run a brewery started at an early age – four years. 'I used to have a small sip of my father's pint and think "I want to make beer when I'm bigger".' Some years later he put his wish into practice when he opened his small plant in 2006 in picturesque but derelict farm buildings on top of the Surrey hills. Four years later he thought all his Christmases had arrived at once when his Mild won Gold in both the Champion Beer of Britain's Mild class and the same class in SIBA's national competition.

A year later, the brewery, with a staff of four, was working at full capacity. Ross took the plunge and installed a smart new 30-barrel plant in part of the Denbies Wine Estate at the foot of Box Hill. The hill marks the summit of the Surrey Downs. The ancient woodland is classified as an area of outstanding natural beauty and has featured in a number of novels, including Jane Austen's *Emma*.

Surrey Hills remains an independent concern: it's not owned by the wine company. Ross and his team deliver to pubs within a 15-mile radius of the brewery. For Hammer Mild, he uses Mild Ale malt and chocolate and crystal malts with two English hop varieties, Challenger and East Kent Goldings. The beer has a fine hop character for a Mild: bitter and peppery. On the nose the hops balance the rich chocolate, creamy malt and dark fruit notes. Chocolate, wholemeal biscuits, burnt fruit and tart hops fill the mouth while the lingering finish finally becomes dry, preceded by a superb blend of rich, creamy and biscuity malt, peppery hops and dark chocolate.

> *I used to have a small sip of my father's pint and think "I want to make beer when I'm bigger".*

TASTING NOTES

APPEARANCE:

AROMA:

TASTE:

OVERALL SCORE:

TASTING NOTES

APPEARANCE:

AROMA:

TASTE:

OVERALL SCORE:

Thwaites Nutty Black

Source: Daniel Thwaites' Star Brewery, Blackburn, Lancashire, England
Strength: 3.3% draught; 3.9% bottle
Website: www.thwaites.co.uk

It's good to find such a big and venerable brewery dedicating itself to cask ales and bottle-conditioned beers. Thwaites was founded in 1807 and its Star Brewery dominates the Blackburn skyline. It's still owned by the Yerburgh family, descendants of Daniel Thwaites, and beer is delivered to local pubs by horse-drawn drays. The family's dedication to brewing has been underscored by plans announced in 2012 to move to a new greenfield site outside the town. Thwaites has also expanded its range of beers, which it supplies to a large estate of 400 pubs throughout northern England and the Midlands.

The success of such cask ales as Lancaster Bomber and Wainwright's – the former promoted with evident relish by cricketer Andrew Flintoff – encouraged Thwaites to rethink a policy that had concentrated for some years on 'smooth' nitro-keg beers. Cask ales have been given prominence, with several new additions to the range, and this was followed by a move into bottle-conditioned beers. Thwaites' longstanding Dark Mild was renamed Nutty Black and the success of the beer was reinforced by the launch of a stronger bottle-conditioned version – initially called Very Nutty Black, but now branded Nutty Black in line with the cask version – with what the company admits is a tongue-in-cheek tag line of 'export strength' – when Mild Ale was in its heyday in the 19th century, it was brewed in vast quantities for thirsty workers in the mill towns and mines of the north-west. Little went abroad.

The beer is brewed with Pearl pale malt, 10% crystal malt and roasted malt. The hops are Challenger, Fuggles and Goldings, which create 23.5 units of bitterness. The beer has a pronounced liquorice and dark toffee aroma, with a delicious hint of blackcurrant fruit and gentle spicy hops. Roasted malt, toffee, dark fruit and hop resins build in the mouth while the finish is bittersweet and complex, with dark fruit, roasted malt, dark toffee, liquorice and peppery hops. The beer is available in the Morrisons supermarket chain, which is giving the entire Mild sector an encouraging boost.

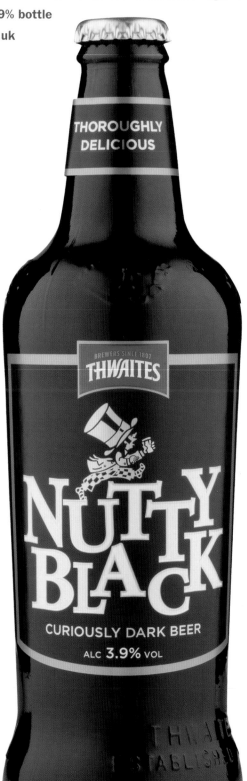

Unibroue 17

Source: Brasserie Unibroue. Chambly, Montréal, Canada

Strength: 10%

Website: www.unibroue.com

Unibroue 17 is a long way removed from a British Mild. This is a strong brown ale and, among many awards, it was named the best dark ale in the World Beer Awards 2010, staged in Britain but with an international panel of judges. The beer is one of many in a large portfolio produced by a brewery that has come a long way from its humble micro plant in 1990. Since 2006, it has been owned by the giant Japanese group Sapporo International and there have no complaints about any diminution in the quality or character of the beers. The company was founded by André Dion and Serge Racine in 1990 to bring a taste of Belgian-style ales to the Francophone area of Canada. Their success led the move to a state-of-the-art plant in Chambly in Montréal, with a major injection of funds from Canadian rock star Robert Charlebois. Today it has 300 employees and warehouses throughout Québec.

Master brewer/*maître brasseur* Jerry Vietz told me he uses pale, chocolate, crystal and wheat malts in his beer, and hops it with American and German 'noble' varieties that create 35 bitterness units. It was Jerry's first brew when he joined the company in 2007 and he planned to make it just once.

But its success in the World Beer Awards and the media attention it gained in Canada has turned it into an annual vintage. The beer is aged in French oak and then re-seeded with fresh yeast for bottling. Jerry says bottles can be laid down for between five to eight years to mature and improve.

The beer has a complex bouquet of smoke, oak and vanilla from the wood, with roasted malt, spicy hops and a delicious hint of coffee. Vanilla is pronounced on the palate and finish but is well balanced by hints of toasted oak, cocoa, mocha coffee and lingering spicy hops.

TASTING NOTES

APPEARANCE:

AROMA:

TASTE:

OVERALL SCORE:

TASTING NOTES

APPEARANCE:

AROMA:

TASTE:

OVERALL SCORE:

West Berkshire Maggs Magnificent Mild

Source: West Berkshire Brewery, Frilsham, Berkshire, England

Strength: 3.8%

Website: www.wbbrew.com

West Berkshire is yet another example of a small brewery that has grown, gone from strength to strength, and picked up a dray-load of medals and awards along the way. The brewery was founded by Dave and Helen Maggs in 1995 in derelict buildings behind the Pot Kiln pub, which was built to refresh people in the local kiln works. There was just room to brew five barrels a week but acclaim for the beers led, in 2006, to a new site based in an old bakery at Yattendon. The brewery, which now supplies some 120 outlets and owns one pub of its own, the Rising Sun at Stockcross near Newbury, moved yet again in 2012 to Home Farm with new equipment that can brew 80 barrels a week. The new site has a shop and a tasting room for visitors. The space has enabled the Maggs and their partners to develop a reed bed system for recirculating and saving waste water. Spent hops and malt are delivered to local farms.

Maggs Magnificent Mild has won awards from SIBA, local CAMRA festivals and has crowned them all with a Gold in the Champion Winter Beer of Britain competition in 2008. It's brewed with Maris Otter pale malt, which is blended with chocolate and crystal malts, roasted barley and wheat. The hops are Fuggles, Goldings and Pioneer, which create 30 bitterness units. The beer has a rich and inviting bouquet of dark chocolate, roasted malt, burnt fruit and peppery hops. Bitter hops provide a solid underpinning in the mouth to a great malt attack of roast and dark wholemeal biscuits, with strong hints of chocolate and dark fruit. The finish is long, with a good hop note at the end balancing the richness of malt and fruit.

The beer has a rich and inviting bouquet of dark chocolate, roasted malt, burnt fruit and peppery hops

Pale Ales

One of the many exhilarating aspects of the modern world of brewing is the cross-fertilisation of beer styles. Pale ale developed in England in the 19th century as an offshoot of India Pale Ale. Pale ale was brewed for the English domestic market: it was an IPA with less alcohol and fewer hops. Unlike IPA, Pale ale did not disappear but its position was muddied early in the 20th century by the arrival of a new type of draught beer known as Bitter. Many writers and even brewers confuse and even combine the new styles as though they are one and the same.

The confusion continues. The year 2012 was the 60th anniversary of the launch of Marston's Pedigree, brewed in the citadel of pale ale brewing, Burton on Trent. To mark the occasion, Marston's produced a 'retro' bottled version of the beer with a label from the 1950s, with the beer clearly described as pale ale. Today, it's called Bitter (see *300 Beers to Try Before You Die!*), even though it's a classic Burton pale ale.

The difference between pale ale and Bitter is easy to determine. Pale ale, in common with its elder brother IPA, was brewed using pale malt and brewing sugar: no darker malts were used. Bitter, on the other hand, is a copper-coloured beer, its hue made possible by the development of a new type of stewed malt in the 20th century known as crystal (see p103). In order to distinguish between the draught and bottled versions of Bitter, many brewers called the latter pale ale, which deepened the confusion.

Before the development of Bitter, pale ale in bottle became a cult drink in England, especially among the new and aspiring middle class. They consumed it in their homes in preference to 'low' public houses where they might – horror! – have to rub shoulders with members of the working class. Bottled pale ale was delivered to people's homes along with the milk and one major London brewer, Whitbread, which had made its fortune from Porter, abandoned darker beers in order to concentrate on the burgeoning demand for pale ale. Two of the great Burton brewers, Bass and Worthington, continued the tradition of the town with pale ales of the highest quality. Worthington's White Shield (see *300 Beers to Try Before You Die!*) not only continues to be brewed but has achieved remarkable sales in recent years as it has been discovered by a new, younger and appreciative audience.

But White Shield swam against the tide. The 20th century witnessed the decline and disappearance of true pale ales, hastened by the loss of many older breweries that had specialised in the style. It was discovered, revived and refashioned by the new wave of craft brewers in the United States with their hunger for beers that had been wiped out by Prohibition in the 1920s. One of the pioneers of the American craft brewing movement, David Geary, launched his pale ale (again, see *300 Beers to Try Before You Die!*) in the late 1980s after studying British brewing methods and history. Geary inspired a legion of American brewers since then, who have developed their own interpretations of the style.

Pale ale first made its mark in North America when such leading British brewers as Allsopp, Bass and Worthington exported their beers in the 19th century. American brewers have returned the compliment. They not only brew fine versions of pale ale but, as this section shows, they have encouraged British brewers to develop beers that tingle with hop character and even carry the name 'American Pale Ale'. There is an additional strand to the revival of the style. English pale ale was once popular in Belgium and brewers exported substantial volumes to the Low Countries in the early and mid-20th century. Now some American brewers are fashioning pale ales that make a deep bow in the direction of both England and Belgium with the use of Belgian malts and even yeast cultures. And to prove that pale ale travels well, there is even an interpretation of the style from Iceland.

The complex fruit character is balanced by cracker wheat malt and booming hop notes

TASTING NOTES

APPEARANCE:

AROMA:

TASTE:

OVERALL SCORE:

8Wired Hopwired

Source: 8Wired Brewing Company, Marlborough, New Zealand
Strength: 7.3%
Website: www.8wired.co.nz

8Wired was named Champion Brewery of New Zealand in 2011 – quite an achievement for a one-man outfit that doesn't actually own a brewery. The brewer is a nomadic Dane named Søren Eriksen who lived in Perth, Australia, with his wife Monique while he was studying for a Masters in biochemistry. He was inspired by the local Little Creatures brewery, which made him realise, he says, 'that beer didn't have to be pale, fizzy stuff'. He started to brew his own beer when Monique bought him a Cooper's home-brew kit. When they moved to Marlborough in New Zealand in 2006, Søren switched to all-grain brewing and then made the leap to commercial brewing two years later. He uses the brewing kit at Renaissance Brewing in Blenheim but his recipes are his own and he is fully in charge of production.

The name 8Wired comes from a type of wire used in electric fencing in New Zealand, though Kiwis also use it for just about every job around the house. Hopwired is Søren's main brand and he believes it's the first Kiwi beer to be brewed exclusively from malts and hops grown in the country. The malts are Gladfield Pale, caramalt, crystal and Munich, while the hop varieties are Motueka, Nelson Sauvin and Southern Cross. The only foreign intruder is an American pale ale yeast culture. Søren says that many American pale ales have pronounced grapefruit aromas but his beer is sharply different with passion fruit, limes, oranges, Sauvignon Blanc and gooseberries. 'When did you last taste a gooseberry?' he asks. The answer is: in many New Zealand wines, such as the Montana range. The complex fruit character is balanced by cracker wheat malt and booming hop notes: the bitterness units are a mighty 70. Rich, toasted malt, ripe fruit and bitter hops dominate the palate, followed by a long, complex finish that ends dry, hoppy and fruity. Søren labels his beer – which is exported to the U.S., Australia and his native Denmark – IPA, but I believe its massive fruit notes make it more at home among New World pale ales.

Adnams Ghost Ship

Source: Adnams Sole Bay Brewery, Southwold, Suffolk, England

Strength: 4.5%

Website: www.adnams.co.uk

For many years, Adnams built its fame on its salty and uncompromisingly hoppy Southwold Bitter. When it was a small, family brewery with little trade outside East Anglia and London, legions of beer lovers would make the trek to Southwold to sample the Bitter in the many fine Adnams' pubs in the town and surrounding areas. Southwold became famous for its pier, brightly-painted beach huts, the whitewashed, inshore lighthouse...and the brewery. Then Adnams added the premium Broadside and it rapidly became one of the most popular beers in the country. (Both Southwold Bitter and Broadside are listed in *300 Beers to Try Before You Die!*) The brewery has expanded rapidly in recent years. A new, eco-friendly brewhouse has been built just outside Southwold with a grassed roof and tanks to catch and recycle rain.

The brewhouse is modern and multi-functional and can produce a wide range of styles. The new, young and enthusiastic head brewer, Fergus Fitzgerald, has been handed the keys to the sweet shop and seasonal and one-off beers have been added to the portfolio, some of them commemorating the fascinating history of the town, with its battles against both the elements and foreign invasion.

One new beer, Ghost Ship, achieved such instant popularity that it's now a permanent fixture. It takes its name from the many wrecks of fighting ships and smugglers' boats off Southwold and the neighbouring village of Walberswick. The Bell pub in Walberswick claims several apparitions, and my wife and I once had a ghostly experience there. We noticed, sitting at the end of the bar, a man in old-fashioned sailors' clothes: peaked cap set a jaunty angle, Guernsey sweater, canvas trousers and knee-length boots. He was smoking a pipe and enjoying a pint. We looked away to continue our conversation and when we looked back a moment later he had gone.

The writer George Orwell, who lived in Southwold for a few years, had a similar experience. He was sitting outside the church in Walberswick one day when he saw a crooked-back man in clothing from a different age come out of the church. Intrigued, Orwell walked to the church but when he turned the corner the man was nowhere to be seen. To add to the shivers, there's Black Shuck, the ghostly dog that roams the marshes in the area. Close to Southwold, the hamlet of Dunwich was once the most important port in Suffolk but cliff erosion has sent most of the town tumbling into the sea. Locals say that at high tide you can sometimes hear the bells of the submerged church tolling.

So Fergus Fitzgerald had no shortage of ghostly happenings to encourage him to fashion a beer called Ghost Ship. Surprisingly, perhaps, it's not brewed solely with pale malt: Fergus blends in rye crystal malt and caramalt. The main hop used is American Citra, with Chinook and New Zealand Motueka in the copper, with a further addition of Citra in the fermenter. Bitterness units are a high 40. The beer has a superb aroma of violets, citrus fruit, spicy hops and lightly toasted malt. Tart fruit, tangy hop resins and a 'malt biscuits' grain note dominate the palate. The finish is long, complex, dry and bitter, but those characteristics are balanced by bittersweet citrus fruit, with grapefruit and lemon to the fore, and rich biscuit malt. It's a beer that sends shivers down your spine.

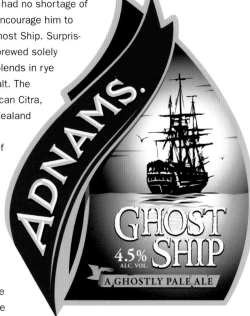

TASTING NOTES

APPEARANCE:

AROMA:

TASTE:

OVERALL SCORE:

Bayou Teche La 31 Bière Pâle

Source: Bayou Teche Brewing Company, Arnaudville, Louisiana, USA

Strength: 5.6%

Website: www.bayoutechebrewing.com

This is a complex beer before you even sample it. It's an American Pale Ale but the founders of the brewery, the Knott brothers, prefer to call it a Louisiana Pale Ale. The brewery is based in a part of the United States that will be familiar to readers of James Lee Burke's atmospheric crime novels that are based around New Orleans and the Bayou Teche. The region was part of the Louisiana Purchase: in 1803 the French agreed to sell a vast tract of land stretching from the Mississippi River to the Rockies and the Canadian border. The asking price was just $15 million and the sale more than doubled the size of the United States. But Louisiana has always remained semi-detached from the union. Its roots are Cajun and Creole with a distinctive culture, language and cuisine of its own.

Byron, Dorsey and Karlos Knott run a brewery by the Bayou Teche, a 125-mile waterway that transported goods for the first settlers in 'Arcadia'. The first major road was called Highway LA-31, which follows the course of the Bayou Teche. The beer commemorates both the river and the highway.

In 2009, the brothers converted a disused rail car into a farmhouse in typical Arcadian style, complete with a small brewery and a 'tasting porch'. Karlos had spent time in Europe, where he fell in love with good beer and Belgian ales in particular. As a result, his pale ale has a Belgian twist. He uses Belgian malts – pale ale, Pilsner, caravienne and biscuit. Caravienne is stewed malt similar to English crystal while biscuit malt is heavily roasted; both are used for colour and flavour. Karlos uses an American yeast culture as he feels Belgian yeast would develop flavours too rich for Arcadians. He uses 'an insane amount of Liberty hops' that create 27 bitterness units: Karlos says he's looking for floral, herbal, aromatic notes without an overpowering bitterness.

The pale gold beer has a big fluffy head of foam and a nutty and fruity aroma with hints of caramel, butterscotch and a resinous/cedar note from the hops. Aromatic hop resins burst across the tongue along with tart orange/citrus fruit and nutty malt reminiscent of old-fashioned Barleycup bedtime drinks. The beautifully-balanced finish has creamy malt, tangy fruit and a continuing hint of butterscotch and tart hop resins. The Knott brothers say the beer is a fine companion for such Louisiana dishes as red beans and rice, shrimp, gumbo (fish or meat stew) and boudin (pork and rice). The local cuisine is rich in peppers, onions and garlic and these heady flavours demand an aromatic beer such as Bière Pâle.

Berkshire Brewing Steel Rail Extra Pale Ale

Source: Berkshire Brewing Company, South Deerfield, Massachusetts, USA

Strength: 5.3%

Website: berkshirebrewingcompany.com

Not to be confused with the West Berkshire Brewery in England, this is an American company and the name is pronounced as it's spelt: not 'Barkshire'. When home brewers Chris Lalli and Gary Bogoff met in the 1990s they shared a similar ambition: to brew the best beer in Massachusetts. Following a long search, they found a disused cigar factory in South Deerfield in the Pioneer Valley. With the aid of friends, including architects, they refashioned the old warehouse into a working brewery with the aim of brewing beer for local people that was 'clean, fresh, well-balanced and in small batches'. Extra Pale Ale was their first brew in 1994, and it went on to become their flagship beer in a portfolio of nine regular beers – both ales and lagers – and many seasonal and occasional beers.

EPA rapidly achieved success. Within two years, BBC – there's another British confusion – had gone from 24 barrels a week to 77. By 1999, Chris and Gary were forced to add an additional 3,000 square feet for warehousing and offices in order to keep pace with demand. Today, they are brewing 580 barrels a week and are officially categorised as a regional rather than a microbrewery. The beers are distributed throughout five states on the east coast.

EPA, in common with all the BBC beers, is unfiltered and unpasteurised and is brewed without chemicals or preservatives. The beer will appeal to 'steam buffs' as well as beer connoisseurs as the label shows a steam locomotive: the brewery's address is 12 Railroad Street. It's brewed with pale, two-row malt and Northern Brewer and Willamette hops, which create 20 bitterness units.

TASTING NOTES

APPEARANCE:

AROMA:

TASTE:

OVERALL SCORE:

The beer has a light bronze colour and an intriguing aroma: how can such a pale beer have a touch of chocolate on the nose? The brewers assure me they use only pale malt. There's a fine grassy and herbal hop note and rich cracker wheat grain. The palate is finely balanced between rich, slightly sweet and juicy malt and solid, peppery hops with a touch of pear-like fruit. The finish is bittersweet with a well-honed hop bitterness vying for attention with ripe malt and fruit. The beer's appeal was summed up by American beer writer Lew Bryson: 'It's what the water in heaven oughta taste like.'

 It's what the water in heaven oughta taste like.

TASTING NOTES

APPEARANCE:

AROMA:

TASTE:

OVERALL SCORE:

Boatrocker Alpha Queen

Source: Boatrocker Brewing Company, Melbourne, Victoria, Australia

Strength: 5%

Website: www.boatrocker.com.au

Matt and Andrea Houghton brewed their first batch of beer in their garage in Melbourne. It was Alpha Queen, so-called because of the alpha acids in the hop varieties they use. The beer was well received and Matt and Andrea put their foot on the gas and built a proper commercial brewery in Kavanagh Street in the city. Matt was inspired to brew by the late Michael Jackson's 1990 television series *The Beer Hunter*. As a result, Matt travelled through such major brewing centres as Bavaria, Belgium and Britain. When he returned home, he studied brewing at Ballarat University, where he met and married Andrea, and they set up shop in their garage.

In typical Aussie fashion, they don't mince their words: 'We don't brew beer like the big boys,' they say, 'no preservatives and no sugar.' That's a dig at giant brewers Down Under who use substantial amounts of sugar cane in their brews, which accounts for the sweet and sticky nature of mainstream lagers. Boatrocker was the first brewery in Australia to list the ingredients it uses.

Alpha Queen is not a beer for the fainthearted. It's brewed with malts imported from Britain: pale, crystal, light Munich, carapils and wheat. The hops are Centennial, Columbus and New Zealand Cascade, which create 42 IBUs – that's a high level of bitterness. The hops are added at the start of the copper boil and as a late addition just before the boil ends. The beer is also 'dry hopped', meaning there's a further addition prior to kegging and bottling.

The beer has a burnished copper colour and has a fine aroma of grassy hops, apricot fruit and caramel and spices. The rich palate is dominated by toasted grain, fruit, spices and herbal and peppery hops, followed by a long finish that is dry, fruity, intensely hoppy and spicy. Leave the car in the garage...

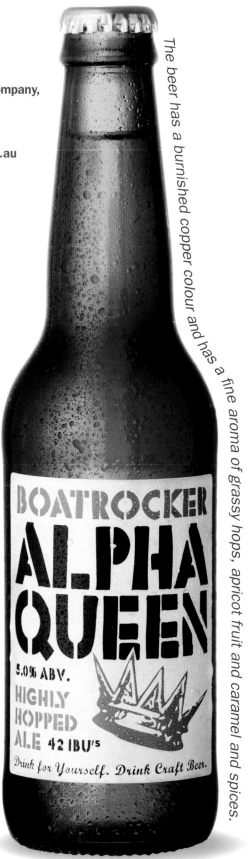

The beer has a burnished copper colour and has a fine aroma of grassy hops, apricot fruit and caramel and spices.

Dark Star American Pale Ale

Source: Dark Star Brewing Company, Partridge Green, West Sussex, England

Strength: 4.7%

Website: www.darkstarbrewing.co.uk

It's fitting that Dark Star's prize-winning beer is called American Pale Ale, for the brewery's history reads like a chapter from the American Dream. The brewery was so small when it started that it was crammed into one part of the cellar of a pub. It has moved twice since then and its current site, with a brewhouse that resembles the launch pad at Cape Canaveral, can produce some 20,000 barrels a year.

The origins of the company go back even further than the original pub cellar. In the 1980s, Rob Jones brewed with his partner Martin Kemp at the Pitfield Brewery in North London, where they were nicknamed the Yeastie Boys after the rap group the Beastie Boys. The plant was tiny but the beers were good and in 1987 Rob's and Martin's strong ale, Dark Star – named after a song by the Grateful Dead – won CAMRA's Champion Beer of Britain competition. When the partners went their separate ways, Rob held on to the name Dark Star, which is now labelled Original. He set up his new brewery in 1994 in part of the cellar of the Evening Star pub in Brighton, the famous Regency seaside resort in Sussex: the pub is just a few yards from the main railway station. He won such acclaim for his beers that, with new partners, he moved to a considerably

bigger site at Ansty in 2001, and then for a third time to Partridge Green, where the custom-built plant can produce 45 barrels per batch.

Dark Star has a wide portfolio of beers, with seven regular beers, monthly brews and seasonal specials, a portfolio that includes English, European and American styles. In 2009, American Pale won the Gold award in the golden ale class in the Champion Beer of Britain competition at the Great British Beer Festival at Earls Court. The company goes from strength to strength, owns four pubs – including the Evening Star – and is now a regional rather than a microbrewery.

In order to give American Pale Ale an authentic character, Rob and his colleagues use not only American hops but a yeast culture imported from the United States. The beer is brewed with low colour Maris Otter malt and hopped with all-American varieties: Cascade, Centennial and Chinook. The pale gold beer has a profound aroma of citrus fruits – orange, lemon and grapefruit – with cedar notes from the hops and biscuit malt. Tart fruit builds in the mouth but is well balanced by creamy malt and intensely bitter hops. The finish is long and complex, with an intertwining of fruit, malt and hops; it finally ends dry and hoppy.

Pale Ales

TASTING NOTES

APPEARANCE:

AROMA:

TASTE:

OVERALL SCORE:

Einstôk Icelandic Pale Ale

Source: Einstôk Ölgerd, Akureyri, Iceland

Strength: 5.4%

Website: www.einstockbeer.com

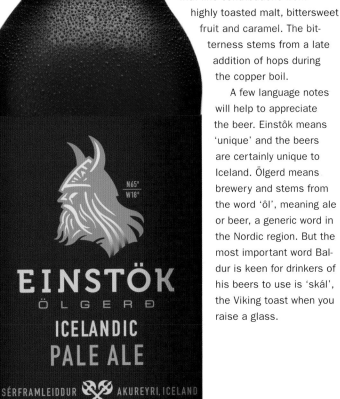

What else could they brew in Iceland but pale ale? The wonder is that anything can be brewed there at all, as prohibition lasted from 1915 until 1989. Several new breweries have started to fill the gap, concentrating on brewing mainstream lagers. The Viking Brewery in the fishing port of Akureyri, 60 miles south of the Arctic Circle, offers something different with its Einstôk subsidiary. Brewmaster Baldur Karason has developed a specialist range of beers that includes Toasted Porter and Doppelbock as well as Pale.

Baldur was born in the town of Siglufjörður but moved to Akureyri where he started work for the Viking Brewery as a food scientist. He was keen to make beer and in 1993 went to the Heriot-Watt University's faculty of brewing in Edinburgh, where he graduated as a brewer. He returned to Viking where the owners, Bernard La Borie, David Altshuler and Jack Sichterman, wanted to develop a range of specialist beers, and gave Baldur free rein to produce new recipes.

He had at his disposal the purest brewing water in the world. It flows from prehistoric glaciers down from the local mountains and through lava fields and is ideal for brewing high-quality beers. For Pale Ale, Baldur uses pale ale, crystal and chocolate malts and a blend of American Cascade and Bavarian Northern Brewer and Hallertauer hop varieties. Bitterness units are not measured and Jack Sichterman told me, 'We're not looking to blow people's heads off as some pale ales do – we want smooth, flavourful and delicious drinkability.' This doesn't mean the beer lacks hop character. It has a pale copper colour with floral, herbal and pine needle hop aromas, and creamy sherbet, caramel/toffee and 'malt biscuits' grain notes. On the palate, tart blood orange fruit emerges with growing hop bitterness, juicy malt and a continuing caramel note. The finish is intensely bitter but with fine contributions from highly toasted malt, bittersweet fruit and caramel. The bitterness stems from a late addition of hops during the copper boil.

A few language notes will help to appreciate the beer. Einstôk means 'unique' and the beers are certainly unique to Iceland. Ölgerd means brewery and stems from the word 'öl', meaning ale or beer, a generic word in the Nordic region. But the most important word Baldur is keen for drinkers of his beers to use is 'skál', the Viking toast when you raise a glass.

Fordham Tavern Ale

Source: Fordham Brewing Company, Dover, Delaware, USA

Strength: 6.1%

Website: www.fordhambrewingco.com

Fordham is a major independent brewery in the eastern U.S., producing a sizeable portfolio of beers that ranges from pale ale through wheat beer and German styles such as Alt and Doppelbock. It also has some history on its side: the first Fordham brewery dates from 1703 when Queen Anne encouraged a young settler from London, Benjamin Fordham, to open a brewery in the new port of Annapolis, named in her honour. Annapolis became the capital of Maryland and was briefly the seat of power in the early United States. Young Benjamin naturally carried out the wishes of his monarch and his brewery flourished as Annapolis became a wealthy port.

Nearly 300 years later, in 1993, a new Fordham Brewery was launched. It quickly acquired a fine reputation for its beers and it moved to a new plant in Dover, Delaware, to keep pace with demand. Along the way it took over the Old Dominion brewery that had been founded in 1989 by Jerry Bailey in Ashburn, Virginia, close to Washington D.C. Old Dominion was a sizeable concern, producing some 27,000 barrels a year. But by the early 21st century, Jerry was happy to take a back seat and hand over to Fordham's Bill Muehlhauser, who now produces both Fordham's and Old Dominion's brands.

The merger was facilitated by investment from the biggest brewer in the U.S., Anheuser-Busch, but A-B plays no part in brewing, recipes or brand development: its interest lies solely in its ability to act as the distributor of the beers.

Tavern Ale, described as an American Pale Ale, is Fordham's flagship beer. It has a complex recipe made up of pale, wheat, Munich and cara malts. The hops are Bravo and Cascade blended together for the first addition in the kettle, with further additions of Cascade after 15 and 45 minutes. Chinook are added in the whirlpool at the end of the boil and the beer is then dry hopped with a blend of Cascade, Chinook and Crystal. Finally the beer is cold conditioned for five days prior to packaging on a deep bed of Cascades. The units of bitterness are 44.

Tavern Ale has a copper colour with a big nutty and toasted malt aroma, balanced by peppery hop resins. There's a chewy 'breakfast cereal' malt note in the mouth with bitter orange fruit and pine-like hop resins. Bitter hops dominate the finish, but the bitterness is balanced by vinous fruit and rich, toasted malt. Tavern Ale and other Fordham brews can be enjoyed in the brewery tap, the Rams Head, in Dover, named after Benjamin Fordham's first tavern. Here's a health unto Her Majesty!

Fordham and Old Dominion beers are exported to Britain.

TASTING NOTES

APPEARANCE:

AROMA:

TASTE:

OVERALL SCORE:

Odell 5 Barrel Pale Ale

Source: Odell Brewing, Fort Collins, Colorado, USA

Strength: 5.2%

Website: www.odellbrewing.com

Odell Brewing's pale ale comes from a pilot brewery where new beers – sometimes as many as 75 a year – are formulated and brewed just five barrels at a time – hence the name. Pale Ale created such interest that it was rapidly turned into a regular member of the portfolio.

This is a beer that's a hymn of praise to the noble hop plant. Three varieties are used – Fuggles, Glacier and Willamette – and they are added four times during the boil in the kettle. There's a further infusion of whole hop flowers in the hop back, the vessel that receives the liquid at the end of the boil. Finally, the beer is 'dry hopped' when it's packaged,

which means a handful of hops are added to kegs or to the vessel used for bottling to give the finished beer a further fine aroma and palate.

The grains used are pale, crystal and Munich malts and the bitterness units are 36. The beer is bronze coloured with a hint of copper. It has superb aroma with an almost Cognac note from fruity hops, balanced by a fresh-bread malt note and peppery hop resins. Ripe fruit – apricots, bitter oranges and gooseberries – dominate the palate but there's an increasingly bitter hop note along with sappy malt. The finish is dry, hoppy and bitter with continuing rich fruit and luscious malt. This is beer of the highest quality.

Porterhouse Hop Head

Source: Porterhouse Brewing Company, Dublin, Ireland

Strength: 4.7%

Website: www.theporterhouse.ie

Brewing has been transformed in Ireland in recent years and the driving force is a remarkable entrepreneur called Oliver Hughes. He worked briefly in the 1980s for two short-lived small breweries, Dempsey's and Harty's, that were ahead of their time and failed to break the mighty duopoly of Guinness and Murphy's. Hughes moved to England and lived for several years in St Albans in a road adjacent to the head office of CAMRA. He was able to see at first hand the dramatic changes to beer and brewing in Britain and, with his partner Liam LaHart, developed a new strategy for Ireland based on brew pubs. In 1996, Hughes and LaHart opened the Porterhouse in Temple Bar in Dublin, an area that was undergoing rapid re-development and became a fashionable place to eat and drink. The first beers, brewed on the premises, were an old Dublin speciality, Plain Porter, along with Oyster

Stout and Wrasslers 4X. Wrasslers brought back a much-missed Irish brewing name and 4X was a stout with potent history, the favourite beer of Irish Republican hero Michael Collins.

The Porterhouse was an overnight success and the demand for the beers soon outstripped the ability of the in-house plant to produce sufficient quantities. A stand-alone brewery was built on the edge of the city, two new pubs were opened in the Glasnevin and Nassau Street areas and Oliver Hughes repaid his thanks to Britain by opening a vast, sprawling Porterhouse in London's Covent Garden. Knowing the British market well, he launched a cask beer, TSB for London, but added, recognising the fast-moving changes in Ireland, Hop Head in cask form for both Dublin and London. His latest venture is a Porterhouse in New York City, based in Manhattan's oldest building, Fraunce's Tavern. General George

Washington said goodbye to his troops at Fraunce's at the end of what the British politely call the War of Independence but is better known in the U.S. as the Revolutionary War. With a mischievous grin, Oliver Hughes says the struggle for independence from Britain in both America and Ireland links his pubs on both sides of the Pond and he is not ruling out opening a Porterhouse in Boston, Massachusetts, with its large Irish-American population.

Hop Head is based firmly on the American Pale Ale style. It's brewed with pale malt only and is hopped with American Cascade and German Hallertau varieties. It has a massive hit of floral, resinous and citrus hops, balanced by juicy and biscuit malt. Hop bitterness and citrus – grapefruit to the fore – build in the mouth with a good underpinning of sappy malt. The lingering finish offers a fine balance of bitter hops, tangy fruit and juicy malt.

Wicked Elf Pale Ale

Source: Little Brewing Co, Port Macquarie, New South Wales, Australia

Strength: 5.4%

Website: www.littlebrewingcompany.com.au

While many British small craft breweries operate from lock-ups on industrial estates, their Australian counterparts have much more space available to them. The Little Brewing Company is on the coast where the River Hastings runs into the Pacific Ocean. It's an idyllic location, with crystal clear waters against a backdrop of hills that are rich in wildlife, including kangaroos. But Port Macquarie – named for a governor of New South Wales during the early colonial period – does have a grim past. It was one of the first penal colonies in the country and criminals transported there from Britain were appallingly treated, repeatedly flogged and given the back-breaking task of clearing scrub and forest.

Port Macquarie was the first place to have sugar cane planted by settlers: the cane was a boon for the first brewers in the country until supplies of barley were available. Big brewers still use substantial levels of sugar cane in mainstream lagers, but that style of brewing is far removed from the brewery founded in 2007 by Kylie and Warwick Little, who fashion beer using only the finest raw materials. They have 59 medals for their beers in both national and international beer competitions.

Wicked Elf is an American-style pale ale and the Littles underscore the integrity of the beer by using an imported ale yeast from the U.S., along with Cascade hops from Oregon. Australian and Tasmanian hop varieties are blended with the Cascades. Pale and crystal malts are used, with a further blend of local and English barleys. The beer has a deep bronze colour with a big punch of bittersweet grapefruit on the nose from the Cascades, backed by nutty malt and bitter hop resins. Tart fruit builds in the mouth with fine contributions from a malt note reminiscent of wholemeal bread and intensely bitter hops. The finish is long and complex, starting with tangy fruit but ending dry and bitter with a continuing rich malt note. The beer has not only won medals but is highly praised by author of *The Beer Bible*, and one of Australia's leading beer writers, Willie Simpson.

TASTING NOTES

APPEARANCE:

AROMA:

TASTE:

OVERALL SCORE:

Wynkoop Silverback Pale Ale

Source: Wynkoop Brewing Company, Denver, Colorado, USA

Strength: 5.5%

Website: www.wynkoop.com

I was attending the Great American Beer Festival in Colorado one year when I met John Hickenlooper running the Wynkoop bar. The Wynkoop drew visitors in droves as it was famous for its tremendous range of American and imported beers. John also owned a major bookstore in town and he asked if I would like to give a talk at the store one evening. I naturally agreed but on the evening in question I found, greatly to my disadvantage, that I was following Colin Powell, a four-star general and chairman of the Joint Chiefs of Staff. He had just published his memoirs and I must admit that he drew a rather bigger crowd to the bookstore than I did. It was nevertheless a pleasant evening and I watched Hickenlooper's meteoric rise to fame with interest. In 1988, he added a brewery at the Wynkoop and soon after ran for office, becoming mayor of Denver. He went on running and at the time of writing he is the Governor of Colorado. A stab at even higher office should not be ruled out.

The Wynkoop is a vast red-brick building opposite the railroad station in a district known as LoDo, short for Lower Downtown. The building dates from 1888 and was originally one of the many warehouses and offices that fed the railroad system. Wynkoop takes its name from Edward W Wynkoop, who was the first mayor of Denver city. The rambling building has a vast bar area, a gigantic pool room, a restaurant serving delicious food and a brewery that produces acclaimed beers. John Hickenlooper and his team are concerned about the environment and are keen to help save endangered species. Silverback Pale Ale is named for the male African gorilla that's the one of the closest animal relatives to humans and is in danger of becoming extinct: money from the sales of the beer is donated to the Mountain Gorilla Conservation Fund.

The pale ale has a complex recipe comprised of pale malt from American two-row barley, aromatic malt imported from Simpson's in England, two types of caramalt and flaked barley. The hops, used at different stages of the kettle boil, are Cascade, Centennial, Columbus and Czech Saaz, which create 45 bitterness units. Added to the malts and hops are Grains of Paradise, a spice from West Africa that's eaten by the mountain gorillas' lowland cousins. In spite of the caramalts, the beer is extremely pale in colour – as pale as a Pilsner. It has a superb spicy and citrus fruit aroma with light toasted malt and peppery hop resins. It's spicy and intensely bitter in the mouth but the bitterness is balanced by biscuit malt and floral, herbal hop resins. The finish is finely balanced between sweet, juicy malt, tart fruit and bitter hops. Who knows – perhaps it will be served in the White House one day.

Bitters

The English are notorious for blunt speaking – they famously call a spade a bloody shovel. When they ask for a bitter beer they expect to get what it says on the label. In the age of American highly hopped beers, an English Bitter may seem tame by comparison. But for visitors, a pint of Bitter may still come as a shock. There is now a substantial range of beers available in England and its Welsh and Scottish neighbours, but Bitter remains the defining style, a beer that reaches perfection in its cask-conditioned form.

Rather like Monty Python's Spanish Inquisition, nobody expected a new style of beer called Bitter early in the 20th century. In the previous century, brewers had made a tidy living and some amassed great fortunes. But changes in how beer was retailed led to an upheaval in pub ownership. Political interference in the brewing industry is almost always a disaster – American Prohibition being the best-known example. In England, the Beer Act of 1830 was a crude attempt by extreme exponents of the free market to allow householders, rather than experienced publicans, to sell intoxicating liquor. As a result, close to 50,000 rudimentary beer houses opened, doubling the number of licensed premises. In the main they were run by people with no knowledge of retailing, or storing and selling beer.

Many of these 'Tom and Jerry Houses' went out of business, owing large amounts of money to brewers that supplied them with beer and loans. The calamity can be measured by the fact that one of the great Burton brewers, Allsopps, went into administration and had to be financially restructured, while in London, brewer Barclay Perkins was owed £2 million by bankrupt publicans, a colossal sum for the time. As a result, brewers rushed to recoup their losses by buying up failed beer houses. Brewers had owned pubs before, but not on this scale. In some cases they were in possession of hundreds of pubs and these estates developed into the 'tied house' system – pubs that were tied to the brewer-landlord for their supplies. The property scramble came with a price tag. Big companies such as Allsopps and Bass moved from family ownership to become public companies and their new shareholders demanded a fast return on their investments.

The brewers were under pressure to improve the turnover of beer in their pubs. They could no longer wait months for Porters, Stouts and pale ales to reach fruition in casks. Brewing chemists developed new strains of yeast that cleared in cask quickly, enabling brewers to produce ales that were served after a few days of secondary fermentation. This brief conditioning was not a problem where dark beers, with their robust malt character, were concerned. But pale ale tasted thin and immature. New malting technology came to the brewers' aid with crystal malt. This is stewed malt, made in a similar manner to toffee, with the starch in the grain converted into sugar and finally, as the temperature is raised, into a tiny ball of crystallised sugar. Crystal malt can't be turned into alcohol in the brewery but it gives a caramel and nutty flavour to finished beer and also – hence its importance to running beers – a mature character known as 'mouthfeel'. Copper and amber coloured running beers were dubbed 'Bitter' by drinkers and a style was born.

Changes in lifestyle, and drinking habits in a post-industrial society witnessed a move to lighter-coloured wine, spirits and beer. From the 1950s, Bitter became the main English beer style, one that marked it out from the rest of the world's beers. For many overseas visitors, asking for 'a pint of Bitter' in a pub is on a par with trips in London's red buses, though many of the visitors must initially be startled by the spicy and peppery character imparted by English hops.

The beers here have an upper limit of 4 per cent alcohol. Above that, beers belong to the Best Bitter category, though confusion can be caused when some brewers call their standard Bitter 'Best', a rare example of the English exaggerating their abilities.

Box Steam Chuffin Ale

Source: **Box Steam Brewery, Trowbridge, Wiltshire, England**

Strength: **4%**

Website: **www.boxsteambrewery.com**

The railway system transformed brewing in Britain in the 19th century, enabling brewers to deliver their beers at speed throughout the country. Nobody is more closely associated with the Iron Horse than Isambard Kingdom Brunel. The great Victorian engineer drove the new transport system at dizzying speed. One of his greatest achievements was the Box Tunnel – cut through a hill in Wiltshire – that allowed a main line to link London and the port city of Bristol.

Brunel's work is commemorated in the beers of the Box Steam Brewery, whose first brewing plant was based close to the famous tunnel.

The brewery was founded in 2004 by the Roberts family, led by Andrew Roberts, and it remains in their hands. In 2012 the family moved to a custom-built new site as demand for their beers grew. They supply outlets throughout the West Country and run two pubs of their own, the Cross Guns in Avoncliff and the Inn at Freshford. Bottled versions of the beers are exported as far as Canada and Finland. The new site was officially opened by long-term fan Pete Waterman, the pop music impresario, who is a passionate steam train buff and owns several loco- motives. He was joined by a Brunel lookalike in his familiar stove-pipe hat, cigar clenched in his teeth.

Andrew Roberts and his head brewer Phillip Downes believe in using the finest raw materials for their beer and sourcing those ingredients as close to home as possible. They are also determined that brewing should be eco-friendly and they installed a collection system at the new brewery that enables spent grains and hops to be delivered to a local farm as animal feed. For Chuffin Ale Andrew and Phillip use Maris Otter pale malt, which makes up 90 per cent of the grain, with crystal and chocolate malts, and a small proportion of wheat to give the beer a good foaming head. Just one hop is used, the Fuggle. The chestnut-coloured beer has a pronounced chocolate note on the nose, with sultana and raisin fruit and spicy hops. Vinous fruit builds in the mouth with tart and bitter hops, biscuit malt and a continuing hint of dry chocolate. The finish is bitter- sweet with dry chocolate, burnt fruit and bitter hops.

Bryncelyn Holly Hop

Source: **Bryncelyn Brewery, Ystradgynlais, Wales**

Strength: **3.9%**

Website: **none**

Bryncelyn is a small brewery with a big reputation, not only for its beer but for the fact that owner Will Hopton is a keen fan – possibly the keenest fan – of the late Buddy Holly, the rock icon who inspired the likes of Elvis Prelsey and the Beatles. As well as Holly Hop, Will, with his brewer Robert Scott, produces a range that includes Buddy Marvellous, Buddy's Delight, Not Fade Away, Maybe Baby, Oh Boy, Buddy Confusing and, for Christmas, That'll Be the Sleigh. Will opened his brewery in 1999 with a tiny, quarter-barrel kit. This was upgraded to three-quarter barrel status the same year and then, in 2008, Will and Robert relocated to a new site with a six-barrel plant acquired from the former Webb's Brewery in Ebbw Vale. (If you're struggling with the Welsh names, 'Y' is pronounced 'U', making the site of the brewery more like 'Ustradgunlice'.)

Holly Hop has won many awards over the years, including Welsh Beer of the Year in 2007. With a name such as Hopton, Will encourages Robert to use a generous amount of the plants in his beers. Holly Hop is a blend of American Cascade and Bobek from Slovenia. The grains are pale, amber and crystal malts with 20 per cent wheat malt for both head retention and flavour. The amber coloured beer has a creamy and fresh-bread malt appeal on the aroma, with floral hop notes and a delicious hint of citrus fruit. Fruit builds in the mouth, balancing the rich malt character and tangy hop resins. The finish is a fine balance of rich malt, bitter hops and juicy citrus fruit.

Perhaps Will and Robert will consider adding a beer called Big Hopper in memory of Big Bopper who died in the same Iowa plane crash as Buddy Holly in February 1959.

Elgood's Cambridge Bitter

Source: Elgood & Sons, Wisbech, Cambridgeshire, England

Strength: 3.8%

Website: www.elgoods-brewery.co.uk

If you'll excuse the alliteration, Elgood's is exceedingly elegant. The striking brown stone facade of the brewery stands proud on the banks of the River Nene in the Fenland town of Wisbech. Once through the gates you find a commodious brewhouse with gleaming copper vessels and a fermentation room packed with high-sided wooden vessels. There are spacious offices and a welcoming visitor centre complete with bar. In addition, there are four acres of gardens that include herbaceous borders, ancient oaks, a lake and a herb garden. There's also a maze in the shape of a yard of ale, where you can get lost even before you touch a drop of beer.

Elgood's is different to the average brewery. It dates from Georgian times, a period of fine architecture and a belief in the beauty of nature. It was one of the first Georgian breweries to be built outside London. The site dates from 1682, it became a granary and was converted to brewing in 1786. The Elgood family took over in 1877 and has been in charge ever since. The '& Sons' in the title is dated. The company is run today by three sisters: Belinda Sutton is the managing director, Jennifer Everall is the company secretary and Claire Simpson is a director and landscape gardener. Those are their married names but they are Elgoods to their roots.

They own 42 pubs, many of them in tiny, isolated villages almost lost in the mysterious Cambridge fens, where much of the land was retrieved from the

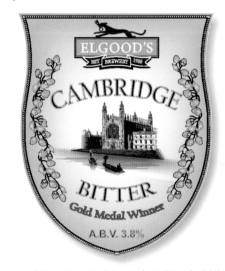

encroaching sea centuries ago. In order to build the business, the sisters sell bottled versions of their beers to major supermarket groups and are also attacking the export market with a 7% Black Eagle Imperial Stout for the United States.

The man about the place, Alan Pateman the jovial head brewer, produces beers that deserve the label 'traditional'. He could follow the trend towards using imported raw materials, hops in particular, but he prefers to remain true to the brewery's traditions. For Cambridge Bitter, which won its class in the 2006 Champion Beer of Britain competition, he uses Maris Otter pale barley malt, with grain grown in the eastern counties of England, mainly from north Norfolk.

TASTING NOTES

APPEARANCE:

AROMA:

TASTE:

OVERALL SCORE:

He blends in wheat malt, roasted barley and invert sugar. The two hops are a mix of Challenger and Fuggles that create 30 units of bitterness. The copper coloured beer has a rich toasted and creamy malt aroma with spicy hop resins and a plum-like fruit note. Biscuit malt, hop resins and tart fruit meld in the mouth, followed by a lingering finish that ends dry and hoppy but with a good balance of creamy malt and vinous fruit.

Visitors to the brewery will note with interest the large copper cooling pans or 'cool ships' that were once used to cool the hopped wort prior to fermentation. When Alan Pateman arrived at Elgood's, one of his first acts was to phase out the cool ships as he was concerned that wild yeasts could infiltrate the brewhouse and inoculate the wort. 'I'm not here to make Belgian lambic,' he jokes. Fortunately, the cool ships have been left in place as a potent reminder of brewing practice from past times. The brewery and gardens are open to visitors from April until September every year: see the website.

TASTING NOTES

APPEARANCE:

AROMA:

TASTE:

OVERALL SCORE:

Emerson's Bookbinder Bitter

Source: Emerson's Brewing Company, Dunedin, New Zealand
Strength: 3.7%
Website: www.emersons.co.nz

The story of Richard Emerson's Rights of Passage tour of European brewing centres is told in the Pilsner section. Suffice it to say, he brews ale as well as lager: his first commercial beer was a Porter. On his visit to Britain he was equally entranced by Bitter and he and his colleagues – the 'brew crew' – have fashioned a Kiwi interpretation of the style. They even dub it 'ordinary bitter', a curious habit of some English brewers – notably Brakspear and Young's – for their less-than-ordinary beers.

The beer was first brewed as a one-off for a festival in Oamaru in 1996. The Criterion Hotel, where the festival was staged, had two of Emerson's beers on sale by hand-pump, but Richard thought a third beer was needed and he designed one on 'the back of an envelope' and brewed it the next day. It was named in honour of two bookbinders, Michael O'Brien of Oamaru and David Stedman of Dunedin. Bookbinder was popular enough to become a regular beer and in 1997, at the Wellington Brewfest, Richard was overjoyed to be handed a silver medal for the beer by the great beer writer, the late Michael Jackson.

As with their Pilsner, the brew crew are keen to use all-New Zealand ingredients where possible. The hops are Fuggles and Riwaka – and the Fuggles, though a famous English hop, are grown in the Nelson area of New Zealand, the main hop-growing region in South Island. The area takes its name from Admiral Lord Nelson who is something of a hero in New Zealand: the main high road in Nelson city is called Trafalgar Street.

The hops create 31 units of bitterness. A complex grist is comprised of ale, lager, crystal and black malts. The amber beer has a perfumy hop aroma with 'malt loaf' grain notes and rich vinous sultana and raisin fruit. Malt and fruit build in the mouth but they are balanced by bitter hop resins. The finish is long and finally becomes dry but with continuing contributions from burnt fruit, nutty malt and bitter hops. A far from 'ordinary' Bitter.

Hawkshead Bitter

Source: Hawkshead Brewery, Staveley, Cumbria, England

Strength: 3.7%

Website: www.hawksheadbrewery.co.uk

Alex Brodie is a rare member of the journalists' profession: he has a good head for business. Most of us couldn't run the proverbial chip shop. Alex for many years was a distinguished BBC broadcaster. He was the corporation's Middle East Correspondent, followed by a stint as one of the presenters on Radio 4's flagship news programme, *Today*. He was also a regular presenter on the BBC World Service. But he tired of the endless travelling and wanted to spend more time with his wife, Anne. They settled in the most beautiful region of England, the Lake District, made famous by the 'Lake Poets' Byron, Shelley and Wordsworth. It's a place of great tranquillity, with deep lakes and high – by English standards – mountains.

In order to make a living, Alex turned to his other love: beer. In 2002 he opened his brewery in an ancient barn near the village of Hawkshead, famous for its Beatrix Potter associations. By 2006 he was forced by the success of his beers to move to a custom-built new brewery in Staveley on the banks of the River Kent. In 2010 he expanded the site, turning it into a glass-fronted building that leads into the Beer Hall where visitors can sample the beers, eat delicious meals, visit the shop and watch the brewing process.

Alex employs a five-man brewing team led by Matt Clarke. The custom-built Moeschle brewing kit can produce 20 barrels per

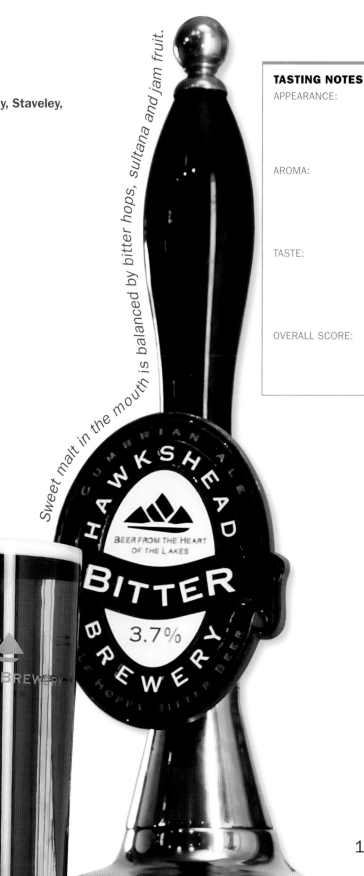

Sweet malt in the mouth is balanced by bitter hops, sultana and jam fruit.

TASTING NOTES

APPEARANCE:

AROMA:

TASTE:

OVERALL SCORE:

brew. Hawkshead currently produces 5,000 barrels a year but it has the capacity to grow production to 9,000 barrels. The vessels include traditional mash tun and copper, with five dual-purpose fermenters that also act as conditioning tanks. Thanks to its location, the brewery has access to some of the finest water imaginable. The water is soft and it's hardened or 'Burtonised' with the additions of mineral salts. The yeast strain, which delivers a fruity character to the beers, originated in a famous and long-closed Sheffield brewery, Stones. The hop store has an impressive collec-

tion of around 12 varieties sourced from England, Europe, New Zealand and the United States.

For Hawkshead Bitter, Matt uses First Gold, an English 'hedgerow' variety, and Styrian Goldings from Slovenia: they create 35 units of bitterness. The grains are Maris Otter pale malt and 4 per cent crystal malt. The beer has a glowing copper colour, with a big aroma of peppery hop resins, nutty malt and tart fruit. Sweet malt in the mouth is balanced by bitter hops, sultana and jam fruit. The bittersweet finish has dark fruit, bitter hops and rich, nutty malt and is finally dry and hoppy.

Kelham Island Pride of Sheffield

Source: Kelham Island Brewery, Sheffield, South Yorkshire, England
Strength: 4%
Website: www.kelhambrewery.co.uk

TASTING NOTES

APPEARANCE:

AROMA:

TASTE:

OVERALL SCORE:

The beer is well named, for Kelham Island single-handedly put the pride back into Sheffield brewing. The capital of South Yorkshire is still known as Steel City even though it lost its steel industry in the 1980s. At the same time, it lost a host of thirsty steel workers and, one by one, the big breweries in the city, two owned by Bass and one each by Ward's and Whitbread, closed. Brewing in Sheffield was revived by Dave Wickett, who lectured in economics at the local polytechnic. He was was an active member of CAMRA and had opened the Fat Cat pub in the Kelham Island district in 1981, defying a trend towards carbonated keg beers from the existing Sheffield brewers. The pub proved such a success that in 1990 he built a brewery next door and within a few years could boast, tongue-in-cheek, that he ran the only commercial brewery in the city as the big brewers were closing their doors. It was the first new brewery in Sheffield for a century and it used equipment bought from a micro-producer in Oxford. In 1999 he was on the move to a bigger plant with five times the capacity of the original but still only

yards from the pub. Dave's first beer was a traditional copper-coloured bitter but he put Kelham Island on the map when he produced a golden ale, Pale Rider (see *300 Beers to Try Before You Die!*). The beer won the Champion Beer of Britain trophy in 2004 and its success forced Dave to expand yet again five years later to keep pace with the clamour for his beers.

Kelham Island has grown from 10 barrels a week to 100 barrels. Dave Wickett, after a long battle with cancer, died in 2012 but his son Ed has taken over at the brewery while brewing is in the hands of head brewer Ian Kenny. For Pride of Sheffield, Ian uses a blend of Maris Otter and Tipple pale malts with a touch of crystal. The hops are Admiral, Fuggles, Golding and Willamette. The amber beer has nose-tingling hop resins on the aroma, with rich biscuit malt and tart fruit and a hint of citrus. Tangy fruit builds in the mouth but is perfectly balanced by soft, creamy malt and solid hop bitterness. The finish is long, quenching, firmly bitter and dry but with continuing contributions from rich malt and citrus fruit. It's a fine tribute to the memory of Dave Wickett.

RCH PG Steam

Source: RCH Brewery, West Hewish, Somerset, England
Strength: 3.9% cask/4% bottle
Website: www.rchbrewery.com

There are a lot of initials connected to this brewery and beer. RCH stands for the Royal Clarence Hotel in the seaside resort of Weston-super-Mare, where the brewery was first based in the 1980s. Brewing was intermittent, with just five barrels of beer produced every fortnight. But the brewers were forced to find new premises when hotel guests complained they couldn't take baths or showers as all available water was being used to make beer. The image of a naked guest lying red-faced with anger in an empty bath while brewers beaver away down in the cellar is an appealing one that could have come straight from a Laurel and Hardy movie.

The brewery moved in 1999 to the hamlet of West Hewish where new 15-barrel brewing equipment was installed. Increasing demand for the beers forced the owners to expand in 2002 to a 30-barrel plant. PG Steam was the first beer brewed with the new kit, which has a steam boiler to heat the copper. PG in the name has nothing to do with one of Britain's most popular brands of tea, PG Tips. The letters come from the first names of managing director Paul Davey and head brewer Graham Dunbaven. Graham uses Optic pale malt and crystal malt with Fuggles and Progress hops. Bitterness units are not measured but this is an intensely bitter beer with a deep gold/amber hue. The aroma has orange and vine fruits with a big spicy Fuggles hop note and nutty malt. The palate is a robust balance of bitter, spicy hops, rich malt and tart fruit followed by a long, dry, bitter and fruity finish.

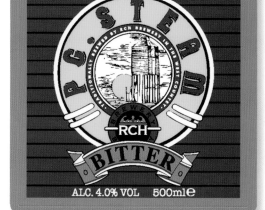

ALC. 4.0% VOL   500ml℮

TASTING NOTES

APPEARANCE:

AROMA:

TASTE:

OVERALL SCORE:

Redoak Bitter

Source: **Redoak Boutique Beer Café, Sydney, New South Wales, Australia**

Strength: **3.5%**

Website: **www.redoak.com.au**

Redoak has become an Aussie legend in a blink of the eye. Beers from the spacious and stylish restaurant at 201 Clarence Street have won more awards than you can shake the proverbial mashing fork at, including Champion International Small Brewer in the Australian International Beer Awards in 2008.

The concept of matching fine beer with equally fine cuisine, rare if not unique to Australia, was launched in 2004. It was the brainchild of brother and sister David and Janet Hollyoak. David had been a keen home brewer from the age of 14, when he made ginger beer. He's a civil engineer by profession, a useful trade, for as well as brewing beer he can turn his hand to building the equipment. Janet brought management and PR skills to the young enterprise, and brother and sister were fortunate to link up with chef Chris Beard, who produces superb food to match David's beers.

As you enter the café, small brewing vessels catch the eye. But most of the brewing is off-site: residents of this up-market area of Sydney objected to brewing taking place in their midst. As well as Bitter, which is one of his best-selling beers, David has a wide portfolio, including chocolate Stout and organic pale ale. His wife is Belgian and, encouraged by her, he turns his hand to several Belgian-style beers. These include Framboise – raspberry beer – that won a gold medal in the World Beer Cup in the U.S. in 2008.

David's first task was to convert his sister to the joys of beer. Janet admits she was a dedicated champagne imbiber until David talked her into joining him in the café venture. Now she is front-of-house, encouraging customers to try the beer-inspired recipes and beer and food matches she has dreamt up with head chef Chris Beard.

Redoak offers beer appreciation dinners and courses, and also simpler tasting boards. On my visit, in mid-morning, Janet took me through a tasting board of cheeses with a variety of her brother's beers. For diners, the menu offers Scotch fillet marinated in Baltic Porter, pappardelle with Honey Ale, barbequed vegetable stack with Irish Red Ale, marinated chicken breast with Kölsch and lamb sausages with Bitter.

Bitter is a confusing term in Australia. Such major brands as Castlemaine XXXX and VB, short for Victoria Bitter, may have started life as warm-fermented ales but they are lager beers today. David's interpretation is a true member of the style and it makes a deep bow in the direction of bitter from the Old Country.

It's brewed with Chateau pale and crystal malts and is hopped with imported Fuggles and East Kent Goldings for bitterness and Centennial for dry hopping. The aroma is full and complex, with rich 'fresh bread' malt, spicy hops and a hint of vinous fruit. Bitterness builds in the mouth but is well balanced by chewy, nutty malt and sultana fruit. The finish is long, ending dry and hoppy, but with continuing contributions from dark fruits and rich malt.

I was delighted to see, among the many framed certificates on the walls of the café, a signed photo of Ricky Ponting who, in 2010, was the captain of the Australian cricket team. He sent his best wishes to all at Redoak. It's comforting to know that, even though the cricket team is officially sponsored by VB lager, at least one member of the squad knows where to go for a good beer when he's back home.

> *The concept of matching fine beer with equally fine cuisine, rare if not unique to Australia, was launched in 2004.*

Ridgeway Bitter

Source: Ridgeway Brewing, South Stoke, Oxfordshire, England
Strength: 4%
Website: none

TASTING NOTES

APPEARANCE:

AROMA:

TASTE:

OVERALL SCORE:

The beer is an oddity, for it's found almost exclusively in bottle-conditioned format (a cask version is occasionally available in the Oxfordshire area). As I explained in the introduction to the Pale Ales section (see p91), bottled versions of Bitter are usually labelled as pale ale. But Peter Scholey, the brewer at Ridgeway, is steeped in Bitter brewing and he feels sufficiently confident to bottle a beer that carries the name. It is, however, brewed with just pale malt and no darker grains such as crystal. Is it a Bitter or a Pale Ale? Let your taste buds decide. (See also Ridgeway in the IPA section.)

Brakspear in Henley-on-Thames, where Peter was head brewer, was one of the oldest breweries in Britain, where beer making had taken place since at least 1700. In 1799, the Brakspear family arrived and put its stamp on the company. The family is distantly related to Nicholas Breakspear, who was the only English Pope and served in that role as Adrian IV in the 12th century. The link between the Pope and the brewing family, despite the small difference in spelling, is the bee logo used by the brewery, which was taken from Adrian's motif on his mitre. The brewery closed in 2002 though Brakspear Bitter (see *300 Beers to Try Before You Die!*) is still brewed, sharing premises with the Wychwood Brewery in Witney.

The history is important, as Peter Scholey was able to take a sample of the Brakspear yeast culture he had used at Henley. It's a culture that gives a rare character to his beers, one that most other brewers fight tooth and nail to remove. If you read any book on brewing or home brewing, you will be told in no uncertain terms that a bi-product of fermentation known as diacetyl must be rigorously removed for fear of distressing drinkers. Diacetyl is a compound that gives a toffee or butterscotch note to beer. It was the hallmark of the old Brakspear beers as a result of the 'double drop' system outlined in the IPA entry.

Peter fashions his Bitter from Maris Otter pale malt and two English hop varieties, Boadicea and Challenger: the first named in a new hop that is the result of careful cross-breeding to produce a plant resistant to attack by aphids and which, as a result, needs low level of pesticides. The beer is gold coloured with a touch of bronze and an aroma of lightly toasted malt, a hint of butterscotch, spicy hop resins and a sulphur note. Toasted malt, butterscotch, lime fruit and bitter hops fill the mouth. Bitterness builds in the finish with notes of butterscotch, tart lemon-and-lime fruit and a malt note reminiscent of fresh-from-the-oven cake.

Salopian Shropshire Gold

TASTING NOTES

APPEARANCE:

AROMA:

TASTE:

OVERALL SCORE:

Source: Salopian Brewery, Shrewsbury, Shropshire, England

Strength: 3.8%

Website: www.salopianbrewery.co.uk

Shropshire Gold hasn't wandered into the wrong section of the book. In spite of the name, it's brewed and promoted as a Bitter, and as such it won the Bitter category of the Champion Beer of Britain competition in 2011. The brewery was founded in an old dairy in 1995 on the outskirts of the magnificent market town of Shrewsbury, which has no fewer than 660 historic listed buildings. They include examples of timber-framed structures from the 15th and 16th centuries, with the higgledy-piggledy pub, Ye Three Fishes, in the heart of the medieval area. The brewery at first concentrated on producing European-style beers, such as Alt and Weiss. But although the beers were greeted with acclaim by beer connoisseurs, sales were limited. In 1999, new owners, Wilf Nelson and Jake Douglas, took a decision to rebuild the brewery, quadruple the capacity and brew beers with wider appeal.

Shropshire Gold was the first beer to emerge from the new plant and was an immediate success. It was designed to offer choice for drinkers in area dominated by national brands: at the time, Draught Bass for example was still widely available in the West Midlands and Welsh Borders region. Gold now accounts for more than half the brewery's production. In order to create an acceptable aroma and flavour, several yeast cultures were tried until one was chosen and is still used today by head brewer Kevin Harris. He also buys the finest whole flower aroma hops on the grounds that a few extra pennies spent on the right varieties pays dividends with the quality of the finished product.

The beer has a pale bronze colour and is brewed with Maris Otter low colour malt along with crystal malt. The hops are well-travelled: Amarillo from the U.S., Brewers Gold from Bavaria and Celeia from Slovenia. The beer has a fine aroma of floral and spicy hops, lemon jelly fruit and sappy malt. Citrus fruit and hop resins build in the mouth but are balanced by a delicious Horlicks-like grain note. The finish offers a good balance of bitter, spicy hops, bittersweet fruit and juicy grain.

Surrey Hill Ranmore Ale

Source: **Surrey Hills Brewery, Dorking, Surrey, England**

Strength: **3.8%**

Website: **www.surreyhills.co.uk**

The story of Surrey Hills is told in the Brown & Mild Ales section. The brewery has fared well in CAMRA's Champion Beer of Britain competition, winning the Bitter class in 2009 for Ranmore Ale. This is a fiercely traditional English-style Bitter with a backbone of the finest malting barley, low colour Maris Otter, and a proportion of caramalt for colour and flavour. The hops are First Gold from England and Green Bullet from New Zealand. First Gold is a popular hedgerow hop that grows to half the height of conventional varieties. Green Bullet is a Kiwi offshoot of a Slovenian hop and as a result offers a fine herbal, floral and spicy note alongside the more fruity contribution of First Gold.

The beer has a sturdy bronze/copper colour with a powerful attack of fruity and floral hop resins on the nose, balanced by a fresh wholemeal bread grain character. The palate is dominated by bitter, spicy hops, chewy and nutty grain and a tangy and tart fruit note from the hops. The finish for a beer of moderate strength is long and complex, ending dry and bitter but along the way there are good contributions from spicy hops, bittersweet fruit and rich malt.

TASTING NOTES

APPEARANCE:

AROMA:

TASTE:

OVERALL SCORE:

Teignworthy Reel Ale

Source: **Teignworthy Brewery, Newton Abbot, Devon, England**

Strength: **4%**

Website: **www.teignworthybrewery.com/www.tuckersmaltings.com**

John Lawton has the ideal setting for an artisan brewery: part of Tucker's Maltings, one of the last Victorian suppliers of malt in England to still use the 'floor' system. Barley from the West Country is washed or steeped in huge tanks of water, then spread across heated floors. The grain is turned by hand while it germinates and is finally loaded into a kiln where it's heated to produce pale malt and darker varieties. The maltings stand alongside the main railway line: before the arrival of gas, coal from South Wales was unloaded straight from trucks into the maltings to fuel the kilns.

All John has to do is walk a few feet and pick up some sacks of grain for his next brew. He's been doing this with growing success since 1994 and he's doubled production to 100 barrels a week. Impressively, he supplies some 300 pubs in Devon and Somerset and he repays the compliment to his hosts by making bottle-conditioned beers under the Edwin Tucker name for the malting's shop.

Reel Ale is John's biggest-selling beer and is named for the fishermen who work the River Teign that flows nearby. The name of the river is pronounced 'Tayn' or 'Tin' depending on which part of Devon you come from. Reel Ale is brewed with Maris Otter pale malt and crystal malt and it has a complex hop recipe comprised of Bramling Cross, Challenger, Fuggles and Goldings. The hops are added at different stages of the copper boil to extract the correct levels of aroma and bitterness. With such a major contribution from the hops, Reel Ale is an intensely bitter beer but the hop character is balanced by cracker wheat grain, cobnuts from the crystal malt and a sharp orange fruit note. Delectable chewy malt fills the mouth and the finish but tart fruit and hops add their own counter-balance. This is a highly drinkable and quenching beer with considerable depth and complexity for its strength.

Tuckers Maltings is open to visitors and the brewery can also be toured at selected times.

TASTING NOTES

APPEARANCE:

AROMA:

TASTE:

OVERALL SCORE:

TASTING NOTES

APPEARANCE:

AROMA:

TASTE:

OVERALL SCORE:

Triple fff Alton's Pride

Source: Triple fff Brewing Company, Alton, Hampshire, England

Strength: 3.8%

Website: www.triplefff.com

In the summer of 2008 I was invited by Graham Trott, owner and founder of Triple fff, to formally open his new brewhouse. As a large crowd gathered outside, Graham and his colleagues draped a ribbon across the entrance for me to symbolically cut. But when the moment arrived, one important element was missing: scissors. When Graham found a pair of nail scissors I held them up and cracked to the crowd: 'Well, it is a micro-brewery!' It got a good laugh but Graham wasn't best pleased. 'I'm not a micro!' he hissed in my ear.

It was a grievous error but all was quickly forgiven for just a few weeks later Graham won the much-coveted Champion Beer of Britain trophy for Alton's Pride at the Great British Beer Festival.

Graham, a keen home brewer, founded Triple fff in 1997 on the outskirts of Alton, a town once famous for its railway, hops and brewing. Both William Thackeray and Charles Dickens praised the beers of Alton, where the water is remarkably similar to the 'liquor' of faraway Burton-on-Trent: rich in natural sulphates from the chalk hills of Hampshire and ideal for brewing bitter beer. Two major breweries in Southeast England, Courage and Fremlins, opened subsidiaries in Alton while the local brewer, Crowley, had the misfortune to be taken over and closed by the London brewer, Watneys. Today, the global giant Molson Coors brews lager on the old Courage site, which passed to Bass and eventually to the Canadian-American company.

Graham Trott has, in every way, restored pride to Alton. His brewery is close to the Four Marks station on the Watercress train line that once carried Courage beers to London. The line was closed in the 1960s but it's been restored and lovingly cared for by steam train devotees. Graham is a quiet and unassuming man and it's something of a surprise to discover that he's a lover of loud rock music and he was determined to make a splash with beers dubbed, in musical terms, triple fortissimo. Some of his beers, such as Moondance, Stairway to Heaven and Pressed Rat & Warthog, take their names from rock titles – and it takes a degree of chutzpah to call a beer Pressed Rat & Warthog.

Alton's Pride may have a relatively humble name but it's a rich and complex beer, brewed with Maris Otter pale and cara gold malts and generously hopped with Amarillo, Fuggles, Goldings and Mount Hood varieties from England and the U.S. The bronze beer has a profound aroma of floral hops, tart citrus fruit and sweet, juicy malt. The palate is full and rounded, with creamy malt, citrus fruit and peppery hops, followed by a lingering bittersweet finish that is hoppy and malty, with a continuing tangy fruit note; it finally ends dry.

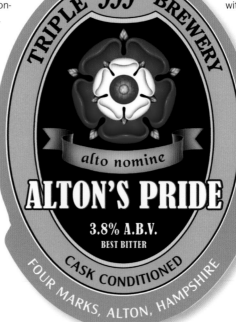

Vale Wychert Ale

Source: Vale Brewery Company, Brill, Buckinghamshire, England

Strength: 3.9%

Website: www.valebrewery.co.uk

TASTING NOTES

APPEARANCE:

AROMA:

TASTE:

OVERALL SCORE:

Vale Brewery was founded in 1994 and was first based in Haddenham, a village so breathtakingly lovely that it's often used as the location for movies and TV series that portray idyllic country life, with a duck pond and green, and the occasional murder thrown in for good measure. The brewery is owned by two brothers, Mark and Phil Stevens, who had previously worked for Allied Breweries and Morrells of Oxford and were keen to run their own business. In Haddenham they found a good location and also history to inform some of the beer names. Wychert is a Saxon word meaning 'white earth' and it was the basis for many of the original buildings in the village. The earth was mixed with water and straw to make pliable mud that was turned into blocks raised one on top of each other. The stone base of the buildings was called 'grumpling', which gives its name to another Vale beer.

The success of the brewery forced the brothers to move a few miles away to a new site in the equally historic village of Brill. The name is a PR person's dream, for Vale can now promote its beers as 'Brill beers brewed in Brill'. The village was used by J R Tolkien as the Middle Earth hamlet of Bree in *The Lord of the Rings*. Capacity at Brill was doubled and then expanded again to 20 barrels. Vale also has a small brewing plant at its pub, the Hop Pole in Aylesbury, where one-off and historic recreations are produced: see introduction. For Wychert, brewers Simon Smith and David Renton use Maris Otter pale malt with small amounts of chocolate and crystal grains. The hops are English Fuggles and German Perle. The amber-coloured beer has a fine aroma of toasted malt, a hint of chocolate and an earthy hop note – the latter fitting well with the notion of wychert. The palate is full and rounded with a continuing hint of chocolate, rich toasted, nutty malt, an orange fruit note and bitter, spicy hops. The finish lingers with bittersweet notes of rich malt, cobnuts, chocolate, tart fruit and hop resins. Brill in every sense.

York Guzzler

Source: **York Brewery, York, England**

Strength: **3.6%**

Website: **www.york-brewery.co.uk**

There can't be many breweries in the world that are given top billing by a historic city. Yet, as visitors to York leave the train station, one of the signs directs you to 'York Brewery'. The brewery is equally fortunate to have a prime location in the heart of the city with its Roman and Viking associations but perhaps the Vikings' notorious passion for ale convinced the city authorities that a brewery was not out of keeping. The brewery dates from 1996 and it was the first new beer maker in the city for 40 years. It has developed in to a major tourist attraction: not only is the brewery open to visitors but a gallery enables them to watch the brewing process below.

The brewery doubled production in 2007 and it now has a brew length of 20 barrels. York also owns three pubs in the city. Ownership changed in 2007, when Mitchells of Lancaster took control. It marked a U-turn on the part of Mitchells, who had once been a major brewer in Lancaster but stopped production in 1999. It kept its toe in the brewing liquor by retaining the rights to the successful cask beer Lancaster Bomber, which is brewed under licence by Thwaites of Blackburn. Now Mitchells is back as a brewing force, but on the opposite side of the Pennines.

Guzzler was first brewed in 2003: the name is slang for someone who drinks fast and greedily and should not be taken as a recommendation by the brewery. Head brewer Nick Webster uses pale and crystal malts and torrefied wheat: the last named is similar to popcorn and is used in tiny

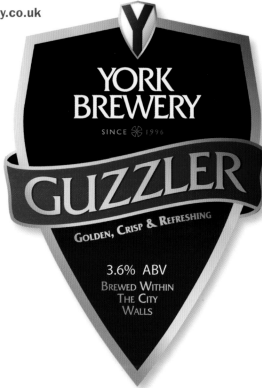

amounts to create a good head on the beer. The hops are English Challenger and Styrian Goldings. The beer is pale bronze with spicy hop resins, sappy malt and luscious citrus fruit on the aroma. 'Fresh bread' grain dominates the palate but there are powerful contributions from tangy fruit and pine-needle hop resins. The finish is quenching, with powerful and continuing notes of cedar and spice from the hops and tart fruit.

 The brewery dates from 1996 and it was the first new beer maker in the city for 40 years.

Best Bitters

'A pint of Best' was once a familiar cry in English pubs. Today, drinkers tend to ask for a beer by name. But whether they use the moniker on the pump or the generic title, pubgoers are carefully seeking a beer that's a step up from the ranks of Bitters that are between 3 and 4 per cent alcohol. Best starts at 4 per cent and can rise as high as 5 per cent. At the top end of the band, beers will have robust malt character and need a generous addition of hops to prevent them becoming too grainy and cloying. Lower down the scale, the beers will be a fine balance of rich grain, fruit and hops.

Before the arrival of golden ales and the other 'new wave' beers of the small brewery revolution in Britain, most brewers concentrated on a small range of Mild, Bitter and Best Bitter. Best was often the last pint of the evening, a fine way to round off a visit to the pub, the malts and hops lingering on the tongue long after closing time. For brewers, Best was evidence of their artistry, to such an extent that they often downplayed their Bitters by calling them, almost dismissively, 'ordinary' or 'cooking' beers. And yet, in some cases, Bitter and Best come from the same gene pool, using identical grains and hops, with Best merely brewed to a higher strength. The two beers can even derive from the same basic liquid, with brewing 'liquor' or water added to achieve the desired final measure of alcohol.

The modern trend, however, is to produce two quite distinctively different beers. While ordinary Bitter may be copper or bronze coloured, Best in sharp distinction will be paler, allowing hops to offer aromas and flavours of spice, pepper, resin, pine cones and citrus to offset the high level of malt needed to make a stronger beer. The reverse can also be the case, with Best presented as a darker alternative to a pale, hoppy ordinary Bitter. The end result, regardless of colour, is a style that offers rich malt, vinous

or citrus fruit and profound hop character. As there are restrictions on the amount of grain that can be packed into the average mashing vessel, some members of the Best category will have specialist brewers' sugars added during the boil with hops in order to achieve the desired level of alcohol.

The invasion of foreign varieties in recent years has encouraged many brewers to be more ambitious with the hop character of their Best Bitters. Hops from North America, central Europe and New Zealand bring new aromas and flavours, with berry and citrus fruits, fresh herbs, newly-mown grass, freshly-planed pine and tobacco tingling the taste buds.

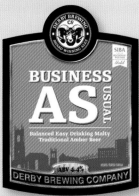

Blythe Palmer's Poison

Source: Blythe Brewery, Rugeley, Staffordshire, England

Strength: 4.5%

Website: www.blythebrewery.co.uk

It's rarely heard these days, but decades ago English drinkers who offered to buy you a beer would ask, somewhat alarmingly: 'What's your poison?' The expression is thought to derive from the activities of Dr William Palmer in the mid-19th century. He was known as the Rugely Poisoner as a result of his role in despatching some of his unfortunate patients and relatives with the use of strychnine. His victims included his mother-in-law and brother and he even killed four children before they reached their first birthdays. He made a considerable amount of money from his victims' insurance policies, mirroring the activities of England's most notorious serial killer of the 20th century, Dr Harold Shipman. Palmer was eventually arrested when he murdered his best friend, John Cook, and he was hanged in public in 1856 in Stafford.

You have to admire Rob Greenway's chutzpah in naming his Best Bitter in honour of Dr Palmer. In spite of the forbidding title, it's won many awards at CAMRA beer festivals. Rob was a keen home-brewer who was made redundant from his full-time job and decided he had a choice: vegetate or brew. He set up shop in 2003 with a 2.5 barrel kit in a barn on a farm in Hamstall Ridware outside Rugeley. He produces several of his beers, including Palmer's Poison, in both cask and bottle-conditioned form.

Poison is brewed with Pearl pale malt, crystal and black malts, with a touch of flaked maize for head retention. The hops are two English varieties, Challenger and Goldings. The darker malts create a tawny-coloured ale with powerful hints of caramel and toffee on the nose, toasted malt and spicy hops. Rich toasted malt, caramel and berry fruits build in the mouth, with a firm balance of spicy and bitter hops. The finish is dry and roasty but is counter balanced by notes of caramel, coffee and a solid underpinning of tart hop resins.

Buffy's Norwegian Blue

Source: Buffy's Brewery, Tivetshall St Mary, Norfolk, England

Strength: 4.9%

Website: www.buffys.co.uk

This is a beer about love, marriage and parrots. If that sounds like something out of a Monty Python sketch, then spot on, for a Norwegian Blue is not only a species of parrot but is the very one used in the famous Dead Parrot sketch, the lifeless bird that had 'gone to meet its maker'. Buffy's also has a Polly's Folly so there's a strong parrot theme running through the brewery.

The brewery was founded in 1993 at Mardle Hall, an impressive country pile that dates from the 15th century and once home to a certain Buffy, whose name lives on as a beer brand. Roger Abrahams had brewed at home for 25 years while he worked for Norwich Union, the major insurance company now known as Aviva. He wanted a better lifestyle, threw in his job and launched Buffy's in 1993. He was joined by Julie Savory, a piano tuner who went to the hall to check Roger's piano, sampled his beer, and married him. Julie still occasionally tunes pianos but she says she can sell 50 firkins of beer in the time it takes her to give one piano a makeover. She's kept busy, along with a staff of five, for Buffy's has established itself as one of the leading independent breweries in the country and now supplies an impressive 150 regular outlets.

Norwegian Blue, available both cask and bottle conditioned, is brewed with barley malt that's grown in Norfolk, the famous 'bread basket of England', renowned for the quality of grain grown in dark alluvial soil, much of it reclaimed from the sea centuries ago. The beer is made with Maris Otter pale malt with small amounts of crystal malt and roasted

barley. The hops are a blend of two English varieties, Fuggles and Goldings, with Mount Hood from the United States. The amber ale has an entrancing aroma of toasted malt and ripe citrus fruit – melon and grapefruit to the fore – with a hint of caramel and a big attack of peppery hop resins. Sweet nutty malt and caramel build in the mouth but they are balanced by tart fruit and increasingly bitter hops. The finish is long and deep, with toasted grain, caramel and citrus fruit vying for attention with a solid backbone of iron-like hop bitterness.

Don't feed it to your parrot...

TASTING NOTES

APPEARANCE:

AROMA:

TASTE:

OVERALL SCORE:

> ❝ *This is a beer about love, marriage and parrots.* ❞

Coniston Old Man Ale

Source: Coniston Brewing Company, Coniston, Cumbria, England
Strength: 4.2% cask/4.9% bottle
Website: www.conistonbrewery.com

Ian Bradley is a very lucky brewer. He has one of the finest locations in England, behind a historic coaching inn, the Black Bull, and at the foot of the Old Man of Coniston mountain: water flows down from the mountain in a stream – called a beck in the local dialect – from where it goes straight into the brewing vessels. In 1998, Ian had just opened his brewery when, to his astonishment and delight, he won the Champion Beer of Britain award at the Great British Beer Festival (see *300 Beers to Try Before You Die!*) for Bluebird Bitter. His success put Coniston and the Black Bull on the map and also helped draw attention to the nascent micro-brewing movement in Britain.

Scroll forward 14 years to the same beer competition in the same location, London's magnificent Olympia Hall, and Coniston again walked off with the top prize, this time for its No. 9 Barley Wine (see Old Ales, Barley Wines & Vintage Ales section). In between, Ian has expanded his range to six core beers and some seasonal brews, and has grown the brewery from a 10-barrel kit to 40. Some 70 pubs in the North West serve his beers and they are distributed nationally by wholesalers. Ian has overcome the loss of a leg in a serious motorbike accident and remains in full-time control of the brewery.

Old Man Ale is brewed with Maris Otter pale malt, crystal malt and roasted barley and has just one hop, the English Challenger, making it in brewers' parlance a 'single varietal beer'. It's a fiercely traditional example of English Best Bitter, with a glowing copper colour, a big aroma of toasted malt with hints of roast and caramel and sharp orange zest fruit and tangy hop resins. There's rich creamy and toasted malt in the mouth, balanced by citrus fruit, chewy caramel and increasing hop bitterness. The finish is long and deep, with powerful notes of tangy fruit, bitter hops, toasted and roasted grain and a continuing caramel/toffee note.

The beer can be enjoyed next door to the brewery in the Black Bull, which is owned by Ian's parents. The inn dates from the Tudor period and is best known as the base for Donald Campbell's ill-fated attempt on the world water speed record on Coniston Water in 1967 in his boat Bluebird. The inn has many photos of Campbell and his team, plus stills from a BBC film about the attempt on the record. Anthony Hopkins played Campbell and looks disconcertingly like him.

Derby Business as Usual

Source: Derby Brewing Co, Derby, England

Strength: 4.4%

Website: www.derbybrewing.co.uk

Trevor Harris is a Derby brewer to his fingertips. In 1991, he installed a small brewing plant in the Brunswick Tavern in the city (see Mild section) and built a nationwide reputation for the beer at the old railwaymen's pub. When the Brunswick was bought by the Leicester brewer Everards, Trevor left and set up his new company, Derby Brewing, in 2004, in a large shed on the site of a former paintworks. The brewery is a family-run concern, with Trevor's wife Kes and their son Paul also heavily involved: Paul manages three pubs in Derby owned by the company, the Greyhound, Queen's Head and Royal Standard.

The brewery has expanded rapidly and has a 12-barrel plant that was due to expand to 20 barrels in 2012. Trevor supplies 400 pubs in the Midlands, Yorkshire and North Wales and is moving south into Oxfordshire. When an additional fermenting vessel is installed he will start to bottle his beers on a substantial scale.

Business as Usual gets its name from Trevor's love of sport. He is a devoted supporter of Derby County football club and also follows cricket and tennis. He likes to attend the Wimbledon tennis tournament every year and was amused to hear that if pigeons invade the ground and attack the hallowed turf, the club phones a man who owns a Harris Hawk. The man says 'business as usual', brings the hawk to the ground and sorts out the pesky pigeons. A hawk named Harris was too good to pass up and the beer was born. It's brewed with Maris Otter pale malt, with a dash of crystal malt and torrefied wheat for a good head. Challenger, Goldings and Perle hops are added in the copper, with a further addition of Goldings at the end of the boil. The hopped wort then passes over a deep bed of Northdown in the hop back prior to fermentation. The finished beer has a newly-minted copper colour and a big fruity, tangerine nose, with rich nutty malt, peppery hops and a fresh tobacco note. Fruit and hops build in the mouth balanced by honeyed malt, followed by a bittersweet finish that interweaves tangy fruit, bitter hops, juicy malt and a lingering hint of tobacco.

> **The man says 'business as usual', brings the hawk to the ground and sorts out the pesky pigeons.**

TASTING NOTES

APPEARANCE:

AROMA:

TASTE:

OVERALL SCORE:

Green Jack Trawlerboys Best Bitter

Source: Green Jack Brewing Co, Lowestoft, Suffolk, England

Strength: 4.6%

Website: www.green-jack.com

I have to declare an interest: in 2009 I officially opened Green Jack's new brewery in Lowestoft but I claim no part in the success of their beers. They have won many awards, culminating in 2012 with Gold in the Best Bitter class at the Champion Beer of Britain competition for Trawlerboys, and a Silver in the overall competition.

Green Jack is run by Tim Dunford, who opened a tiny brewery in 2003 in the Triangle Tavern in Lowestoft. Thanks to the acclaim for his beers, he moved to a new custom-built plant in 2009 housed in a refurbished fish smoking building, where he can produce 35 barrels per brew. Green Jack is the most easterly brewery in Britain and its beer names reflect the long tradition of fishing, trading and trawling in the ancient port town of Lowestoft: other beer include Red Herring, Gone Fishing and Baltic Trader. The Trawlerboys pump clip shows an image of the Lowestoft-built Boston Sea Stallion trawler that was launched in 1978 by none other than Margaret Thatcher.

The name of the beer takes its name from the nickname of Lowestoft Town football club, the Trawlerboys. In Suffolk, they're fond of the word 'boy' – Ipswich town FC is known as the Tractor Boys. Boy or 'bor' derives from a local dialect word meaning neighbour and you're likely to be greeted in those parts with 'Y'arl roit, bor?' or 'You all right, neighbour?'

Trawlerboys is a highly complex beer, brewed with Flagon barley malt grown in Norfolk that's blended with cara, chocolate and crystal malts, plus some dark cane sugar. The hops are Bramling Cross and Challenger. The beer is copper/tawny coloured and has a rich aroma of chocolate, toasted malt, dark burnt fruits, bitter hops and caramel. The palate offers dark fruit, chocolate, caramel, toasted malt and bitter and spicy hop resins. The finish is long, deep and lingering, with continuing toasted malt, chocolate, burnt fruit and bitter hops. It's a drop of y'arl roit.

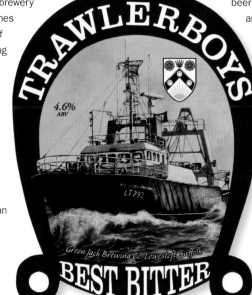

Hogs Back TEA

Source: Hogs Back Brewery, Tongham, Surrey, England

Strength: 4.2%

Website: www.hogsback.co.uk

Hogs Back Brewery takes its name from a famous narrow ridge that runs along the North Downs in Surrey. Writing in 1813, Jane Austen, visiting the area from London, told her sister, 'I never saw the country from the Hogs Back so advantageously'. With such a backdrop, the brewery has one of the finest locations in England, set in half-timbered 18th-century farm buildings. Hogs Back is one of the oldest and most successful of the new wave of independent brewers, dating from 1992, when it produced just 10 barrels a week. Today, after many expansions, it can brew 10,000 barrels a year: no 'micro' this!

TEA, short for Traditional English Ale and a wry comment on the English addiction to the leaf of the tea bush, was one of the company's first beers and is now its flagship brand. It has garnered many awards, including gold in the Best Bitter category at the Champion Beer of Britain competition in 2000. Rupert Thompson, who became chairman of the brewery in 2012, says the brewers use just Fuggles in TEA for historic reasons as well as for aroma and flavour. The Farnham area of Surrey, where the brewery stands, once used to rival Kent as a hop-growing region. As agriculture declined and brewers switched to lager beer in the 1970s and 80s, the hop farms disappeared. Hogs Back buys its hops from the one remaining hop grower in the area and there are plans to encourage more farmers to return to hop growing to meet the demands of the ale revival.

Rupert brings a wealth of brewing experience to Hogs Back. He has worked with such diverse beer brands as Carling Lager, Old Speckled Hen and Brakspear before joining Hogs Back. One of his first acts was to rebrand all the main beers with bright new pump clips and labels and he plans to expand sales vigorously. He says the word Traditional in TEA's name is not accidental: Hogs Back is eschewing the modern trend towards extreme

beers packed with fruity hops. 'At Hogs Back, we're malt heads, rather than hop heads,' he says.

TEA is brewed with Pearl pale malt, with a touch of crystal malt and wheat. Fuggles create 21 units of bitterness: in spite of Rupert's caveat, this is not a beer that lacks hop character. The amber/tawny ale has a rich honeyed malt aroma, with a hint of nuts and caramel from the crystal malt and a spicy note from the Fuggles.

Lightly toasted malt offers a solid backbone in the mouth but there are good contributions from orange fruit, caramel, and earthy hops. The finish is long and interweaves honeyed malt, caramel, tart fruit and gentle but lingering spicy Fuggles resins.

TASTING NOTES

APPEARANCE:

AROMA:

TASTE:

OVERALL SCORE:

TASTING NOTES

APPEARANCE:

AROMA:

TASTE:

OVERALL SCORE:

McMullen's Country Bitter

Source: McMullen & Sons, Hertford, England

Strength: 4.3%

Website: www.mcmullens.co.uk

If I describe McMullen as an old-fashioned brewery, it's meant as a compliment. They brew beer in a slow, ruminative fashion, in close proximity to the barley fields of eastern England and handily based for the hop orchards of Kent and the Midlands. As the family name suggests, they have an ancient Irish connection but they have been brewing in England since 1827, when a cooper named Peter McMullen decided it would be sensible to make a liquid to put in the casks he made. Today, Fergus McMullen continues the family control of the company, which has a substantial estate of 140 pubs, including the imposing red brick Victorian Nags Head in London's Covent Garden, immediately opposite the Underground station.

The original 19th-century brewery in Hertford has been replaced by a new, modern and highly flexible plant that enables McMullen to produce a wide range of one-off and seasonal beers alongside the key ales: AK (see *300 Beers to Try Before You Die!*) and Country Bitter. It makes much of the fact – down to signs on its delivery vehicles – that it's the 'Whole Hop Brewery', using hop flowers in their freshly-picked whole cone form and not reduced to pellets or extract. Country Bitter is brewed with either Flagon or Tipple pale malts, which are blended with crystal malt, wheat malt and flaked maize. The hops are all English: Bramling Cross, Fuggles and Progress, which create 30 units of bitterness. It's a 'fully attenuated beer', which means it has a long fermentation that turns all available malt sugars to alcohol and creates a finished ale that drinks stronger than its ABV would suggest. It has the McMullen hallmark of bitter orange fruit on the aroma and palate, balanced by a 'fresh bread' malt note and profound hop character reminiscent of pine cones, cedar wood and spice, with a rich butterscotch note. The finish is long and complex, ending dry, but with a fine interweaving of rich, nutty malt, tart fruit and bitter and spicy hops.

Skinner's Betty Stogs

Source: Skinner's Brewing Company, Truro, Cornwall, England

Strength: 4%

Website: www.skinnersbrewery.com

Steve Skinner has built a reputation as both an adroit brewer of fine ales and also a man with a sharp sense of humour that he harnesses to help sell his beers. He started his brewing career on the Channel Island of Jersey where he ran brewpubs. He moved to Cornwall with a similar plan but when that didn't work for him he decided to launch a stand-alone commercial brewery.

The brewery opened in 1997 and moved to bigger premises in 2003 where Steve and his team can now produce 375 barrels a week on a 25-barrel plant. A visitor centre and shop have been added to the site and while Steve sells three-quarters of his beer in Devon and Cornwall he also has nationwide outlets for them, including the influential Wetherspoon chain of pubs.

With an annual turnover of £4 million, Skinner's Brewery is no laughing matter. But humour always bubbles to the surface. Betty Stogs is the flagship brew and its name comes from a Cornish folklore about a woman with that name who was a legend in the west of the county for her lifestyle: she was lazy, unkempt, boozed, couldn't cook or sew and never washed her child. The child was taken from her by 'the small folk', a mysterious tribe of tiny people who live among the flowers and rocks on the coast and help people living in poverty. They washed Betty Stogs' child in the morning dew and returned it to her fresh and clean. Such was the shock that Betty improved her ways and became a model mother.

Not only does Betty Stogs live on as a beer but Steve uses every occasion, including the Great British Beer Festival, to organise a parade of Cornish musicians thumping out loud, strident music. They are led by a Cornish actor dressed as Betty, with curled hair and brightly rouged cheeks. In spite of the jokiness, Betty Stogs is a serious beer and proved the point by winning the Best Bitter class in the Champion Beer of Britain competition in 2008. It's brewed with Cornish Optic pale malt, crystal malt and a touch of roasted barley. The hops are Celeia from Slovenia and English Northdown. The copper-coloured beer has a rich biscuit malt nose with a touch of roast, tangy citrus fruit and floral hop resins. Chewy toasted malt builds in the mouth but is balanced by hops that add an increasing bitter note, along with roast and tart fruit. The finish is long and interweaves between toasted malt, citrus fruit and bitter, floral hop resins.

 She was lazy, unkempt, boozed, couldn't cook or sew and never washed her child.

TASTING NOTES

APPEARANCE:

AROMA:

TASTE:

OVERALL SCORE:

TASTING NOTES

APPEARANCE:

AROMA:

TASTE:

OVERALL SCORE:

Westerham William Wilberforce Freedom Ale

Source: Westerham Brewery Co, Crockham Hill, Kent, England

Strength: 4% draught; 4.8% bottle

Website: www.westerhambrewery.co.uk

Robert Wicks at Westerham (see IPA section) launched Freedom Ale in 2007 to commemorate the 200th anniversary of Wilberforce's success in gaining parliamentary support for the abolition of the slave trade. But Robert was keen to stress that while the 18th-century slave trade – thanks to the efforts of great reformers such as Wilberforce – had been ended, human trafficking continues in the 21st century. As a contribution to tackling this shocking and degrading business, a financial contribution from each pint or bottle of the beer is made to the international charity Stop the Traffik.

Robert is also a keen supporter of the Fairtrade movement that buys food and ingredients direct from small farmers in Third World countries, avoiding global cartels that reduce the farmers' income. For Freedom Ale, he buys demerara sugar from a small farmers' co-operative in Malawi in Africa. The sugar makes up 20 per cent of the fermentable ingredients. There's a subtle historic undertone to the use of demerara sugar, for in the 18th century some British brewers imported demerara from plantations in the Caribbean where slaves from Africa were put to work.

The other ingredients in the beer are Maris Otter pale malt, crystal malt and Kent Goldings and Northdown hops. The hops create 36 units of bitterness. Maris Otter malt comes from Warminster Maltings in Wiltshire that specialises in buying barley from designated farmers. They tell Warminster which fields produce the best grain, enabling brewers to get supplies from the same fields each year to ensure consistency of grain and beer character.

The deep gold beer has a profound pear drop note on the aroma from the sugar, allied to sherbet lemons, biscuit malt and nose-tingling hop resins. The palate has a malt note reminiscent of a freshly-harvested barley field, with ripe fruit and increasingly bitter hops. The long finish is a superb balance of biscuit malt, tangy lemon and pear fruit, and peppery hops. It's a beer with heart.

The long finish is a superb balance of biscuit malt, tangy lemon and pear fruit, and peppery hops.

Worthington E

Source: William Worthington's Brewery, Burton-on-Trent, Staffordshire, England

Strength: 4.8%

Website: www.nationalbrewerycentre.co.uk

The inclusion of Worthington E will raise an eyebrow or two among older British readers who recall the early struggles of CAMRA in the 1970s against the national brewers and their carbonated keg beers. Didn't E rank alongside Watney's Red and Ind Coope's Double Diamond as the beers of the devil that attempted to kill cask ale? Up to a point: the history of both E and Double Diamond is not that simple. Both were once fine cask ales that were bowdlerised by their owners – Allied Breweries in the case of DD, Bass where E was concerned – in the pell-mell rush to dominate the keg market in the 1960s and 70s.

William Worthington was one of the great Midlands brewers who helped turn Burton into the most important brewing town in the world in the 19th century. Worthington was a cooper from Leicestershire who went to work at Joseph Smith's brewery in Burton and bought Smith out in 1760. Worthington's became so successful with their pale ales that in the 19th century they not only joined the other Burton brewers in exporting to India and other colonies but broke into the lucrative London market. Worthington's owned a warehouse close to St Pancras station where beer arrived by train from Burton via Derby. The rubric E comes from the simple cask branding used by Worthington's before brand names became the vogue in the 20th century. Some brewers branded their casks with Xs to denote strength, others used letters. In the case of Worthington's, its mild and pale ales were marked A, B, C and so on, with E denoting strong pale ale. The addition of crystal malt in the early 20th century meant that this particular beer became a member of the bitter class, rather than pale ale.

Worthington's stood out from the Burton crowd by brewing acclaimed bottled beers as well as draught. Its White Shield, a true Burton IPA, remains a classic of the style and featured in *300 Beers to Try Before You Die!* In the 1920s, Worthington's merged with its Burton neighbour, Bass, but its beers continued to carry the Worthington name. After its brief hey-day as a keg beer, E disappeared from sight but reappeared this century thanks to the new William Worthington's Brewery within the National Brewery Centre in Burton. The centre is the former Bass Museum that was closed in 2008 by the new owners of the Bass breweries, Molson Coors. Following a vigorous campaign, the museum reopened in 2010. It's run by a private company, Planning Solutions, but Molson Coors makes a substantial annual contribution to the centre and also supplies beer to the bar and restaurant. There had been a small White Shield pilot brewery on site for many years, but at the end of 2010 Molson Coors invested £1 million in the new Worthington plant, which becomes both a visitor attraction and a working brewery. Steve Wellington, who had run the White Shield brewery, was given free rein to brew new beers and recreate old Bass brews. Before he retired, Steve brought back the cask version of Worthington E in all its glory and his successor, Stefano Cossi, continues to produce the beer. It's available in the bar at the brewery centre and also in selected Mitchells & Butlers pubs. It's certainly worth the trip to Burton to both sample the beer and tour the centre with its fascinating story of brewing in Burton: see the website above for full information about opening hours and tours.

The beer is brewed with pale and crystal malts and is hopped with Challenger and Fuggles, with a late addition of Northdown. Units of bitterness are 29. The pale copper beer has an inviting aroma of pine cones and resins from the hops, balanced by ripe damson fruit and biscuit malt. The palate is dominated by growing and intense hop bitterness but with a good balance of juicy malt and ripe fruit. The finish is long and delicate, with hops still dominating but with fine contributions from tart fruit and nutty malt. Welcome back, old timer!

TASTING NOTES

APPEARANCE:

AROMA:

TASTE:

OVERALL SCORE:

Wye Valley Butty Bach

Source: Wye Valley Brewery, Stoke Lacy, Herefordshire, England

Strength: 4.5%

Website: www.wyevalleybrewery.co.uk

Butty bach is Welsh for 'little friend' and the beer was first brewed for Welsh drinkers just over the border from Wye Valley's Herefordshire base. It was greeted with acclaim and was voted the top beer three years in succession at CAMRA's Cardiff beer festival. It's now widely available throughout Britain and its sales have grown in step with the brewery's development, which has gone from micro status to a fully-fledged regional brewery, producing around 20,000 barrels a year. It started life as a pub brewery at the Nags Head in Canon Pyon in 1985, the brain-child of Peter Amor. Peter was an established brewer who had worked for Guinness at its now-closed London plant at Park Royal. Peter became a leading member of the Society of Independent Brewers (SIBA), and went on to become its distinguished and voluble chairman for several years.

The brewery relocated to outbuildings at the Barrels pub in Hereford and finally, as demand required greater capacity, to the former Symonds cider works at Stoke Lacy. One of the first tasks at Stoke Lacy was to scrape years of cider yeast from the walls to prevent contamination of the beer. The range of beers has grown considerably and includes the specialist Dorothy Goodbody range: its stout appeared in *300 Beers to Try Before You Die!* Several of the beers, including Butty Bach, are available in bottle-conditioned form as well as draught.

Butty Bach is brewed with Maris Otter pale malt, with crystal and wheat malts and a touch of flaked barley. The complex hop recipe includes Bramling Cross, Fuggles and Goldings: the Fuggles, a major Herefordshire hop, are sourced from a local farm. The deep bronze beer has a fine hop aroma of spice and citrus fruit, with a cracker-like malt note and a hint of almond from the crystal malt. The palate is dominated by malty sweetness but there's a good balance of spicy hops and tart fruit. The finish is long, with rich biscuit malt cut by spicy hops, citrus fruit and a continuing hint of almonds.

Extra Strong Beers & Bitters

The yardstick for this section, the beer by which all others are judged, is Fuller's ESB or Extra Special Bitter (see *300 Beers to Try Before You Die!*). The 5.5 per cent London beer started life as a winter ale in 1969 and, with a little help from the arrival of CAMRA in 1971, achieved cult status and regular production. The deep bronze beer with an explosion of marmalade fruit and peppery hops was admired to such an extent that it has three times been judged the Champion Beer of Britain and in addition has won its class several more times in the competition.

Fuller's jealously guards the title and its legal team swoops on any other British brewer who dares to use the title ESB. With fellow beer writer, the late Michael Jackson, I appeared as a special witness in a court case brought by Fuller's against a hapless individual who imported a French beer into Britain with a title almost identical to ESB's. He lost the case and deservedly so as the French beer in question was a lager.

When Fuller's exported ESB to the United States it quickly acquired cult status there, too. The Chiswick brewery can't control trademarks in the U.S. and brewers there started to brew their own interpretations, to such a degree that there's now a class labelled Extra Special Bitter in the annual competition staged at the Great American Beer Festival. The style has travelled even further as I found when I went to Australia, where English pale ales and bitters are much admired among the growing ranks of craft brewers.

Long before ESB, brewers in mainland Europe had their own interpretations of strong ale. This is especially the case in Belgium, which had a ban on the sale of strong spirits in bars and cafés early in the 20th century. To make up the shortfall in alcohol, brewers filled the gap with beers of exceptional strength. Critics of strong beers claim they tend to be sweet and cloying as substantial amounts of malt and special brewing sugars are needed to achieve high levels of alcohol. Modern brewers have responded by balancing the malt and fruit created by alcohol with generous amounts of hops that cut the sweetness and impart not only bitterness but also tart and tangy notes of citrus, pine, resins and herbs.

Fuller's Brewery brews the definitive English ESB

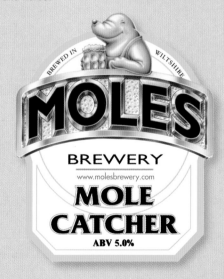

16 Mile Old Court Ale

Source: 16 Mile Brewery, Georgetown, Delaware, USA

Strength: 6.1%

Website: www.16milebrewery.com

New world and old world have powerful historic links here. Georgetown is in Sussex County where another principal town is called Lewes – a town closely associated with brewing for many British readers. The links are even closer where beer is concerned for Brett McCrea, who founded 16 Mile with Chad Campbell, worked in 1991 as an overseas research student at the House of Commons in London thanks to the Hansard Scholarship Programme. In his spare time he discovered London pubs and fell in love with English ale. His brews at 16 Mile are, he says, his tribute to 'my favourite style of beer'.

Brett and Chad studied at the same school and are proud natives of Delaware. They've been brewing since the 1990s and are based in spacious buildings in a field on the edge of town. Georgetown is now an important manufacturing centre but when Delaware became a state of the union the town was so remote it was described as being 'sixteen miles from any-where'. Old Court Ale pays homage to the Old Court House that has been dispensing justice since 1791.

16 Mile has a 15-barrel brew house and uses mainly barley malt imported from England to give what Brett describes as the 'characteristic flavour' he wants for his beers. The success of the brewery means it now employs a large staff but Brett and Chad are hands-on, brewing beer and acting as tour guides. Brett describes Old Court as a 'dark pale ale' and he uses pale malt, caramalt and small amount of Munich malt. The hops are Northern Brewer for bitterness with Cascade added halfway through the copper boil and at the end for aroma. The hops create 35 units of bitterness. The beer has a pale bronze colour with a dense head of foam, followed by sultana and raisin fruit on the nose with a 'malt loaf' grain character and peppery hop notes. Bitter hops build in the mouth, with rich burnt fruit and chewy malt. The finish is dry with a creamy malt character balanced by peppery hops and dark fruit.

Bitter hops build in the mouth, with rich burnt fruit and chewy malt.

Black Sheep Riggwelter

Source: Black Sheep Brewery, Masham, North Yorkshire, England

Strength: 5.9%

Website: www.blacksheepbrewery.co.uk

The famous brewing town of Masham, which is also home to the Theakston brewery, owes its wealth to sheep and wool. Black Sheep makes a deep bow to its four-footed, woolly friends with the name of both the brewery and Riggwelter, a Yorkshire dialect expression for a sheep that's fallen on its back and can't get up without assistance. The brewers feel this is the ideal name for their strong ale and its possible side effects. There are many other sheep connections at the brewery, which has a visitor centre and a bar – known as the Baa. A video of the brewery and its beers is called Ewe Tube.

The brewery was founded in 1992 by Paul Theakston, who left his family's company when it was taken over by the national giant Scottish & Newcastle (Theakston's is now independent again). Paul's wife Sue said he would be 'the black sheep of the family' when he launched a rival company separated by just a wall from the family brewery and based in an old maltings. Paul thought it was too good a name to pass up and, with a brilliant eye for marketing as well as a keen sense of humour, he turned Black Sheep into one of the major independent British breweries with close to 1,000 free trade outlets and bottled beers in major supermarkets. A new brewhouse was added in 2003 and Black Sheep now produces 80,000 barrels a year and has further plans to expand. 'Don't call me a micro!' Paul says sternly. He's reached retirement age and has handed over day-to-day running of the brewery to his sons Rob and Jo but he keeps a paternal, mature ram's eye on the business, which uniquely for such a substantial brewery, doesn't own a single pub and relies on the free trade for its success.

Black Sheep is dedicated to using the finest natural ingredients: crystal-clear water from the surrounding Yorkshire Dales, Maris Otter malting barley and English hops. The brewery's signature is its Yorkshire Square fermenting system, which

TASTING NOTES

APPEARANCE:

AROMA:

TASTE:

OVERALL SCORE:

In order to maintain an active fermentation, some of the yeast on the top deck has to be washed back down. Every six hours, a pump draws beer from the lower chamber and sprays it over the top deck, washing the yeasty liquid down the organ pipe. This is known as rousing and it aerates the fermenting beer. It's rare for oxygen to be introduced into the fermentation process and rousing alters the metabolism of the yeast, which creates a fruity, vinous note in the beer. The other characteristic of the Yorkshire Square system is an astringency known as 'yeast bite', the result of separating beer from the yeast during the cleansing on the top deck.

The Riggwelter that emerges from this exhaustive system of fermentation is brewed with Maris Otter pale malt, crystal malt and pale chocolate malt. Hops for bitterness are Challenger, Fuggles, Goldings and Progress, which are added at the start of the one-hour boil. For aroma, a substantial amount of Goldings are added to the hop back, the vessel that receives the hopped wort. The hops from the copper and are also added to the hop back. Units of bitterness are 38.

the Theakstons believe is crucial to the taste and character of their beers. Yorkshire Squares were developed in the 19th century to cleanse pale ale of yeast sediment: a similar development happened in Burton-on-Trent with the invention of the 'Burton Union' method of yeast separation. A square is a two-storey vessel, with a closed bottom chamber topped by an open deck with a raised surround. Fermenting beer rises from the bottom chamber to the top through a central manhole. The yeast is trapped on the top deck but the beer runs back to the bottom chamber down an 'organ pipe'.

Riggwelter is an amber-coloured beer with a smoky, roasted grain aroma, powerful notes of ripe banana and espresso coffee, all underscored by resinous hops. Rich coffee, fruit, smoky roasted grain, liquorice and tart, bitter hops build in the mouth, followed by a long and complex finish that interweaves roasted grain, vinous fruit and bitter hops. In the depths of winter, Paul Theakston likes to add a tot of rum to the beer, which he calls Rigg and Rum. If that doesn't put you flat on your back, nothing will.

Greene King Hen's Tooth

Source: Greene King, Westgate Brewery, Bury St Edmunds, Suffolk, England

Strength: 6.5%

Website: www.greeneking.co.uk

This strong bottle-conditioned beer is a spin-off from Greene King's hugely successful beer Old Speckled Hen, the bottled version of which is now the best-selling premium ale in Britain, having overtaken the legendary but much-diminished Newcastle Brown. Old Speckled Hen was brewed by Morland in Abingdon to commemorate the fiftieth anniversary of the MG sports car, which was built in the Oxfordshire town. A factory run-around MG was used to try out new body paints and as a result of its dappled appearance was given the nickname of the 'Owd Speckled Un', which became Old Speckled Hen when the beer was launched. As a result of the beer's success, Morland added Hen's Tooth. The name indicates that despite its strength it's not sweet and cloying but has a good hop balance: something as rare as hen's teeth.

Morland was bought and closed by Greene King in 2000 and production was transferred to Bury St Edmunds. The original Morland yeast is used to brew Hen's Tooth and to continue bottle fermentation. The malts are Tipple pale malt and crystal malt, and the beer has a complex hop regime that includes Admiral, Boadicea, Challenger, First Gold, Goldings and Pilgrim: several are new varieties that would not have been available to Morland. The units of bitterness are a redoubtable 42, which perfectly balances the rich malt character. The beer is amber bright with lively foam. It has a big caramel-verging-on-toffee aroma with fruitiness reminiscent of raspberries and a freshly-baked bread malt note, underscored by herbal and resinous hops. The palate is fruity and malty with chewy caramel and increasing hop bitterness. Sweet malt, fruit and caramel combine in the finish but with a solid underpinning of herbal and spicy hops.

The palate is fruity and malty with chewy caramel and increasing hop bitterness.

TASTING NOTES

APPEARANCE:

AROMA:

TASTE:

OVERALL SCORE:

Hargreaves Hill Extra Special Bitter

Source: Hargreaves Hill Brewing Company, Yarra Glen, Victoria, Australia

Strength: 5.4%

Website: www.hargreaveshill.com.au

Brewer Simon Walkenhorst is frequently challenged over his ESB: 'People ask me whether it's a true ESB or an APA – American Pale Ale. I always thought ESB was a descriptor and my beer is a re-interpretation of a classic English dry-hopped style using New World ingredients.' The fact that Simon uses Australian-grown crystal and Munich malts alongside pale ale malt proves his point. He uses a variety of hops – 'whatever is available to give a good punch of hops to balance the rich malt,' he says. His hop of choice is Nelson Sauvin from New Zealand – so-called because of its similarity to the flavours of the Sauvignon Blanc grape. But he also uses Citra, Galaxy and Simcoe from the U.S.

Simon and his partner Beth Williams opened their brewery and restaurant in 2004 with the launch of their first beer, Hargreaves Hill Pale. They have since added a lager and an imperial stout but it's ESB that has won the most plaudits. In just a

few years he has acquired cult status among beer aficionados and the revered Australian food and drink writer James Halliday named it one of his top 20 beers in 2011. ESB is used in beer and food matching events at the Hargreaves Hill restaurant situated in the spectacular Yarra Valley one hour from Melbourne.

The beer, available on draught and in bottle, has 35 to 40 units of bitterness but this level increases as a result of dry hopping the finished beer. The copper-coloured ESB has a mighty punch of grassy and fruity hops on the nose, balanced by toasted, nutty malt. Hop bitterness builds in the mouth, providing a solid backbone to the massive malt character – toasted, smoky, nutty – with further spicy and fruity contributions from the hops. The finish is long and complex, rich toasted malt interweaving with powerful spicy hop resins and ripe fruit.

Hesket Newmarket Catbells Pale Ale

Source: Hesket Newmarket Brewery, Hesket Newmarket, Cumbria, England

Strength: 5%

Website: www.hesketbrewery.co.uk

This brewery has a special place in the annals of British brewing. It stands behind the Old Crown pub in Hesket Newmarket and both are run as co-operatives to maintain their role as vital hubs of the rural community. The village is set in beautiful Cumbrian countryside on the opposite side of Skiddaw – England's fourth highest mountain – to Keswick. Pub and brewery were run in the 1980s by Jim and Liz Fearnley. When the work became too much for them, they decided to close the

brewery but both locals and beer lovers from further afield formed a co-op to buy it and keep it in production. It began its new life with 100 shareholders in 1999 and on its opening day a message of support was received from the legendary mountaineer Sir Chris Bonington, who lives in the area, enjoys the beer and was climbing in Nepal at the time. When the Fearnleys retired in 2002, a second co-op was created to run the pub, making the Old Crown Britain's first co-operatively

The brewery has been substantially updated and enlarged and can produce 50 barrels a week. The beers are now more widely available in pubs in Cumbria and the Lakes. Most of the beer names are drawn from mountains and fells, including Haystacks, Skiddaw, Helvellyn and Scafell. Catbells is one of the most popular fell walks in the area, much praised by the famous walker and writer Alfred Wainwright. While the brewery calls its beer named for the mountain a pale ale, I think the balance of malt and hops bring the beer into the Strong Bitter category.

Catbells, available both in cask and bottle-conditioned formats, is brewed with 100% Maris Otter pale malt and is hopped with Challenger and Northdown varieties, with a final late addition of Styrian Goldings at the end of the copper boil. The golden ale has a superb aroma bursting with hop resins, pine needles, tart fruit and juicy malt. Biscuit malt, bittersweet fruit and tangy hops fill the mouth, followed by a long, lingering finish well-balanced – like a fell walker – between bitter hops, rich malt and ripe fruit.

owned pub. The shareholders in both co-ops can own just one share each, to avoid well-heeled people buying a majority of shares with a view to takeover and private ownership.

Holgate ESB

Source: Holgate Brewhouse, Woodend, Victoria, Australia

Strength: 5%

Website: www.holgatebrewhouse.com.au

If Holgate's Hopinator (see IPA section) had a determinedly New World emphasis of powerful citrus hops, Paul Holgate's interpretation of ESB stresses his British roots in Manchester and his strong love for traditional ales from the Old Country. The beer is served cask conditioned from handpumps in the bar of the adjoining hotel with a serving temperature of 8 to 10 degrees C. This may seem a tad on the warm side to Australians used to ice-cold stubbies, but it's a temperature that allows the full malt and hop notes to express themselves.

ESB is brewed with pale and crystal malts with a dash of roasted barley – the use of roast is rare in this style, though several breweries use touches of darker malts, including chocolate, for colour and flavour. The hops are English to their core: Fuggles and Goldings, which create 35 units of bitterness.

The amber coloured ale has a big punch of peppery and spicy hops on the nose, balanced by nutty and biscuit malt and a smoky, roasted grain note. The palate is a rich balance of clean, succulent malt, roast grain, a hint of caramel and big peppery hop resins. The finish is long, clean and quenching, with powerful notes of rich malt, caramel, smoky roast flavours and bitter, spicy hops.

The beer is a splendid companion for Natasha's spicy dishes in the hotel.

TASTING NOTES

APPEARANCE:

AROMA:

TASTE:

OVERALL SCORE:

Moles Mole Catcher

Source: Moles Brewery, Melksham, Wiltshire, England

Strength: 5%

Website: www.molesbrewery.com

Moles Brewery is one of the longest-surviving small craft breweries in Britain. It was founded in 1982 by Roger Catte, who had brewed with Ushers in Trowbridge, Wiltshire. Ushers brewery had the grave misfortune to become part of the Watneys group, one of the reviled producers of extremely bad keg beers in the 1970s. Ushers suffered a double indignity: when it closed in 2000 its equipment was sold to North Korea to make lager.

Roger Catte, whose nickname is Mole, fared better than his previous employers. His custom-built plant, originally ten barrels and expanded to 25, produces half-a-dozen regular beers as well as seasonal brews, all promoted with the aid of a cheery cartoon mole character. Brewing remains firmly traditional, with mash tun, copper, open fermenter and whole leaf hops.

Moles owns ten pubs in the West Country and supplies a further 200 outlets. It was given a substantial boost in 2011 when Mole Catcher won the Strong Bitter class in the Champion Beer of Britain competition. It's brewed with Maris Otter pale malt and crystal malt. It's a 'single varietal beer', which means only one hop is used, the American Cascade. The copper-coloured beer has a spicy and fruity hop note on the nose, balanced by a freshly-baked malt note with hints of roast and nuts. Sappy malt and bitter hops dominate the palate with a solid underpinning of tangy fruit. The finish is long, finely balanced between rich malt, tart fruit and bitter hop resins.

Oakleaf Blake's Gosport Bitter

Source: Oakleaf Brewing Company, Gosport, Hampshire, England

Strength: 5.2%

Website: www.oakleafbrewing.co.uk

There's history mixed into the mash of a beer that commemorates Blake's Gosport Brewery. Blakes was founded in 1897 and lasted until the 1920s, when it was bought and closed by the much larger Brickwoods Brewery in Portsmouth. Brickwoods fell victim in the 1960s to a curious device known as 'the Whitbread Umbrella'. Whitbread, a London brewery with national reach, offered to take substantial stakes in a number of regional breweries to save them, Whitbread said, from possible takeover. The Whitbread Umbrella proved to be poor protection: many of the regional breweries that huddled under its frame soon found themselves swallowed by the holder of the handle. In the case of Brickwoods, it was merged with another victim of the umbrella, Strongs of Romsey, to become Whitbread Wessex. Both breweries eventually closed.

Oakleaf was founded in 2000 by Dave Pickersgill and his son-in-law Ed Anderson on a wharf alongside Portsmouth Harbour, with a staff of five. They own no pubs but they have 350 free trade outlets and the beers are widely available through wholesalers.

Blake's Gosport Bitter is available in bottle-conditioned format on a regular basis and is also produced in cask form as a seasonal beer. It's brewed with Maris Otter pale malt and crystal and chocolate malts. The single hop used is the Golding. The dark ruby-coloured beer has a peppery hop aroma with rich toasted malt, a delightful dry chocolate note and a hint of bittersweet fruit. Chewy toasted malt, chocolate, bitter hops and ripe, juicy fruit build in the mouth, followed by a long finish dominated by dark malt, chocolate, bittersweet fruit and peppery hops.

Shepherd Neame 1698

Source: Shepherd Neame Brewery, Faversham, Kent, England

Strength: 6.5%

Website: www.shepherd-neame.co.uk

There are breweries with history, and then there's Shepherd Neame. The official date for the opening of the brewery in Court Street, Faversham, is 1698 – hence the name of the beer – but ale has been brewed on the site, with its supply of fresh water from a well, since at least the 12th century. In 1147 King Stephen founded an abbey in Faversham that had its own small brewery to supply ale to the monks and visiting pilgrims. The abbey was dissolved at the time of the Reformation but small-scale brewing continued on the site, and a commercial company was formed in 1698.

In the intervening centuries, Faversham had become a major port, responsible for important trade with the European mainland. For a period, it was also the court of the kings of Kent. The town holds 17 royal charters and the collar of the bottled beer has three royal lions to denote this long association with the monarchy.

In 1732 the Shepherd family took over the brewery in Court Street and in 1864 a local hop farmer, Percy Beale Neame, formed a partnership with the Shepherds. The Neames remain in control to this day and they have turned part of the building into a museum that traces the long and fascinating history of the brewery. In a cobbled passageway, it's possible to see the top of the 200-feet deep artesian well that has supplied chalk-filtered pure brewing liquor since the time of the abbey.

1698 was first brewed in 1998 to celebrate 300 years of commercial brewing on the site. It was then a filtered and pasteurised beer but since 2005 it's been bottle conditioned, brewed using the finest raw ingredients from Kent. Pearl pale malting barley is joined with crystal malt and the extract is hopped three times with Target and East Kent Goldings: the copper boil starts with an infusion of Target while Goldings are added late in the boil. There's a further addition of Goldings in the whirl-pool where the hopped wort is separated from spent hops and unwanted protein. Following fermentation, the beer is filtered and then has a dosage of fresh yeast.

1698 is a pale bronze beer with an enormously complex aroma of hop resins, marzipan, vanilla, butterscotch, toasted grain and vinous fruit. Rich, sweet, sappy malt and butterscotch coat the tongue, balanced by tangy hops and blood orange fruit. The finish is dry with continuing contributions from toasted grain, bitter hops, tart fruit, butterscotch and vanilla.

Along with all the Shepherd Neame beers, 1698 is protected by an ordinance from the European Union known as a PGI – Protected Geographical Indication – that allows the brewery to use the term 'Kentish Ales'. This gives the brewery's beers the same protection as French Champagne and means that no brewer outside the county can use the term 'Kentish' on its labels.

TASTING NOTES

APPEARANCE:

AROMA:

TASTE:

OVERALL SCORE:

Wells & Young's Special London Ale

Source: Wells & Young's Brewing Company, Bedford, England

Strength: 6.4%

Website: www.wellsandyoungs.co.uk

Unlike Kent, 'London' in a beer's title is not protected by a PGI. Special London Ale is brewed in Bedford, some 45 miles north of the capital. It started life at Young's Brewery in Wandsworth, south London, but when the brewery closed in 2006, production of all its beers moved to Charles Wells in Bedford. Special London Ale has had an even more peripatetic existence: it was first called Young's Export and was aimed at the Belgian market, where strong ales are in vogue. The beer was even brewed under licence in Belgium for a period to stress the importance of the trade there. At the time it was a filtered beer but it became bottle conditioned when production moved back to Wandsworth in 1998. Its popularity soared when it was named CAMRA's Champion Bottled Beer of Britain in 1999.

It's brewed with Maris Otter pale malt and crystal malt and is hopped with Fuggles, Goldings and Target varieties. Following fermentation, the beer is warm conditioned for three weeks on a bed of Goldings and Target. The beer is then cold conditioned, filtered and re-seeded with fresh yeast. With such a high level of alcohol, it's a beer that will mature and improve for a year or two if carefully stored.

The bronze beer has all the hallmarks of a Young's ale, with a pronounced orange fruit note, intensely bitter hops and juicy malt on the nose. Bitter hop resins, tart fruit and biscuit malt build on the palate while the finish is a fine meld of marmalade fruit, peppery hops and sappy malt.

West Berkshire Dr Hexter's Healer

Source: West Berkshire Brewery, Yattendon, Berkshire, England

Strength: 5%

Website: www.wbbrew.com

This beer, with its image of an imposing doctor in Victorian or Edwardian garb, including a top hat, recalls an age when society regarded beer as a tonic with important medicinal properties made from such wholesome ingredients as barley malt, hops and pure water. West Berkshire is good at creating fetching names for its beers: we have already encountered Maggs Magnificent Mild. Dr Hexter, it turns out, was not a family doctor from a previous age but is the landlord of a pub in Wantage for whom Healer, along with Dr Hexter's Wedding Ale, were specially developed by the brewery. He's not a practising doctor – it's his nickname.

The beer – and the good doctor's name – took on national significance in 2009 when it won the Strong Bitter class in the Champion Beer of Britain competition. It's brewed with Maris Otter pale malt with chocolate and crystal malts, and is hopped with three English varieties: Cascade, Fuggles and Goldings. As a result of the popularity of American Cascades, the hop is now grown in England. The amber beer has a rich and inviting aroma of toasted malt, a powerful hint of chocolate, orange fruit and spicy hops. Fruit develops in the mouth, taking on a more complex marmalade character, balanced by peppery hop resins, toasted malt and chocolate. Rich, tart fruit, chocolate, dark malt and bitter, peppery hops combine in the long finish that finally ends dry and hoppy.

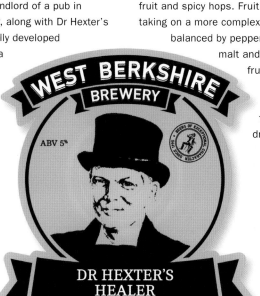

> *West Berkshire is good at creating fetching names for its beers: we have already encountered Maggs Magnificent Mild*

York Centurion Ghost's Ale

Source: York Brewery, York, England

Strength: 5.4%

Website: www.york-brewery.co.uk

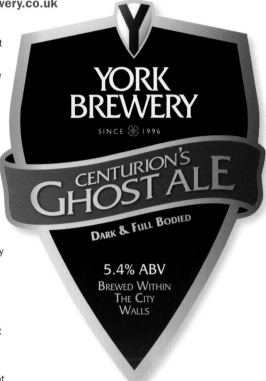

When York Brewery opened in 1996 it was the first new beer maker in the city for forty years and is still the only one within the city walls. As you leave the railway station, among the signs directing visitors to the city's many places of historic interest, there's one for 'York Brewery', an indication of the company's rapid success in just a few years and its role as a tourist attraction.

Centurion won the Strong Bitter class in the Champion Beer of Britain competition 2007 and it celebrates a city with a potent history that dates from AD 71, when it was founded by the Romans. It was called Eboracum, which became Jörvik when the Danes invaded, and finally the more familiar York. Over the centuries it has become a major manufacturing city, a seat of ecclesiastical power based on the mighty Minster or cathedral, and in the 19th century an important hub in the new railway system. But it remains best known for its Roman associations that include occasional ghostly sightings.

The brewery opened in Toft Green with equipment bought from the closed Matthew Brown Lion Brewery in Blackburn. Centurion was added to the portfolio in 2000 and has become the centrepiece of production in a 20-barrel brewhouse that can be viewed from a visitors' gallery. There's also a Tap Room where all the beers can be sampled on draught.

Centurion is brewed with pale, chocolate and crystal malts and is hopped with Bramling Cross, Challenger and Fuggles varieties. The dark ruby beer has roasted grain, chocolate and berry fruits on the nose, underpinned by a solid base of spicy and floral hops. Dark, chewy grain, chocolate, fruit and hop resins combine on the tongue, followed by a long, quenching finish that is finally hoppy with spice notes, chocolate and dark fruits.

This section has referred several times to breweries that were the unfortunate victims of takeovers. In the case of York, a 2008 takeover seems to have worked to the brewery's advantage. It's now owned by Mitchells of Lancaster, a brewery that stopped making beer in 1999 in order to concentrate on running pubs. As a brewery, it was best known for its premium bitter, Lancaster Bomber, which is now brewed under contract by Thwaites of Blackburn. Mitchells has brought its experience of brewing and retailing to York and its beers are now available on both sides of the Pennines, as well as in five pubs – four in York and one in Leeds.

Old Ales, Barley Wines & Vintage Ales

One of the many joys of the revival of good beer is the restoration of ancient styles that were once part of brewing history, not modern practice. This is especially true of old ale and barley wine, beers with deep roots in the history of British brewing in the 18th century, later forgotten and ignored, but now bringing pleasure and interest to drinkers in the new millennium.

Old ale, also known as stale or stock ale, was a beer aged in wooden vessels known as tuns. During a maturation period that could last for a year or longer, the beer picked up a sour note from the action of wild *Brettanomyces* yeasts along with *lactobacilli* and tannins in the wood. Old, stale and stock ales were invariably blended with younger, fresher beers that smoothed out and made palatable the acetic nature of the aged beer. Few modern old ales are made in this way: one exception is Greene King's Strong Suffolk Ale, which featured in *300 Beers to Try Before You Die!* This method of blending old and fresh beers is similar to the 'solera' system used by sherry makers in Spain. In Belgium the method is more widely used to produce the sour red beers of West Flanders, of which the best-known example is Rodenbach (also discussed in *300 Beers to Try Before You Die!*), while Belgian *gueuze* is also a blend of aged and fresh *lambic* beers: the *solera* link is a potent one here, as many *lambic* brewers import wooden casks from the sherry industry in Jerez.

Old ales are not necessarily strong and can have modest strengths of around 4.5%. Barley wines, in contrast, are designed to be strong, as the name suggests. The style was once the preserve of the English aristocracy, either brewed in small breweries on their estates or commissioned from commercial companies. When England was more or less permanently at war with France, the aristocracy considered it their patriotic duty to abandon French wine and drink home-brewed ale. Barley wine was a term used in the 18th century and was in the same vein as other powerful ales such as Dorchester Beer, malt liquors, malt wine and October Beer. They were beers brewed in October, using malts and hops fresh from the harvest and matured until the following spring or summer. They were exceedingly strong and clearly improved with age: recent research suggests that the first India Pale Ales exported to the sub-continent were October Beers that were sufficiently high in alcohol and hops to withstand the long sea journey.

The decline of the English aristocracy and their country homes in the 20th century led to barley wine being brewed solely by commercial brewers. The style dwindled and was kept alive by a handful of producers, the best-known being Whitbread's Gold Label, which had the indignity of ending up in cans. But new wave brewers on both sides of the Atlantic have restored interest in barley wine along with the welcome development of vintage ales – brewed once a year and recalling the days of October Beers.

British producers of strong beers have not been helped by a government decision to levy additional rates of duty on beer above 7.5%, increasing the price of a pint by 25%. The government says the measure is designed to tackle 'binge drinking' but the notion that people who sip a delectable barley wine do so on a park bench with the bottle inside a paper bag is risible.

TASTING NOTES

APPEARANCE:

AROMA:

TASTE:

OVERALL SCORE:

Bare Arts Dark Barley Wine/Pale Barley Wine

Source: Bare Arts Brewery, Todmorden, West Yorkshire, England
Strength: 9%/9.8%
Website: www.barearts.com

If drinking barley wine brings on a hot flush, there's no better place to get your kit off than Bare Arts, which combines a small brewery with a gallery specialising in nude art work. Owners Trevor and Kathryn Cook believe it's the only nude art gallery in the world that is licensed to sell alcohol: we would be pleased to hear from other contenders. The Cook family ran a pub in Bacup for many years and opened their four-barrel plant alongside the gallery in 2005. As well as artwork by local artists, including Kathryn, the gallery also features poetry readings, live music and beer tasting events.

Trevor produces 500 litres of beer with each brew. The beers are available to buy from the shop or online in bottle-conditioned form and mini-casks and can be found in local pubs. Trevor is adamant he will only use British malting barley and hops, and he ages his beers for lengthy periods to allow them to develop rich, round and warming flavours.

His Dark Barley Wine is made with Maris Otter pale malt, dark crystal malt and Goldings hops, with the crystal malt developing an attractive deep amber colour. The beer has a pleasing note of toffee on the aroma and palate from the stewed malt, with toasted malt, rich burnt fruits and peppery hops on the nose. The toffee turns to marzipan on the palate with raisin and sultana fruits, chewy malt and bitter hop resins. The finish is long, deep and warming, dominated by rich toasted malt, burnt fruits, peppery hops and the continuing note of marzipan.

There's a clear Belgian influence at play, as Trevor follows his dark beer with an even stronger pale one: Dubbel followed by Tripel. Pale Barley Wine is made with lager malt – British grown – and Goldings hops. A long copper boil with the hops, followed by ageing, delivers a deep bronze colour with a pronounced toasted malt aroma, lemon and lime fruits, and Goldings hop resins. The palate is sappy and fruity, with hints of leather and fresh tobacco, all balanced by a solid underpinning of peppery hops. The finish has a big, warming kick of alcohol, ripe juicy malt, bitter hops and continuing hints of leather and tobacco.

Burton Bridge Tickle Brain

Source: Burton Bridge Brewery, Burton-on-Trent, Staffordshire, England
Strength: 8%
Website: www.burtonbridgebrewery.co.uk

This is an historic beer with literary allusions. Tickle Brain was a phrase used in Tudor times to mean both strong ale and someone who over-indulged in it. In Shakespeare's *Henry IV Part One*, Falstaff – who else? – says irreverently to Mistress Quickly, owner of the Boar's Head tavern in London's Eastcheap,

'Peace, good pint pot. Peace, good tickle brain'. Geoff Mumford and Bruce Wilkinson, founders of Burton Bridge (see the Burton Ales section, p195, for more on their careers) set out to recreate a beer they thought would be similar in style to the strong ales made with hops in the 16th century, when the

hop plant was starting to be more widely used by brewers. The label of the beer has an image of Henry VIII who allowed his court brewer to make both unhopped ale and hopped beer. The Burton Bridge beer is brewed with Pipkin pale malt and chocolate malt and is hopped with a single variety, English Northdown. The deep brown ale is aged in casks for a minimum of four months before it's bottled with live yeast. It has a big, pungent, grassy hop aroma with rich toasted malt and hints of chocolate and vinous fruit. Cracker-like malt builds in the mouth, underscored by uncompromising hop bitterness, ripe fruit and chocolate. The finish is long, warming, bitter-sweet, with vinous fruit, strong hints of caramel and chocolate, toasted grain and grassy/woody hops.

> **TASTING NOTES**
> APPEARANCE:
>
> AROMA:
>
> TASTE:
>
> OVERALL SCORE:

Coniston No 9 Barley Wine

Source: Coniston Brewing Co, Coniston, Cumbria, England
Strength: 8.5%
Website: www.conistonbrewery.com

No 9 was the surprise winner of the 2012 Champion Beer of Britain competition – and no one was more surprised than brewer Ian Bradley, who went on holiday during the Great British Beer Festival in London in August. When the award was announced, brewing consultant David Smith, who had supplied the equipment for the brewery and remained in close touch, came up to accept the prize and the plaudits. As he admitted, it was unusual for someone from Yorkshire to accept an award for a beer brewed on the other side of the Pennines.

The beer's name stems from the fact that it's the ninth beer to be brewed in the plant behind the Black Bull Inn in Coniston. It's only brewed three or four times a year as each batch is aged for three months before it's released on draught or in bottle. The batch sent to GBBF was quickly drained dry by the crowds at London Olympia and drinkers had to wait patiently for the second brew to be ready in the autumn.

No 9 is brewed with Maris Otter pale and crystal malts and is hopped with English Challenger and Goldings varieties. Ian uses a German technique known as *kräusening* to encourage a strong secondary fermentation while the beer is ageing. He adds a batch of fresh, young beer to the older brew. The fresh beer is Coniston Bluebird, which won the Champion Beer of Britain competition back in 1998 and put the brewery on the road to fame and success. David Smith says: 'You're getting two champion beers in one glass'.

The deep copper-coloured beer has a superb aroma of toasted malt, vinous fruits and peppery hops resins. Toffee malt, blood orange fruit and a rich cedar wood note from the hops fill the mouth, followed by a long, lingering, complex finish that delivers warming alcohol with an almost cognac-like note, bitter fruit, creamy malt and bitter hops with spice and cedar.

> **TASTING NOTES**
> APPEARANCE:
>
> AROMA:
>
> TASTE:
>
> OVERALL SCORE:

TASTING NOTES

APPEARANCE:

AROMA:

TASTE:

OVERALL SCORE:

Fuller's 1845

Source: Fuller, Smith and Turner's Griffin Brewery, Chiswick, London, England
Strength: 6.3%
Website: www.fullers.co.uk

The visitors' book in the reception room at Fuller's brewery is kept under glass, open at a page from February 1995 that bears the signature of Prince Charles, the Prince of Wales. The prince attended the brewery to start the mash and add the hops in the copper for a new beer that marked the 150th anniversary of the founding of the partnership of John Bird Fuller, Henry Smith and John Turner. Brewing on the site, close to the banks of the Thames, has been going on for far longer: it started 350 years ago, during the time of Oliver Cromwell's republic. The partnership took over in 1845 and portraits of the founders hang in the brewery and the pub next door. Smith bears a remarkable resemblance to Karl Marx, who may just possibly have enjoyed the brewery's ales when he was resident in London in the last half of the 19th century.

The heady blend of Cromwell, the heir to the throne and Karl Marx is matched by 1845, which has been brewed with due reverence to the type of ales produced during the middle of the 19th century. It's bottle conditioned, in tune with Victorian practice, uses amber malt for colour and flavour – amber is rarely used today – and Goldings hops, which date from that period. It's brewed with Tipple and Concerto spring barleys, with crystal and amber malts and a touch of chocolate malt for colour adjustment. The Goldings create 52 units of bitterness. In total, the beer enjoys 100 days of conditioning and ageing: following primary fermentation, the beer rests in conditioning tanks and is then filtered and re-seeded with fresh yeast. A further period of conditioning follows before the beer leaves the brewery.

With the aid of barley called Concerto, this is a symphony in the glass.

The amber bright beer has Fuller's orange fruit note on the nose with harvest-fresh malt, a hint of chocolate and tangy Goldings hop resins. Burnt raisin fruit joins orange in the mouth, with chocolate and chewy malt, and growing and intense hop bitterness. The finish is long and deep, dominated by tart orange fruit, raisins, chocolate, biscuit malt and bitter and peppery hop resins. With the aid of barley called Concerto, this is a symphony in the glass. 1845 has twice won the bottled beer category of the Champion Beer of Britain competition.

Harveys Elizabethan Ale

Source: Harvey & Son, Lewes, East Sussex, England
Strength: 7.5%
Website: www.harveys.org.uk

This is a beer rich in history. It was first brewed to commemorate the coronation of Elizabeth II in 1953 but brewer Miles Jenner says it's based on the type of strong ales produced during the reign of the first Elizabeth in the 16th century. The beer was recreated in 2012 to mark the Royal Jubilee and uses the same recipe and ingredients: Maris Otter pale malt, black malt and flaked barley, with Fuggles and Goldings hops – the hops are grown by Stuart Highwood at Collier Street farm in Kent, the source of the hops for the 1953 beer.

The beer is almost black in colour with toffee, raisin and sultana fruit, aromatic coffee, rich chocolate and peppery hops on the nose. Chocolate and coffee coat the tongue with roasted grain, vinous fruit, a port wine note, toffee and spicy hops. Toffee malt dominates the long finish but is balanced by dry chocolate, latte coffee, port wine and gentle spicy hops. Miles Jenner says the beer will improve with age and adds that a batch of the 1953 brew 'is still drinking well', which scotches the notion that beer can only be aged for a year or two. In the Lewes area, lovers of the beer called for 'a Lizzie', which in Tudor times would probably have earned them a spell in the Tower of London.

TASTING NOTES

APPEARANCE:

AROMA:

TASTE:

OVERALL SCORE:

Miles Jenner says the beer will improve with age and adds that a batch of the 1953 brew 'is still drinking well'

TASTING NOTES

APPEARANCE:

AROMA:

TASTE:

OVERALL SCORE:

Hogs Back A Over T

Source: Hogs Back Brewery, Tongham, Surrey, England

Strength: 9%

Website: www.hogsback.co.uk

The polite people who run Hogs Back claim that A Over T stands for 'Aromas Over Tongham'. Given the strength of the beer, those of us with a more vulgar turn of mind might think it recalls the old expression that indicates someone has tumbled backside over apex as a result of imbibing powerful ale.

The beer is one of Hogs Back's earliest brews (see history of the brewery in Best Bitter section) and is available both in cask-conditioned and bottle-conditioned formats. It was launched in 1993 and the draught version was named Champion Winter Beer of Britain in 2006. It's brewed with Pearl pale malt and crystal malt and is hopped with Bramling Cross and Goldings varieties that create a redoubtable 70 units of bitterness: the hops are added in large amounts to counter any cloying sweetness from the malts. The amber/red beer has vinous fruits, fresh tobacco and powerful spicy hop resins on the aroma. Rich cracker biscuit malt, massive fruit notes – ranging from sultana and raisin to blackcurrant – and tart and peppery hops fill the mouth. The finish has a big kick of warming alcohol, with a ripe malt note, vinous fruits and bitter, spicy hops that balance all the rich malt and fruit notes. Mind how you go...

The polite people who run Hogs Back claim that A Over T stands for 'Aromas Over Tongham'

Hopshackle Restoration

Source: Hopshackle Brewery, Market Deeping, Lincolnshire, England

Strength: 9%

Website: www.hopshacklebrewery.co.uk

Nigel Wright follows in Belgian brewers' footsteps with a strong ale inspired by beers from our neighbour across the North Sea, and one that has close links to the church as is also the case with Belgian Trappist and abbey beers. The beer came about when the vicar of St Guthlac's in Market Deeping approached Nigel and asked for help in raising funds for the upkeep of the church. Nigel ran a competition to choose the best name for a beer and the winner was Restoration. A donation of 25 pence from every bottle sold goes to the church.

The beer is brewed just once a year and enjoys a long ageing process. Nigel says 9% alcohol can reach 10% as a result of secondary fermentation in the brewery and in bottle. While the beer is undergoing primary fermentation, the Rev Philip Brent pops over from his church and blesses the brew.

Restoration is brewed with Pilsner malt, chocolate malt and a malt known as Special B, which is a type of dark crystal from Belgium. Nigel also adds candy sugar, which is widely used in Belgium, including in Trappist breweries, to encourage a strong fermentation and to add colour and flavour to the beer.

The hops are German Hersbrucker and American Mount Hood that create 28 units of bitterness.

Following primary fermentation and the vicar's blessing, the beer is aged in a conditioning tank in the cellar for six months, during which time it mellows, matures and purges itself of unwanted rough alcohols. It's then primed with brewing sugar and a fresh yeast culture that Nigel describes as 'an alcohol-tolerant strain', meaning it doesn't fall asleep on the job, overcome by the level of alcohol. A further four to six weeks is allowed for secondary fermentation before the beer is allowed to leave the brewery. Only some 1,500 bottles are produced each year and Nigel says the beer will continue to improve if laid down. He keeps bottles from each vintage in the brewery and compares them as they age.

The dark amber beer has ripe vinous fruit, a powerful hint of port wine, rich creamy malt and light floral hop resins on the nose. Cherries and plums dominate the palate, balanced by sweet creamy and chewy malt and a good underpinning of floral and herbal hops. The finish has more vinous and sultana fruits, with rich creamy malt and a lingering gentle spicy hop bitterness.

Pitfield 1890 Stock Ale

Source: Pitfield Brewery, Epping, Essex, England

Strength: 10%

Website: www.pitfieldbeershop.co.uk

I said in the introduction to this section that stock ales need not necessarily be strong but this interpretation, which is based – as the date suggests – on a late 19th-century recipe, shows they could reach high levels of alcohol. The term stock is believed to have meant a beer that was stored for a long period in contrast to 'running beers' designed to be consumed once fermentation was complete. Stock ales would often be used to blend with beers of a lower strength but Pitfield's beer is offered at full strength and is a fascinating example of a style that went into rapid decline and disappearance in the 20th century.

Based on a farm in Essex, Martin Kemp and brewer Andy Skene use organic ingredients to fashion their beers. Maris Otter pale malt and crystal malt are supplied by Warminster Maltings in Wiltshire while Northdown hops comes from the major hop merchants, Charles Faram in Malvern, Worcestershire. Martin and Andy produce their Stock Ale as an annual vintage. The sample described here is a bottle from the 2008 vintage and was some four years old when tasted. The beer is bottle conditioned and there was a good 'hiss' of natural carbon dioxide when the cap was lifted: the CO_2 plus the lively head indicated the beer was in good condition. The glorious pale bronze colour and rich fruity nose have the appearance and aroma of fino sherry: the fruit develops on the nose with bitter oranges to the fore and hints of lime marmalade. The malt has a rich marzipan note, and fruit and malt sit on a solid base of gentle but persistent cedar wood hop resins. Tart fruit, a warming hit of alcohol, lightly toasted malt and increasing hop bitterness combine on the palate while the finish is bone dry with not a hint of cloying sweetness. The fruit is over-ripe, dominated by blood oranges, the marzipan note continues and the beer ends with firm hop bitterness, leaving a lingering finale of tangy fruit and hop resins at the back of the throat.

Porterhouse An Brain Blásta

Source: Porterhouse Brewing Co, Dublin, Ireland

Strength: 7%

Website: www.theporterhouse.ie

The blending of English and Irish needs no translation: this is a strong beer that should be treated with reverence to avoid damage to the brain cells. The story of Porterhouse is told in the Pale Ale section. When Oliver Hughes had established his first Porterhouse bar in Dublin, he added An Brain Blásta to his range as a beer for sipping rather than quaffing: the ideal companion for the meals served in all three Dublin bars and their counterparts in London and Manhattan.

The beer is a true Irish style, blending pale malt with roasted barley, with a touch of black malt and flaked barley. The hops are East Kent Goldings, Galena and Nugget. The deep copper-coloured beer has a luscious aroma of roasted grain, ripe raisin and sultana fruit and powerful bitter hop resins.

A cracker-like malt character develops in the mouth, melding with dark, burnt fruit and hop resins that offer a powerful herbal and bitter note. The finish is long and not sweet, the roasted grain providing its own bitter note, beautifully balanced by dark fruits and bitter hops. The beer poses a modest threat to the brain cells but beware the cocktail they serve in the Porterhouse bars, a blend of peach schnapps layered with Baileys and a dash of grenadine. It's called Brain Haemorrhage.

Sharp's Massive Ale

Source: Sharp's Brewery, Rock, Cornwall, England

Strength: 10%

Website: www.sharpsbrewery.co.uk

Sharp's has grown – boy, how it's grown! I was on holiday in Cornwall in 1994 and dropped in – to my family's despair – to a new small brewery at Rock. I discovered owner Bill Sharp inside a brewing vessel and, as it was a one-man operation able to produce 1,500 barrels a year, too busy to spend much time talking to me (to my family's delight). Today, despite its remote location, Sharp's is one of the biggest and most successful breweries in the country. It has changed hands twice, the last switch being a £20 million takeover in 2011 by the global brewing giant Molson Coors, whose British operation is based in Burton on Trent.

Doomsters, myself included, opined that this would spell the end of Sharp's as an independent brewery. Molson Coors, we added, would quickly close the Rock operation and would cherry pick the main Sharp's brands, Doom Bar in particular, and produce them in Burton. So far, we've been gloriously wrong. The group has invested £7.5 million at Rock, enabling production to rise to 200,000 barrels, and the group has not attempted to curb the enthusiasm of head brewer Stuart Howe. Stuart has a passion for both British and Belgian

beer and he often melds the two countries' styles in the beers he produces.

Massive is a case in point, with the use of dark candy sugar – a Belgian speciality – for colour, flavour and fermentability. The grains are Cocktail pale malt, crystal malt and roasted barley and three hops are used: Northdown, Northern Brewer and Perle. The amber-coloured beer has a rich fruity (blood orange) aroma with toasted malt and floral, grassy hop resins. In the mouth, the slightly sour fruit note builds, allied with ripe grain and increasingly bitter hop notes. The finish is long and bittersweet, the rich fruit blending well with ripe grain and bitter hop resins.

The beer enjoys a long ageing process. It's conditioned in cask for 18 months prior to bottling. It's then both warm and cold conditioned for six months before being released.

> *Stuart has a passion for both British and Belgian beer and he often melds the two countries' styles in the beers he produces.*

TASTING NOTES

APPEARANCE:

AROMA:

TASTE:

OVERALL SCORE:

Woodforde's Headcracker

Source: Woodforde's Norfolk Ales, Woodbastwick, Norfolk, England

Strength: 7%

Website: www.woodfordes.co.uk

TASTING NOTES

APPEARANCE:

AROMA:

TASTE:

OVERALL SCORE:

Woodforde's is named for an infamous Norfolk diarist and drinker called Parson Woodforde who was renowned for falling out of his pulpit after too much grog. But the religious connection might help explain how the brewery, founded in 1981, survived a disastrous fire at an earlier site and has gone on to great success in the pretty Broadlands village of Woodbastwick. The large brewery, with a capacity of 18,000 barrels a year, is based in attractive old farm buildings. Two former farm cottages have been converted into a brewery tap, the Fur & Feather, which not only sells the full Woodforde's range but has a resident chef who prepares excellent meals to accompany the beers.

The brewery has enjoyed remarkable success over the years in the Champion Beer of Britain and Champion Winter Beer competitions, winning gold and silver awards for Wherry Best Bitter, Mardler's Mild, Norfolk Nog and Headcracker. Headcracker has won the best barley wine award no fewer than three times in cask-conditioned form: it's also available bottle conditioned. It's brewed with Maris Otter pale malt and caramalt and is hopped with Goldings and Styrian Goldings. The colour is amber bright and the nose offers tempting aromas of caramel, vanilla, a muesli-like grain note, peppery hops and rich vinous fruits. Fruits, caramel and chewy grain build in the mouth, balanced by a solid contribution of spicy and bitter hops. The finish is long and bittersweet, the peppery hops countering the rich malt, tart fruit and caramel notes.

Headcracker has won the best barley wine award no fewer than three times in cask-conditioned form

Porters & Stouts

A frequently asked question at beer tastings and other events is: 'What *is* Porter?' The simple answer is 'A type of Stout' but that doesn't begin to explain the intriguing history of the style. When Porter burst upon the world in London early in the 18th century, it was the custom for brewers to call their strongest beers, regardless of colour, Stout. The description indicated strength, not the impact on the waistlines of regular drinkers. The clamour for Porter became so enormous – 'almost the universal cordial of the population', according to one contemporary writer – that brewers were forced to produce more than one version, of which the strongest was dubbed 'Stout Porter'. Over time, the Porter tag was dropped and the strong versions became known simply as Stout. Porter lingered on as the junior partner of the style but it largely disappeared from view in the 20th century as a result of the worldwide success of the Irish interpretations of Stout.

Courage Russian Imperial Stout

The great beer revival of the late 20th century and early 21st has led to brewers delving into old brewing books and records. As a result, hundreds of brewers, mainly in Britain and the United States and, more recently, a new wave of brewers in Ireland, has led to Porter and Stout enjoying a revival that was once considered impossible, due to the global hegemony of one brand: from the late 19th century to the close of the 20th, Stout was Guinness and Guinness was Stout.

There is considerable dispute over the origins of Porter: otherwise amicable beer writers engage in verbal fisticuffs on the subject. Put aside the hyperbole and finger-jabbing, it now seems clear that Porter was first brewed in the 1720s. Far from being 'invented' by Ralph Harwood at the Bell Brewhouse in Shoreditch, East London, Porter was a development of the brown beers popular at the time. Harwood, as many 18th century writers reported, undoubtedly produced a beer called 'entire butt'. But he was not the only brewer in town and his site was too small to meet the demand for well-hopped and refreshing beer.

The capital was changing rapidly from a number of loosely-connected boroughs and villages into a sprawling metropolis. Workers forced from the countryside as a result of land enclosures were herded into factories, docks and markets in London and they needed constant refreshment from beer rich in protein. A popular beer of the time was called 'three threads' or 'three thirds', a mixture of 'twopenny ale', brown ale and stale. Twopenny was pale ale, produced by country brewers and sold at twice the price of London beers, hence the name. Country brewers were able to produce pale ale as they had access to coal-fired kilns which gave maltsters much more control over the tempreature of the kilning process, allowing paler malts to be produced. A tax on the use of coal in cities forced London brewers to kiln their malt over wood fires, which produced a darker malt, ideal for brown ale, but which was no use for producing their own pale ale. Stale was a beer aged in wooden vats for a year or more, which had a sour and lactic tang as a result of attack by wild yeasts and other organisms in the wood. Harwood and other London brewers and publicans jibbed at the cost of twopenny ale. They needed to produce and sell beer as cheaply as possible for a fast-growing population of poorly-paid workers. To achieve this aim, the London brewers were determined to break the grip of their country cousins.

Curious Porter

The Barclay Perkins brewhouse at Southwark in the mid-nineteenth century

Harwood and other brewers were aided by the development of better-quality brown malt – 'high-blown' malt – in the Hertfordshire town of Ware that supplied most of the malt to the capital, delivered by boats along the River Lea. The new malt and generous amounts of hops enabled London brewers to produce a beer that met with favour among their customers. It was first called entire butt beer as it was served from just one cask or butt in pub cellars instead of being blended from three different casks. It was cheaper to produce than three threads and was easier to deliver from cellar to bar. It served the twin aim of cutting out the country brewers and their twopenny ale and making bigger profits. It rapidly took on the name of Porter as a result of its popularity among the thousands of porters who worked the streets, the docks and the markets of London.

In *The Complete English Brewer* by George Watkins, published in 1773, he described Porter brewing as follows: 'Thus, in brewing Porter, they [brewers] make three and sometimes four mashes; strengthening them with a little fresh malt, or running them as they call it a greater length, that is, making more beer from the same malt, according to their pleasure. These several worts they mix and make the whole of such strength as experience shews them Porter ought to have; and this they work up and barrel accordingly. In the same manner, if a butt of Porter be too mild, they will throw into it a small quantity of some that is very strong and too stale, first dissolv-ing in it a little isinglass. This produces a new tho' slight fermentation; and the liquor, in 18 or 20 days, fines down and has the expected flavour.'

Books on brewing in the early 18th century contain few if any mentions of Porter and Stout. Yet by the 1750s it had become the dominant style in London. Samuel Whitbread, who became one of the most successful, and richest, Porter brewers, opened a small brewery in Old Street in 1742. He was close to Harwood's brewhouse and the bigger Calvert's brewery and he monitored the rapid development of Porter. Whitbread at first brewed amber beer but within just three years he moved to bigger premises in the Barbican district, where he brewed just Porter and Stout. The Whitbread brewery became one of the wonders of the industrial age. Beer had never been produced on such a scale before. In 1787, King George III and Queen Charlotte went to see the 'stupendous' steam engine installed by James Watt. The Porter Tun Room had an unsupported roof span 'of which it is exceeded in its majestic size by that of Westminster Hall', one report said.

At first Whitbread rented 54 buildings in London to store his beer, where it was aged for between four and five months. But from 1760 the beer was matured in enormous underground cisterns at the brewery, each one containing 4,000 barrels. The cisterns were cooled by internal copper piping through which cold water was pumped to keep the maturing beer in good condition during hot weather.

Brewing was no longer a seasonal activity: the technical advances made by the Industrial Revolution enabled beer to be made all year round.

One of the advances was the widespread production of pale malt cured or 'kilned' over coke fires. The lifting of the coal tax made the production of pale malt widespread. It contained a far higher proportion of the enzymes that turn starch into fermentable sugar during the brewing process than was present in brown malt cured over wood fires. As a result, brewers needed less malt to produce beer, which improved their profitability. In order to give Porter and Stout the necessary colour expected by drinkers, brewers added molasses, Spanish liquorice and muscovado sugar to their brews. Less scrupulous brewers added opium, tobacco and extract of poppies. In 1816 the government banned all 'adulterants', as some brewers were poisoning their customers.

The brewers' dilemma of how to colour their Porter was solved for them a year later when Daniel Wheeler invented a malt roaster based on the principle of the coffee roasting machine. The roaster kilned malt to high temperatures of around 450 degrees Fahrenheit or 210 degrees Celsius. The deep brown or black malts had little or no fermentable sugars but, said Wheeler, 'will suffice for the purpose of colouring beer or Porter.' Porter and Stout changed from dark brown beers into the jet black brews recognised today.

The use of roasted grains changed the flavour of Porter and Stout, adding a bitter, charred and slightly acrid taste. This was especially true of the Irish versions of the style. The whole of Ireland was part of the United Kingdom and there were no fetters to imports from the mainland. Irish brewers were dismayed by the vast quantities of Porter and Stout that poured into the country from London, Bristol, Liverpool and later Edinburgh and Glasgow. In the manner of Sam Whitbread, Arthur Guinness had started out as humble producer of ale in Dublin. But by 1787 he was brewing Porter, too, and in 1799 he phased out all other types of beer in order to concentrate on Porter and Stout. In Cork, Beamish & Murphy followed suit and they were later joined by the Murphy brothers in Ireland's second city. The Guinness family astutely built its business internally and externally with such beers as X, XX and Foreign Export Stout until it was for a period the biggest

brewer in the world. Single X was known as Plain Porter in Dublin, immortalised by Irish writer and humorist Flann O'Brien in his book *At Swim-Two-Birds*. Plain was dropped by Guinness in the 1970s but has been revived by the Porterhouse Brewery in Dublin. The use of substantial amounts of roasted malt – changed to unmalted roasted barley in the 1930s – gave Irish Stouts a distinctive dry and bitter character.

The rise of the Irish Stout brewers did not stop its growth in Britain. It spread out from its working-class base with stronger versions such as 'robust Porter' that appealed to the better-off. By 1845, the East London brewer Truman, Hanbury & Buxton brewed 305,000 barrels a year of Porter and Stout and was second in size only to Bass in Burton on Trent. On the other side of the Thames, Barclay Perkins and Courage were also major producers of the style and became leading exporters with their imperial Porters and Stouts for the Baltic states.

Burton pale ales and milder brown beers started to nibble away at the dominant position of Porter and Stout but the biggest blow came in World War One. The government was determined that nothing should stand in the way of the war effort and the manufacture of dark, roasted malts was banned as a result of the extra energy they consumed. Such a ban could not be imposed on the increasingly rebellious Irish.

> ❝ *The new malt enabled London brewers to produce a beer that met with favour among their customers. It was first called entire butt beer as it was served from just one cask or butt in pub cellars instead of being blended from three different casks.* ❞

As a result, Irish Stout reigned supreme. Today, the British drink more Guinness Stout per head than any other country in the world. But slowly in the 1990s and now with gathering pace, brewers in Britain and the U.S. have proved there is more to Porter and Stout than just one global brand while in Ireland craft brewers are daring to challenge the Dublin behemoth. Once again in the bars of the Irish capital drinkers can raise a glass of the black stuff and sagely announce 'A pint of Plain is your only man'.

Acorn Gorlovka Imperial Stout

Source: Acorn Brewery, Barnsley, South Yorkshire, England

Strength: 6%

Website: www.acorn-brewery.co.uk

We encountered Dave Hughes and his Barnsley brewery as the very first entry in this book, a man with a great passion for India Pale Ale. But he has also turned his attention to another English beer style that achieved fame in the 18th and 19th centuries. A major London brewer, Thrales – later Barclay Perkins – based in Southwark on the south bank of the Thames exported strong versions of its Porter to Russia and the Baltic States. The beer found favour at the court of Catherine the Great and it was given a royal warrant, allowing it to be called Imperial Stout. The full story is told in this section under Courage.

Acorn's interpretation is named in honour of Gorlovka, Barnsley's twin town in Ukraine. It's available in both cask and bottle-conditioned form and is brewed with Maris Otter pale malt, crystal malt and roasted barley. A single hop variety is used: Challenger. It has a ruby/black colour and a thick collar of foam. The aroma is rich in liquorice, cocoa powder, roasted grain, dark fruit and peppery hops. Bitter hops build in the mouth along with roasted grain, liquorice, cocoa and burnt fruit. The long and bitter finish offers spicy hops, burnt fruit, liquorice, cocoa and roasted grain.

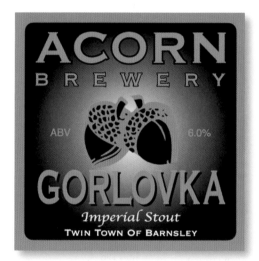

Acorn's interpretation is named in honour of Gorlovka, Barnsley's twin town in Ukraine

Bartrams Comrade Bill Bartram's Egalitarian Anti-Imperialist Soviet Stout

Source: Bartrams Brewery, Rougham, Bury St Edmunds, Suffolk, England

Strength: 6.9%

Website: www.bartramsbrewery.co.uk

Marc Bartram proves that a sense of humour helps brew and sell good beer. There was a Bill Bartram who ran a brewery in Suffolk in the late 19th century but Marc – no relation – has turned him into a local folk hero of mythical proportions. Even the usually cynical media has swallowed the story that Bill served with Admiral Lord Nelson at the Battle of Trafalgar and was also Lord Kitchener's batman in World War One. If true, Bill would have had a remarkable life span. The stout named in his dubious honour suggests he was also around at the time of the Russian Revolution in 1917, which would have made him a very Old Bolshevik indeed.

Marc's brewery, founded in 1999, is based on Rougham Airfield that was an important base for the United States Air Force during World War Two. It's now used for light aircraft and open air events – plus brewing. Marc has a four-barrel plant that produces a large range of beers, 17 in all, in both cask and bottle. His Stout is brewed with Maris Otter pale malt, both light and dark crystal malts,

amber and chocolate malts, and a small amount of roasted barley – 'not too much, as it makes the beer too bitter', Marc says. He uses Galena hops for a long, two-hour boil in the copper and finishes with an addition of East Kent Goldings.

This anti-imperialist imperial Stout has a deep ruby colour with a robust aroma of chocolate, bitter coffee, dark fruit, roasted grain and peppery hops. Chocolate builds in the mouth with continuing contributions from espresso coffee, raisin fruit, smoky grain and bitter hop resins. The finish is long and complex with rich smoky malt, dark fruit, chocolate, coffee and peppery hops making bold contributions.

The beer has won many awards, including CAMRA's Best East Anglian Stout and a gold from the Society of Independent Brewers. It was – with a delicious touch of irony – named Best Stout at a beer festival in St Petersburg in modern Russia. Comrade Bill would have been proud to win the award but sad to find that his beloved Leningrad had returned to its old Tsarist name.

TASTING NOTES

APPEARANCE:

AROMA:

TASTE:

OVERALL SCORE:

Batemans Salem Porter

Source: George Bateman & Son, Salem Bridge Brewery, Wainfleet, Lincolnshire, England
Strength: 4.7%
Website: www.bateman.co.uk

The pump clip for this beer shows a witch on a broomstick and while Wainfleet is some distance from Salem in Massachusetts, scene of the infamous witchcraft trials in the late 17th century, there is a possible connection. Salem Bridge crosses the River Steeping in a market town that was once an important port. Wainfleet is close to the bigger port of Boston, sailing point for many of the Puritans who left for New England. They took East of England names with them, such as Boston and Essex County, where the city of Salem stands. In Massachusetts, the received wisdom is that Salem is derived from the Arabic *salaam* or the Hebrew *shalom*, meaning peace. But in Lincolnshire the name comes from 'safe home': sailors and fishermen braving the North Sea who returned to harbour in Wainfleet were said to be safe home and you wonder whether that could be the source of the American city's name.

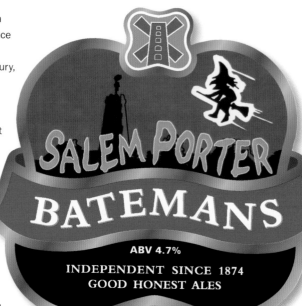

We can be certain of the following: Batemans enjoys an idyllic location by the river, the site dominated by a creeper-clad old windmill where grain for brewing used to be ground. The company was founded by George Bateman in 1874 and has been in family hands ever since. It's now run by siblings Stuart and Jaclyn: Stuart is managing director and looks after sales to both 68 pubs and a large free trade, while marketing director Jaclyn busily exports beer to many countries, including Russia, Scandinavia and the United States. I don't know if Salem Porter has reached Massachusetts but it's a beer that deserves to be given a trial there.

Batemans is living proof that dark beers can find approval. Its Dark Mild featured in *300 Beers to Try Before You Die!* and Salem Porter is a regular cask ale. Head Brewer Martin Cullimore has moved from such traditional malting barleys as Maris Otter

and prefers more modern varieties. He uses Flagon but may also use Concerto, Optic or Tipple. He blends in crystal malt, roasted barley and invert sugar: the finished beer has 120 colour units. The hops are Challenger and Goldings, which create 36 units of bitterness. The deep brown/black beer has a powerful aroma of roasted grain, almonds and liquorice with spicy hop notes. Roasted grain, dark vinous fruits, liquorice, nuts and peppery hops fill the mouth while the finish offers continuing contributions from liquorice, bitter, spicy hops, roasted barley and burnt fruits.

The brewery is just a few yards from Wainfleet railway station, on the line from Grantham or Nottingham to Skegness. It has a visitor centre and small museum, and you can enjoy a beer in a spacious bar inside the old windmill.

Beowulf Dragon Smoke Stout

Source: Beowulf Brewing Company, Brownhills, Staffordshire, England
Strength: 4.7% draught; 5.3% bottle
Website: www.beowulfbrewery.com

The story of Beowulf Brewery is, of course, a saga (see also Dark Raven in the Mild & Brown Ales section). When founder Phil Bennett launched his brewery in 1996, he was determined to dedicate his beers to the epic poem of Anglo-Saxon England, while the brewery's helmet logo was inspired by an item of military headgear found, along with fabulous treasure, in the burial ship of a king of East Anglia unearthed at Sutton Hoo, near Woodbridge in Suffolk, in 1938. Many of the brewery's beers are dark, reflecting the type of ale that would have been drunk in the medieval period.

In 2004, Beowulf relocated to Chasewater Country Park in Staffordshire – famed for its superb brewing water – with units designed and built to reflect medieval architecture. Cask beers are delivered to pubs within a 50-mile radius of the brewery while bottle-conditioned versions are sold further afield.

The Stout, which won an award in the 2010 Champion Winter of Beer of Britain competition, commemorates the dragon slain by Beowulf in the saga. It's brewed with pale and black malts, roasted barley and flaked barley. The hops are Goldings and Pilgrim. As the name promises, it has a smoky aroma and palate from the dark grains with a smooth and creamy note from the flaked barley, which is popcorn by another name, and gives a good head of foam to the finished beer. Bitter chocolate and espresso coffee give a tempting character to the nose and are given full expression in the mouth, along with dark and mysterious fruits, as befits the inspiration for the Stout. There's a good underpinning of peppery hops and a long, smooth finish packed with rich fruit and grain. The bottled version is primed with sugar to encourage a strong second fermentation.

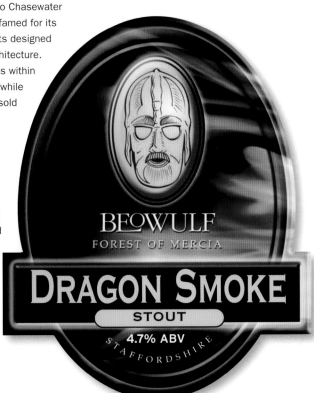

Bristol Beer Factory Milk Stout

Source: Bristol Beer Factory, Bristol, England

Strength: 4.5%

Website: www.bristolbeerfactory.co.uk

They're keen on stouts at this brewery, so much so that for Christmas 2012 they brewed 12 different versions of the style. Bristol Beer Factory is a 10-barrel plant in the Ashton district of the city, once famous or infamous for its tobacco factories. The current brewery is in part of the Ashton Gate Brewery that closed in 1933: the premises give manager Andrew Cooper and brewers Chris Kay and Brett Ellis plenty of room to expand – and demand for the beers suggests they will have to spread their wings.

The devotion to porter and stout fits the brewing history of Bristol. In the 18th and 19th century, George's Brewery achieved fame as one of the great English porter brewers. It used the port and sea to export widely and once sent a salesman on a daunting tour of Ireland by horseback to drum up sales. George's became part of the large Courage group, which eventually closed the plant in 1999.

Bristol's Milk Stout won the porter and stout category of the Champion Winter Beer of Britain competition in 2009. Milk stout is yet another variant of the style and was once one of the most popular beers in Britain post World War Two, when Mackeson Stout was a massive brand. The beer was developed in 1907 by the Mackeson brewery in Hythe, Kent, and used lactose – milk sugar – along with conventional malt and hops. Lactose, a by-product of cheese making, cannot be fermented by conventional brewer's yeast and gives a creamy but not overly sweet note to beer. As a result of several takeovers, Mackeson became a Whitbread beer in the 1920s. In bottled form in the 1950s and 60s, it was for a period the biggest beer in Whitbread's substantial portfolio, accounting for half its annual production. During the war, the government forced the brewery to remove a milk churn from the label as it gave the impression it was brewed using real milk rather than lactose powder (the milk churn returned later). After the war, Whitbread employed a well-known actor, Bernard Miles – the founder of London's Mermaid Theatre, who was later knighted – to advertise the beer with the slogan 'It looks good, it tastes good and, by golly, it does you good', sensible advice that would be illegal today. It was one of the earliest advertisements to appear on commercial television in Britain in the 1950s.

Mackeson, now owned by AB In-Bev, is difficult to find today and it's good to see that the Bristol Beer Factory has revived this fascinating twist on the Stout theme. Lactose powder is added to the copper during the boil with Challenger and Fuggles hops. The grains are Maris Otter pale malt, with crystal and chocolate malts and roasted barley. The black beer has a rich and inviting aroma of creamy malt, chocolate, roasted grain and dark fruits, with a gentle underpinning of spicy hops. Creamy and slightly sweet malt builds in the mouth but is well balanced by hops, burnt fruit and chocolate. The finish is complex, creamy malt vying for attention with fruit, chocolate and hops. The beer is available in both cask and bottle-conditioned forms.

Chiltern The Lord Lieutenant's Porter

Source: **Chiltern Brewery, Terrick, Buckinghamshire, England**

Strength: **6%**

Website: **www.chilternbrewery.co.uk**

Porters & Stouts

The Jenkinson family that runs the Chiltern brewery take a deep interest in local history. The area was a key battleground during the English Civil War in the 17th century. The brewery's pub, the King's Head in Aylesbury, was used as his headquarters by Oliver Cromwell during the protracted battles with the king's forces. One of Chiltern's beers is named in honour of John Hampden, the local Member of Parliament and deputy lieutenant of Buckinghamshire, who died fighting for the parliamentary cause. He is equally revered in the United States, where several towns in New England bear his name as well as an entire county in Massachusetts.

Chiltern Brewery was founded by Richard and Lesley Jenkinson in 1980 and was at the forefront of the micro-brewing revolution. The company is now run by their sons Tom and George and in 2000, to celebrate 20 years of brewing, they launched their Porter, with the mash started by the then-holder of the office of Lord Lieutenant of Buckinghamshire, Sir Nigel Mobbs.

The beer, head brewer Tom Jenkinson says, was inspired by the London Porters of the 18th century and he uses only English materials: Maris Otter pale malt with chocolate and crystal malts and Challenger, Fuggles and Goldings hops. In the style of the early porters, it's a ruby red rather than jet black beer with a lively collar of foam. It has a smoky aroma from the dark and roasted malts, a hint of green apple fruit, bitter chocolate, fresh tobacco and spicy hops. The palate is bittersweet with dark roasted grain, tart fruit, chocolate and hop resins. The finish is notable for its dry chocolate character along with green apple, tangy hops, tobacco and spicy hop resins.

Cigar City Marshal Zhukov's Imperial Stout

Source: **Cigar City Brewing, Tampa, Florida, USA**

Strength: **11%**

Website: **www.cigarcitybrewing.com**

You can tell the Cold War is dead and buried when a brewery in Florida names a beer in honour of a Hero of the Soviet Union. Marshal Georgy Zhukov was the most decorated soldier in the history of the USSR. It was his military skills that helped defeat the Nazi invasion of his country and enabled him to lead the march on Berlin that effectively ended World War Two. He later became Minister for Defence.

The story of Cigar City Brewing is told in the Brown & Mild Ales section. Their Stout is a true imperial with an impressive and historically true level of alcohol. It's brewed every summer then aged in the brewery before it's released for winter drinking. The grains are two-row pale malt, with black patent malt, crystal, chocolate and Munich malt and roasted barley. The hops – Brewers Gold and Magnum – create a mighty 80 units of bitterness. Brewer Wayne Wambles occasionally replaces Brewers Gold with Mount Rainier, which, he says, gives a liquorice note to the beer. It has a head the colour of mocha coffee with a massive aroma of espresso coffee, dark chocolate and liquorice, with some peppery hops bold enough to show their head. The palate is a stunning blend of roasted grain, bitter hops, burnt fruit, coffee and chocolate, while the finish has some lingering sweetness from the rich blend of dark malts. But peppery hops, coffee and burnt fruit continue to make their mark.

Courage Imperial Russian Stout

Source: Wells & Young's Brewing Company, Bedford, England

Strength: 10%

Website: www.wellsandyoungs.co.uk

A beer of profound historical importance has been revived by Wells & Young's. There is neat symmetry in the revival, for head brewer Jim Robertson brewed one of the last batches of Imperial Russian Stout at Courage's brewery close to Tower Bridge in London. Jim is therefore in a strong position to recreate an authentic interpretation of a beer that was exported in vast quantities to Russia and the Baltic in the 18th and 19th centuries.

The story of Russian Stout begins at the Anchor Brewery in Southwark on the south bank of the River Thames. The brewery was built on the site of Shakespeare's Globe Theatre, which was destroyed by fire: in another piece of neat history, the revived Globe Theatre, opened in 1997 as a near-as-possible recreation of the original, now stands on the site of the old Anchor Brewery. In 1693 the brewery was bought by Edmund Halsey, the son of a miller from St Albans in Hertfordshire. He bought his nephew Ralph Thrale into the business and eventually sold it to him for £30,000. In 1758 Ralph Thrale passed the business to his son Henry, who turned the site not only into a successful and expanding business, producing 30,000 barrels a year, but also into a vibrant centre for respectable society. He married the socialite Hester Salusbury, who encouraged the essayist and lexicographer Dr Samuel Johnson to lodge and work in rooms in the brewery. Johnson in turn urged Mrs Thrale to write and he presented her with journals in which she recorded social life in Southwark under the title of Thraliana. Lavish dinners were held at the brewery. One took place in a new copper and was attended by such luminaries of the arts as Johnson, Sir Joshua Reynolds, Sir Oliver Goldsmith and David Garrick.

> *The story of Russian Stout begins at the Anchor Brewery in Southwark on the south bank of the River Thames.*

Henry Thrale died in 1781 and the business was sold within a month to the brewery clerk John Perkins and David Barclay, a rich Quaker and member of the banking family. They paid £135,000 for the business and Dr Johnson was so keen to cash in his shares in the brewery that he coined the less than harmonious aphorism: 'We are not here to sell a parcel of boilers and vats, but the potentiality of growing rich beyond the dreams of avarice.'

The new company, Barclay Perkins, grew apace. By 1809 it was the biggest brewery in London, with an annual production of 205,000 barrels. In common with most brewers in the capital, including its near neighbour John Courage at Horselydown, Barclay Perkins concentrated on producing Mild ale, Porter and Stout, beer styles best suited to London's sodium-rich water. Before the change of ownership, Thrale from the 1780s had started to export substantial quantities of strong Porter to Bremen, Stettin, Kaliningrad and other Baltic ports. A writer who visited the brewery in 1796 recorded that he had drunk Porter that was brewed specially for Catherine, the Empress of Russia, and 'would keep for seven years'. The author of *The History and Antiquities of the Parish of St Saviour, Southwark* wrote that 'the reputation of enjoyment of Porter is by no means confined to England. As proof of the truth of this assertion, this house [Thrale's] exports annually very large quantities; so far extended are its commercial connections that Thrale's intire [Porter] is well known, as a delicious beverage, from the frozen regions of Russia to the burning sands of Bengal and Sumatra. The Empress of All Russia is indeed so partial to Porter that she has ordered repeatedly very large quantities for her own drinking and that of her court.'

Exports to Russia and the Baltic were organised for Barclay Perkins by a Belgian businessman, Albert Le Coq. His name was discovered a century later when cargo was retrieved in 1974 from the wreck of a Prussian ship, the Oliva, which had ended up on the Baltic seabed in 1869. The cargo included a batch of Barclays Imperial Russian Stout, embossed with the name 'A Le Coq'. The Belgian had been granted an imperial warrant from the Russian court for donating 5,000 bottles of stout to soldiers wounded in the Crimean War and the warrant enabled the beer to carry the title of Imperial. In the early 20th century, heavy tariffs were imposed on exports to Russia and Le Coq's company decided to build a brewery in Tartu, now in modern Estonia, to supply beer free from import tax. But the venture was short lived. The Bolshevik government in 1917 nationalised the brewery, which then concentrated on lager beer. (See *300 Beers to Try Before You Die!* for Harvey's Imperial Extra Double Stout, based on Le Coq's recipe, and Le Coq Porter, brewed once again in Estonia).

With exports to the Soviet Union difficult if not impossible in the 20th century, Barclays Russian Stout became a small niche brand in Britain. In 1955, Barclays Perkins merged with its neighbour, Courage, and the beer was re-branded Courage Imperial Russian Stout. When the Courage brewery closed in the 1980s, production of Stout was transferred to John Smith's in Tadcaster, Yorkshire. Both breweries had become part of Scottish & Newcastle and the production of the small volume of Stout soon ceased. In 2007, Wells & Young's bought the rights to the Courage brands and it fell to Jim Robertson to rekindle the beer he had brewed near Tower Bridge in the 1980s. Jim says the Stout is different to any other beer he has ever brewed and the computer software at the Bedford brewery had to be rewritten to make production possible. Twice the levels of raw materials are used to brew the stout than for regular beers and only 120 hectolitre/73 barrel batches can be made at a time. A total of 6,326 kilos of grain and syrup are used. The grain is comprised of pale, amber and chocolate malts, with the addition of wort syrup to reach a starting gravity of 1100 degrees. Amber and chocolate malts account for 25 per cent of the grist.

Jim adds 55 kilos of Styrian Goldings hops in the copper: Fuggles were originally used in the days of Thrales and Barclay Perkins. The finished beer has 60 units of bitterness and 200 colour units. The first fermentation is 'fierce', Jim says, and after 80 hours

the fermenting wort is cooled to stop fermentation going too far. Some of the yeast is cropped out and the 'green', unfinished beer is transferred to a warm conditioning area of the brewery, where it's aged for two months on a bed of Styrians. This, Jim says, is critical for the formation of the beer's character. At the end of warm conditioning, the beer is chilled to minus one degree Celsius to drop out yeast and protein, and the unfiltered beer is then bottled. There are sufficient yeast, protein and hop materials left in the beer to enable it to mature: Jim Robertson says it will continue to age and improve for 13 years. Historically, Jim adds, the beer – sent in magnum bottles and hogshead casks – was inoculated with a second yeast strain but he feels this is unnecessary and uses his house culture throughout the process.

The first batches were exported to the U.S. and Australia in 2012. It was made available in Britain in 2013.

The jet black beer has a stunning aroma of leather, tobacco, freshly-roasted coffee beans, dark, burnt fruits, liquorice, newly-planed wood and spicy hops. Smooth, creamy malt, bitter hops, dark fruits, liquorice, coffee and rich chocolate coat the mouth, followed by a finish of enormous length in which dark malts, fruit, coffee, chocolate, liquorice and spicy hops vie for attention.

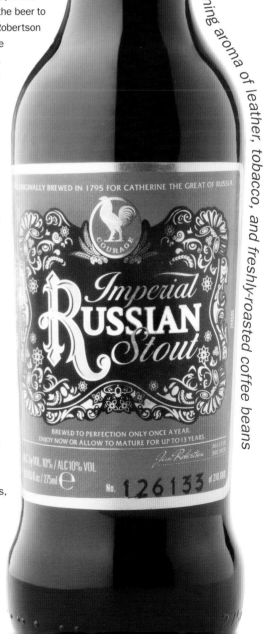

The jet black beer has a stunning aroma of leather, tobacco, and freshly-roasted coffee beans

TASTING NOTES

APPEARANCE:

AROMA:

TASTE:

OVERALL SCORE:

Curious Porter

Source: English Wines, Tenterden, Kent, England
Strength: 5%
Website: www.chapeldown.com

We encountered Curious IPA earlier in this book. English Wines has continued its association with Andy Hepworth at his Horsham brewery, with a faithful recreation of a London Porter from the 18th and 19th centuries. English Wines, whose products are sold under the Chapel Down Vineyard label, works closely with Andy to ensure the beers are made strictly to recipe and aged to develop full, rich flavours. In the case of the Porter, the beer is conditioned with oak to replicate the character of the original style.

The beer is brewed with a complex grist of pale, amber, black, chocolate and crystal malts and is hopped with Admiral, a rare hop grown in Sussex, with a late addition of Goldings in the copper. This is what American beer competitions call a brown porter, topped by a big fluffy head of foam. There is a smoky, oaky aroma with hints of our old breakfast friend: toast and Marmite, and a spicy hop note. Vanilla from the oak makes a marked presence in the mouth with creamy malt, dark macerated fruit and increasingly bitter hops. The finish is bittersweet, with bitter hops balanced by creamy malt, dark fruit and continuing vanilla and oak notes. The beer has a modest strength for the style but is refreshing and rewarding.

Einstök Icelandic Toasted Porter

Source: Einstök Ölgerd, Akureyri, Iceland

Strength: 6%

Website: einstokbeer.com

Einstök means unique in Icelandic and brewmaster Baldur Karason and his team believe there isn't a brewery anywhere in the world quite like theirs. The story of the brewery is, like a Viking saga, the quest for the finest brewing water on the planet (see Pale Ale section). It was founded in Akureyri, just 60 miles south of the Arctic Circle in a fishing port where water flows down from prehistoric glaciers and through lava fields. Baldur describes it as the purest water in the world and ideal for brewing.

Baldur worked as a food scientist at the Viking Brewery, also based in Akureyri. In 1993, to develop his brewing skills, he studied at Heriot-Watt University's School of Brewing in Edinburgh and returned to take up the role of brewmaster at Viking. The owners of the brewery agreed to set up a subsidiary, Einstök, to produce handcrafted ales while Viking concentrates on mainstream lager beers.

Toasted Porter is brewed with lager, Munich and chocolate malts. Bavarian hops are used and Icelandic coffee is added during the kettle boil. The brewery describes the colour of the beer as 'sinister' and says 'don't be afraid of the dark'. There's no need to approach it with trepidation as it has a delightful aroma of freshly-ground coffee beans, liquorice, chocolate and toffee, with a gentle underpinning of floral hops. Coffee and chocolate build in the full, rich palate while the finish offers a pleasing note of spicy hops that balance the rich, creamy dark malt and chocolate and coffee notes.

The brewery describes the colour of the beer as 'sinister' and says 'don't be afraid of the dark'

TASTING NOTES

APPEARANCE:

AROMA:

TASTE:

OVERALL SCORE:

TASTING NOTES

APPEARANCE:

AROMA:

TASTE:

OVERALL SCORE:

Elland 1872 Porter

Source: Elland Brewery, Elland, West Yorkshire, England

Strength: 6.5%

Website: www.ellandbrewery.co.uk

Elland's Porter, based on an authentic Yorkshire recipe from 1872, has won an impressive number of awards, including a gold medal in 2004 in the International Brewing Awards competition; Supreme Champion Beer in CAMRA's winter competition in 2010; and a further gold medal from the Society of Independent Brewers in 2011.

The brewery was first called Eastwood & Sanders following the amalgamation in 2002 of the Barge & Barrel Brewery and West Yorkshire Brewery. It was renamed Elland in 2006 to stress its links with the town. It can produce 50 barrels a week and beers are supplied to some 150 outlets.

The 1872 Porter, available in both cask and bottle-conditioned formats, is brewed with pale, amber, brown and chocolate malts, and the hops are two English varieties, Northdown and Target. As a result of its strength, the beer has a rich and entrancing aroma of coffee and bitter chocolate, with a delicious port wine note and good peppery hop note. Coffee, chocolate, roasted grain, dark fruit and bitter hops build in the mouth while the long, dry and bitter finish is balanced by dark fruit and continuing notes of coffee, chocolate and port.

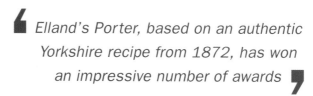

Elland's Porter, based on an authentic Yorkshire recipe from 1872, has won an impressive number of awards

Firestone Walker's Reserve Porter

Source: Firestone Walker Brewing Co, Paso Robles, California, USA

Strength: 5.8%

Website: www.firestonebeer.com

The 'Burton Union' system of fermentation travels well. Adam Firestone and David Walker, founders of the brewery, were so entranced by the system still used by Marston's in Burton on Trent in central England that they designed their own version.

The system was developed in the 19th century to cleanse pale ale of yeast, delivering a sparkling glass of beer to the consumer. It involves a series of wooden casks linked together – 'held in union', the Victorians said. As wort ferments, natural carbon dioxide drives some of the liquid and yeast from the casks and up into receiving trays above, where the yeast is retained.

Firestone and Walker are brothers-in-law whose passion for good beer encouraged them to open their own brewery. They use the union system as they believe it not only removes yeast from beer but delivers fullness of palate and enhanced hop character. They claim to be the only American brewery to use the method.

Unlike the Burton brewers, Firestone and Walker don't build new oak casks but source 60-barrel containers from the bourbon whiskey business. Fermenting beer stays in the barrel for six days before it's racked into stainless steel vessels where a second fermentation takes place. Some of the brewery's special reserve beers are then aged in wood for up to three years and gain whiskey, espresso coffee, plum, cherry and tobacco notes.

Robust Porter is brewed with American two-row barley malt, imported Maris Otter pale malt, crystal, carafa and chocolate malts, with wheat and oats. American Goldings are used as the bittering hop, with a late addition of East Kent Goldings in the kettle. Cascades are used in the hop whirlpool prior to primary fermentation. The finished beer has 45 units of bitterness.

The beer has a deep ruby-red colour with a head of foam the colour of custard cream biscuits. The aroma has a rich cappuccino coffee note, with powerful hints of oak, bourbon, vanilla, liquorice, burnt fruit and smoked grain. Rich roasted grain, dark fruits, coriander, dried herbs and peppery hops fill the mouth. The finish has smoked malt, bitter hops, dark, rich fruits and coffee and chocolate notes. It's an amazingly deep and complex beer that won a silver medal in the 2009 World Beer Championship and has twice won major awards in Australia's international beer competition.

TASTING NOTES

APPEARANCE:

AROMA:

TASTE:

OVERALL SCORE:

Franciscan Well Shandon Stout

Source: Franciscan Well Brewery, Cork, Ireland

Strength: 4.3%

Website: www.franciscanwellbrewery.com

The modern brewery and pub on Cork's North Mall stands on a site that housed a Franciscan monastery from 1216. As the name suggests, the monastery had its own well, which the monks used to brew ale. Sadly, while the well can be viewed, it has dried up and head brewer Peter Lyall and his team use the public supply. The brewery opened in 1998 and is at the heart of the Irish beer revival. Every year Franciscan Well is host to a gathering of the 20-or-so small craft breweries operating in Ireland that are bringing much needed choice and diversity to an island dominated for decades by two giants, Guinness and Murphy's. As those giants are now owned by foreign companies – Diageo and Heineken – there is plenty of scope for small breweries to expand in a country proud of its independence.

The pub is wonderfully atmospheric. From the street, you walk down a long corridor framed by ancient curved brick walls, and turn right into the dimly-lit, cavernous main bar. Beyond there are more spacious bars and a beer garden while to the right is the large brewhouse where Peter and his team create half-a-dozen regular beers and many seasonal brews on their 11.5 hectolitre plant imported from Canada, which includes four stainless steel conical fermenting vessels. Peter is meticulous in his choice of raw materials and also his yeast cultures: he has three different cultures for ale, lager and wheat beers. He uses 11 varieties of pellet hops from Britain, the Czech Republic, Germany and the United States and imports the finest Maris Otter pale malt from England as the base for many of his beers. Peter bubbles with enthusiasm for brewing and conducts tours of the brewery. He looks upon himself as a chef as much as a brewer: 'beer is like making a stew,' he says, 'and I add the vegetables – the hops – at the start of the boil in the kettle.'

He is equally passionate about beer styles and says Cork Stout is subtly different to the Dublin version. The beer, named after the Shandon district of Cork, is unfiltered and is served by mixed gas at the bar. It's brewed with Irish ale malt, roasted barley and wheat malt and the hops are two English varieties, Fuggles and Target. The ruby/black beer has a powerful aroma of chocolate and coffee, roasted grain and spicy hops. Coffee and roasted grain dominate the palate, with further contributions from burnt fruit and peppery hops. Smoky malt, dark fruit, coffee and bitter hops combine in the long finish.

In late 2012, Shane Long, owner of the brewery, announced he was planning a new, stand-alone brewery in Cork that would have four times the capacity of the original site, which will remain in operation. In 2013 Molston Coors bought the company and will concentrate on brewing Stout for the American market. But the original brewpub will remain in operation.

Every year Franciscan Well is host to a gathering of the 20-or-so small craft breweries operating in Ireland that are bringing much needed diversity

Hop Back Entire Stout

Source: Hop Back Brewery, Downton, Salisbury, Wiltshire, England

Strength: 4.5%

Website: www.hopback.co.uk

Hop Back has come a long way since John Gilbert installed a four-barrel plant in the cellar of his pub, the Wyndham Arms, in Salisbury in 1987. John had previously brewed in London before taking over the pub with his wife, Julie. The distinctive logo, used on all the beers, shows the Greek hero Heracles, whose face is carved over the entrance to the pub. The demand for John's beers led to the creation of Hop Back Brewery Ltd in 1991, which set up shop in industrial units at Downton. Two years later, with support from the government's Business Expansion Scheme, £565,000 was raised to develop the brewery. New units were added and the company now produces some 16,000 barrels a year and owns 10 pubs. John and his team have won many awards for their beers, Hop Back Summer Lightning in particular (see *300 Beers to Try Before You Die!*).

Entire Stout has also picked up trophies. The cask version won gold in its class in the Champion Winter Beer of Britain competition in 2008 while the bottle-conditioned version won the Tucker's Maltings Beer competition in 2004 and 2006.

The beer is brewed with pale, chocolate and wheat crystal malts, with roasted barley. The hops are Challenger and Goldings. It has an appealing dark ruby colour with a powerful aroma of coffee, caramel, roasted grain, dark fruit and peppery hops. Dark chocolate, coffee, roasted grain and peppery hop resins build in the mouth, while the finish is quenching and complex, with rich roasted malt, bitter hops, coffee and chocolate notes dominating.

TASTING NOTES

APPEARANCE:

AROMA:

TASTE:

OVERALL SCORE:

Hopshackle Imperial Stout

Source: Hopshackle Brewery, Market Deeping, Lincolnshire, England

Strength: 9.8%

Website: www.hopshacklebrewery.co.uk

Nigel Wright's fascination with old beer styles is told in the IPA section. He dedicates his Imperial Stout to the brewers who exported strong Porters and Stouts to the Baltic in the 18th and 19th centuries. With a neat twist, he uses just one hop in the beer, the German Northern Brewer: the original London imperial Stouts made their way to the Baltic via ports in Germany.

Nigel's interpretation is brewed just once a year and is aged for six months. The beer is then bottled and held in the brewery for a further month to ensure natural carbonation takes place. The beer can then be drunk but Nigel stresses that, as it is bottle conditioned with live yeast and proteins, it will continue to improve with age.

The grains used are Maris Otter pale, crystal, black and chocolate malts with roasted barley. The beer has a colour rating of 250. The Northern Brewer hops contribute 66 units of bitterness. A powerful and unmistakeable aroma of espresso coffee bounces out of the glass of the jet-black beer. There's a creamy malt note reminiscent of that ancient confectionery known as milk drops with bitter chocolate notes and herbal hops. Rich creamy malt coats the tongue, with major contributions from hop resins, coffee and chocolate. The finish is long, with bittersweet notes of rich malt, coffee, chocolate and herbal, spicy hops and a late hint of liquorice.

With a neat twist, he uses just one hop in the beer, the German Northern Brewer: the original London imperial Stouts made their way to the Baltic via ports in Germany.

Invercargill Pitch Black Stout

Source: Invercargill Brewery, Invercargill, New Zealand

Strength: 5%

Website: www.invercargillbrewery.co.nz

Invercargill is the southernmost small craft brewery in the world, founded in 1999 by father and son Gerry and Steve Nally. Gerry was thinking of retiring when Steve convinced him they should put their love of good beer to good use by opening a brewery.

Steve had a degree in chemistry and spent some time touring Europe, including a spell living in the Champagne region of France where he played rugby and enjoyed the local tipple. Back home, he and his father leased an old dairy on the outskirts of Invercargill and brewed pale ale before adding this beer to the portfolio. Pitch Black Stout was a wise choice, as it's become their leading brand. It has won prizes three times in the Australian International Brewing Awards – and a Kiwi beer has to be good to win prizes in Australia.

Pitch Black is a long way removed from the familiar dry Irish version. While no lactose is used in the production, it has a smooth, velvety and creamy character reminiscent of the style, while Pacific Gem hops contribute just 13.4 units of bitterness. The grains are lager malt, dark caramalt, black and chocolate malts, with roast barley. In spite of the name, the beer has a glowing ruby edge in the classic Stout fashion. The aroma offers caramel, milk chocolate, burnt toast and a gentle hint of floral hops. There's a charred note from the roasted grain on the palate but it's balanced by creamy malt, chocolate and gentle hops. The finish is a delicious blend of roasted grain, milk chocolate, caramel and light hop resins. The Nallys have added a fruit version of the beer called Boysenberry.

TASTING NOTES

APPEARANCE:

AROMA:

TASTE:

OVERALL SCORE:

James Squire Jack of Spades Porter

Source: Malt Shovel Brewery, Camperdown, New South Wales, Australia

Strength: 5%

Website: www.malt-shovel.com.au

Clear evidence that the Australian beer scene has changed out of all recognition came when I entered the Malt Shovel Brewery in the suburbs of Sydney. There, clanking round on the bottling line, were endless bottles of Porter – in the land of 'the amber nectar'!

Dr Charles Hahn – Chuck to his legion of friends and admirers – who runs the brewery, is an American who brewed in his native country and worked in New Zealand for several years – 'I brewed a lot of Steinlager', he admits with a rueful grin – before launching Malt Shovel. His company flourished to such an extent with the success of his Original Pilsener (see *300 Beers to Try Before You Die!*) that he became part of the giant Lion Nathan brewing group, part of Kirin of Japan. In the northern hemisphere, such a takeover would mean the kiss of death for a small craft brewer, but Lion is both a benign and generous presence. It has invested heavily in Malt Shovel and funded the opening of brewpubs under the James Squire label in Melbourne, Perth and Sydney. More are planned and even isolated Darwin may eventually have a James Squire pub.

Squire was a convict transported to Australia in 1785 for the shocking crime of stealing a chicken in Kingston, Surrey. While still a convict, he brewed ale for the governor of New South Wales and, on his release, was encouraged to brew commercially to counteract the illicit importing of rum. He developed the first hop gardens in Australia and opened a brewery on the shores of the Parramatta River at Kissing Point. He followed this with the Malt Shovel Tavern near Sydney and is hailed today as the father of Australian brewing. The main beers for the pubs are brewed at Camperdown but each pub has a small plant that produces short-run beers.

Squire's brewery would have been a tad different to the brewery named in his honour. It's a modern Steinecker plant, with stainless vessels attractively clad in wood. The kit stands close to the entrance and attracts many visitors. It comprises a mash mixer that doubles as the brew kettle: when the mash is made, it's filtered in a lauter tun and then returns to the mixer for the boil with hops. Brewing liquor for ales is Burtonised with the addition of salts. Beyond the brewery, steps lead up to an attractive visitor centre and saloon where the Malt Shovel range can be sampled.

The Porter is brewed with pale, chocolate, crystal and roasted malts and is hopped with Super Alpha: units of bitterness are 23. The jet black beer has a fine aroma of coffee and liquorice, roasted grain, dark fruits and fruity hops. Roasted notes, coffee and hops build in the mouth, with a long, satisfying finish that's a fine meld of rich, roasted malt, fruit, coffee and bitter hops, with a lingering note of liquorice.

O'Hara's Irish Stout

Source: Carlow Brewing Co, Bagenalstown, County Carlow, Ireland
Strength: 4.3%
Website: www.carlowbrewing.com

Carlow is at the forefront of the Irish brewing revival. It was founded in Carlow town in 1996 by the O'Hara family with the aim, Seamus O'Hara says, of restoring flavour along with natural brewing methods and ingredients to the island's beers. The company's fortunes were boosted when its Stout won a gold medal in the prestigious International Brewing Awards competition in 2000. In 2006 the brewery moved to a custom-built site in Bagenalstown, the O'Hara family's birthplace. Seamus with a brewing team led by Cieran Kelly produces 15,000 hectolitres a year on plant built in Canada. The kit comprises a mash tun that requires a long, three hour conversion from starch to sugar, a lauter tun for clarification and a brew kettle: hops are added at the start of the boil and at the finish. Hard water, ideal for brewing Stout, Seamus says, lies on a bed of limestone.

The beer range offers pale, red and wheat ales as well as Stout. Carlow exports to 20 countries, including the U.S., Britain, Italy, France and Scandinavia: 60 per cent of annual production is now exported.

Seamus sources his raw materials from Ireland wherever possible. He uses Irish ale malt but buys specialist malts such as caramalt, chocolate malt, roasted barley and flaked barley from Fawcetts in Yorkshire, England. Flaked barley is used in all the beers for head retention: a high proportion is used in Stouts. Hops include Fuggles and Goldings from England, Cascade and Chinook from the U.S. and Saaz from the Czech Republic. They are used in pellet form.

For O'Hara's Stout, pale malt, roasted barley, flaked barley and chocolate malt are joined by English Fuggles and Goldings. The finished beer, nitrogenated in draught form, has a massive rich chocolate aroma with smoky roasted grain. Peppery hops break through in the mouth, with burnt grain, bitter chocolate and dark berry fruits.

The finish is bittersweet, with a good balance of bitter hops, roasted grain, burnt fruit and chocolate. A stronger Stout, Leánn Fóllain (Wholesome Stout), was introduced to celebrate 10 years of brewing.

TASTING NOTES

APPEARANCE:

AROMA:

TASTE:

OVERALL SCORE:

Porters & Stouts

TASTING NOTES

APPEARANCE:

AROMA:

TASTE:

OVERALL SCORE:

Pitfield 1850 London Porter

Source: **Pitfield Brewery, Epping, Essex, England**

Strength: **5%**

Website: **www.pitfieldbeershop.co.uk**

Martin Kemp's passion for recreating old beer styles is boundless, as his previous beers in this book show. He brews three Porters and Stouts: as well as this porter there's 1792 Imperial Stout and Shoreditch Stout. I've chosen the middle one from the range as Martin's original site, in Old Street, North London, was close to where the likes of Calvert, Harwood and Whitbread fashioned the first porters in the 18th century and in so doing lit the touch paper for commercial brewing on a grand scale to develop in the capital city.

Martin's revivalist beers have been inspired by the work of the Durden Park Beer Circle, founded by the late Dr John Harrison. The circle diligently digs out old recipes and brews the results. The circle also makes its work available to both home and commercial brewers. Its major book, *Old British Beers and How to Make Them*, has been reprinted many times and the latest edition is illustrated by a handpump with a clip promising Stout Porter (see www.durdenparkbeer.org.uk).

1850 London Porter is an organic beer brewed with Maris Otter pale malt, brown malt and roasted barley and is hopped with English Goldings. The ruby/black beer, which throws an enormous barley white head in its bottle-conditioned version, is notable for the way peppery Goldings make their presence felt through a massive array of dark roasted grain, coffee and chocolate notes on the nose. The beer is intensely bitter in the mouth – a bitterness that comes from roasted grain as well as hops. The bitterness is well balanced by coffee and chocolate and all the flavours linger into the long finish, which ends dry, hoppy and fruity, with continuing delicious notes of roasted grain and chocolate.

Porterhouse Plain Porter

Source: Porterhouse Brewing Co, Dublin, Ireland

Strength: 4.3%

Website: www.porterhousebrewco.com

Oliver Hughes, the founder of Porterhouse – Ireland's first brewpub, which now has branches as far away as London and New York – describes his Plain Porter as 'the jewel in our crown'. He has restored to the bars of Ireland's capital a famous Dublin beer style that was once the chief type of beer served in the city's pubs. Guinness's main brands were X and XX, the single X denoting Porter, the double denoting Stout. Stout, being stronger and more expensive, was mainly the preserve of better-off drinkers, while X, dubbed Plain, was the drink of the working class. It was enshrined in Irish folklore in 1939 by the acclaimed Irish humorist Flann O'Brien in his book *At Swim-Two-Birds*:

'We sat in Grogan's with our faded overcoats finely disarrayed on easy chairs in the mullioned snug. I gave a shilling and two pennies to a civil man who brought us in return two glasses of black porter, imperial pint measure. I adjusted the glasses to the front of each of us and reflected on the solemnity of the occasion. It was my first taste of porter...[it]

was sour to the palate but viscid, potent. Kelly made a long noise as if releasing air from his interior. I looked at him from the corner of my eye and said: "You can't beat a good pint!" He leaned over and put his face close to me in an earnest manner. "Do you know what I am going to tell you," he said with his wry mouth, "a pint of plain is your only man".'

Guinness phased out plain in the 1970s and it has been a long wait for the style to be revived. The Porterhouse version is brewed with pale, black and crystal malts with roast barley and flaked barley. The hops are Galena, Nugget and East Kent Goldings. The ruby/black beer has a delightful aroma of smoked grain, hints of chocolate and coffee and a solid underpinning of pine-like hop resins. Smooth, velvety dark malt, roasted grain, gently bitter hops, coffee and chocolate fill the mouth followed by a lingering finish in which smooth, creamy malt dominates but with continuing notes of tangy hop resins, coffee, chocolate and roasted grain. It's a succulent and refreshing beer.

Red Squirrel London Porter

Source: Red Squirrel Brewery, Potten End, Hertfordshire, England

Strength: 5%

Website: www.redsquirrelbrewery.co.uk

Red Squirrel was founded in 2004 and its London Porter has won a number of plaudits including a bronze award in the CAMRA's Champion Winter Beer of Britain competition. The owners of the brewery, Greg Blesson and Jason Duncan-Anderson, built up a substantial business importing South African wine and have moved into brewing with evident success.

All their beers carry the logo of a red squirrel. The brewery supports the Red Squirrel Survival Trust and a donation is made from every pint sold

to help the trust stop the ubiquitous grey squirrel killing off the native red variety.

London Porter is brewed with pale malt, chocolate malt and dark crystal malt. The hops are Goldings and Magnum. The beer has a tempting aroma of toasted wholemeal bread, dark berry fruits, black chocolate, and tangy, floral and piny hops. Smooth creamy malt, chocolate, dark fruits and gently bitter hops fill the mouth, while the finish is a superb blend of malt, chocolate, fruit and hops.

Ridgeway Foreign Export Stout

Source: Ridgeway Brewing, South Stoke, Oxfordshire, England

Strength: 7%

Website: none

Peter Scholey, as seen in his IPA and Bitter entries, creates traditional recipes which he then brews on other people's equipment: namely Hepworth in Sussex and Cotswold in Gloucestershire. His interpretation of Foreign Export Stout is radically different from the best-known version of the style, Guinness FES, which featured in *300 Beers to Try Before You Die!* Peter's version has a more complex malt makeup of Maris Otter pale, amber, black, crystal and oat malts along with roasted barley. The hops are Challenger and Styrian Goldings, used in whole flower form – Peter is a passionate supporter of whole hops, which he feels give a far better aroma and bitterness than pellets.

The jet black beer has a rich and tempting aroma of creamy malt, chocolate and coffee, with a solid underpinning of peppery hops and notes of roasted grain, burnt fruit and tobacco. Raisin and sultana fruit are evident on the palate, with ripe, sweet malt, hop resins, coffee, chocolate and tobacco. The finish is long and complex, ending dry and hoppy but balanced by rich malt, roasted grain, chocolate, coffee, dark fruits and tobacco.

Salopian Entire Butt

Source: Salopian Brewery, Shrewsbury, Shropshire, England

Strength: 4.8%

Website: www.salopianbrewery.co.uk

In spite of being tagged a Salopian beer, Entire Butt is another Peter Scholey brew (see previous entry). It was first brewed by Salopian as cask ale, with a recipe devised by the late Martin Barry, one of the brewery's founders. But it has been licensed for several years to Peter at Ridgeway, who produces it in bottle-conditioned format mainly for export to the U.S., Italy and Scandinavia. It represents his honourable attempt to recreate an entire butt beer from London in the 18th century: wouldn't it be wonderful to be able to borrow a time machine for a few days and travel back in time to discover what the first Porters really did taste like and the ingredients used!

Peter's interpretation doesn't solve the riddle of whether entire butt got its name as the result of being blended in pub cellars or was a mix of different mashes in the brewery. But it's a remarkable beer by any standards with possibly the most complex recipe in the world of brewing. The grains are as follows: Maris Otter pale, amber, black, brown, carapils, crystal, dark crystal, pale chocolate, dark chocolate, lager and wheat malts, with roasted barley and torrefied wheat and malted oats. The hops are whole flower Fuggles, Goldings and Styrian Goldings.

The end result is a wonderfully full-tasting and complex beer, as quenching as it needed to be in 18th-century London to refresh the small army of porters working the streets and markets. It has a rich creamy chocolate aroma and palate: no lactose is used but it has something of the appeal of a milk stout. There's chewy raisin fruit, spicy and herbal hops and coffee notes in the mouth with a long, lingering finish with a good solid bitter hop base overlain with creamy malt, burnt fruit, coffee and chocolate. It's a rewarding and fascinating beer.

The good people at Salopian tell me that though they're brewing to capacity they still occasionally produce a cask of Entire Butt. They also have some bottles for sale that are three years old – a good excuse for a visit.

Thornbridge Saint Petersburg

Source: Thornbridge Brewery, Bakewell, Derbyshire, England
Strength: 7.4%
Website: www.thornbridgebrewery.co.uk

Thornbridge Brewery has rapidly established itself as one of the key players in the modern craft brewing movement in Britain. While Jaipur IPA (see *300 Beers to Try Before You Die!*) has won most attention and prizes, Saint Petersburg is widely admired as a superb example of an Imperial Russian Stout. It's aged for 55 days prior to bottling and is primed with a blend of sugars to encourage a good second fermentation in bottle: the beer is also available cask conditioned. Samples of the stout have also been aged in oak casks from several Scottish malt whisky distilleries and French wine and cognac makers at the original plant at Thornbridge Hall.

It's brewed with Maris Otter pale malt, chocolate malt, peated malt, dark crystal, and roasted barley and Demerara sugar, and hopped with Sorachi Ace, Mount Hood, Warrior and Willamette varieties. It's a ruby/black colour with a stirring aroma of smoke and peat, biscuit malt, rich chocolate, espresso coffee, liquorice and fruity and spicy hops. There's a pronounced bittersweet fruit note on the palate and finish, balanced by roasted and smoked grain, chocolate, coffee and fruity, bitter hops.

In 2012 the beer was the victim of a new tax introduced by the government, whose attitude is 'if we need more revenue, tax beer'. Higher Strength Beer Duty (HSBD) brought in a 25 per cent increase on beers of 7.5 per cent and above. Saint Petersburg was originally 7.7 per cent but the company has reluctantly reduced it to 7.4 per cent, drastically changing the recipe to give more malt and hops character to balance the slight lowering of strength. The government's aim is to reduce binge drinking but it's scarcely credible that a small minority of people who abuse alcohol would seek out Saint Petersburg Imperial Russian Stout as their chosen tipple.

TASTING NOTES

APPEARANCE:
Dark, good thick head 4

AROMA:
Liquorice chocolate fruity 3

TASTE:
Chocolate biscuit burnt 3

OVERALL SCORE:
10

175

Wickwar Station Porter

Source: Wickwar Brewing Company, Wickwar, Gloucestershire, England

Strength: 6.1%

Website: www.wickwarbrewing.co.uk

Brewer Neil Challis's fortunes took off when his Porter was named Supreme Champion Winter Beer of Britain in 2008. Neil launched his brewery in 1990 in the cooper's shop of the former Arnold Perrett Brewery, a substantial company founded in 1820 which ceased brewing in 1924. Neil's original plant was 10 barrels, but in 2004 he moved over the road to part of the old brewery and expanded to 50 barrels. He now supplies some 400 outlets with his beer.

Station Porter is named for the local train station that played a vital role in moving Arnold Perrett's beers around the country. The railway line is long gone but its memory survives thanks to a robust beer – cask and bottle conditioned – that's made with Maris Otter pale malt, black malt and crystal malt and hopped with one English variety, the Fuggle. Shortly after Neil won his award, I had the pleasure of meeting him and sampling the beer in the Old Spot pub in Dursley, Gloucestershire, that had also won a top award from CAMRA: National Pub of the Year. I agree with Neil that there's a distinct port wine note on the aroma and flavour of his ruby/black beer. The wine note is underscored by raisin and sultana fruit, liquorice, coffee and chocolate, with a spicy note from the Fuggles. The finish is long and deep, with continuing notes of rich wine, dark fruit, chocolate, coffee, liquorice and hops. It's worth missing a few trains for.

Golden Ales

Since *300 Beers to Try Before You Die!* was first published in 2005, golden ales have gone from a trickle to a tidal wave. The number of beers fitting the description is now so huge in Britain that CAMRA has had to add a new category to its annual Champion Beer of Britain awards. The style has dared raise its head in Australia and New Zealand, challenging the hegemony of 'amber nectar' lagers.

The beer revival in Ireland has also seen a number of golden ales nestling among new wave Stouts and red ales while the undiminished interest in Belgian beers keeps gold and white beers – including those made by Trappist monks – firmly on the map. Curiously, when you consider their passion for new styles and powerful hop flavours, American brewers have been slow to embrace golden ales. They place so much emphasis on such historic styles as pale ale and IPA that golden ales have yet to feature on North American radar. But American craft brewers will not ignore the bandwagon for long.

Lager was the unlikely genesis of golden ales. Small craft brewers in Belgium and Britain, faced by what seemed in the 1980s to be the unstoppable rise of lager and what is dubbed Pils in the Low Countries, started to develop paler ales they hoped might appeal in particular to younger drinkers weaned on what beer writer Michael Jackson brilliantly dubbed Ersaztenbräu.

In Britain, beers such as Exmoor Gold, Hop Back Summer Lightning and Kelham Island Pale Rider (see *300 Beers to Try Before You Die!*) were produced by brewers who lacked the capital to invest in lager equipment. They set out to prove that ales light in colour and rich in hops could be a more flavoursome alternative to mass advertised global brands. The awards garnered by Pale Rider and Summer Lightning proved there was both demand and support for the style. Now just about every brewer in the country has a golden ale in his or her locker.

What distinguishes golden ale from pale ale? The answer is malt, hops and serving temperature. Many golden ales are brewed with exceptionally pale malt: lager malt is used or low colour versions of English barleys. Traditional English pale ales, in comparison, often have a copper colour from the use of crystal malt. Brewers frequently underscore the difference between golden and pale ales by using hops, such as Bavarian, Czech and North American varieties, which give profound floral, herbal and citrus characteristics, unlike the more restrained pepper and spice notes of English hops. Where possible, golden ales are served at a lower temperature than pale ales: special coolers below the pub bar give the beers a final chill before hitting the drinker's glass.

The pleasing irony of the current situation is that while sales of golden ale are in the ascendancy, global lager brands are in free-fall. Once again, flavour has won the day.

TASTING NOTES

APPEARANCE:

AROMA:

TASTE:

OVERALL SCORE:

Ballard's Nyewood Gold

Source: Ballard's Brewery, Nyewood, Hampshire, England

Strength: 5%

Website: ballards-brewery.co.uk

Ballard's – it's good to find a brewery retaining the possessive apostrophe – is a paradigm for Britain's small brewery movement. It was launched in 1980 by Mike Brown in an old cow shed on his family farm. Mike is a lawyer with a passion for cask beer. He felt the obvious name for the brewery – Brown Ale – didn't fit the bill and used his wife's maiden name instead. Once the company was up and running, having made its first move to the back of a nearby pub, Mike returned to the legal world and Carola Brown, née Ballard, became head brewer and managing director.

As well as moving yet again to an old sawmill at Nyewood, near Petersfield, Carola became a leading member of the Small Independent Brewers Association, formed in the same year that Ballard's was founded. Micro brewers were refused membership of the industry's umbrella organisation, the Brewers' Society, and SIBA set out to be a strident voice for the small fry of the brewing world and to campaign in particular for lower rates of duty for its members. Carola became an articulate spokesperson for the association which, renamed the Society of Independent Brewers but retaining the acronym,

won the battle for progressive beer duty in 2002. PBD has helped fuel the astonishing growth of the small brewery sector since then.

Today, Ballard's has expanded into other buildings on the site, and can produce 1,500 gallons of beer a week. It brews only with malt and hops, avoiding sugars and cheaper grains. Several of the draught beers are also available in bottle-conditioned form, including Nyewood Gold. The beer was first brewed for the annual Beauty of Hops competition in 1997, where it won the top award for the use of the Phoenix variety. The draught version went on to win gold in the Strong Bitter category in the 1999 Champion Beer of Britain competition – this was before CAMRA added a 'golden ale' category.

The beer label shows pheasants against a wooded background: 'nye' is an old name for a brace of the birds. Nyewood Gold is brewed with Pearl pale malt, a touch of torrefied wheat for head retention, and the aforementioned Phoenix hops. It has a lilting fruity aroma, with tart lemons to the fore, along with hop resins and sappy malt. The palate and finish are bittersweet: a fine melange of cracker-like malt, orange and lemon fruit and bitter hops. It's a superbly refreshing beer.

Batemans Yella Belly Gold

Source: George Bateman & Son, Salem Bridge Brewery, Wainfleet, Lincolnshire, England

Strength: 3.9%

Website: www.bateman.co.uk

TASTING NOTES

APPEARANCE:

AROMA:

TASTE:

OVERALL SCORE:

Batemans featured in the previous section on porter and stout. Along with their Dark Mild (see *300 Beers to Try Before You Die!*) the family brewery is dedicated to producing traditional dark beers. But Stuart and Jaclyn Bateman, in common with all family brewers, visit their pubs on a regular basis and monitor their customers' views and drinking habits. Batemans' pubs had for several years sold Castle Rock's Harvest Pale as a guest beer and were impressed with its success. As a result, in 2012 Stuart and Jaclyn, with the sage advice of head brewer Martin Cullimore, launched their own distinctively different golden ale.

Yella Belly is a popular term in Lincolnshire, a vast county given over mainly to agriculture. Nobody is quite certain about the origin of the name. Some think it comes from the distinctive yellow waistcoats once worn by members of the Lincolnshire Regiment. Others say it derives from the yellow-breasted marsh frogs that live in low-lying land, much of it reclaimed from the sea over the centuries. A third point of view is farm workers who used to pick mustard seed were called Yella Bellies as they returned from the fields covered in pollen.

Choose your theme then savour the beer. It's brewed with lager malt and American Cascade and Chinook hops. At 42 units of bitterness, this is a beer with great hop bite and makes the point that golden ales are far removed from mainstream lagers. The beer is bright gold in colour and has a big bittersweet aroma of citrus fruits, toasted malt and tart hop resins. Citrus, rich malt and bitter hops fill the mouth while the finish has a long and lingering grapefruit note from the American hops and biscuit malt, but ends dry and hoppy.

> *Yella Belly is a popular term in Lincolnshire, a vast county given over mainly to agriculture.*

Brakspear Oxford Gold

Source: Brakspear Brewing Co, Witney, Oxfordshire, England

Strength: 4%

Website: www.brakspear-beers.co.uk

One of the many fascinations of the modern British brewing industry is its ancient and modern traditions. Ballard's (see p178) is a spirited member of the new breed of craft brewers while Brakspear is a venerable institution: one of the country's oldest beer makers. The original site in Henley-on-Thames dates from 1700 and was bought by the Brakspear family in 1779. The family was distantly related to Nicholas Breakspear, the first and, to date, only English Pope, enthroned in the 12th century as Adrian IV. The Henley Brakspears stressed the connection by using as their company logo the bee, which was the symbol on Adrian's papal mitre.

The brewery expanded, building a sizeable pub estate in Oxfordshire. In common with many regional brewers that had lost family control, Brakspear had the misfortune in 2002 to fall into the hands of new owners whose interest lay in running pubs and not a brewery. The Henley site closed but to the relief of lovers of Brakspear's beers they were resurrected two years later when production moved to Witney. Brakspear now shares the site with the Wychwood Brewery, best known for its Hobgoblin strong bitter (see *300 Beers to Try Before You Die!*). The brewing water in Witney is identical to Henley's and the character of the Brakspear beers has been ensured by moving the brewing vessels to the new

site. They include the last remaining example of a 'double drop' fermentation system. This is based on ancient wooden vessels ranged on two storeys. Fermentation starts on the top floor and after 16 hours the liquid is literally dropped – by opening the base of the vessels – in to the fermenters below. Dead yeast cells and unwanted protein, known as 'trub', are left behind, enabling a fresh, clean fermentation to continue below. The end result is beer with a fine clean and quenching taste, malt and hops joined by a delicious hint of butterscotch. This is the result of the impact of a by-product of fermentation known as diacetyl. Most brewers avoid it like the plague and lager brewers consider diactyl in beer to be a fault but it adds to the complexity and pleasure of traditional warm-fermented ales.

In spite of its bronze colour, Oxford Gold has the Brakspear hallmark of a sulphurous nose with a distinctive hint of butterscotch allied to a rich 'fresh bread' malt note and a whole sweet shop of confectionery, with orange and sherbet lemons to the fore. Bitter hops dominate the palate with fruit, malt and creamy butterscotch making substantial contributions before the tart, tangy and fruity and finally dry and hoppy finish.

This is an organic beer brewed with pale and crystal malts and hopped with Goldings and Target. The packaged version (4.6%) is no longer bottle conditioned.

Castle Rock Harvest Pale/Elsie Mo

Source: Castle Rock Brewery, Nottingham, England

Strength: 3.8%/4.7%

Website: www.castlerockbrewery.co.uk

Castle Rock is an astonishing success story, yet another example of how tiny breweries can blossom and become major players in the industry. Along the way, it has also restored brewing to Nottingham. As a result of takeovers, the city lost such major producers as Hardys & Hansons and Shipstone but there are now half a dozen breweries practising the art of creating good beer.

Chris Holmes is the inspirational founder of Castle Rock. Chris was national chairman of CAMRA in its formative years of the 1970s. He was a college lecturer but gave up teaching to run pubs dedicated to cask beer in Nottingham and its environs. In 1998 he added a small, 30-barrel brewery to his pubs and by 2005 he was forced to expand to 70 barrels. Five years later, he and his partners raised the daunting sum of £600,000 to build a brand new brewery close to the site of the original plant alongside the Vat & Fiddle pub. The pub's name comes from the fact that it's close to the local offices of Revenue & Customs. I'm not certain I would make a joke of the tax inspectors but they seem to take it in good part. (For non-British readers, Vat not only means a brewery vessel but Value Added Tax, a form of sales tax, deeply unpopular with brewers.)

The year 2010 was a good one for the brewery. Not only did it open a new plant with a capacity of 20,000 barrels a year but it won the Champion Beer of Britain award for Harvest Pale, propelling it to national attention. Capacity may have to be expanded again to cope with demand. Castle Rock believes in putting something back into the local community and every month produces a special beer with a proportion of sales going to help the work of the Nottingham Wildlife Trust, which campaigns to save endangered species.

Both the beers reviewed here are brewed with special version of Maris Otter malted barley called Low Colour. This enables brewers producing golden ale to use a traditional English barley, rather than lager malt. The malt is known for short as LCMO, enabling wits at the brewery to come up with the name of Elsie Mo for the stronger of the two beers. The name in turn led to the bottle label and pump clip depicting a voluptuous young woman.

Harvest Pale is brewed with Low Colour Maris Otter and torrefied wheat. Bittering hops at the start of the copper boil are Cascade and Centennial, with Cascade and Chinook added towards the end of the boil. The beer has 30 units of bitterness and has a superb aroma of tart grapefruit, biscuit malt and tangy hop resins. Bittersweet fruit builds in the mouth but is well balanced by aromatic malt and cedar-like hops. The finish lingers, with continuing ripe grapefruit, gently bitter hops and creamy malt.

Elsie Mo, available in bottle-conditioned form as well as draught, has the same grains as Harvest Pale but the hops are English Challenger and Bobek from Slovenia. Bobek is also used as a late hop in the copper. Bitterness units are 34. The beer has a powerful blast of citrus fruit – lemon leading – on the nose with creamy malt and bitter hop resins. Bitter hops build in the mouth but are balanced by 'Rich Tea biscuit' malt and tart lemon and grapefruit. The finish is long, deep and complex, with tart fruit interweaving with bitter hops and creamy malt.

TASTING NOTES

APPEARANCE:

AROMA:

TASTE:

OVERALL SCORE:

TASTING NOTES

APPEARANCE:

AROMA:

TASTE:

OVERALL SCORE:

Cumbrian Legendary Ales Loweswater Gold

Source: Cumbrian Legendary Ales, Esthwaite Water, Cumbria, England

Strength: 4.3%

Website: www.cumbrianlegendaryales.com

Cumbrian Legendary Ales has enjoyed some spectacular settings. When I first visited it was a tiny three-barrel plant in the Kirkstile Inn at Loweswater, with Melbreak Mountain looming at the rear. The brewery was added in 2003 by the pub's owner, Roger Humphreys, and in 2009 he moved to the current site in order to expand and was joined by experienced brewster Hayley Barton. The new site has an equally superb setting, overlooking Esthwaite Water with Helvellyn towering in the background. The brewery, which now produces 50 barrels a week, is based in ancient barns. One, a cruck barn with curved wooden timbers, was built in the 16th century, the second was added a century later.

On my second visit, in the winter of 2012, snow lay thick on the ground and crusted the mountains, with mist rising eerily off the still, icy waters of Esthwaite. This is a magical part of the world that has inspired both poets and brewers. Hayley Barton was sufficiently inspired to win the top award in the golden ales section of the Champion Beer of Britain competition in 2012. Her brewhouse was built locally in Kendal and is of traditional design, with mash tun and copper feeding five fermenters.

Hayley 'Burtonises' her brewing water with gypsum and magnesium salts to enhance the aroma and flavour of the whole flower hops she uses.

For Loweswater Gold she uses just one hop, the German Brewers Gold, and a single grain, Maris Otter pale malt. The aroma has a creamy, oatmeal note allied to delicate hop resins and tart lemon fruit with a hint of sulphur and butterscotch. The fruit note builds in the mouth but is well balanced by juicy malt and cedar-like hops with lingering butterscotch. The finish is bittersweet and quenching with tart lemon fruit vying for attention with bitter hop resins, butterscotch and creamy malt.

Flushed by the success of Loweswater Gold and Langdale, an ale that won a silver in the CBoB awards in 2012, new fermenters are on order at the brewery. Like the mountains that form a backdrop to the brewery, Cumbrian Legendary Ales is reaching for the stars.

 This is a magical part of the world that has inspired both poets and brewers.

Dark Star Hophead

Source: **Dark Star Brewing Co, Horsham, West Sussex, England**

Strength: **3.8%**

Website: **darkstarbrewing.co.uk**

The amazing rags-to-riches story of Dark Star is told in the Pale Ale section. Hophead is one of the brewery's most popular beers and is brewed with Low Colour Concerto malt and American Amarillo and Cascade hops. Units of bitterness are between 28 and 30. The gold/pale bronze beer has a big hit of grapefruit, tropical fruits and elderflower on the nose with cookie-like malt and tart hop resins. Bittersweet fruit builds in the mouth with compensating bitter, pine wood hop notes and delectable oat malt biscuits from the malt. The finish continues the powerful fruit character but ends dry, hoppy, with a lingering cracker wheat note from the malt.

TASTING NOTES

APPEARANCE:

AROMA:

TASTE:

OVERALL SCORE:

Dungarvan Helvic Gold

Source: **Dungarvan Brewing Company, Dungarvan, Co Waterford, Ireland**

Strength: **4.9%**

Website: **dungarvanbrewingcompany.com**

This is one of the new breed of small artisan breweries, riding on the wave of increased interest in beer, that are bringing much-needed choice to Irish drinkers. Dungarvan was launched in 2010 by two couples, Cormac and Jen O'Dwyer and Claire and Tom Dalton: Cormac is the head brewer. They produce most of their beer in bottle-conditioned form for restaurants and bars and, spurred on by consumer response, they plan to branch out into cask beer as well. Their success is an indication of how fast the Irish beer scene is changing.

The compact brew house, with attractive, wood-clad vessels, has a brew length of six barrels, based on traditional mash tun and copper that can produce two to three brews a week. Fermentation lasts for a week, then the beers are bottled flat and warm conditioned to allow the yeast to work again and create a natural carbonation. 'Natural' is a word you hear many times at Dungarvan – natural brewing water from a limestone source, the best natural ingredients such as Maris Otter malt from England and whole flower hops from several countries, and no filtration or pasteurisation. Following warm conditioning, the beers are cold conditioned for four to six weeks before leaving the brewery.

Helvic Gold is brewed with Maris Otter pale malt with a touch of Munich malt. The bittering hops are English Goldings and German Northern Brewer, with American Cascade used as a finishing hop at the end of the copper boil. The pale gold beer has a big citrus/grapefruit aroma with a fresh herbal note, juicy malt and spicy hop resins. A big grapefruit note in the mouth is balanced by growing hop bitterness and rich creamy malt. The finish is long and lingering, with juicy malt, bitter, resinous hops and continuing bittersweet citrus fruit.

TASTING NOTES

APPEARANCE:

AROMA:

TASTE:

OVERALL SCORE:

Duvel Triple Hop

Source: Brouwerij Duvel Moortgat,
Breendonk, Belgium
Strength: 9.5%
Website: www.duvel.com

Duvel is the golden ale by which all others are measured. The regular beer appeared in *300 Beers to Try Before You Die!* but this is a stronger version with, as the name suggests, more hops and greater hop character. The success of Duvel is reflected in a change of name at the brewery. Originally the Moortgat brewery, it has been retitled Duvel Moorgat.

The brewery was founded in 1871 and has always been a specialist ale producer though in recent years it has added a couple of Pilsner-style lagers that are highly rated. In 1923, when Scotch Ale was popular in Belgium, Moortgat asked the renowned brewing scientist Jean De Clerck of Leuven University to analyse the yeast in a bottle of McEwan's Export. The Scottish brewery was unaware that its house yeast culture was pirated by a respectable professor and used to brew a new beer at Moortgat. In common with Scotch Ales, it was an amber-red beer at first and it was greeted by one of the brewery workers with the cry: 'This is the devil of a beer'. The Flemish for devil is duvel (pronounced doo-v'l) and the name stuck. In 1970, the brewery decided to alter the recipe and change Duvel into a golden ale in a bid to counter the inexorable rise of Pils beers in Belgium at the time. It did so with astonishing success. Duvel became a legendary beer, exported to 40 countries and spoken about by beer lovers in hushed, reverential tones.

It's brewed with Belgian and French two-row spring barley that is specially malted at the brewery. The beer has a colour rating of just seven, only fractionally higher than for a Pilsner. Hops are added to the copper boil in three stages and Triple Hop is dry hopped with Styrian Goldings. Dextrose is added before primary fermentation to boost the level of alcohol and encourage the yeast to turn most of the sugars to alcohol.

Primary fermentation last for six days and is followed by three days of secondary fermentation at a cold temperature. The beer is then cold conditioned for a month, filtered, and given a fresh dosage of yeast and dextrose. The beer is finally bottled and held for two weeks, during which time it undergoes a third fermentation. The finished beer is renowned for its 'Poire William' fruit aroma and flavour, overlain by tangy hops and juicy malt. In the case of this stronger version, Saaz and Styrian Goldings hops are joined by American Amarillo. This gives an additional note of citrus fruit and cedar wood, while the malt takes on a freshly-baked bread note. The third hop will change annually: in 2012 it was Citra. The palate is bittersweet, with creamy malt, ripe pear fruit and bitter, woody hop resins. Fruit builds in the finish but is beautifully balanced by spicy, leafy hops and rich biscuit malt. A heavenly beer that's popular in Hades.

Hawkshead Lakeland Gold

Source: **Hawkshead Brewery, Staveley, Cumbria, England**

Strength: **4.4%**

Website: **www.hawksheadbrewery.co.uk**

As the crow flies, Hawkshead and Loweswater breweries are neighbours. But crows don't have to navigate their way round and across Cumbria's spectacular lakes and visiting the two breweries means a lengthy drive round majestic Windermere and then across the lake's chain ferry. The story of Alex Brodie's transition from leading British radio journalist to successful craft brewer is told in the Bitter section. For Lakeland Gold, head brewer Matt Clarke uses Maris Otter pale malt with Cascade, Fuggles and Goldings hops. The pale bronze beer has a big fruity/citrus nose with biscuit malt and earthy/peppery hop resins. Orange and lemon fruit build in the mouth with juicy malt and spicy and peppery Fuggles and Goldings hop notes. The finish is long, with tart citrus fruit, peppery hops and an oatcake note from the malt.

Hepworth Prospect

Source: **Hepworth & Co, Horsham, West Sussex, England**

Strength: **4.5%**

Website: **www.hepworthbrewery.co.uk**

Andy Hepworth has restored brewing in Horsham. He was head brewer at King & Barnes, a large Horsham brewery that went out of business in the 1990s. Andy set up shop in old railyard buildings at Horsham station: the company logo is based on a traditional lozenge-shaped platform nameplate. The brewery is flexible and can produce both ale and lager, and the equipment is used by other brewers, notably Brakspear's last head brewer Peter Scholey, to fashion their own brews.

Andy is committed to using locally sourced raw materials and draws both malts and hops from Sussex suppliers. His beers carry a warranty of origin that guarantees the source of the ingredients he uses. Prospect is brewed with organic barley malt grown on the Goodwood Estate in Sussex. Goodwood is famous for its horse and car racing circuits but it's also a stately home that's been in the hands of the Dukes of Richmond for centuries. The family is committed to organic and sustainable agriculture and produces organic cheese as well as grain.

The beer is certified as organic by the Soil Association. Along with pale malt, there's a touch of crystal malt and the hops are Admiral and Goldings. Prospect is a gold/bronze beer with a buttery malt, peppery hops and a touch of lemon fruit on the nose. Hops build in the mouth but there's a fine balance provided by smooth malt and tart fruit. The finish has buttery malt, lemon fruit and an increasingly bitter and peppery hop note. It's available both cask- and bottle-conditioned.

TASTING NOTES

APPEARANCE:

AROMA:

TASTE:

OVERALL SCORE:

Holden's Golden Glow

Source: Holden's Brewery, Woodsetton, Dudley, England

Strength: 4.4%

Website: www.holdensbrewery.co.uk

Holden's is a delight, a bright, spick-and-span brewery alongside its brewery tap, the Park Inn. Brewery and pub are Black Country institutions, a region of the Midlands that gained its name from the number of factory chimneys pumping black smoke into the air at the height of the Industrial Revolution. The company has been in family hands since 1898, when Edwin Holden married Lucy, daughter of a publican who encouraged them to run one of his pubs. In 1915 the couple took on the Park Inn, which had a small brewery attached. They brewed Black Country Mild and Bitter and gradually expanded both the brewery and the number of pubs.

Today, Holden's runs 20 pubs and supplies around 70 other outlets. Jonathan Holden is in charge and he launched Golden Glow, a beer that sits between his traditional Mild and Bitter. Golden Glow won a bronze award in the Bitter class of the 2009 Champion Beer of Britain competition, before a golden ale category was introduced. It's brewed with Maris Otter pale malt, a dash of crystal and is hopped with a single variety, Fuggles. It has a woody and spicy hop aroma with restrained fruit and a rich biscuit malt note. Leafy hops build in the mouth with chewy malt and light fruit. The finish is bittersweet to start, with rich biscuit malt and tangy fruit, but ends dry and hoppy, with a powerful spicy and leafy Fuggles character. A new brewhouse is planned to keep pace with the demand for Holden's beers.

> 'Golden Glow won a bronze award in the Bitter class of the 2009 Champion Beer of Britain competition'

Ironbridge Gold

Source: Ironbridge Brewery, Ironbridge, Telford, Shropshire, England

Strength: 4.4%

Website: ironbridgebrewery.co.uk

The brewery takes its name from the world-famous Iron Bridge that crosses the River Severn and is heralded as the birthplace of the English Industrial Revolution in 1779. The claim is debatable, as the revolution developed in several parts of the country. But nevertheless the bridge, built of cast iron by Abraham Derby, using coal from the mines at Coalbrookdale, did lead to iron smelting on a vast scale. The bridge, with its striking position over the Severn Gorge, is now a Unesco World Heritage Site and draws visitors from all around the world.

The brewery opened in 2008 and enjoys a fine position in Victorian warehouses alongside the river in the delightfully named Merrythought Village. Beer is brewed in a 12-barrel plant and a visitor centre was added in 2009. The brewers have adopted a system they call 'mash hopping', introduced for Gold and now used for all their beers. The method is an ancient one and is thought to have been developed by German wheat beer brewers, who want low bitterness in their beers. At Ironbridge, whole hop flowers are placed on top of the grain bed in the mash tun at the end of the mashing cycle. As the hops are not boiled, their presence doesn't give bitterness to the mash but does impart hop flavour. The hops are then added in the usual fashion during the copper boil.

Gold is brewed with Maris Otter pale malt with Bravo and Centennial hops. It has a superb aroma of cookie-like malt, a touch of lemon and grapefruit and leafy hop notes. The palate has rich biscuit malt, tart fruit and woody, bitter hops. The finish ends dry but is preceded by rich malt and tangy bittersweet fruit.

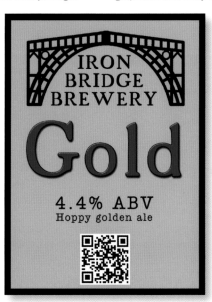

IRON BRIDGE BREWERY

Gold

4.4% ABV
Hoppy golden ale

TASTING NOTES

APPEARANCE:

AROMA:

TASTE:

OVERALL SCORE:

Itchen Valley Pure Gold

Source: Itchen Valley Brewery, New Alresford, Hampshire, England

Strength: 4.8%

Website: www.itchenvalley.com

Both this beer and its brewery have a convoluted history. Pure Gold takes its name from the gold bullion lost at sea in 1916 when a British armoured cruiser was shipwrecked en route to Russia. The ship was named *HMS Hampshire* and the founders of the Hampshire brewery, with a strong sense of history, named their most successful beer after the event. The ship had fought in the Battle of Jutland and a few weeks later set sail for Russia with a crew that included Field Marshall Lord Kitchener, the most senior British army officer. The ship hit a German mine and sank, losing both Kitchener and the stash of gold bullion.

The brewery was founded in 1997 and moved to a new site in 2006 with an expanded 20-barrel plant. Three years later the brewery achieved national fame when it appeared in a TV series, *Gerry's Big Decision*. It was fronted by businessman Sir Gerry Robinson who invested in companies that were in trouble but which, in his view, could be saved and restored to profitability. Owners Malcolm Gray and Jane Fuller gratefully accepted Sir Gerry's largesse.

Pure Gold is brewed with Maris Otter pale malt and hopped with American Cascade and Czech Saaz. It has a massive aroma of tropical and citrus fruits – a veritable confectioner's shop offering orange, lemon, grapefruit and pineapple. There's a solid underpinning of honeyed malt and nose-tingling hop resins. Creamy malt, ripe bittersweet fruit and tangy hops fill the mouth, followed by a long finish packed with rich malt, tangy fruit and leafy hops.

Pure Gold takes its name from the gold bullion lost at sea in 1916 when a British armoured cruiser was shipwrecked en route to Russia

Little Creatures Bright Ale

Source: Little Creatures Brewing, Fremantle, West Australia

Strength: 4.5%

Website: littlecreatures.com.au

You have to pinch yourself when you go to Australia and discover – oh joy! – that there's far more to Aussie beer than Foster's and XXXX. On my first visit to Beer Expo in Melbourne I was surrounded by enthusiastic young brewers who pressed on me samples of their IPAs, Stouts, American-style pale ales and their interpretations of all things beery from Belgium. Dozens of bottles were delivered to my hotel room and when I left I told the concierge: 'There's a lot of beer in my room and I can't take it home so please distribute it among your colleagues.' Being a good hotel man, he merely said 'Thank you, sir' but I could tell from the glint in his eye that there would be a right old knees-up in Room 303.

As I explained in the IPA section, one of the pace-setters in Australia is Little Creatures in Fremantle. The brewery has won more awards than you can shake a mashing fork at and they now have a second operation in Melbourne. They have a substantial portfolio of beer, including one called Rogers. I thought for a moment... but no, it honours two pioneers of Aussie craft brewing, Roger Bailey and Roger Bussell. I guess I'll just have to wait for Protzenbräu Pils.

Bright Ale is Little Creatures' contribution to the sparkling ale segment of the beer market made famous by Cooper's of Adelaide (see *300 Beers to Try Before You Die!*). The Fremantle interpretation has a complex grain makeup consisting of pale, carapils, Munich and Vienna malts. Whole flower East Kent Goldings are used as bittering hops while aroma varieties Cascade, Pacifica and Summer are added in the hop back. The beer has 24 units of bitterness and 15 colour units, which means that despite the use of some darker grains this is indeed a pale, golden beer. But Munich and Vienna malts give a rich toasted and vanilla note to the aroma and palate of the beer with citrus fruit, floral notes and woody resins from the hops. It has a long, quenching finish, ending dry but with good contributions from leafy hops, tart fruit and toasted malt.

TASTING NOTES

APPEARANCE:

AROMA:

TASTE:

OVERALL SCORE:

Mighty Oak Maldon Gold

Source: **Mighty Oak Brewing Co, Maldon, Essex, England**

Strength: **3.8%**

Website: **www.mightyoakbrewing.co.uk**

Mighty Oak can rightfully call itself an award-winning brewery. It has won the supreme Champion Beer of Britain award for Oscar Wilde dark Mild (see *300 Beers to Try Before You Die!*) while Maldon Gold won the top award in the golden ale category in in 2007 and went on to take silver in the overall competition.

The brewery was founded in 1996 by John Boyce and his business partner Ruth O'Neill. Ruth is an accountant: a handy person to have around. John worked for many years for Ind Coope in Romford, part of the Allied Breweries national group and which closed in the 1990s. John departed and set up Mighty Oak, and moved to bigger premises in 2001 where he now produces 70 barrels a week for pubs in Essex and East London: we have enjoyed a glass of Maldon Gold together after a football match at West Ham United.

John told me that when he worked at Ind Coope he never knew that brewing malt was pale in colour as the giant brewery seemed to use malt that was yellow and black. This may account for the poor reputation of Ind Coope's beers. John certainly knows now that malt can be pale, fresh, crisp and lusciously biscuity as he uses the finest Maris Otter pale in Maldon Gold along with English First Gold and American Mount Hood hops. First Gold is a hedgerow hop that grows to half the height of conventional varieties and is relatively free from pests and disease. An offspring of Whitbread Golding Variety, it gives a fine spicy note to the beer while Mount Hood contributes a typical blast of American citrus fruit. The beer has a rich palate of 'custard cream' malt, spicy and fruity hops with building bitterness, while the finish is dry and hoppy but with solid contributions from bittersweet fruit and creamy malt.

Mighty Oak is in good family hands. When John Boyce came to pick up his champion beer plaque at CAMRA's annual awards lunch in 2011, he booked a whole table and brought his large extended family, several of whom now work in the brewery. The future is assured.

TASTING NOTES

APPEARANCE: LIGHT PALE - LIGHT HEAD
4.

AROMA: Fruit, citrus Dry Nutty
4

TASTE: STRONG CITRUS FRUIT - HOP AFTERTASTE
5

OVERALL SCORE: 13

Oakham Citra

Source: **Oakham Ales, Peterborough, Cambridgeshire, England**

Strength: **4.2%**

Website: **www.oakham-ales.co.uk**

Oakham may be a small craft brewery but in every other respect it's a big and successful company. It has won many awards in both the Champion Beer of Britain and Winter Beer of Britain competitions, including supreme champion for its JHB in 2001 (see *300 Beers to Try Before You Die!*). It's also got bigger. It was once the biggest brewpub in Europe – based in central Peterborough – but it has now built a 75-barrel plant in the suburb of Woodston. The six-barrel plant remains at the pub and produces special and trial brews. It also brews beers recommended by customers who join its 'Oakademy of Excellence'.

Citra was launched as a seasonal beer but it achieved such acclaim that it rapidly went into permanent production as a cask-conditioned beer, followed by a filtered bottled version. Oakham was the first British brewery to use the new American hop, which, as its name suggests, has so much citrus fruit on the aroma and palate that it puts some other American hops to flight. But this hop has more than the usual grapefruit: there's passion fruit, lychees and gooseberries, too. The beer is all about hop character (55 units of bitterness) but Maris Otter pale malt holds up well with compensating honey and cracker notes.

Otley 01

Source: Otley Brewing Company, Pontypridd, Mid-Glamorgan, Wales
Strength: 4%
Website: www.otleybrewing.co.uk

01 was the first beer brewed by the Otley brothers, Nick, Charlie and Matthew, hence the name and the subsequent numbering of the beers that followed. 01 won the golden ale section of the Champion Beer of Britain competition in 2008 and remains one of the brewery's most popular beers. It has also been named Champion Beer of Wales three times.

Otley is a remarkable success story, all the more so in an area of South Wales that has lost its traditional industries such as mining and hence the thirsty workforce that went with them. The Otley family has run pubs in and around Pontypridd for generations and the three brothers now run the pubs and added a brewery in 2005. The pubs act as a showcase for the brewery. This is particularly the case with the Bunch of Grapes, where Nick Otley, who is also a trained chef, stages regular beer-and-food matching events.

The brewery has been such a success that it doubled in size by 2012 and was producing 4,000 barrels a year. New conditioning tanks are on order to increase capacity further and a move to new, bigger premises is planned.

The brothers use the letter O in their name to good effect in the branding of their beers, starting with 01 and moving up in strength. 01 is brewed with pale and lager malts and hopped with Brewers Gold and Styrian Goldings varieties. The pale gold beer has a luscious aroma of lightly toasted malt and lemon-and-lime fruit, backed by zesty floral hops. The palate balances rich malt with tart fruit and bitter hops, followed by a long finish that ends dry, quenching and hoppy but is preceded by continuing notes of fresh bread malt and tangy fruit.

The palate balances rich malt with tart fruit and bitter hops

TASTING NOTES

APPEARANCE:

AROMA:

TASTE:

OVERALL SCORE:

Otter Bright

Source: **Otter Brewery, Luppitt, Honiton, Devon, England**

Strength: **4.3%**

Website: **www.otterbrewery.com**

Otter enjoys one of the finest locations in Britain, alongside a river at the foot of the Blackdown Hills. It's far removed from many small craft breweries that use second-hand vessels from farms or dairies. David McCaig is an experienced brewer who joined West Country Breweries in the 1960s at the age of 19 and moved around the Whitbread empire, brewing in Stroud (where he met and married Mary Ann), Luton and Liverpool before moving to Devon with four children to run a bed & breakfast.

But the brewing bug had not gone away. After two years of planning, Otter opened in 1990 with modern stainless steel kit that can produce 80 barrels at a time. More than 500 pubs take Otter beers and it has its own outlet, the Holt in Honiton.

David and Mary Ann are still heavily involved in running the brewery but day-to-day running of the company has passed to their son Patrick. The McCaigs are passionate believers in supporting the environment. They draw brewing water from their own spring and return waste water to a water course that feeds reed beds. Excess yeast is used to feed pigs on local farms and spent grains become cattle feed. Used hops make fine garden mulch. In 2009 the McCaigs built an 'eco cellar' with a living sedum roof that collects rain water that is used to wash brewing vessels and vehicles. The brewery boiler is fired by recycled wood chips.

Otter Gold has a simple but tried-and-tested recipe with Extra Pale Maris Otter malt and Fuggles hops and a touch of torrefied grain and wheat for clarity and head retention. Critics of English hops who say such varieties as Fuggles and Goldings lack the fruit of American or Australasian varieties should think again when they sample Otter with its pungent spicy and tart orange aroma and palate, beautifully complemented by creamy and honeyed malt. The finish is long, packed with juicy malt, tart fruit and spicy hop resins.

The McCaigs are passionate believers in supporting the environment.

Burton Ales

In 1712, writing in the London magazine the *Spectator*, Joseph Addison noted that 'We concluded our walk with a glass of Burton ale'. The same journal reported that beer from Burton was in great demand in Vauxhall Pleasure Gardens in the capital. Long before India Pale Ale from Burton-on-Trent transformed brewing on a world scale, Burton on Trent had already established itself as a major brewing town and it was selling beer far beyond Staffordshire.

The ability to deliver beer as far away as London was made possible by important improvements to transport. For centuries, roads in England were badly maintained and were often impassable in winter. Water, always so crucial to brewing in Burton, came to the rescue, this time not from wells and springs but from rivers and canals. In 1699 the Trent Navigation Act made the river navigable from Burton to Shardlow. Early in the 18th century, work started that eventually allowed cargo to be carried along the Trent to Gainsborough and then Hull. Finally in 1777 the opening of the Trent and Mersey Canal completed a link between Hull and Liverpool, two important ports on the east and west coasts of the country.

The driving force behind the Trent and Mersey was a potter in Stoke-on-Trent called Josiah Wedgwood who wanted new markets for his products. But the waterways and the docks also gave the Burton brewers the opportunity to sell their beer further afield. Beer was delivered to Hull and then shipped to London where the celebrated diarist Samuel Pepys developed a taste for what he mistakenly dubbed 'Hull ale'. The Burton brewers were also building trade far beyond the shores of England. Along with textiles, iron and rope, the town of Burton was developing lucrative business with the Baltic States, Scandinavia and Imperial Russia. Peter the Great and the Empress Catherine enjoyed the nut brown ales from Burton, which were brewed strong – around 11 or 12 per cent – and well hopped to withstand the rigors of the long sea journeys from Hull via Danzig to St Petersburg.

The Burton brewers grew wealthy thanks to their Baltic trade. As well as delivering beer to the region, they imported large amounts of timber, Polish oak in particular, which was needed to make beer casks. They sold on surplus timber to brewers in other parts of England. So much money flooded into Burton that some of the brewers, including members of the Wilson family, whose brewery later became known as Allsopps, and William Worthington became bankers as well as beer makers. William Bass, who sold his successful carrying business to concentrate on brewing, rapidly grew to rival Wilson and Worthington. By the turn of the 19th century, he had set up agents in St Petersburg, Riga, Danzig, Bremen, Hamburg and Hanover. When Thomas Salt opened a new brewery in Burton, Bass and Wilson intensified their drive for new markets, managing to sell English ale to Scotland and then venturing as far as the Caribbean, North America and even Australia.

Early in the 19th century, the lucrative trade to the Baltic collapsed. The trade had become less profitable when Russia imposed high tariffs on British imports and it ceased altogether when France's Bonaparte blockaded all the key ports in the Baltic. Ships from England had to sail in convoy and the Royal Navy was unwilling to divert its vessels to protect traders. Burton was plunged into crisis. Several breweries closed and those that survived had to concentrate their efforts on the domestic market. The new technologies of the Industrial Revolution came to their aid. Coke was replacing wood as the fuel that fired malt kilns and as a result malt became lighter in colour. Samuel Allsopp, who had taken over Wilson's brewery, was in the forefront of developing a version of Burton Ale more suited to the home market. He knew from his customers' remarks in many parts of Britain that he needed to make his beer lighter in colour. He asked his London agent to send him a 'bottle of the Windsor ale – in a Box safe and say how much is sold pr. Barrell' so he could model his beer on it. Windsor ale was made from pale malt with the addition of honey. Allsopp also learned from customers that they wanted beer with less malt sweetness and more hop bitterness.

> ❛ *Burton was plunged into crisis. Several breweries closed and those that survived had to concentrate their efforts on the domestic market.* ❜

The new versions of Burton Ale paved the way for India Pale Ale, which propelled the town to world attention. But before the arrival of IPA, Burton Ale became a major beer style in its own right. Its impact was so profound that just about every brewer in the country found it necessary to have 'a Burton' in his portfolio. A 19th-century price list in the now closed Young's Brewery in Wandsworth, south London, included a Burton and it survives today as Young's Winter Warmer. Fuller's renowned Extra Special Bitter (see *300 Beers to Try Before You Die!*) developed from the brewery's Burton.

In 1891, when the Suffolk brewer Sir Edward Greene died following 55 years in the business, the London Star newspaper said in an obituary: 'He was one of the first country brewers to discover that beer need not be a vile, black turgid stuff, but brewed a bright amber-coloured liquid of the Burton type which he sold at one shilling a gallon and made a fortune'. It's highly likely that Greene King's Abbot Ale (see *300 Beers to Try Before You Die!*) is descended from a beer 'of the Burton type'.

In the 20th century Burton Ale went out of fashion, replaced by Bitter, pale ale and IPA. But it was still sufficiently in demand in World War Two to give rise to a macabre saying among pilots in the air force: when one of their comrades was shot down over the English Channel he was said to have 'gone for a Burton'.

Sadly, I cannot include in this section Bass No 1, a beer of true historic importance. Although it's called a barley wine today, it's a true Burton Ale of the old type, before paler versions were introduced for domestic trade. Although its strength has varied, it was usually brewed to 10.5 per cent and only pale malt was used: its dark colour was the result of an exceptionally long boil in the copper with Fuggles and Goldings hops, during which time some of the malt sugars were caramelised. Bass No 1 was also the beer used to make special brews to mark such royal occasions as a coronation and jubilee: the monarch of the day would visit Burton and ceremonially press the button to start the mash for the beer. The name No 1 is derived from the fact that at the height of Burton Ale's fame Bass produced no fewer than six versions of the style, ranging in strength from moderate to very strong. No 1 was produced in bottle-conditioned form and also occasionally on draught for CAMRA beer festivals. But at the time of writing there are no plans to brew it again in the William Worthington craft brewery within the National Brewery Centre. It appears to have 'gone for a Burton'.

Burton Bridge Bridge Bitter

Source: Bridge Brewery, Burton on Trent, Staffordshire, England
Strength: 4.2%
Website: www.burtonbridgebrewery.co.uk

Burton Ales fly under different flags these days. This beer may be labelled 'Bitter' but Geoff Mumford and Bruce Wilkinson say it's their interpretation of a Burton. They should know, as they have a long and honourable track record of brewing in the town. They worked for several years at the Ind Coope breweries in both Burton and Romford and then launched their own company in 1982. They are veterans of the craft brewing movement and they now own six pubs and supply around 300 outlets with their beers.

The brewery stands behind the Burton Bridge Inn: as the name suggests, the pub is at the foot of the bridge that crosses the Trent and effectively joined the town to the outside world and enabled brewers to sell their beers more widely. The pub is opposite the site of Benjamin Printon's brewery, the first commercial brewery in the town founded early in the 18th century. Later such key brewers as John Thompson, Boddingtons, Salt and John Nunneley all brewed within yards of the pub. It was first called the Fox & Goose and was bought by Bass in the 19th century but it closed in 1982. Geoff Mumford was driving over the bridge one day in that year, saw the 'for sale' sign and thought it would make the ideal location for a small brewery.

Bridge Bitter was the first beer to emerge from the brewery. Bruce and Geoff were determined to use only the finest raw materials, having been unimpressed by the poor hops and grains used at Ind Coope. Their version of a Burton is brewed with Pipkin pale malt and crystal malt, and is hopped with three English varieties, Challenger, Northdown and Target. Styrian Goldings are used as a late hop in the copper. The bright amber beer has a waft of sulphur on the aroma – the famous 'Burton snatch' – that gives way to rich juicy malt, orange fruit and tangy and spicy hops. Sappy malt and fruit build in the mouth, underscored by herbal, floral and spicy hops. The finish is long and complex, dominated at first by malt and fruit but it becomes finally dry and hoppy.

Draught Burton Ale

Source: J W Lees & Co, Greengate Brewery, Manchester, England
Strength: 4.8%
Website: www.jwlees.co.uk

This is the beer that put Burton Ale back on the map. It was once a major cask beer brand but due to the machinations of brewing giants it has been passed from pillar to post and is now brewed some distance from its birthplace. When it was launched in 1976 by Allied Breweries, owners of the Ind Coope and Allsopp breweries in Burton, the Campaign for Real Ale was in its infancy. Draught Burton Ale helped spark the revival of cask beer among Britain's bigger brewers. It had found favour among family and regional brewers but national companies remained aloof from cask beer, preferring to concentrate on keg beer and lager. When DBA, as it was known for short, was launched in 1976, it bore the name of Ind Coope and it proved to be an overnight sensation.

Allied had intended to serve the beer in a handful of carefully-chosen pubs but the clamour forced the company to rapidly increase production and to supply the beer to thousands of outlets. Such was the demand that the Birmingham firm of Gaskell & Chambers had to put its workers on permanent overtime to produce sufficient beer engines for pubs demanding to sell the beer.

In a sane world, DBA would have remained a leading, popular beer. But there's little sanity among global brewing groups. As a result of cataclysmic changes in the brewing industry in the 1970s, 80s and 90s, Allied Breweries changed owners twice and its production centres were sold to Carlsberg in 1992. Even though the Ind Coope brewery in Burton survived and is now owned by Molson Coors, production of DBA was moved to Tetley in Leeds. Carlsberg had little interest in the brand and hived it off to the family-owned J W Lees in Manchester. The beer is now produced in tiny volumes and is sold to only a handful of pubs. It's worth seeking out: it's frequently available in the Roebuck, 101 Station Road, Burton, just a few yards from the railway station and opposite the former Allsopps brewery.

Draught Burton Ale is something of a hybrid beer. Geoff Mumford and Bruce Wilkinson, now at Burton Bridge, worked at Ind Coope when the beer was launched and they say it was based on the recipe for a strong bottled version of Ind Coope's famous Double Diamond pale ale. However as the recipe is comprised of pale and chocolate malts and liquid sugar, the beer has the amber colour and rich malt and hops character of a true Burton rather than a pale ale. The hops are unspecified English bittering hops with Styrian Goldings for aroma and dry hopping in cask. While the level of alcohol is given as

4.8%, Allied Breweries used to warn both publicans and drinkers that, as a result of secondary fermentation in cask, the finished strength could be as high as 5.1 or 5.2%.

The beer has a massive aroma of marmalade fruit, biscuit malt and peppery hops, followed by a palate dominated by rich malt, bittersweet fruit and tangy hop resins. The finish is long, with ripe fruit and fat grain to start but becoming bittersweet and finally bitter and hoppy. Seek it out!

Fuller's Old Burton Extra

Source: Fuller, Smith & Turner's Griffin Brewery, Chiswick, London England
Strength: 7.3%
Website: www.fullers.co.uk

In 2010, Fuller's launched a new series under the Past Masters title that recreates beers from the company's old brewing books. Old Burton Extra is based on a recipe from 1931: to be more precise, 10 September 1931, the date chosen by head brewer John Keeling from the brewing book for that year. John feels that some interpretations of Burton

TASTING NOTES

APPEARANCE:

AROMA:

TASTE:

OVERALL SCORE:

Ale are not true to style. He says his beer restores the type of beer that was still popular before World War Two.

The beer is brewed with pale and crystal malts, maize and brewing sugar. The hops are Fuggles and Goldings and the beer is dry hopped before bottling. A rich and tempting aroma of toasted malt, vanilla, caramel, orange fruit and peppery hops bounces from the

> *He says his beer restores the type of beer that was still popular before World War Two.*

glass. The palate is complex, offering ripe honeyed grain, caramel, tart fruit and bitter hops resins. The long, deep finish is a superb balance of ripe malt, caramel, vanilla, orange fruit and peppery hops. It ends dry, hoppy and fruity. Only one batch is produced of each beer in the series but stock is kept at the brewery shop and can be ordered online: www.shop.fullers.co.uk.

TASTING NOTES
APPEARANCE:

AROMA:

TASTE:

OVERALL SCORE:

Tower Salt's Burton Ale/Gone for a Burton

Source: Tower Brewery, Burton on Trent, Staffordshire, England
Strength: 3.5%/4.6%
Website: www.towerbrewery.co.uk

John Mills' brewery is rich in Burton history, based in the water tower of the maltings that supplied grain to Thomas Salt. Salt was one of the giants of Burton brewing in the late 18th and 19th centuries, a maltster who took to making beer with considerable success. He became the fourth biggest brewer in the town and was taken over by Bass in 1927. The maltings were in the Walsitch area of the town: Walsitch is an Anglo-Saxon word meaning a stream that acts as a boundary. John Mills worked as a brewer for 10 years before branching out on his own. He opened his brewery in 2001 and as a result of his painstaking work he was given an award by the Civic Society for the restoration of an historic industrial building.

The top floor of the tower, reached by narrow spiral stairs and walkways, is heavily beamed and contains the original water tanks used by Salt's, which had three maltings in the town. As the windows of the top floor were broken, John's conversion of the building started with daunting task of shovelling some four tons of pigeon droppings into

sacks and dropping them down to the ground floor. The depth of the droppings was measured by the fact that some of the beams were hidden from view. When they were restored to sight some fascinating inscriptions could be seen, such as 'T.S. [Thomas Salt] 1875' and 'Alf Tyler – maltster 1957'.

The ground floor is occupied by John's impressive brewhouse where he can produce 12,000 barrels a year – a sizeable amount for a small brewery. He has also added a visitor centre and reception area with his beers on tap: guests can enjoy a beer while surveying the fascinating collection of Burton memorabilia. Proud of his brewing roots in his birthplace, John brews two versions of Burton Ale. Salt's Burton Ale is brewed with pale and crystal malts and hopped with Pilgrim and Northdown varieties. At 3.5 per cent, it's on the low side for the style but, as John says, it punches above its weight. It has a bright amber colour and has a nutty/malt aroma underscored by lemon fruit and woody hop resins. The palate is a fine blend of juicy malt, tart fruit and spicy hops, which continue in to

TASTING NOTES
APPEARANCE:

AROMA:

TASTE:

OVERALL SCORE:

the finish. John's sadness at the loss of the great brewers in the town is mirrored by his stronger beer. Gone for a Burton's label and pump clip show a shattered version of the famous bass red triangle, the first trademark to be registered under new legislation in 1876 to prevent unscrupulous companies copying their rivals' logos – and the Bass triangle had been copied and misused around the world. John's beer is brewed with pale and crystal malts and the hops are Fuggles and Northdown. Once again, the colour is amber and the rich cracker-like malt is balanced by tart bitterness and a spicy note from the Fuggles. Biscuit malt fills the mouth but it complemented by a bitter note from the Northdown and a woody, spicy contribution from the Fuggles. The finish is long and deep, with nutty and sappy malt balanced by light citrus fruit and spicy hops.

Young's Winter Warmer

Source: Wells & Young's Brewing Co, Bedford, England

Strength: 5%

Website: www.wellsandyoungs.co.uk

There was great sadness in 2006 when Young's Ram Brewery in south London closed. It brewed delicious and uncompromisingly hoppy beers and the site was renowned for its live ram mascot and a stable of dray horses that delivered beer to local pubs. But the brewery site in Wandsworth was effectively a giant roundabout that created terrible traffic jams. When the Young family failed to find an alternative site in London, the reluctant decision was taken to merge the brewing operation with Charles Wells in Bedford. Young's head brewer, Ken Don, spent several months at Bedford carefully and scientifically reproducing his beers on the Wells plant. It was not an easy task, as Young's had used open fermenters while Wells is a highly mechanised, modern brewery with enclosed conical fermenters where yeast drops to the bottom of the vessels rather than rising to the top. But in spite of these difficulties it's generally thought that Ken made a good fist of recreating his beers in Bedford.

Winter Warmer is brewed every year between November and January but it was once produced all year round when it was known as Burton. The beer is so loved by Young's aficionados that some of them meet every year to taste the new vintage and mark it against previous versions. It's brewed with Maris Otter pale malt and crystal malt, with a large amount (20 per cent) of dark brewing sugar. The hops are Fuggles and Goldings: the colour is 65 units, bitterness 26-30. The ruby coloured beer has a massive port wine aroma with sultana fruit, strong hints of caramel and toffee, and a solid underpinning of spicy and peppery hops. Vinous fruit fills the mouth with chewy malt, butterscotch and peppery hops. The finish is long, bittersweet, finally dry but with strong contributions from burnt fruit, butterscotch, caramel and bitter, peppery hops.

Scottish Ales

'Revolution' may be an over-used word in the world of brewing but it neatly sums up the profound changes that have taken place in Scotland in recent years. Scottish brewing developed at a slower pace than in England.

The quality of most Scottish barley was poor and was best used to make whisky. And the absence of hops – which don't grow well in northern climes – also meant ale lacked the balance of beers brewed south of the border. For centuries ale brewing in Scotland tended to be a domestic affair and the end results were rudimentary. Not surprisingly, many Scots, especially in the harsh northern area, preferred to drink the distilled version of barley malt. As a result of the 'Auld Alliance' between Scotland and France against Perfidious Albion, better-off Scots drank large amount of imported French wine. But supplies dried up during the Napoleonic Wars and commercial brewing start to develop in the Lowlands around Alloa, Edinburgh and Glasgow, where more suitable barley grew. Refugees from revolutionary France who settled in Scotland were pleased to find rich, dark and malty ales they dubbed 'Scottish Burgundy'.

From the 1800s through most of the following century, Scottish beer meant a dark, malty type of ale, a style that reflected a country with a cold climate and an absence of hop growing: Export, the Scots' interpretation of India Pale Ale in the 19th century, for example, tended to be darker, sweeter and less heavily hopped than the English version. However, Scotland developed lager brewing much earlier than England. The reason was twofold: before the arrival of refrigeration, the Scottish climate made it easier to ferment beer at lower temperatures while many Scots who worked abroad discovered lager in North America and Australasia and returned with a taste for the style.

Malty ales and thin lagers dominated Scottish brewing as a result of a wave of takeovers and mergers from the 1960s that created two giants: Scottish & Newcastle (S&N) and Tennent Caledonian. S&N is now owned by Heineken and no longer brews in Scotland. Tennent, once part of the Bass group and then InBev, has passed to the Irish company C&C, best known for Magners cider. There is now sufficient slack in the market for smaller brewers to offer distinctive brews that meet with a demand from drinkers for beer with character and flavour. The result is a flowering of Scottish beer that has both underscored traditional styles and which also reflects the impact of ales from England and the United States. There are now more than 50 breweries in the country and the result is a rekindling of interest in such styles as 60, 70 and 80 Shilling ales. The names come from a 19th-century system of invoicing for beer based on strength. 60 Shilling ale in Scotland is roughly equivalent to English Mild ale and, regardless of colour, is known as 'Light', while 70 and 80 Shilling are the Scottish versions of Bitter and Best Bitter and are called 'Heavy'.

The traditional Lights and Heavies are today complemented by golden ales, pale ales and IPAs, while Scottish Stout, once a largely forgotten style, has made a welcome return. There is much to enjoy in Scotland, not least ales with a more generous use of the hop plant.

Black Isle brewery

TASTING NOTES

APPEARANCE:

AROMA:

TASTE:

OVERALL SCORE:

Black Isle Hibernator Organic Oatmeal Stout

Source: Black Isle Brewing Co, Old Allengrange, Ross-shire, Scotland
Strength: 7%
Website: www.blackislebrewery.com

'Save the planet – drink organic' are the watchwords of this brewery that stands in converted farm buildings in the Highlands region of Ross and Cromarty, names familiar to those who listen to the BBC's shipping forecast. The Black Isle is in fact a peninsula set in beautiful countryside, with many castles, both ruined and intact. David Gladwin, who founded the brewery in 1998, is, as his slogan makes clear, a passionate supporter of organic production. He grows his own barley on 120 acres and his malts and hops are free from pesticides and herbicides. Spent grain is fed to cows, horses and sheep, including David's own cow called Molly. The brewery has won prizes in the Soil Association's food and drink awards in 2009 and 2010, and Oatmeal Stout was named Beer of Scotland by the Society of Independent Brewers in 2009 and won a similar prize from CAMRA in Scotland the following year.

For 11 years the brewery had a small five-barrel plant but £1 million was invested in 2010 on new 30-barrel equipment that includes four fermenting vessels. Brewers Andrew Fraser and Colin Stronge use a traditional mash tun with a copper and whirl-pool heated by direct flame to produce their range of beers. Using oatmeal in stout is an old Scottish tradition that gives a rich creamy character to the beer and creates a style that is radically different from the more acrid and bitter flavours of Irish Stout. Black Isle's stout is made with pale and chocolate malts and unmalted oats, with just one hop, the First Gold hedgerow variety. The jet black beer has an enticing aroma of creamy malt, chocolate, liquorice and dark fruits, with a solid underpinning of spicy hops. The palate is bitter-sweet, with creamy malt, berry fruits, espresso coffee, chocolate, liquorice and light hop resins, followed by a long and deep finish in which malt, dark fruits, liquorice, coffee and chocolate are beautifully melded and balanced by spicy hops.

Brewboys Seeing Double Wee Heavy

Source: Brewboys, Croydon Park, Adelaide, South Australia

Strength: 8%

Website: www.brewboys.com.au

Stephen Nelsen and Simon Sellick are based close to the acclaimed Cooper's of Adelaide: the brewery that kept the ale flag flying in a sea of ice-cold, fizzy lager. Cooper's saw off their detractors and are now a major force in Australian brewing (see *300 Beers to Try Before You Die!*). Stephen and Simon brew on a different scale. They run a brew shop, lecture on beer and have worked at several craft breweries. Their production system is unusual: due to the cramped facilities at their shop, they start the brewing process at friendly micros then take the hopped wort – the sugary extract that has been boiled with hops – to the shop, where they have a couple of fermenting vessels in a back room.

They are passionate about brewing old and new beer styles. Wee Heavy is a traditional Scottish style that is now a rarity in its own country. It's a type of barley wine and, under the old Scottish system of rating beer, was also known as 90 Shilling Ale. The beer usually came in a small nip bottle and many Scots drinkers would add a Wee Heavy to their pint to give it extra body and flavour. The Brewboys interpretation is meticulous. Stephen and Simon import Scottish malt, including peated malt from Inverness normally used in the whisky industry, and blend it with local malts. The recipe is made up of Maris Otter pale malt, chocolate, crystal and peated malt with imported East Kent Goldings and Fuggles. The units of bitterness are 27.

In order to reach the required strength and character, yeast is pitched three times to turn all the malt sugars to alcohol. The beer is brewed in what passes for winter in Australia and is aged in the fermenters for six weeks. The beer is then hand bottled with a further dosage of yeast. The amber/tawny beer that emerges from this exhaustive process has a pronounced peat nose with caramel, toffee and ripe bananas. A hint of peppery hop makes itself felt on the palate and finish of the beer, which is otherwise dominated by massive notes of ripe fruit, caramel, toffee and peat. After a couple of bottles, you'll realise why it's called Seeing Double.

A hint of peppery hop makes itself felt on the palate and finish of the beer

Cairngorm Black Gold

Source: Cairngorm Brewery, Aviemore, Highlands, Scotland

Strength: 4.4%

Website: www.cairngormbrewery.com

In the 1990s I visited breweries in Scotland – my version of the Grand Tour – and discovered the Tomintoul plant in the Highlands village of the same name. It was based in an 18th-century water mill and was one of the most dilapidated breweries I had ever seen: the vessels held together with sealing wax and string. In the winter, the brewer said his water often froze. He was Andrew Neame, a member of the Shepherd Neame brewing dynasty in faraway Kent. In spite of the unprepossessing nature of the plant, Andrew produced some delicious beer and his Wildcat strong bitter won both plaudits and prizes.

I wasn't too surprised to learn that the brewery went into receivership a few years later. Its brands (but not the brewing kit) were bought by the Aviemore Brewery. Aviemore had been set up in 1997, and in 2001, following the acquisition of Tomintoul, changed its name to Cairngorm. The brewery is based in a small town famous as a ski resort, set in the Cairngorms National Park. Local materials have been used to both protect the environment and to blend the brewery buildings with the majestic surroundings of the snow-capped Highland mountains. The brewery is clad in larch from the Rothiermurchus Estate while thermalite blocks maintain a constant temperature, ideal for brewing. Superb,

crystal-clear water for brewing comes down from the Cairngorms – and it no longer freezes in winter!

Demand for the seven regular cask beers and seasonal ales has led to the brewery expanding. The current kit can produce 20 barrels per brew and 140 barrels a week. Black Gold is a superb example of a Scottish Stout and it has won several awards, including CAMRA's Scottish Beer of the Year in 2005 and SIBA's Supreme Champion Beer in 2009. It's brewed with pale, crystal and chocolate malts, with roasted barley and lactose sugar. The hops are Challenger and Fuggles that create 35 units of bitterness. It's charcoal black in colour with a deep collar of foam and an inviting aroma of coffee, molasses, velvety smooth malt, hints of roasted grain and light floral and spicy hops. Smooth grain, coffee, molasses and chocolate dominate the palate with a hint of burnt and roasted grain and spicy hops. The finish is bittersweet with rich creamy malt, roasted grain, chocolate, coffee, molasses and gentle hop resins.

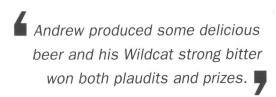

Andrew produced some delicious beer and his Wildcat strong bitter won both plaudits and prizes.

Il Chiostro Scottish Ale

Source: Il Chiostro Microbirrificio Artigianale, Nocera Inferiore, Campania, Italy

Strength: 8%

Website: www.ilchiostro.net

The world of beer gets ever more fascinating. In the spring of 2012 I discovered a Scottish Ale brewed by an Italian named Porta at the foot of Mount Vesuvius who had been inspired by a visit to the Caledonian brewery in Edinburgh. I was in the region of Campania, centred on Naples, at the invitation of Gianluca Polini and Yuri Di Rito, who run a restaurant dedicated to beer: Ottavonano, in the small town of Atripaldi.

Ottavonano means 'the eighth dwarf': it loses something in translation but is based on a joke about Snow White and Seven Dwarfs having to expel an eighth member of the fraternity for his drunken behaviour.

I conducted a beer talk and tasting at the restaurant and sampled beer brewed by Simone Della Porta. Next day we made the short journey to his small brewery at Nocera Inferiore. Simone, with a heavily bearded face, generous girth and hint of a tonsure, could easily pass for a monk and would no doubt be welcomed at the nearby monastery of Monte Cassino, birthplace of St Benedict – the inspiration for today's Trappist brewers – and scene of a crucial battle in World War Two in 1944. The name of the brewery means The Cloister and the bottles carry the image of a monk. Simone first studied law and then brewing at a specialist brewing faculty in Udine. His visit to Edinburgh encouraged him to turn his skills as a home brewer into commercial success.

As well as his Scottish ales, Simone makes several other beers (including, naturally, a Porta Porter) with some of his brews matured in oak, using casks made by the last remaining barrel maker in the region. His beers are bottle conditioned, a rare species in Italy. The brewery is based on a conventional mash tun and copper system, with the copper fired by direct flame, as is the case at Caledonian. He can produce 150 litres at a time. Soft brewing water comes from a well on the site, in a garden lush with lemon trees. His beers are strong, as Italians like doppio malto,

> *A Scottish Ale brewed by an Italian named Porta at the foot of Mount Vesuvius who had been inspired by a visit to the Caledonian brewery in Edinburgh.*

and are brewed with malt imported from Crisps in England. He uses hops from both England and the United States. For his Scottish Ale, Simone brews with Maris Otter pale malt and East Kent Goldings and Northdown hops. The gold/amber beer has a pronounced orange fruit aroma with peppery hops and honeyed malt. Rich malt, peppery hops and tart fruit build in the mouth, leading to a long, deep, bittersweet finish with a fine balance of juicy malt, orange fruit and tangy hop resins.

Following my visit to the brewery, I was taken on a white-knuckle ride around the hairpin bends of the spectacular Amalfi coast. I needed a soothing beer at the end of the journey and enjoyed more of Simone's ales with a superb lunch at the Al Convento restaurant in a former Franciscan convent.

It's dark and lonely work being a beer writer, but someone has to do it...

TASTING NOTES

APPEARANCE:

AROMA:

TASTE:

OVERALL SCORE:

Highland Dark Munro/Scapa Special

Source: Highland Brewing Company, Swannay, Orkney, Scotland
Strength: 4%/4.2%
Website: www.highlandbrewingcompany.co.uk

Rob Hill is proof that there's life after redundancy. He worked at the Orkney Brewery, one of Scotland's most successful craft breweries (see below and *300 Beers to Try Before You Die!*) until he was declared surplus to requirements during a takeover battle for the company. Bloodied but unbowed, Rob – who hails from Lancashire and earned his brewing spurs at Moorhouse's in Burnley – set up his own brewery on a tiny five-barrel plant in Swannay in 2006. He has been brilliantly successful and now sells his beer to some 300 outlets. He kept his original plant but has since added a 20-barrel kit: he uses both plants and brews four times a week. Among other staff, Rob has been joined by his son, Lewis.

Dark Munro is a strong Mild ale with a Lancastrian twist: when he was at Moorhouse's, he brewed Black Cat Mild, which was named Champion Beer of Britain in 2000. His Highland beer takes its name from the Munros: the group of Scottish mountains first listed by Sir Hugh Munro in 1891. To classify as a Munro, a mountain must be at least 3,000 feet high. There are, to date, 282 Munros and every year doughty hikers and climbers tackle as many as they can. The king of the Munros is Ben Nevis, Britain's highest mountain, which rises to a majestic 4,409 feet. (I once set out to conquer Ben Nevis but after an hour's clambering sensibly returned to the Ben Nevis Inn for a soothing pint.)

Rob's beer is brewed with Maris Otter pale malt, chocolate and crystal malts and is hopped with one variety, Fuggles. It has a luscious aroma of chocolate, vinous fruit, cocoa beans and spicy hops. Rich malt, vinous/port wine fruit and chocolate dominate the palate but Fuggles spicy hop resins in the finish balance the richness of roasted malt, vinous fruit, chocolate and bitter hops: this is a very hoppy interpretation of Mild.

Scapa Special is described as 'a Highland pale ale' and takes its name from Scapa Flow, the famous natural harbour on Orkney that was used by Viking ships 1,000 years ago but is best known as the main base for the Royal Navy in both world wars of the 20th century. At the end of World War One, the Germans scuttled their fleet at Scapa Flow in preference to handing them over to the British. Rob's beer is brewed with Maris Otter pale malt and has a complex hop makeup of varieties from Germany, New Zealand, Slovakia and the United States: namely Hallertauer, Green Bullet, Styrian Goldings and Willamette. The pale gold beer has a massive aroma of tart citrus fruits, herbs and fresh grass, with honeyed malt and tangy hop resins. Fruit, juicy malt and bitter and floral hops build in the mouth, leading to a long, quenching finish with honeyed malt, citrus and bitter hop resins.

Inveralmond Lia Fail

Source: Inveralmond Brewery, Inveralmond, Perth, Scotland
Strength: 4.7%
Website: www.inveralmond-brewery.co.uk

If Scotland gains its independence, Inveralmond brewery will no doubt launch a celebratory beer and may be one of the first to change the '.uk' tag in its website address. The brewery has its heart on its sleeve: one of its beers is called Independence while Lia Fail is the Gaelic for Stone of Destiny. The stone has iconic status in Scotland. It was kept at Scone Abbey near Perth and was used as part of the ceremony to crown Scottish kings. In 1296, Edward I of England removed the stone and took it to Westminster Abbey in London, where subsequent English monarchs were crowned. The stone was only returned to Scotland in 1996 and now rests in Edinburgh Castle.

Inveralmond brewery opened one year later and was the first new brewery in Perth for more than 30 years. It has expanded from a 10-barrel to a 30-barrel plant and plans further expansion. The quality of its beers is based on crystal-clear water from the Grampians and the best quality malts and hops. Lia Fail is a fine representative of traditional Scottish brewing: a rich, dark and robust malty ale brewed with Maris Otter pale malt, dark crystal and chocolate malts, and malted wheat. The hops are American Cascade with English Challenger and Fuggles.

from the heart of scotland
Lia Fail
distinctively rich
A.B.V 4.7%
The Inveralmond Brewery
Perth Scotland

The beer has a rich aroma of roasted and toasted grain, chocolate, dark fruit and spicy hops. Creamy malt, chocolate and fruit dominate the palate but there's a fine underpinning of bitter hop resins while the finish is long and bittersweet, with notes of creamy and roasted grain, smooth chocolate, vinous fruit and a good balance of gently bitter hops. Lia Fail won a silver medal in the 2007 Champion Beer of Britain competition and has also won gold awards from SIBA Scotland in 2003 and 2006.

 The brewery has its heart on its sleeve: one of its beers is called Independence ,

TASTING NOTES
APPEARANCE:

AROMA:

TASTE:

OVERALL SCORE:

TASTING NOTES

APPEARANCE:

AROMA:

TASTE:

OVERALL SCORE:

Kelburn Cart Blanche

Source: Kelburn Brewing Company, Barrhead,
East Renfrewshire, Scotland

Strength: 5%

Website: www.kelburnbrewery.com

Cart Blanche, which was named CAMRA's Champion Beer of Scotland in 2006, is a fine indicator of the way in which brewing is changing in the country. It's a golden ale with a pronounced hop bite, a long way removed from traditional 'Heavies' and reaching out to a younger generation of drinkers. The brewery was launched in 2002 by Derek Moore who graduated in science at Paisley university with a passing knowledge of brewing and a keen love of good beer. He brewed at home and decided to go the extra mile with a commercial operation, which he opened with the support of his son Ross and daughter Karen. Derek joined CAMRA back in 1978 and helped form the Renfrewshire branch in 1981 when cask beer was hard to find as a result of the overarching duopoly of Scottish & Newcastle and Tennent Caledonian. The brewery has gone on to win some 40 awards from industry and consumer competitions with beers that challenge drinkers with profound hop character.

Cart Blanche takes its name from Paisley's river, White Cart Water. It's brewed with Maris Otter pale malt, crystal and wheat malts and is hopped with Challenger and Styrian Goldings. The beer has a big punch of spicy hop resins on the nose with a cracker-like malt note and tart citrus fruit. Hop bitterness grows in the mouth, complemented by creamy malt and tangy fruit. The finish is refreshing and lingering, finally becoming dry after a bittersweet battle between creamy malt and spicy hops.

> Cart Blanche, which was named CAMRA's Champion Beer of Scotland in 2006, is a fine indicator of the way in which brewing is changing in the country.

Orkney Skull Splitter

Source: Orkney Brewery, Quoyloo, Orkney, Scotland

Strength: 8.5%

Website: www.sinclairbreweries.co.uk

This beer is a cross between a barley wine and a traditional Wee Heavy. It has won a shelf-load of awards from CAMRA, SIBA and international competitions and it's a pity that it became mired in a silly controversy in 2008, when a complaint was made to the Portman Group that the name encouraged people to drink strong beer to excess. The Portman Group is funded by the brewing industry and monitors the manner in which beer is sold and marketed. If the complainant had spent a few minutes researching the name he or she would have discovered that Skull Splitter was the nickname given to Thorfinn Einarsson, the seventh earl of Orkney: the Vikings invaded the islands in the eighth century and took control from the ninth. Norman Sinclair, owner of the brewery, mounted a strong defence of a name he said commemorated the history of Orkney and was not an invitation to drink immoderately. Fortunately, common sense prevailed and Skull Splitter remains on sale and is widely exported, including to the United States.

Orkney Brewery was founded in 1988 by Roger White and his wife Irene. They have now retired but they put their stamp on a company that was one of the first breweries to restore craft beer to Scotland. Ironically, Roger White, who first brewed Skull Splitter, is teetotal and could scarcely be accused of encouraging binge drinking.

The original plant was based in an old schoolhouse at Quoyloo and brewing was along strict ecological lines, with waste water treated in two lakes to support fish and Mallard ducks. The brewery is run by Sinclair Breweries, which owned the Atlas Brewery on the Scottish mainland but transferred all production to Orkney in 2010. Capacity has doubled on an adjacent site and the original building is being converted to a visitor centre. The company supplies beer to some 600 outlets in Scotland and uses wholesalers for the English market.

Skull Splitter is brewed with Maris Otter pale malt, chocolate and crystal malts and is hopped with East Kent Goldings. The deep amber beer is immensely complex with a massive aroma of creamy malt, berry fruits, molasses, caramel and peppery hops. Dates and figs appear on the palate to meld with rich malt, hints of chocolate, molasses, caramel and vanilla. Peppery hops keep a watching brief in a long, bittersweet finish dominated by malt, dark fruits, chocolate, dates, figs, caramel and molasses. This is a beer to sip, savour and admire.

TASTING NOTES

APPEARANCE:

AROMA:

TASTE:

OVERALL SCORE:

Renaissance Stonecutter

Source: Renaissance Brewing Company, Blenheim, New Zealand

Strength: 7%

Website: www.renaissancebrewing.co.nz

New Zealand's links with Scotland are so powerful – Dunedin, for example, is the ancient version of Edinburgh – that a Kiwi Scottish Ale was inevitable: except Stonecutter is produced by two Americans. Andy Deuchars, despite having a good Scottish name, hails from California, along with his business partner and brother-in-law, Brian Thiel. Andy is a trained brewer while Brian is a mechanical engineer and is 'good at putting things together and taking them apart' – a useful man to have around a brewery.

They launched their brewery in 2005 in Blenheim, in the Marlborough region of New Zealand's South Island. It's a famous wine-making area but Andy and Brian were determined to bring good beer to local bars and restaurants. Their plant is based in a building that has been an ice cream factory and a winery. In the short time they have been brewing, they have picked up awards in both New Zealand and Australian brewing competitions – and Kiwi beer has to be good to get noticed in Australia.

Stonecutter is an immensely complex beer, brewed with no fewer than nine malts. They include pale malt made from locally grown Optic two-row spring barley from the Canterbury area, with imported specialist malts from Britain and Germany. The grist is comprised of pale malt, crystal, caramalt, chocolate malt, roasted malt and peated malt – the latter imported from Scottish maltsters in Inverness who supply the whisky industry. Two hops used are both locally grown – Southern Cross for bitterness and Pacific Jade, which is added in the hop back, the vessel that receives the boiling hopped wort from the copper. The beer has 38 units of bitterness and a colour rating of 20. The beer is fermented with a culture called London ESB.

The deep bronze/amber beer has an immense aroma of coffee, chocolate, liquorice, caramel, roasted grain and notes of whisky, which continue into the palate. The finish is long, deep and complex, with roasted grain, caramel, whisky, chocolate, coffee and floral and grassy hops.

The name Stonecutter has links to Freemasonry and, says Andy Deuchars, reflects the fact that the beer is 'handmade, deep, mysterious and intense'.

Stewart Brewing Edinburgh No 3/80/-/Edinburgh Gold

Source: Stewart Brewing, Loanhead, Midlothian, Scotland

Strength: 4.3%/4.4%/4.8%

Website: www.stewartbrewing.co.uk

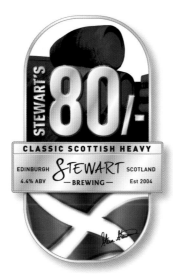

Stewart Brewing was launched in 2004 and in just a decade has established itself as one of Scotland's leading craft breweries. It's a family affair, run by Steve and Jo Stewart. Steve became a keen home brewer at the age of 16, starting with a Boots kit (for non-British readers, Boots is a high street chain of pharmacies that used to sell home brewing equipment). He moved on to full mash brewing and then studied at the world-famous Brewing and Distilling course at Heriot-Watt university in Edinburgh. He met Jo when he went on to study for a Masters in energy and the environment.

It was time to put theory in to practice. Steve worked with the leading British brewing group Bass where he learnt the entire business, from malt and hops to sales and marketing. But it was when he went on secondment to the small craft brewery Harpoon in Boston, Massachusetts, that he was fired with the enthusiasm to launch his own company. Back home and with the help of Jo's father, Steve built his 10-barrel brewery close to Edinburgh and opened for business in 2004: he brewed and Jo looked after sales. Today they have a staff of nine and are looking for new premises to keep up with demand.

Two of the three beers make a deep bow in the direction of traditional Scottish brewing. No 3 recalls a famous Edinburgh ale, Younger's No 3, which still causes older drinkers in the capital to blink away a tear or two. However, the Younger's beer was also labelled 'Export' and it was a Scottish interpretation of India Pale Ale, brewed only with pale malt. Dave Stewart's No 3 is brewed with Maris Otter pale malt, chocolate and crystal malts and wheat, and hopped with one English variety: Challenger (16 bitterness units). The amber beer has an aroma of toasted malt, chocolate and cobnuts, balanced by spicy hops. Malt, chocolate and spicy hops build in the mouth, leading to a lingering, bittersweet finish with toasted malt, chocolate and gentle but persistent Challenger hop resins.

80/- helps restore one of the key styles of Scottish brewing. It's a fine example of a Heavy, brewed with Maris Otter pale malt, chocolate, crystal and cara pils malts and wheat. Unlike No 3, this beer has a complex hop grist made up of Challenger, German Magnum and Tettnanger and Styrian Goldings (18 units of bitterness). The auburn coloured beer has a malty aroma – roast, chocolate and Ovaltine – with sultana fruit and spicy and floral hops. Creamy malt, chocolate and dark fruit dominate the palate with a gentle balance of floral and spicy hops. The finish is bittersweet but ends dry, with rich malt, dark fruits, chocolate and light hop resins.

Edinburgh Gold is a horse of a different colour. It's a modern beer style brewed with Maris Otter pale malt, cara pils and wheat, and hopped with Challenger, Magnum, Tettnanger and Styrian Goldings (23 bitterness units). It has a rich and inviting citrus fruit aroma with juicy malt and grassy, herbal and spicy hops. The palate offers a fine blend of tart and tangy fruit, sappy malt and herbal hops, with a long and lingering finish packed with tart fruit, bitter and spicy hops, and juicy malt.

Sulwath Black Galloway

Source: Sulwath Brewers, Castle Douglas, Dumfries & Galloway, Scotland
Strength: 4.4%
Website: www.sulwathbrewers.co.uk

Sulwath is yet another family concern, one that's based in the south of the country in a region forever associated with Robert Burns. The poet died in Dumfries and was a frequent visitor to inns and taverns in the area: he scratched his poem 'Epigram to a Scrimpit Nature' on the window of the Black Bull in Moffat (the window is now in a museum in Moscow). Sulwath is an ancient name for the Solway Estuary that marked the border between Scotland and England in the 13th century. The brewery was founded in 1996 in old farm buildings, with Allan Henderson as managing director and his father Jim as general manager and advisor. It moved to its present site, which includes a visitor centre, with equipment that can produce 500 gallons of beer a week.

Black Galloway is brewed with Maris Otter pale malt, chocolate and crystal malts and roasted barley. The hops are English Challenger and Goldings. What style is it? The *Good Beer Guide* hedges its bets by calling it a 'Porter/Stout'. The strength suggests a Porter but the use of roasted barley makes it more of a Stout. Roasted and toasted grain features on the nose and palate of the beer, with a big chocolate note, hints of molasses and dark fruits and spicy hops. The finish is long and complex, with roasted grain, burnt fruit, chocolate and a good underpinning of peppery hops. It's a refreshing and rewarding beer.

Irish Red Ales

Alongside Stout, Irish Red Ale defines brewing in the republic. Brewing has deep and ancient roots in Ireland: archaeologists have found evidence of small domestic breweries dating back to 1000 BC. Saint Patrick is believed to have had his own brewer and monasteries continued the tradition. In common with Scotland, commercial brewing was slow to develop in Ireland and was mainly a domestic affair carried out by women or 'ale wives'. The industrial revolution of the 18th and 19th centuries created improved methods of brewing and commercial ale became widely available. The style persisted despite the popularity of Porter and Stout.

While it was possible to brew pale ale along English lines, Irish brewers preferred a darker style. Beer in Ireland had always had a strong malt character as the damp climate makes hop growing difficult. As late as the early 18th century, some brewers were using such herbs as gentian in place of hops. Goldings were grown in the Kilkenny area in the 18th and 19th centuries but they were used sparingly and no hops are grown in Ireland today. (As an experiment, hops were grown in 2012 at the White Gypsy Brewery in Templemore but the crop was destroyed by torrential rain and floods.) Historically, the use of roasted malts made up for low hop bitterness and gave Irish ales their distinctive character and colour.

The increasing dominance of Stout and Guinness in the 20th century tended to dilute interest in Red Ale. The style became confined to breweries, such as Smithwick's, that Guinness had taken over. But interest in Irish Red was rekindled, oddly, due to a French connection. My first encounter with Irish Red was not in Ireland but in Paris in the 1980s, when Métro stations carried large posters advertising George Killian's Bière Rousse. The beer was brewed by Pelforth, a large brewery based in the Lille area, famous throughout France for its pelican symbol. It's now part of Heineken. Research revealed that the beer was originally brewed by Letts Brewery in

Enniscorthy in County Wexford. The brewery started life in an abbey in the 15th century: the address of Friary Hill confirms this while a photograph from the 1950s shows the brewery was powered by a waterwheel. In 1864 it came into the hands of George Henry Lett and passed to his grandson, George Killian Lett.

The brewery closed in 1956 but George Killian Lett, who died aged 84 in 2010, sold the rights to his main brand, Red Ale, to Pelforth and to Coors in the United States. In France it remained a true ale, made by warm fermentation, but Heineken had no interest in the brand and ceased production. In the U.S., it remains a popular beer but is made by cold fermentation and is closer to a Vienna-style lager than Irish ale.

The craft brewing revival in Ireland has rekindled interest in the style with most of the new breweries producing their interpretations. As a result, Red Ale can now proudly take its place once again on the podium of Irish beers.

TASTING NOTES

APPEARANCE:

AROMA:

TASTE:

OVERALL SCORE:

Samuel Adams Irish Red

Source: Boston Beer Company, Boston, Massachusetts, USA

Strength: 5.8%

Website: samueladams.com

No apologies for starting this section with an American beer, as Boston is famous for its large Irish community and powerful links with the Old Country. I have only twice been told to keep my mouth shut so people couldn't hear my British accent. One occasion was in a backstreet pub in Cork where drinkers have long memories and recall the Black and Tans, British auxiliaries, burnt part of the city to the ground as a reprisal against the IRA in the 1920s. The second occasion was when I was in Boston, where support for Irish republicanism remains strong. So I toured the Sam Adams brewery but otherwise kept shtum on the streets and in bars.

The story of the Boston Beer Company is told in *300 Beers to Try Before You Die!* and in the IPA section of this book. Irish Red is brewed with two-row pale malt and Caramel 60, stewed malt that gives the beer its red colour. The hops are two English varieties, East Kent Goldings and Fuggles, with Hallertauer Mittelfruh from Bavaria, which create 25 units of bitterness. Thanks to its strength and hop rate, this is a full-flavoured and complex beer with a big aroma and palate of nuts, butterscotch, caramel and cherries, balanced by an earthy Fuggles note, pepper from the Goldings and grassy note from the Mittlefruh. The beer ends dry, with good hop notes, but with continuing contributions from caramel, butterscotch and toasted malt.

❝ I have only twice been told to keep my mouth shut so people couldn't hear my British accent. ❞

Dungarvan Copper Coast

Source: Dungarvan Brewing Company, Dungarvan, County Waterford, Ireland

Strength: 4.3%

Website: dungarvanbrewingcompany.com

Dungarvan brewery opened in April 2010 and has quickly built up sales in bars, restaurants and supermarkets. It's run by two couples, Cormac and Jen O'Dwyer, and Claire and Tim Dalton. Cormac was a devoted home brewer and he mans the conventional mash tun, copper and four fermenters. The brew length is six barrels and he brews two or three times a week. Most of the beers are bottled and contain live yeast, a bold step in a country where drinkers are used to filtered beers served by a mix of applied gasses. The couples plan to move into cask-conditioned ale as well: have I mentioned there's a beer revolution underway in Ireland?

Beer is bottled flat straight from the fermenters and warm conditioning encourages the yeast to work again and develop natural carbonation. The bottles are then allowed to condition for a further four to six weeks before leaving the brewery.

Copper Coast recalls the former mining industry in the area: old quarries and tumbledown buildings can still be seen in the countryside. The beer is brewed with Maris Otter pale and crystal malts and is hopped with Challenger and Northern Brewer. The bright amber beer has a luscious aroma of barley twist confectionery, light hop resins and a herbal note. Toasted and nutty malt builds in the mouth, balanced by a growing hop note. The finish is bitter-sweet with rich biscuit malt balanced by hop resins and a late sultana fruit note.

The bright amber beer has a luscious aroma of barley twist confectionery

TASTING NOTES

APPEARANCE:

AROMA:

TASTE:

OVERALL SCORE:

TASTING NOTES

APPEARANCE:

AROMA:

TASTE:

OVERALL SCORE:

Eight Degrees Sunburnt Irish Red

Source: Eight Degrees Brewing, Mitchelstown, County Cork, Ireland

Strength: 5%

Website: www.eightdegrees.ie

Irish craic – conversation in a pub with a pint – takes on a distinctly edgy note at Eight Degrees. It's run by an Australian, Cameron Wallace, and a New Zealander, Scott Baigent. Aussies and Kiwis famously don't get on, especially when they're playing or talking cricket or rugby. But Cam and Scott rub along famously, though there's a lot of caustic asides as they brew and sell beer. Cam is an accountant and Scott an engineer. They were both keen home brewers back home and honed their skills at the famous VLB School of Brewing in Berlin. They married Irish women and decided to tackle the Irish market with a distinctive range of beers.

The 15-barrel brewing kit came from O'Hara's at Carlow when that company upgraded. It's a mash mixer, kettle and whirlpool system using hop pellets. No additives or preservatives are used in brewing and the beers are not filtered: 'Filtration strips out hop aroma and flavour,' Scott says. Natural carbonation created by fermentation is used for both kegs and bottles. Draught beers are dry hopped in keg: draught and bottled beers are sold nationwide to off-licences, bars and restaurants, and Cam and Scott are signing up two to four new accounts a week.

Why Eight Degrees? Because Mitchelstown, in the beautiful Ballyhoura district, is 8 degrees west Longtitude and it's also the perfect serving temperature for their beers. The name Sunburnt for their Red Ale is a gentle dig at the expense of the Irish who, with their pale skins, arrive on holiday Down Under and burn like a crisp within an hour or two. The beer is brewed with Maris Otter pale malt, caramalt, crystal, Munich and roasted malt and is hopped with New Zealand Cascade and Pacific Gem varieties. The hazy red beer has a big hit of raisin and sultana fruit on the nose with rich wholemeal biscuits from the malt and gentle hop resins. Nutty malt, burnt fruit and increasing hop bitterness build in the mouth, followed by sweet, juicy malt in the finish that's balanced by dark, burnt fruit and tangy hops.

Franciscan Well Rebel Red

Source: Franciscan Well Brewery, Cork, Ireland

Strength: 4.3%

Website: www.franciscanwellbrewery.com

'There's many a slip, twixt cup and lip'. In between writing the Porters and Stouts section of this book and Irish Red Ale, the Irish brewing industry was shaken by the news that the mighty global brewer Molson Coors, best known for Carling lager, had bought Franciscan Well in January 2013. The group plans to build a new 75,000 hectolitre brewery on the edge of Cork. Its research indicates that the Irish craft brewing sector will grow by 10 per cent between 2013 and 2017 and it wants a slice of the action. It will also busily export the brewery's beers to the United States, Shandon Stout in particular. It's always sad when a small craft brewery loses its independence but Molson Coors' record in Britain, where it took over Sharp's brewery in Cornwall and has not interfered with the product range, suggests that Franciscan Well may prosper. The chairman of the new company is Shane Long, founder of the original brewery, which will continue to operate within the pub.

It's unlikely that Rebel Red will be exported to the U.S. as Molson Coors brews Killian Irish Red for that vast market and it withdrew another Irish beer, Caffrey's, from North America to avoid affecting sales of Killian's. Let's hope Rebel Red will continue to entrance visitors to the pub as it's a fine version of the style. Brewer Peter Lyall uses Maris Otter pale malt and 12 per cent dark stewed malt, crystal 150, with a small amount of roasted barley, which, Peter says, is like a chef adding garlic. The hops are both English varieties, East Kent Goldings and Fuggles.

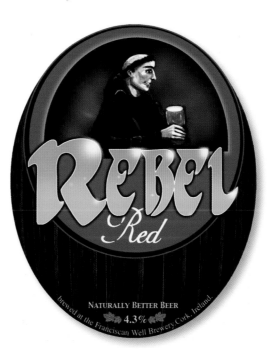

Rebel Red commemorates Cork's role as one of the main bastions of opposition to British rule, though my accent was no bar to being greeted warmly and taken on a tour of the brewery. The amber/red beer has nutty malt, bitter orange fruit, caramel, fresh tobacco and grassy hops on the aroma. Rich toasted malt, tart fruit, spicy hops and caramel fill the mouth, while the finish is bittersweet, dominated by toasted malt, caramel, orange fruit and bitter hop resins.

TASTING NOTES

APPEARANCE:

AROMA:

TASTE:

OVERALL SCORE:

TASTING NOTES

APPEARANCE:

AROMA:

TASTE:

OVERALL SCORE:

O'Hara's Irish Red

Source: **Carlow Brewing Company, Bagenalstown, County Carlow, Ireland**

Strength: **4.3%**

Website: **Website: www.carlowbrewing.com**

As one of the leading craft breweries in Ireland (see Porters & Stouts section), Carlow naturally has a Red Ale in its quiver. The hard limestone water of the area is ideal for brewing what is effectively pale ale with some colour in its cheeks. Seamus O'Hara and brewer Cieran Kelly add 10 kilos of hops to their brews and in the case of Irish Red the variety is American Mount Hood.

The grains are pale Irish malt with cara malt, roasted barley and a touch of flaked barley for head retention.

The beer has a big roasted grain nose with sultana fruit and herbal, spicy hops. Chewy fruit and toasted malt build in the mouth with gentle grassy hops. The bittersweet finish offers smoked malt, dark fruit and light but persistent spicy hops.

Porterhouse Red

Source: **Porterhouse Brewing Company, Dublin, Ireland**

Strength: **4.4%**

Website: **www.porterhousebrewco.com**

TASTING NOTES

APPEARANCE:

AROMA:

TASTE:

OVERALL SCORE:

As the man at the forefront of the Irish brewing revival, Oliver Hughes has a keen eye for tradition and, along with Plain Porter and two Stouts, he has what he calls in his retiring way 'a superior red ale'. The beer writer Michael Jackson was similarly and more objectively overwhelmed and said 'it makes Caffrey's taste like Tizer'. Tizer, if you don't know it, is a red-coloured soft drink or soda while Caffrey's was a Belfast brewery that was taken over first by Bass, then InBev and finally Molson Coors. It had major success in the 1990s with its Irish Ale but since it was sidelined by Molson Coors the beer has become a supermarket canned cheapie. The Belfast brewery closed and I have no idea where Caffrey's is brewed today.

Porterhouse Red is brewed with pale, crystal and chocolate malts, with wheat for head retention, and is generously hopped for the style with East Kent Goldings, Galena and Nugget. The beer has a rich fresh-bread malt note with strong hints of chocolate, raisin fruit, cobnuts and peppery and grassy hops. Juicy and toasted malt build in the mouth, balanced

by nuts, dark fruit and bitter hop resins. The finish is long and bittersweet, rich toasted grain vying for attention with dark fruit, chocolate and peppery hops.

A final thought: before it was run by the Caffrey family, the Belfast brewery was owned by a man with the remarkable name of Clotworthy Dobbin. Surely the time is ripe for a new craft brewery in the north of Ireland called Clotworthy Dobbin's Fine Ales.

Wheat Beers

Making beer with wheat is an ancient tradition dating from the time when breweries were based mainly in the countryside and bought grain direct from farmers, many of whom also brewed. Brewers and farmers took grain from the fields and – depending on the crop, the soil and the climate – the grains might be oats, rye and wheat as well as barley.

Barley has long been the preferred grain for beer making: as well giving a rich biscuit character to the finished beer, the grain has a husk that acts as a natural filter during the brewing process. Wheat on the other hand lacks a husk and can become glutinous when mashed with water and gums up pipes and other outlets. As a result, it became common practice to blend wheat with barley malt. Modern wheat beers continue that tradition and are made from a blend of the two grains.

In Bavaria, the character of wheat beer comes from a special yeast culture that creates an aroma and flavour strongly reminiscent of Juicy Fruit chewing gum, along with cloves and banana. The yeast produces natural compounds called phenols and guaicols that resemble the sap from tropical trees that's used in the manufacture of chewing gum.

Over the centuries, interest in wheat beer has waxed and waned. Today, Belgium and Germany are the two most notable countries producing wheat beer but the style has been taken up with enthusiasm in Australasia, Britain and the United States. In Britain, revival would be a fair description, for wheat-based beer used to be popular in the 16th and 17th centuries. Brewing historian Martyn Cornell, in *Beer: the Story of the Pint*, records that in 1568 the brewers of Oxford were banned from having their 'wheate malte' ground anywhere except at the 'Castell Mills' while in London the Lord Mayor told the Privy Council, comprised of leading parliamentarians, that wheat was used in the ratio of one-to-ten with barley to make 'stronge bere'.

A type of wheat beer called Mumm was also popular in England. Its origins are obscure but it seems to have first been brewed in Brunswick (Braunschweig) in Germany in the late 15th century. It was exported to England and was sufficiently popular to be taken up by local brewers. The *Receipt* [recipe] *Book of John Nott* in the late 1600s includes his version of Mumm that used three malts – wheat, oats and barley – along with such flavourings as myrica, cardamom seeds, wild thyme, spearmint, marjoram and bark. Hops are not listed, which indicates that use of the plant was still making slow progress in England, and herbs and spices remained in common use. It's also possible that, by trial and error, brewers found that hop bitterness didn't blend well with the tart note given to beer by wheat. Even today, wheat beers are lightly hopped – 12-14 units of bitterness are common – and in Belgium spices are still used as an additional flavouring.

In Bavaria, the biggest wheat beer region in the world, the style is inextricably linked to the *Reinheitsgebot*, the Purity Pledge of 1516. The pledge originally stipulated that

only barley malt and water could be used to make beer. The workings of yeast were not fully understood at the time, but as the science of brewing progressed, yeast was added to the pledge. Then, as hop growing spread, the plant was also included. It's noticeable that wheat was missing from the list of ingredients. It was not an oversight. The pledge was drawn up by the Bavarian royal family, the House of Wittelsbach, which in feudal times exercised a monopoly over the supply of both barley and wheat. Wheat beer, pale in colour, was considered a refined drink, suitable only for the nobility, while the common people were restricted to brown beer made from barley. The Royal Court Brewery, the Hofbräuhaus, opened in Munich in 1589 to make wheat beer. At one stage there were 30 royal brewhouses in Bavaria that made wheat beer exclusively for the nobility. The style became available for general consumption only in 1859 when the royal family licensed a Munich brewer, Georg Schneider, to brew it. Demand became so great that Schneider was forced to buy a second brewery in Kelheim in the heart of the Hallertau hop-growing region.

Other brewers in Munich and Bavaria followed Schneider and added wheat beer to their portfolios.

But as sales of golden lager, in the shape of Helles (light) and Pils, took off in the 20th century, wheat beer went into steep decline until it was rediscovered in the 1980s by the 'green' generation. Young people decided that a beer with natural yeast sediment and rich in protein was healthier than lager beer. Such has been the surge in wheat beer sales since then that the style today accounts for around half of beer sales in Bavaria.

The language of wheat beer can be difficult to disentangle. In Bavaria it's called both *Weizenbeer* – wheat beer – or *Weisse*, which means white and comes from the colour of the beer, its collar of foam in particular. But there are also dark versions of the style, known as *Dunkel Weisse/Weizen*, and strong ones known as *Weisse/Weizen Bock*. In Belgium the problem is compounded by the use of two languages. There wheat beer is labelled both *bière blanche* and *wit bier* (white beer) and is also known as *bière de froment* or *tarwebier*, which stand for wheat beer in French and Dutch.

German wheat beers, along with all other styles, no longer have to adhere to the *Reinheitsgebot*. Following complaints by brewers in other countries, mainly French brewers in the Strasbourg area, that the pledge was a restraint of trade, the European Court ruled in 1987 that the pledge should be lifted. This has allowed beers, including French ones, to be sold in Germany. However, most German brewers remain true to the pledge for beers sold on the domestic market, though exported beers produced by bigger breweries, many of which are now owned by global companies, may contain ingredients, such as maize, previously frowned upon.

Otley O-Garden

Ballast Point Wahoo Wheat Beer

Source: Ballast Point Brewing Company, San Diego, California, USA

Strength: 4%

Website: www.ballastpoint.com

A classic Belgian-style wheat beer brewed in California: the beer world spreads and contracts at the same time. Jack White was a keen home brewer who wanted to help fellow practitioners by supplying equipment and ingredients. He opened Home Brew Mart in San Diego in 1992, where he teamed up with Yuseff Cherney. Four years later they built a small brewery at the back of the store and started to brew on a commercial scale. They met with sufficient success to force a move to bigger premises in 2004, but they have maintained the home brew business.

The brewery has boomed and won a gold medal in the small brewery category in the 2010 World Beer Cup. Jack, Yuseff and their team brew a wide range of beers, including IPA and Porter. With a meticulous eye for detail, they use a special Belgian yeast culture to produce Wahoo, which is made with barley malt, oats and wheat and is spiced with coriander and orange peel. The hops are German Northern Brewer, which create 15 units of bitterness. The beer has a hazy gold colour and a spicy nose with coriander and peppery hops to the fore. Spicy and herbal notes dominate the palate with rich grain, tart citrus fruit and gentle hop bitterness. The finish has sweet grain balanced by orange fruit, herbs, spices and light hops. It's a refreshing and flavoursome beer.

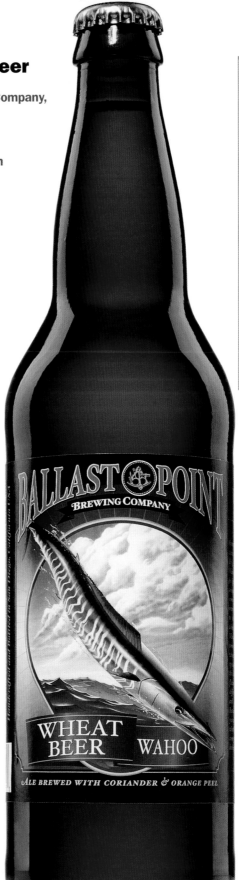

TASTING NOTES

APPEARANCE:

AROMA:

TASTE:

OVERALL SCORE:

Erdinger Weissbier/Pikantus Weizenbock

Source: Erdinger Weissbräu, Erding, Bavaria, Germany
Strength: 5.3%/7.3%
Website: www.erdinger.de

Erding is a picture-postcard Bavarian town with pastel-coloured buildings and onion-domed churches. It was set on fire during the Thirty Years War and was largely rebuilt in the 17th and 18th centuries. The town once had nine small breweries: one survives and it has become the biggest producer of wheat beer in the world. Erdinger's production currently stands at 1.5 million hectolitres a year, in stark contrast to its humble origins. Its original site dates from 1537: the site is now a brewery tap and hotel. The brewery came into the hands of the Bombach family in 1935 and is run today by Werner Bombach, who built a new brewery in 1983 on a greenfield site on the edge of town and has subsequently doubled production.

Bombach and his brewers are painstaking about the raw materials they use. The brewery supplies local farmers with seed to grow barley and wheat to Erdinger's precise specifications. The soft, aromatic quality of the beer comes from wheat with a low level of protein while brewing 'liquor' comes from an on-site bore hole and is softened. Hops are from the Hallertau region and are Perle and Tettnang varieties. They are added three times during the boil and are used primarily for aroma rather than bitterness.

Erdinger produces a filtered Kristall version of its main beer but the unfiltered *Weissbier* – labelled '*mit Hefe*' or 'with yeast' – is the classic version. A double decoction mash is used (see Glossary) and primary fermentation is in horizontal tanks: Werner Brombach is against the use of cylindro-conical tanks as he feels a 'dirty tasting beer' can result. Before it's bottled or run into kegs, the beer is re-seeded with a lager yeast culture, *kräusened* with fresh wort, and warm conditioned for two to four weeks. The use of lager yeast for conditioning is controversial in Bavaria but brewers such as Werner Bombach believes it gives the finished beer greater stability and shelf life. The beer has a hazy gold colour, a superb aroma of banana, cloves, a

hint of vanilla and gentle, spicy hops. The finish is quenching, fruity, full of delicious creamy malt and a good underpinning of herbal hops.

Pikantus – piquant – is a strong *Weizenbock* with an amber colour from the addition of darker roasted malts, both barley and wheat. The malts give a delicious liquorice note to the beer, which blends with rich roasted and creamy grain, a bigger note of vanilla and fruit, and a more pronounced spicy hop character.

Emerson's Weizenbock

Source: Emerson's Brewing Company, Dunedin, New Zealand

Strength: 8%

Website: www.emersons.co.nz

Success comes with a price. The brewers of the popular Pilsner included earlier in this book have been bought by Lion, the giant Australasian brewing group owned by Kirin of Japan. The reaction in New Zealand to the purchase was highly critical: drinkers were concerned that an admired craft brewery had lost its independence while a number of bars in the Dunedin area refused to stock the brewery's beers. The terrible trail of takeovers and closures in the 1970s and 80s helped spark the world-wide development of the craft beer movement but giant global brewers are more benign – or canny – these days. In countries such as Australia, New Zealand, Britain and the United States, where mainstream beers are in decline, big brewers are buying smaller ones because they recognise their brands are in demand. The record of Lion in Australia and Molson Coors in Britain, despite initial misgivings, has not impeded the likes of Malt Shovel and James Squire in Australia or Sharp's in Britain. Even the takeover of Goose Island by the world's biggest brewer of all, AB InBev, has so far led to wider distribution of the Chicago beers.

So it's finger crossed for the future of Emerson's and in particular its Weizenbock. Local beer writer Neil Miller says: 'The annual release [in August] of this wonderfully dark and strong wheat beer is a highlight on the New Zealand beer calendar.' Brewed with locally-grown ale and lager malts, with German wheat, roasted malt, carapils, cara aroma malt and chocolate malt, the beer is hopped with New Zealand Cascade and has 34 units of bitterness – high for the style. It has an immense aroma and palate of bananas, cloves and other spices, chocolate, raisins and Christmas cake. The finish is long, deep and complex, with continuing notes of bananas, cloves, chocolate, raisins, roasted grain and gentle hop resins. The beer won a gold medal in the 2010 Australian international beer awards and gold in the wheat beer section of BrewNZ in 2009.

> **The annual release [in August] of this wonderfully dark and strong wheat beer is a highlight on the New Zealand beer calendar.**

TASTING NOTES

APPEARANCE:

AROMA:

TASTE:

OVERALL SCORE:

TASTING NOTES

APPEARANCE:

AROMA:

TASTE:

OVERALL SCORE:

Kaiserdom Hefe-Weissbier

Source: Kaiserdom Privatbrauerei, Bamberg, Germany

Strength: 4.7%

Website: www.kaiserdom.de

The full story of the Kaiserdom family brewery is told in the Pilsner section. It's far and away the biggest brewery in the spell-binding town of Bamberg, famous for its smoked or *Rauch* beers. Kaiserdom's wheat beer is, as the name implies, a cloudy, unfiltered beer and the label carries the tag line '*Naturtrüb*', which also means unfiltered. The brewery reveals little about ingredients and brewing methods – it's descended from a Benedictine monastery and maintains a belief in strict observance – but the beer is a blend of malted barley and wheat, with hops from the Hallertau.

The beer has a gold/orange colour with a massive banana and cloves aroma and palate, with some apple notes, too. Creamy malt, fruit and spices dominate the palate followed by a dry finish with a pronounced banana note, creamy malt and gentle hop resins.

Kaltenberg Weissbier Dunkel/Hell

Source: Kaltenberg Marthabräu, Fürstenfeldbrück, Bavaria, Germany

Strength: 5.5%

Website: www.royal-bavarian-beer-selection.com

TASTING NOTES

APPEARANCE:

AROMA:

TASTE:

OVERALL SCORE:

Crown Prince Luitpold of Kaltenberg is a member of the Wittelsbachs, the royal Bavarian family that lost power at the end of World War One. Nevertheless, he still enjoys the title of His Royal Highness, though he was quick to tell me to call him Lui. He is famous and admired for restoring the fortunes of *Dunkel* – dark lager – at his brewery in the castle at Kaltenberg: see *300 Beers to Try Before You Die!* But he is also a major producer of wheat beer. In the mid-1980s he bought the Martha brewery in the town of Fürstenfeldbrück, close to Munich, which was founded by a woman of that name in 1573. It was bought by Sebastien Müller who died without leaving children and the brewery passed into the safe keeping of the local church until it was bought by Prince Luitpold. An old wooden beer cask with a halo of hops and an inscription informing visitors that 'God gives us malt and hops' leads into a brewhouse with gleaming copper mashing and boiling vessels that feed open fermenters made of stainless steel set in attractive blue-tiled surrounds.

Prince Luitpold is strict about all aspects of brewing. 'Few wheat beer brewers produce a proper bottle-conditioned beer,' he says. 'We produce a fresh yeast culture for each brew. If you use the same yeast from the normal run there will be some dead cells present. One hundred per cent fresh yeast gives greater stability and freshness to the bottle: remember, 40 per cent of the flavour of beer comes from the yeast.' He uses a fruity, warm-fermenting yeast culture for primary fermentation and a lager culture for secondary fermentation. The bottles are warm conditioned for two weeks, longer in cold weather, to encourage a powerful secondary surge, and is then cold conditioned. Pale and Munich malts are used with Hersbrucker, Perle and Tettnang hops, which produce 12-13 units of bitterness.

I sampled the beers in a rustic tavern attached to the brewery, which serve hearty Bavarian food and has a *Stammtisch*, a large table set aside for locals: woe betide you if you occupy their hallowed places. The Dunkel Weisse, which has added darker roasted grain, is packed with delicious chocolate flavours with earthy hop notes and a hint of sourness. The Helles or light version is a classic of the style, with a fruity, spicy and peppery aroma, with more fruit and spices in the mouth, followed by a long finish packed with citrus fruit and creamy malt, with gentle hop resins.

Krombacher Weizen

Source: Krombacher Brauerei, Kreuztal-Krombach, North Rhine Westphalia, Germany

Strength: 5.3%

Website: www.krombacher.de

It's a sign of the enormous interest in wheat beer in Germany that one of the country's biggest brewers based in the north, a hot-bed of Pils production, has added a warm fermented beer to its portfolio. It took a long time to get around to brewing wheat beer. Its Weizen was launched in 2007, some 200 years after the brewery was founded in a town then spelt Crombach. It was opened by Johannes Haas, whose father owned a tavern in the town, an important consideration as an ancient law said beer could only be brewed for local inns. Krombach is in a region known as Siegerland, which is not only heavily wooded but has pure spring water filtered through rock. The brewery has access to 48 springs from an area called the Zimberg Tunnel, hidden in dense forest. The water is low in minerals, ideal for brewing both Pils and wheat beer.

The brewery was bought from Haas by the Schaderberg family, which continues to run the company today. Their fortunes coincided with the industrial revolution. Mining, iron and steel became major industries in

Siegerland and created a large army of thirsty workers. When the railway linked the region with the Ruhr, the driving force of north German industry, Krombacher had a vast new market in which to sell its beer. Pils was first brewed in the 1890s when the brewery was rebuilt to accommodate steam engines and ice-making machines for cold fermented beer. Following the difficult period of the 1930s and World War Two, Krombacher's fortunes revived in the 1950s and its sales boomed as a result of German re-unification in the 1980s. Today production stands at five million hectolitres a year.

Weizen is brewed with a meticulous devotion to both detail and raw materials. Barley and wheat malts are sourced from within Germany while hops come from the Bavarian Hallertau. The beer has a gold/pale bronze colour and a massive hit of cloves on the nose, with creamy malt and a developing banana note. Spice and fruit build in the mouth, balanced by rich creamy malt and light hop notes. Cloves and rich malt dominate the finish with gentle hop notes. It finally ends dry.

TASTING NOTES

APPEARANCE:

AROMA:

TASTE:

OVERALL SCORE:

Little Valley Hebden's Wheat

Source: Little Valley Brewery, Cragg Vale, Hebden Bridge, West Yorkshire, England
Strength: 4.5%
Website: www.littlevalleybrewery.co.uk

It's a fair bet that if you're called Wim van der Spek and learned your brewing skills in the Netherlands you will have a passing knowledge of wheat beer and would want to brew it even if you're some way from the source in remote West Yorkshire. We have already encountered Wim in the IPA section and now we turn our attention to his spiced wheat beer, a style locked into the history and culture of the Low Countries.

In common with all Wim's beers, Hebden's Wheat – named after the nearby town of Hebden Bridge – is made entirely from organic materials and has the seal of approval of the Soil Association. The malt grist is half and half barley and wheat malts and the hops are Hersbrucker from the Bavarian Hallertau. Coriander seeds and lemon peel are added following the copper boil and prior to fermentation. The beer is available both cask- and bottle conditioned: the draught version won a silver medal in the 2007 Champion Beer of Britain competition.

The golden beer has a spicy and lemon aroma with hints of herbal hops and bubblegum. Peppery hops and tart lemon fruit build in the mouth with honeyed malt and light hop resins. The finish is quenching, full of lemon zest and spices and a gentle underpinning of herbal hops.

Otley O-Garden

Source: Otley Brewing Company, Pontypridd, Glamorgan, Wales
Strength: 4.8%
Website: www.otleybrewing.co.uk

You have to admire the chutzpah of the Otley brothers. They are a remarkably successful brewery in South Wales but they are a pipsqueak compared to the power and legal muscle of AB InBev, the world's biggest brewer, which owns a famous spiced Belgian wheat beer that I shall not name but which featured in *300 Beers to Try Before You Die!* To date, Otley hasn't heard from the global giant's lawyers, who are probably too busy fighting the battle of the Budweisers.

O-Garden has won many awards, including the speciality class of the Champion Beer of Britain competition in 2008 and the wheat beer class in CAMRA's Welsh beer awards in 2010.

The story of Otley Brewery is told in the Golden Ales section. For their wheat beer, the Otley brothers use pale malt, wheat, American Amarillo and Celeia hops from Slovenia, with the addition of orange peel, coriander and cloves. The beer is both cask- and bottle-conditioned and it has a spicy clove and coriander aroma with orange and creamy malt. The palate is fresh, zesty, full of tart fruit and spice with a hint of hop resins. The finish is dry, quenching, crisp, fruity and spicy.

O-GARDEN
ABV 4.8%
500ML

TASTING NOTES

APPEARANCE:

AROMA:

TASTE:

OVERALL SCORE:

TAP 5.

Schneider Weisse Tap 4/Tap 5

Source: Privatbrauerei G Schneider & Sohn, Kelheim, Bavaria, Germany
Strength: 6.2%/8.2%
Website: www.schneider-weisse.com

Erdinger may be the biggest wheat beer brewer in the world but Schneider is regarded by many as the master of the style. For decades the brewery was best known for its Original Weisse and Aventinus Weizenbock (see *300 Beers to Try Before You Die!* But the company has spread its wings and introduced several new beers.

The brewery at Kelheim is an odd blend of Spanish and Gothic architecture. It was built in 1607 and is almost certainly the oldest continuous wheat beer brewery in the world. All the sons of the Schneider family are named Georg and Georg VI is now in charge, with his father Georg V and mother Margaretta on hand to give advice. The family is linked to the Bavarian royal family who licensed Georg Schneider in 1859 to brew wheat beer commercially. This meant that for the first time wheat beer was made available to the 'common people' and was no longer the preserve of the nobility. Schneider – a name that means Taylor in English – brewed first at the Hofbräuhaus, the royal court brewery, in Munich but moved to a tavern and brewhouse at the Tal, the Dale, near the Gothic town hall. Again, as demand for his beer soared, Schneider added the second plant at Kelheim. The tavern in Munich still stands but the brewery was destroyed by the British Royal Air Force in World War Two: there are graphic photos of the air raid and the destruction of the brewery on display.

The Kelheim brewery, which can produce 300,000 hectolitres a year, has open fermenters, which are rare in Germany where brewers are terrified of contamination by wild yeasts. Malts are blended in the proportion of 60% wheat to 40% barley, which is a large amount of wheat. Some Vienna and darker malts are used to give the beers their bronze/copper colour. Hersbrucker hops from the neighbouring Hallertau are the main aroma hop. Water filtered through Jurassic stone is softened to remove some of the minerals. The modern brewhouse was built in 1988 with stainless steel mashing vessels and kettles set on marble floors. Primary fermentation lasts for between three and five days and the beer is then bottled or kegged at warm temperature. The beer is *kräusened*

with wort and re-seeded with yeast – the house culture not a lager yeast: the Schneiders frown on the modern tendency to use lager yeast in bottle and keg. The beer is matured for a week, during which time a second fermentation takes place and the beer is naturally carbonated. Finally, the beer is cold conditioned to stabilise it.

The new beers mark a dramatic change from tradition. Tap 4 is tagged 'Mein Grünes' – My Green – and is made entirely with organic malt and hops. The blend of malts is slightly different to Original: 50-50 barley and wheat malts. The hop variety is New Zealand Cascade which creates 20 units of bitterness (Original has 14-15 units). This is a major departure, the first time I've come across a German brewer using imported hops.

Tap 5 is, in every sense, stunning. It's tagged 'Meine Hopfenweisse' – My Hop Weisse – and breaks with the belief that wheat beers should be lightly hopped as the plant's aromas and flavour do not blend well with the character of wheat malt. The beer, again, is a 50-50 blend of barley and wheat malts: the wheat malt varieties are Arthus, Dekan and Hermann while the barley malt is Grace. The Saphir hop variety from the Hallertau creates 40 units of bitterness and is also used to dry hop the beer following fermentation. Dry hopping was not permitted during the days of the *Reinheitsgebot* but can now be used following the relaxation of the law.

Unlike Original, both beers are made only with pale malts. The Green version is exceptionally pale, with a straw colour. It has a yeasty, fresh bread aroma with light spice notes, rich malt and a touch of citrus fruit. Citrus builds in the mouth with creamy malt, tangy hop resins, spices and a hint of banana. The banana note builds in the finish as the beer warms in the glass with continuing notes of spice, citrus and creamy malt.

The Hopfenweisse has a stunning aroma of floral, herbal and fruity hops with fresh toasted malt, tart fruit and spice. Tangy hop resins dominate the palate with rich fruit, juicy malt and spices. The finish is long and bittersweet with spices, zesty fruit, creamy malt and herbal hop resins.

Thornbridge Versa Weisse Beer

Source: Thornbridge Brewery, Bakewell, Derbyshire, England

Strength: 5%

Website: www.thornbridgebrewery.co.uk

'Innovation, Passion, Knowledge' are the watchwords of Thornbridge, one of the most successful of the new craft breweries in Britain. It has grown at a phenomenal rate. It opened in 2005 in a few garden sheds at Thornbridge Hall, a former stately home that had fallen into disrepair and was rescued by Emma and Jim Harrison. On the back of the success of its beers, including the much-garlanded Jaipur IPA (see *300 Beers to Try Before You Die!*) and St Petersburg (see Porters & Stouts section), the brewery moved to a custom-built new site in 2009 at Crompton Mill near Bakewell. The mill is of historic importance as it was here that Richard Arkwright in the late 18th century harnessed the power of the River Derwent to make a spinning frame driven by water power that sparked the start of the industrial revolution.

Jim Harrison and his brewing team have harnessed not only the water but a modern, flexible brewing kit built in Italy that cost £1.6 million and enables them to produce 30,000 barrels a year.

All the Thornbridge beers are produced strictly to tradition and recipe. Versa, as the name implies, is inspired by the Bavarian wheat beer style and is unfiltered. Both the yeast culture and the wheat malt are imported from Bavaria and the malts are blended with pale barley malt, caramalt and crystal malt. The single hop variety is Tettnanger. The golden beer throws an enormous fluffy head of foam, followed by a spicy/clove aroma with a yeasty, fresh wholemeal bread note and gentle, floral hops. Creamy malt, clove, banana and bubblegum dominate the palate followed by a tart and refreshing finish with a fine blend of spice, banana, creamy malt and light hops.

Creamy malt, clove, banana and bubblegum dominate the palate

TASTING NOTES

APPEARANCE:

AROMA:

TASTE:

OVERALL SCORE:

227

Three Boys Wheat

Source: Three Boys Brewery, Christchurch, New Zealand

Strength: 5%

Website: www.threeboysbrewery.co.nz

The brewery started life in 2006 in a shed at Ralph Bungard's home then moved to a commercial building in Christchurch. It was forced to move yet again following the disastrous earthquake of February 2011. As a result, Ralph and his sons Marek and Quinn – the three boys – now have a 1,800 hectolitre plant in smart new buildings in the Woolston district of the city.

Ralph is a scientist who worked in Sheffield in the early years of the 21st century where he acquired a taste for British beer, Black Sheep and Timothy Taylor in particular. When he returned home he found jobs in academia hard to find and decided to brew commercially. The brewery quickly found favour with New Zealand drinkers and the beers have won several awards in competitions. Ralph is sufficiently highly regarded to be handed the president's role in the New Zealand Brewers' Guild.

The Belgian-style *wit* is brewed with 40% lager malt from Gladfield Malt in New Zealand and 60% Weyermann wheat malt from Germany. The bittering hop is Green Bullet and Motueka is added at the end of the copper boil: both are NZ varieties. Ralph says: 'We add dry ground coriander seed from India and our favourite lemon zest comes from the variety Yen Ben. We only use zest and not juice in the brew. Lemons are a much more "Kiwi" form of citrus – most home gardens have a lemon tree – and we feel lemon zest adds a little more local NZ flavour to the brew.'

The beer has a zesty/spicy aroma of lemon and coriander with creamy malt and floral hops. Citrus builds in the mouth, balanced by creamy malt, light hops and peppery spice. The finish is long and quenching, with rich, creamy malt, spice, gentle hops and a tangy and tart lemon note.

The finish is long and quenching, with rich, creamy malt, spice, gentle hops and a tangy and tart lemon note

Abbey & Trappist Beers

In a beer world undergoing tumultuous change and innovation, we must not overlook the history, culture and deep social roots of brewing. Beer making is as old as time, and for centuries it was controlled in European countries by the church.

Mont des Cats
Bière Trappiste

That control was largely broken at the time of the Reformation but the link has been maintained by a handful of monasteries that continue to make beers of quality in Belgium and the Netherlands. The monastic breweries in those countries featured in *300 Beers to Try Before You Die!* but they have since been joined by monks in both Austria and France. In the case of the French monastery, the beer is currently brewed by Chimay in Belgium but the monks plan to install their own brewing equipment. There is also the possibility of a second Dutch monastery, the Abbey of Maria Toevlucht near Breda, starting to brew beer, but this is such a closed order that the ale may be just for the monks own consumption.

The story of Trappist brewing is one driven by necessity, not commercial gain. The Trappists are properly known as the Cistercian Order of the Strict Observance. Their order was founded at the abbey of La Trappe in Normandy in 1664. At the time of the French Revolution, the monks' churches were sacked and the monks headed north to the Low Countries. They built new places of worship and in several cases added small breweries to make beer to accompany their meals, to help sustain them during Lent and to refresh visiting pilgrims. Following World War One, small amounts of Trappist ale were made available commercially to help the monks rebuild churches damaged during the fighting. Commercial sales became more widespread after the Second World War: the invading German army had stripped many of the breweries of their copper vessels and the costs of restoration were high.

Until the 1980s, Belgium was a small brewing country of which we knew little. But since the profusion of beers in the country became better known, Trappist ales have become more widely available. In 1997,

members of the Strict Observance met to discuss how to protect their beers from the shrill demands of the modern world of supermarkets and the confusion caused by the increasing number of Abbey beers produced by commercial brewers. The result was the creation of the International Trappist Association that places a common seal 'Authentic Trappist Product' on the monks' beers. The monks are at pains to explain that the label does not imply there is such a thing as a 'Trappist style' of beer. The only similarity from one monastery to the next is that the beers are ales, made by warm fermentation, but each beer has evolved in its own way. Save for occasional religious gatherings, there is little contact between the monasteries. Crucial to the authenticity of the beers is the ruling that production must be overseen by the monks in each abbey, even when lay workers are employed in the breweries.

Abbey beers, like the famous curate's egg, are good and bad in parts. Some are the result of crude commercialism, where big breweries cash in on the popularity of Trappist ales with bottles adorned with images of stained glass windows and abbeys that confuse the consumer. In other cases, however, abbey ales are the result of legitimate co-operation between a religious house and a commercial brewery. In these cases, the monks have licensed breweries to brew for them using where possible original recipes and in return receive royalties from sales that help with the upkeep of their churches.

For this section I have spread the net wider than just the Low Countries. There are a few British breweries producing ales that have strong link to abbeys and the theme has been picked up as far away as Australia, proving that beer can be made by mates as well as brothers.

TASTING NOTES

APPEARANCE:

AROMA:

TASTE:

OVERALL SCORE:

Ampleforth Abbey Beer

Source: Ampleforth Abbey/Little Valley Brewery, Hebden Bridge, North Yorkshire, England

Strength: 7%

Website: www.ampleforth.org.uk/www.littlevalleybrewery.co.uk

Benedictine monks at Ampleforth and the Little Valley Brewery have restored a brewing tradition lost in England at the time of the Reformation. Ampleforth Abbey Beer, a russet-coloured ale, is the result of fusing the methods of modern Trappist breweries in Belgium with fragments of knowledge garnered from the period in the 17th century when English Benedictines, living in exile in France, brewed and sold an ale dubbed 'la bière anglaise'. The beer is brewed by the Little Valley Brewery, run by Wim van der Spek and Sue Cooper, who we have already encountered in the IPA and Wheat Beer sections. Following the Belgian method of designation, this means the Ampleforth beer – with the subsidiary term Double/Dubbel – is an Abbey Beer rather than a monastic one brewed by the monks themselves. However the brothers have been closely involved in the development of the beer and may consider moving production to the abbey. They have produced cider and cider brandy for several years and, with 2,000 acres at their disposal, have sufficient space to build a small brewing plant.

Dogged research went into the creation of the beer. Wim has visited the Trappist breweries in the Low Countries to study their recipes and methods of production. Father Wulstan from Ampleforth accompanied him, as he was determined to produce a beer with an authentic monastic character. As a result of their travels and research, Wim has used both modern brewing techniques and information about the original recipe made available by the monastery of Dieulouard near Nancy in Lorraine. The English Benedictines settled there when they fled to France in 1608 and built a brewery to support their pastoral work. When Elizabeth I replaced Mary Tudor on the throne, the monks expected persecution: one monk who stayed at the order's mother church, Westminster Abbey, was tried for

Rich fruit and malt dominate the palate but they're balanced by spicy hops

Ampleforth Abbey

treason and executed. The English monks met up with French and Spanish members of the order at Dieulouard. They took over a church, which they turned into the Abbey of St Lawrence. The beer from their brewery was widely available throughout France and enjoyed a fine reputation. In 1793 the Benedictines returned to England, this time escaping the anti-clerical French Revolution. Some of the monks settled in Yorkshire where a major landowner, Lady Anne Fairfax, had granted a house to her priest-in-residence, Father Anselm Bolton. Lady Anne, while a devout Roman Catholic, was a member of the Fairfax family whose generals had fought with Oliver Cromwell during the English Civil War. Father Bolton's house was developed first into a priory and then into the current abbey. Work on the abbey finished in 1897 and included a boys' school: the school today is co-educational.

La Bière Anglaise was brewed with barley malt, wheat, hops, yeast and water. It would have been a deep amber, russet or brown colour as malt at the time was cured over wood fires that resulted in brown malt. The beer from Dieulouard was said to be 'double fermented' and even 'sparkled like Champagne'. This raises the intriguing thought that the English monks may have had contact with Dom Perignon and other French Benedictines who developed sparkling wine in the 17th century, also in north-east France.

What is certain is that the monks' beer would have enjoyed a first fermentation in the brewery and a second in oak casks. Wim van der Spek's beer for Ampleforth has a second fermentation in bottle rather than cask. It's called Double in the Trappist tradition of producing beers in rising order of strength: Single, Double and Triple. The beer is brewed with pale and wheat malts and the colour is the result of using three darker malts: chocolate, crystal and Munich, which add nutty and toffee-like notes. Soft brown sugar, another Trappist tradition, is also used. There are two hop varieties: Northern Brewer from Germany and Savinjski Goldings from Slovenia. The yeast culture comes from an unnamed Belgian Trappist brewery but the Ampleforth beer is so strongly reminiscent of the ales produced at the Rochefort monastery in French-speaking Wallonia that the origin of the yeast is not difficult to determine.

The beer has a spicy and peppery aroma from the hops, backed by roasted grain, chocolate and sultana fruit. Rich fruit and malt dominate the palate but they're balanced by spicy hops, while the finish is bittersweet with dark fruit, roasted grain, chocolate and gentle hop resins. The beer was launched in the summer of 2012 and within six months had sold close to 30,000 bottles. It can be bought direct from the abbey or via their website; the beer is also on sale in Booth's and Tesco supermarkets in Yorkshire and from specialist beer shops.

Caulier Abbaye Paix-Dieu

Source: Brasserie Caulier, Péruwelz, Belgium

Strength: 10%

Website: www.brasseriecaulier.com

This beer can genuinely be described as history in a glass. Both brewery and abbey have ancient roots and have known turbulence, closure and reorganisation. The abbey, whose name means Peace of God, was run by nuns who employed monks to brew for them. The abbey started life as a convent in the early 13th century in the diocese of Liège. It transferred to its present site in 1244 and became a Cistercian abbey run by an abbess. There were also monks on site who worked under the direction of the nuns, tilling the fields, husbanding animals and brewing ale to sustain the community. Nuns and monks were dispersed in 1797 during the French Revolution and the site fell into disrepair. It was restored by the government of Wallonia and is now run as a heritage centre. Archaeological digs at the site found evidence of a small brewery.

The commercial brewery in Péruwelz, between Mons and Tournai and close to the French border, is now run by the Caulier family but brewing in the small town dates from 1628. The local brewery stopped production and became a beer distribution company. It was bought by a miner, Charles Caulier, in 1933, and his family continued the distribution business until the third generation under Roger Caulier decided to brew as well. They were able to buy equipment from a closed brewery and started production in 1994 in former tannery buildings. They quickly established a good reputation for a range of beers in swing-top bottles, gold, amber and brown, called Bon Secours – Good Help.

Government officials running the former abbey decided to launch a beer to commemorate brewing on the site. Caulier won the tender and in 2010 launched Abbaye Paix-Dieu. In common with all Caulier's beer, Paix-Dieu is brewed with the finest raw materials, without artificial fertilisers or stabilisers, and continues to ferment in the bottle. The most fascinating aspect of the production of the abbey beer is that it's fermented at night, during full moon in the autumn. Roger Caulier discovered this method when he visited a French wine maker: brewing at full moon, it seems, speeds up fermentation and cuts the primary stage from seven to five days. This becomes utterly believable after several glasses of the 10% beer.

Following fermentation, the beer is cold conditioned for several weeks, during which time it clears naturally. It's brewed with Pilsner malt and pale candy sugar and hopped with Goldings from Kent in England. The pale bronze beer has a big honey malt, floral hop and candy sugar aroma. Peppery hop resins build in the mouth with rich, sweet, lightly toasted malt, honey and spice. The finish is bittersweet, with gentle peppery hops, biscuit malt and a continuing honey note.

Durham Benedictus

Source: Durham Brewery, Bowburn, Co Durham, England
Strength: 8.4%
Website: www.durhambrewery.co.uk

It's one of the finest views in the whole of England. As trains roar through Durham, with the line perched high above the city, there are quick snatches of the awesome cathedral and the chunky castle. This is border country and the castle, one of many in the north east of England, was built to keep the marauding Scots at bay. It was the duty of the leading monks, known as 'prince bishops', in the Benedictine cathedral to go beyond ordinary clerical duties and organise the defence of the region. Work on the Norman cathedral started in 1093 and was completed within 40 years. Its position is stunning, based on a great loop in the River Wear and standing high above a deep gorge.

The Durham Brewery commemorates the cathedral with several of its beers, including Bede's Chalice, Cloister and Evensong as well as Benedictus. Labels and pumps clips are designed with a suitably ecclesiastical typeface and symbols. The brewery was founded in 1994 by two school teachers, Christine

and Steve Gibbs. The immediate success of the brewery sent Steve out of the classroom into full-time running of the brewery. The original five-barrel plant was replaced in 1999 by a 10-barrel kit that produces a wide range of cask-conditioned and bottle-conditioned beers.

Benedictus falls into the second category. Steve and his brewing team use an especially active yeast culture that turns as much malt sugar into alcohol as possible, to avoid the finished beer being sweet and cloying. It's brewed with Maris Otter pale malt with crystal and wheat malts. The hop recipe is complex, using Columbus, Goldings, Saaz, Styrian Goldings and Target varieties. The result is a golden beer in the Tripel style with rich peach and peardrop aromas on the nose, with a fudge-like malt character, caramel notes from the crystal malt and earthy hop resins. Rich malt, powerful spicy and peppery hops and caramel coat the mouth, followed by a long, profound finish with juicy malt, ripe fruit and bitter, earthy and spicy hops.

TASTING NOTES

APPEARANCE:

AROMA:

TASTE:

OVERALL SCORE:

TASTING NOTES

APPEARANCE:

AROMA:

TASTE:

OVERALL SCORE:

Engelszell Gregorius

Source: Stift-Engelszell Abbey, Engelhartszell, Austria

Strength: 9.7%

Website: www.stift-engelszell.at

Engel is the German for angel and someone somewhere must be looking after the abbey of Stift-Engelszell, for it's had a tumultuous and even tragic history. The monks started brewing again in 2012 following a long gap: brewing had ceased in 1932 when the equipment was sold to a major Austrian group, Brau AG, now BrauUnion, part of Heineken. The present abbot, Marianus, needed additional funds for the upkeep of the buildings. He has only six other brothers left in the community that stands in a wooded valley in Upper Austria, close to Munich over the border in Bavaria.

A priory was founded on the site by Cistercians in 1293. It was later promoted to the rank of abbey and it's considered to be one of the finest rococo buildings in central Europe, with many exquisite works of art. The community was dissolved in 1786 by Emperor Joseph II and was re-founded in 1925 by German Trappist monks who had been expelled from Alsace in World War One. They faced even greater upheaval following the Nazi takeover of Austria – the Anschluss – in 1938. A year later the 73 monks were evicted from their monastery. Four of them were sent to the Dachau death camp and others were forced to join the German armed forces, the Wehrmacht.

When Austria gained its independence following the defeat of Nazi Germany, the abbey was able to function again. The monks made cheese, bread and spirits and added a brewery in 2012 to boost their income. The monks turned for help to Peter Krammer, who runs the family-owned Brauerei Hofstetten some 25 miles away. Peter designed and built a 15-hectolitre plant with stainless steel vessels and small enclosed conical fermenters. The plant is half the size of the Achel monastery brewery in Belgium.

Both Peter and the monks were determined to produce a beer that was unique to the abbey and was not a clone of any of the Trappist beers produced in Belgium and the Netherlands. The abbey is the eighth Trappist establishment to brew beer and only the second outside Belgium. Gregorius is named in honour of a former abbot, Gregorius Eisvogel.

As well as malts and hops, the beer is also infused with local honey: Peter Krammer says the honey is fully fermented and helps make the finished beer dry. He says its use is similar to that of candy sugar used in many Belgian Trappist ales. The recipe is comprised of Pilsner malt from Austria and darker stewed caramunich and caravienne malts from the specialist Weyermann company in Bamberg in Franconia. The hops are local Aurora with Magnum from the Mühlviertel hop-growing region on the other side of the Danube. Fermentation is with a wine yeast culture from Alsace that helps create the high level of alcohol. The beer is aged for six months before it's bottled with yeast sediment. It's been awarded the official Trappist logo. The amber/red beer has a pronounced spicy hop nose, with roast chestnuts, toasted malt, vinous/port wine fruit and chocolate. Dark vinous fruit dominates the mouth with dry chocolate, roasted and toasted grain, and peppery hop resins. The finish starts sweet with rich grain notes, port wine and chocolate but spicy hops kick in to make a dry end.

The monks plan a second beer, Benno, a 7% golden ale. They were not satisfied with trial brews in 2012 and decided, with Peter Krammer's advice, to reformulate the recipe and production regime. Watch for further information on the abbey's website.

Franciscan Well Purgatory

Source: Franciscan Well Brewery, Cork, Ireland

Strength: 4.5%

Website: www.franciscanwellbrewery.com

As befits a brewpub based on the site of a monastery founded in 1216, Franciscan Well brews a strong pale ale that celebrates its connection with the Franciscan friars who founded the original establishment. It's brewed with Maris Otter pale malt only and is hopped with American Cascade and English Target varieties. It has a pungent aroma of grapefruit/citrus, tangy hops resins and sappy malt. Citrus fruit dominates the palate with growing hop bitterness and lightly toasted malt. The long and intensely bitter finish has toasted malt, tart fruit and pungent and bitter hop resins.

Growler Augustinian Ale

Source: Growler Brewery, Pentlow, Essex, England

Strength: 4.5%

Website: www.growlerbrewery.com

I visited Growler brewery when it was based in Clare in Suffolk but it moved to a bigger site near Pentelow in 2005, just over the border in Essex. When I attempted to find it, I got hopelessly lost down country lanes and phoned the brewery for help. 'Where are you?' I was asked. 'Next to a field of barley,' I replied. There was a pause and then the voice said: 'We've got rather a lot of that around here.' It's handy being surrounded by your basic raw material and Growler uses the finest Maris Otter malting barley in its brews. The brewery was originally called Nethergate but, under new ownership, has changed its name to Growler to reflect the success of its multi-award-winning Old Growler Porter (see *300 Beers to Try Before You Die!*).

That book also included a beer called Augustinian Ale but that was a 5.2% bottle-conditioned beer aimed at the American market and made with the addition of coriander. This version is available only in draught cask-conditioned format and is a seasonal or occasional brew: you will have to monitor the website to find when it's available. It's a genuine abbey beer as it's brewed in collaboration with Clare Priory, which receives a royalty from sales. The priory, now a modern building near Clare Castle on the banks of the River Stour that marks the boundary between Essex and Suffolk, is the mother house of the Augustinian Order in England. The original priory was established in 1248 and was one of the first to be suppressed in 1538 during the dissolution of the monasteries under Henry VIII. At the time, there were 800 Augustinian friars in England and Ireland and they were all dispersed by the monarch. In 1953 friars from Ireland came to Clare and re-established the community.

The beer brewed to mark the history and community work of the priory is made with Maris Otter pale malt, crystal malt, and torrefied wheat. The hops are Challenger and Styrian Goldings. The pale bronze beer has an entrancing aroma of orange and lemon fruit, with a hint of caramel from the crystal malt and a fine herbal and grassy hop note. The palate is full, with a solid earthy hop resin note balancing tart citrus fruit and a rich biscuit malt character. The finish is bittersweet with bitter and spicy hops balancing the rich malt and citrus fruit notes.

Clare Priory, against all the odds in an increasingly secular society, has reported an increase in the number of monks joining the community. I hesitate to suggest that the occasional glass of Augustinian Ale has anything to do with this desire to live and work in the priory.

TASTING NOTES

APPEARANCE:

AROMA:

TASTE:

OVERALL SCORE:

Maredsous Blonde

Source: Abbaye de Maredsous, Denée/Brouwerij Duvel Moortgat, Breendonk, Belgium

Strength: 6%

Website: www.maredsousbiere.be/www.duvel.com

Neither the monks at Maredsous nor the Moorgat brewers can be accused of jumping on the commercial abbey beer bandwagon, for this collaboration dates from 1963, before the Breendonk company had achieved international acclaim for its strong Duvel golden ale. The beers are meticulously made and they are a remarkable achievement, as they bridge a linguistic divide in Belgium that seems increasingly to look like a gulf beyond repair. (I once asked a brewer in a Dutch-speaking area if he thought Belgium could survive as one country and he replied tersely: 'I hope not.') The monks were seemingly undeterred by the fact that Duvel is a Flemish word meaning Devil. Perhaps the beer is made with a long spoon.

The monastery is a Benedictine community near Namur. It started life as a small church founded by German monks on land donated by a local family. It lost its brewery and the monks were dispersed during the French Revolution. The new abbey was built in the 19th century and is regarded as one of the great Gothic masterpieces of its time. It developed a major role in the wider community around Dinant and Namur thanks mainly to the work of Joseph Marmion, an Irish Benedictine monk who, as Abbot Columba, presided over the abbey from 1905 until 1923. Today it has an acclaimed school of arts and crafts and makes cheese for general sale.

The monks approached Moortgat to brew beer for them to help fund their activities and the up-keep of the monastery. The Brune and Triple beers appeared in *300 Beers to Try Before You Die!* and I am adding Blonde to this book: in common with many brewing monasteries in Belgium, a Blonde beer has joined the portfolio to appeal to younger drinkers and as a comparatively low-strength beer for the monks to enjoy with their meals.

All the beers are brewed to what are called original recipes held by the monks and said to be secret. This is frustrating for those of us that revere the beers and would like to know the grains and hops used in their manufacture. Understandably, Moortgat cannot break the vow of silence, though it seems odd that Benedictines are more tight-lipped than Trappists: the Trappist brewers are quite happy to reveal their recipes. I will hazard a guess and suggest the malt for Blonde is grown in either Belgium or France while the hops are likely to come from a similar source or from Bavaria.

The bottle-conditioned beer has a powerfully aromatic hop nose, with peach-like fruit and grassy resins, balancing rich honey-like malt. Spritzy hops and perfumy grain build in the mouth with a smooth fruit note, while the finish is long with good bitter hop resins, creamy and honeyed malt and a continuing bittersweet fruit note.

Mont des Cats Bière Trappiste

Source: Abbaye de Notre-Dame de Scourmont, Chimay, Belgium/
Abbaye Mont des Cats, France

Strength: 7.5%

Website: www.chimay.com/www.abbaye-montdescats.fr

This new Trappist beer was launched in 2012 and is the result of collaboration between the biggest Belgian Trappist brewery, Chimay, and monks at the Abbey of Holy Mary just over the border in French Flanders. Mont des Cats has nothing to do with felines: Cats comes from a German tribe, the Chatti, who lived in the area many centuries ago. The abbey stands on a small hill at Godewaersvelde and it lost its brewery when the abbey was closed during the French Revolution. Trappist monks built a new priory in 1824 and it was given the official designation of an abbey in 1847. The importance of beer to the monks' way of life encouraged them to install a brewery that year – the ale they produced was solely for their consumption. A new 100-hectolitre plant was built in 1896 and beer was sold commercially to raise funds for the abbey's upkeep. The quality of the beer was praised. In 1898, Father Eugene Arnoult wrote: 'The trade of beer of the Trappist fathers extends far, in the large cities of the north, in Paris, and in all France. Their product, under the name of "fine beer", has a well-deserved reputation: its blond colour, its lightness, and the smoothness of the hops employed make it a worthy rival of the so-famous Pale Ales.'

The separation of church and state in France early in the 20th century forced many of the monks to leave the abbey and brewing ceased in 1905. Worse was to follow: in 1918, a bombardment during the war destroyed the community and the brewery was never rebuilt when the abbey was re-established. In 2011 the abbot at Mont des Cats approached his opposite number at Chimay with a view to adding a beer that could be sold alongside the monks' cheese, with the income adding to the abbey's funds.

Both abbeys are keen to stress that the beer is produced solely for Mont des Cats and is not a re-badged existing Chimay ale. It's brewed with Pilsner malt and caramalt and is hopped with German Hallertau varieties and American Galena. The russet/amber bottle-conditioned beer has a massive bouquet of peppery and spicy hops with blood orange fruit and cookie-like malt. Bitter hops build in the mouth with a fine balance of tart fruit and chewy malt. The finish is long and complex, with tangy citrus fruit, peppery hops and rich toasted malt. At the time of writing, the beer has yet to be awarded the official Trappist logo. Is it an abbey beer or a Trappist one? Either way, it's fine ale and a worthy addition to the family.

TASTING NOTES

APPEARANCE:

AROMA:

TASTE:

OVERALL SCORE:

Red Hill Christmas Ale

Source: Red Hill Brewery, Red Hill South, Victoria, Australia
Strength: 8.3%
Website: www.redhillbrewery.com.au

We brew this with almost religious fervour,' Karen and David Golding say. It's their interpretation of a Belgian abbey beer and it's brewed for the Christmas period in the summer: this is the southern hemisphere, where Santa Claus comes in shorts and flip-flops. The story of the Goldings, their brewery and hop farm in the Mornington Peninsula of Victoria state is told in the Pilsners section. Their beer range is eclectic and ranges from cold-fermented Pils to this powerful ale, one of the most popular in their portfolio. It's brewed with Pilsner malt, Maris Otter pale malt, crystal and wheat malts and is hopped with the Goldings' own Hallertau and Tettnang varieties. They also dry hop the beer before it's released. They say the bottle-conditioned beer will improve with age for a few years.

The beer has a hazy orange colour with a massive creamy malt, tart fruit and spicy hop nose. Silky smooth malt, tangy citrus fruit, and spicy and grassy hops fill the mouth followed by a long and lingering finish that's bittersweet, full of warming alcohol, tangy fruit, spicy hops and rich creamy malt. As one Australian writer noted, it may be a Christmas Ale but it's not one for a Silent Night.

> *it may be a Christmas Ale but it's not one for a Silent Night.*

Sint Bernardus Tripel/Prior 8/Abt 12

Source: Brouwerij St Bernard, Watou, Belgium
Strength: 7.5%/8%/10%
Website: www.sintbernardus.be

The relationship between the St Bernard commercial brewery and the monks at the Westvleteren monastery is a complex one. For more than 40 years, St Bernard brewed identical beers to those produced by the monks. This was the result of an agreement signed in 1946 that allowed the St Bernard brewery to make beers for commercial sale. The monks, who belong to one of the most reclusive Trappist monasteries in Belgium, preferred to make beer strictly for their own consumption and didn't want any connection with the outside commercial world. (See *300 Beers to Try Before You Die!* for the Westvleteren entry.)

The St Bernard brewery has an even older connection with Trappists. At the time of the French Revolution, monks from the abbey at Mont des Cats (see p239) left for the comparative safety of the Low Countries and set up a farm they called Refuge Notre Dame de St Bernard in Watou, where they made cheese. In 1934, in a different political and religious climate, descendants of the monks returned to France and the farm and cheese making was taken on by Evarist Deconinck. Following World War Two, Deconinck held discussions with the monks at the Sint Sixtus abbey at Westvleteren and the result was the agreement to produce beers labelled St Sixtus. The abbey brewmaster, Mathieu Szafranski, of Polish origin, handed over his recipes and even his yeast culture. Deconinck prospered as a brewer to such an extent that he sold his cheese business to concentrate on making beer.

In 1992 the agreement between brewery and abbey came up for renewal. The monks' attitude had changed. They had seen the success other Belgian Trappist breweries were enjoying and decided they would sell beer on a restricted basis themselves. St Bernard was allowed to continue to brew but he had to change the name of its beers from St Sixtus to St Benardus. The monastery asked the brewery to remove the image of a monk

from beer labels. This has not been done but the labels do contain the tagline 'Abbey Ale'. What is not in dispute is the quality of the St Bernardus beers. Tripel is brewed with pale malt, pale candy sugar and Northern Brewer hops. It has a hazy gold colour and a big herbal and spicy hop resins aroma with cookie-like malt and apricot fruit. There's rich fruit in the mouth with creamy malt and bitter hop resins. Hop resins dominate the finish with ripe fruit, creamy malt and tangy, spicy hops. Prior 8 is made with pale malt, dark candy sugar and Northern Brewer hops. It has a deep russet colour with chocolate on the nose along with raisin fruit, roasted grain, freshly-peeled walnuts and spicy hops. The palate is rich and bittersweet, with roasted grain, chocolate, dark burnt fruit and spicy hops. The finish has a big chocolate hit with roasted grain, raisin fruit and spicy hops. Abt (Abbot) 12 has an identical recipe to Prior 8 but with greater amounts of malt and sugar to achieve the level of alcohol. It's a burnished ruby colour, with dry chocolate, liquorice, sultana fruit, dark roasted grain and peppery hops on the aroma. Rich chocolate builds in the mouth with liquorice, burnt fruit, silky malt and a light touch of spicy hops. The long, warming finish is dominated by a nutty/chestnuts note with dry chocolate, liquorice, smooth creamy grain and light hop resins.

In 2010, in the company of fellow beer writer Tim Webb, author of the influential *Good Beer Guide Belgium*, I set out to visit both St Bernard and Westvleteren. We found St Bernard closed for the day while we had the good fortune to arrive at the abbey on one of its open days, when beer is sold to visitors. We not only bought beer but also toured the brewery with brewmaster Father Joris. A commercial brewery closed and a Trappist one open: God moves in a mysterious way...

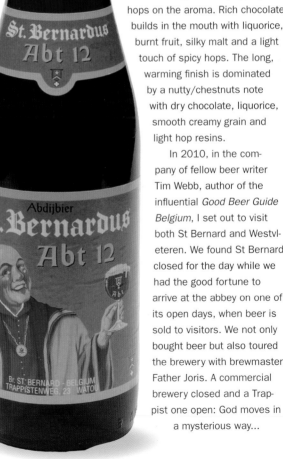

Van Steenberge St Stefanus Blonde

Source: Brouwerij Van Steenberge, Ertvelde, Belgium

Strength: 7%

Website: vansteenberge.com

The St Stefanus beer is the result of collaboration between a fiercely independent Belgian family brewery and an abbey that has survived two attempts to destroy it. The brewery started life on a farm in the 1820s. It grew in size and influence in the early 20th century under the guidance of Paul Van Steenberge, a remarkable figure in Belgian life. He became mayor, entered the national parliament as an advocate of the Flemish cause, and built a Flemish university in Ghent.

His main beer was in the *Oud Bruin* (Old Brown) style but following World War Two and the increasing popularity of lager, the brewery launched its own Pils. But the brewery found it difficult to compete with the big brands and in the 1960s the family decided to return to ale brewing. As Trappist beers grew in popularity, Van Steenberge approached the Augustinian monks of Sint Stefanus, who were keen to have a beer that carried their name. The monastery in Ghent had brewed for centuries but production stopped in the 1970s. The monastery dates from 1295 when Augustinian monks arrived in Ghent and were given four hectares of land to build a shrine to Stefanus – Saint Stephen. The abbey that grew up around the shrine was destroyed by Calvinists in the 17th century but it was rebuilt with the support of Ghent city council. The buildings were then seized and partially destroyed during the French Revolution. Lay people in Ghent raised money to buy back one third of the land to rebuild part of the abbey. The monks restored their brewing tradition but falling numbers forced them to abandon beer making in the 1970s.

As a result of discussions with Van Steenberge, a beer called Augustijn was launched in 1978. The beer is still known by that name in Belgium but in 2012 it was rebranded as St Stefanus for export. The monastery receives a royalty from beer sales. According to Jef Versele, the brewery's sales manager and a member of the Van Steenberge family, the monks insisted that the beer should be re-fermented in bottle. They handed over their recipe and, crucially, the yeast culture. The culture was developed by Janis Jerumanus. He was raised by Augustinian monks, became a micro-biologist and was appointed a professor at the University of Leuven. He was invited to become an advisor to the brewery at the Ghent monastery and later discussed recipes and the yeast culture with Jozef Van Steenberge.

In total, three yeast cultures are used to make the beer, which is re-fermented in both bottle and keg. Blonde is made with pale, Pilsner and Munich malts with a small amount of brewing sugar, and is hopped with Saaz, with the addition of some bittering hops and some German Hallertau. The brewery uses hard water that's filtered and then Burtonised with sulphates. At the end of primary fermentation, some yeast is removed by centrifuge but sufficient remains for a four-week maturation at 2 degrees Celsius. The original yeast is then filtered out and two new strains, including the 'wild yeast' *Brettanomyces*, added. 'Brett' is best known as the catalyst used to make lambic and gueuze beers. Bottles are stored at 24 degrees for two weeks, allowing for secondary fermentation to take place. The bottles are then moved to a cellar for a minimum of three months before being released. Jef Versele says the beer will improve in bottle for three years. For the keg version, he says a careful measure of sugar is used to avoid the kegs exploding. He has worked out how many yeast cells are needed to convert the remaining sugars: around 85 per cent of the sugar is turned to alcohol. Van Steenberge is one of few Belgian breweries to condition beer in keg.

At the brewery I was able to taste samples of the beer at different ages. At six weeks, the pale gold St Stefanus has a big spicy and peppery hops aroma with tangerine fruit, a custard cream malt note and a hint of 'horse blanket' from the Brett. Tart hops and tangy fruit fill the mouth, balanced by creamy malt and a hint of sourness. The finish is dry, with tangy hop resins, tangerine fruit and rich malt. At six months, the fruit character is more pronounced, with a big spicy hop note and more restrained malt. Bitter hops and tart fruit dominate the palate while creamy malt builds in the finish with bitter hops and tangy fruit.

TASTING NOTES

APPEARANCE:

AROMA:

TASTE:

OVERALL SCORE:

Welbeck Ernest George

Source: Welbeck Abbey Brewery, Welbeck, Nottinghamshire, England

Strength: 4.2%

Website: www.welbeckabbeybrewery.co.uk

It's a public relations dream – a monk brewing at an English abbey. But in this case the monk is a woman, Claire Monk, and the estate has not been a functioning abbey since the dissolution of the monasteries under Henry VIII. Welbeck Abbey nevertheless has a long and fascinating history, and today offers talks and seminars on arts, crafts, cooking – and beer tastings led by Claire.

Welbeck Abbey was founded in 1140 and was the principal religious house of the Premonstraten-sian or Norbertine Order in England. Following the dissolution of the monasteries, it became the coun-try estate of the noble Cavendish family and passed through the family line to the Dukes of Portland, enormously wealthy landowners who still own large swathes of central London, including Portland Place, home of the BBC, and Harley Street, famous for its specialist doctors' consultation rooms.

In 2010, the organisers of food and drink events at the abbey approached Dave Wickett, founder and owner of Kelham Island Brewery in Sheffield, with the idea of restoring the abbey's long-lost brew-ing tradition. They felt that beer events would add interest to the courses staged at Welbeck. Dave responded by installing the original Kelham Island 10-barrel brewing equipment in former stables. He put Claire Monk in charge and since the brewery opened in 2011 she has not only supplied beer to the abbey but also sells it in cask and bottle to pubs and other outlets in the region.

Claire Monk came to brewing in an unusual way. She studied biology and biochemistry at Sheffield University and, as part of her studies, visited Kel-ham Island to see how beer was made. She came away fascinated by the processes she had seen and found she wanted to pursue not an academic career but a brewing one. When she left university she contacted Kelham Island to see if they had a job for her. Dave Wickett took her on and started her out the hard way, washing casks for her first week. Undaunted, she learnt the skills of brewing until she was ready to take over at Welbeck.

Her beers commemorate the history and the personalities of the abbey. Ernest George, her only bottle-conditioned beer to date (also available in cask as a seasonal beer), is named after the architect who restored part of the abbey that was destroyed in a major fire in 1900. It's brewed with Maris Otter pale malt, dark crystal and roasted malts, a small amount of black malt and a healthy dose of chocolate malt. Two hops are used, English Challenger and American Willamette. At the end of fermentation the beer is racked into nine-gallon casks. The beer destined for bottling is not fined with clearing agents but is packaged with a dosage of brewing sugar. There's sufficient yeast in the beer to encourage a second fermentation.

The ruby beer throws a deep collar of foam with a strong sour fruit note reminiscent of Belgian lam-bic. A cracker-like malt note develops, with spicy and woody hop resins. Dry and bitter chocolate makes an appearance in the mouth, with vinous fruit, spicy hops and biscuit malt. The note of sourness is still present in the finish, balanced by increasing hop bit-terness, chocolate and toasted grain. A challenging but rewarding beer.

Belgian Ales

Beer is locked and intertwined in the history of Belgium. The region that is now the modern kingdom of Belgium has over the centuries been part of the Netherlands, Spain and the Habsburg Empire with incursions by the French and the Germans. A long struggle for independence and national identity led to a gritty determination to hang on to icons that were proudly Belgian – and they include beer.

Many of the invaders and conquerors came from wine-drinking countries. But Belgians drink beer, as the roistering peasants in the paintings of the Brueghels make clear. Today, as dissention between Dutch and French speakers shows no sign of abating, beer at times seems the cement that holds the country together.

Since the end of World War Two, lager – always called Pils – has developed a powerful presence. But beers made by warm fermentation have maintained their grip and have enjoyed a resurgence in recent years. The discovery by the outside world that Trappist monks, defying history and the Reformation, still brew beer has led to other fascinating styles being unearthed, not least lambic and gueuze made by 'wild fermentation' (see next section). Both abbey breweries and those in the secular world had to recover from two world wars in the 20th century that had seen their copper equipment ransacked by the invading German armies. Some took the opportunity to convert to Pils brewing but soon found they were no match for emerging giants such as Stella Artois and quickly returned to the ale fold.

Belgian ale has had an impact in several sections of this book, where we have encountered brown ales, golden ales, wheat beers and abbey and Trappist brews. This section is devoted to such styles as saison and strong ales. Saison is a beer that is also known as farmhouse ale: it originated as a seasonal beer, hence the French name, on farms in Wallonia where it was brewed to refresh the workforce, especially at harvest time. The style has a close affinity with *bière de garde* brewed over the nominal border in French Flanders. Saisons can range in colour from pale to dark, are usually refermented in the bottle and in some cases have an addition of spice.

Visitors to Belgium are often surprised and even bowled over by the strength of beers. This is the result of a period of partial prohibition in the early 20th century that outlawed the sale of spirits in bars. Brewers rushed to fill the gap by producing beers with high levels of alcohol. It's best to follow the local tradition of sipping and savouring: British-style pint quaffing is not advisable. Strong Belgian ales offer rich and rewarding aromas and flavours of fruit as well as malt and hops. Belgian brewers traditionally ferment ales at higher temperatures than is the norm in other countries. While English ale brewers ferment at between 16-22 degrees Celsius (61-72 degrees Fahrenheit), Belgian brewers often ferment as high as 32 degrees Celsius (90 degrees Fahrenheit). The result is the production of a high level of esters: natural flavour compounds that resemble such fruits and confectionery as pear drops, apple, apricot, banana, orange, prune and marmalade, with honey and perfume.

The fascination with Belgian beer has spilled out from that small country across the world. As this section shows, craft brewers as distant as Australia and the United States have become addicted to Belgian beer styles and moules frites.

On the palate there's chewy grain, tart fruit and spicy hop

TASTING NOTES

APPEARANCE:

AROMA:

TASTE:

OVERALL SCORE:

Antwerpse Seef

Source: Antwerpse Brow Compagnie, Antwerp, Belgium

Strength: 6.5%

Website: www.seef.be

Brewer Johan Van Dyck will have to put up with being called 'an artist in beer' as his product, Seef, takes Belgium and the wider brewing world by storm. It was the top talking point at the Beer Passie festival in Antwerp in June 2012 and earlier that year it won a gold medal in the World Beer Cup in the U.S. just a short time after its launch.

Seef – pronounced 'safe' – is a recreation of an old beer style in Antwerp that was lost in the 20th century due to what Johan calls 'the rise of industrial lager'. When his recreation of the beer was launched in Antwerp City Hall the mayor hailed it as the city's second greatest beer – he was careful not to overshadow Antwerp's iconic De Koninck pale ale (see *300 Beers to Try Before You Die!*).

Johan was marketing director at the large Duvel Moortgat brewing group but left to set up his Antwerpse Brouw Compagnie when he developed a passion for Seef and its history. In the 18th and 19th centuries it was a major style in Antwerp and the surrounding region. It was produced by many small breweries and its name is thought to come from one of those early companies. It was so popular that one part of Antwerp was nicknamed Seef. The beer was consumed mainly by industrial workers who found its pale, cloudy appearance and blend of malt, hops and fruit wonderfully refreshing. One contemporary writer described it as 'the poor man's champagne' as a result of its natural fermentation in bottle and the lively, spritzy head of foam when poured.

> *Johan Van Dyck will have to put up with being called 'an artist in beer' as his product, Seef, takes Belgium and the wider brewing world by storm.*

But, Johan explains, the style disappeared with the arrival of mass-marketed lager. The problem was made worse during World War One when the Germans seized copper brewing vessels in order to make tanks and bullets for the war effort. When Johan set out to recreate the style he found that the original recipe for the beer had been kept a closely-guarded secret. But after months of pains-taking work he came across the descendants of one of the brewers and they gave him the recipe, which had been kept in an old shoebox. With the help of scientists at the University of Leuven's department of brewing and bio-chemistry, he discovered from the recipe that the beer was made with a blend of malted barley, wheat, buckwheat and oats, along with locally-grown Belgian hops.

That was the easy part. He couldn't recreate the beer without yeast and he wanted an authentic culture. Leuven has a yeast bank with samples of every known Belgian culture and the scientists came to the conclusion that the yeast used to ferment Seef was a mutated version of baker's yeast. It was not unknown centuries ago for small businesses to make beer and bread alongside one another.

The university's brewing department created a yeast culture they believed to be as close to the original as possible. Johan was now in business and all he needed was a brewery prepared to make the beer for him. He found salvation at the large Roman Brewery in Oudenaarde, best-known for its Oud Bruin beer (see Brown & Mild Ales section). He is delighted by Roman's devotion to the beer but, as a result of Seef's remarkable success, he plans to build his own plant in Antwerp to give it greater authenticity.

Seef has a double fermentation, first in the brewery and then in bottle. Following primary fermentation, it's matured for seven weeks to develop its full flavours and natural carbonation before being bottled. The finished beer is 6.5% alcohol and it has a hazy pale gold colour: it's not filtered. The appealing aroma offers a pronounced lemon/citrus fruitiness with a 'fresh bread' grain note and a spicy and resinous hop appeal. On the palate there's chewy grain, tart fruit and spicy hops, while the bittersweet finish is dominated by hops and fruit. It's finally dry and superbly quenching. It's deceptively easy to drink despite the level of alcohol.

I joked with Johan that he's become such a local hero in Antwerp that they've already erected a statue in his honour. On closer inspection, this turns out to be an older man with a chin beard. But a second Van Dyck will surely not be overlooked for long by the burghers of the city.

Binchoise Blonde/Brune

Source: Brasserie la Binchoise, Binche, Belgium

Strength: 6.2%/8.2%

Website: www.brasserielabinchoise.be

A lot of Belgium's tangled history is bound up in the ancient town of Binche, founded in the 14th century, along with the beers from its brewery. In the 16th century the Holy Roman Emperor, Charles V, gave the medieval castle to his sister Queen Mary of Hungary, who was also governess of the Netherlands, a country that included modern day Belgium. The brewery for a while produced a beer called Marie de Hongrie and it's a pity it's been discontinued. Today Binche has been proclaimed a Masterpiece of Heritage and Humanity by UNESCO, mainly as a result of its annual carnival that takes place for three days before Ash Wednesday. Thousands parade through the streets, with men wearing masks that look remarkably similar to those worn by modern-day protesters against global big business and bankers. The brewery logo shows men in the masks.

Binche had a brewery and maltings for several centuries that stood opposite the medieval ramparts. The brewery closed in the 1920s but the maltings survived until World War Two. The buildings remained intact and were used again in the late 1980s when André Graux, an out-of-work photographer, was inspired to launch his brewery in part of the old maltings by his father, who was a keen home brewer.

I visited while I was touring breweries in Wallonia as a guest of the local tourist board, which feels the beers of the French-speaking region of Belgium unfairly play second fiddle to those from the north. The plan was to end the day in Pernode with a visit to Du Bocq's brewery but heavy snow prevented that and I was glad to seek shelter and sample a warming beer at Binchoise.

In 2001 the brewery was bought by Bruno Deghoran who has upgraded the brewing kit and added a restaurant, Brasserie Binchoise, that specialises in matching food with the house beers. The beers are all re-fermented in bottle and 750ml versions have Champagne-style corks in wire cradles. Blonde, the biggest-selling beer, is made with pale malt, is hopped with unspecified varieties and is spiced with Curaçao orange. The pale bronze beer has a fine aroma that combines peppery hops and tart orange fruit with honeyed malt. The palate is a lively balance of tart fruit, peppery hops and silky malt, with a quenching, fruity and hoppy finish. Brune is made with an addition of dark, roasted malt and star anise as a spice. The aroma is full of toasted, cookie-like malt, chocolate and spice, followed by a palate rich with dark malt, spice, chocolate and spicy hops. The finish is warming and well-balanced between toasted malt, spice, dark chocolate and spicy hops.

> *The pale bronze beer has a fine aroma that combines peppery hops and tart orange fruit with honeyed malt.*

Bootleg Raging Bull

Source: Bootleg Brewery, Wilyabrup, Western Australia, Australia

Strength: 7.1%

Website: www.bootlegbrewery.com.au

Raging Bull is a Belgian-style dark ale brewed at a brewery the owners describe as an 'oasis of beer in a wine desert'. Bootleg is based in the Margaret River wine-growing region and is run by the sixth generation of the Reynolds family who arrived in Australia from Britain in the 1830s. Over the years the Reynolds have played leading roles in the theatre and education, and branched out into brewing in 1994. Another settler from the Old Country is Michael Brookes from Buxton in Derbyshire. His family migrated in 1974 and when Michael came of working age he started as a bartender at the Bootleg restaurant alongside the brewery but quickly rose through the ranks to become head brewer.

Michael brews a wide range of ales, including pale and amber along with several wheat beers. His interpretation of Belgian dark ale is made with pale and crystal malts with roasted barley. The single hop is Pride of Ringwood from Tasmania. The tawny/copper beer has an intense aroma of rich and roasted grain with coffee and chocolate, underscored by berry fruits from the hops. Coffee and chocolate build in the mouth with a solid balance of roasted grain, dark fruit and bitter hop resins while the finish is long and complex, coffee and chocolate dominating with berry fruits, roasted grain and lingering fruity and bitter hop resins.

TASTING NOTES

APPEARANCE:

AROMA:

TASTE:

OVERALL SCORE:

Bridge Road Saison Chevalier

Source: Bridge Road Brewers, Beechworth, Victoria, Australia

Strength: 6%

Website: www.bridgeroadbrewers.com.au

Ben Kraus studied wine-making – not an unusual profession in Victoria, a major wine-growing region – but he got an itch to try his hand at brewing. He started with some second-hand kit in his father's garden shed in 2004 and when people liked his beers he moved to a 150-year-old coach house and stable block behind a Victorian hotel in Beechwood. With his partner Maria, he has added a bar, pizza parlour, beer garden and children's play area: Maria's pizzas are the talk of the town and other dishes are matched with Ben's beers.

Ben is meticulous with his recipe for Saison, down to importing a Saison yeast culture from Belgium to create the right balance of aromas and flavours. He brews the beer with 93% Pilsner malt, 5% pale wheat and 2% cara malt: the last two grains are imported from Weyermann of Bavaria. The hops are Bavarian Hersbrucker and Czech Saaz. The straw-coloured beer has grassy hops, tart fruit and silky malt on the nose, with a full, rich palate of creamy malt, spicy hops and tangy fruit. The finish is long and quenching with a superb balance of juicy malt, citrus fruit and grassy/herbal hop resins.

One of Maria's dishes in the restaurant is mussels poached in Saison. You can't get more Belgian than that.

The Bruery Saison de Lente

Source: The Bruery, Placentia, Orange County, California, USA

Strength: 6.5%

Website: www.thebruery.com

Patrick Rue gave up the legal business to become a brewer: a wise switch. He started to brew to alleviate the boredom of lessons at law school and his passion grew until he decided that his future lay in making beer. His first serious batch was made in his kitchen with his brother Chris while his wife Rachel wondered if the stove would ever recover. She was delighted when Patrick moved into a commercial site where he now brews a wide range of beers that are bottle-conditioned, unfiltered and unpasteurised. Several, such as the Saison – a seasonal beer for the Lenten period – make a deep bow in the direction of Belgium.

Saison is made with two-row pale malt and Vienna malt and is hopped with Sterling and Warrior from the U.S. and Styrian Goldings from Slovenia: Sterling has been cloned from Saaz and Cascade while Warrior is

a similar clone to Simcoe. The hops create 35 units of bitterness. Two yeast strains are used, the house strain complemented by a *Brettanomyces* culture bought from Belgium.

Patrick says the beer will continue to improve for two years in bottle. It has a hazy gold colour and pours with an enormous fluffy head of foam. The aroma is astonishingly complex, with hop resins, pine kernels, zesty orange and lemon fruit, rich malt and a sour note from the *Brettanomyces*. Woody hop resins dominate the mouth, with pine kernels, orange and lemon fruit, honeyed malt and a continuing hint of sourness. The finish is long and lingering, with further contributions from malt, hops and fruit before the beer finally becomes dry and uncompromisingly bitter with a lingering sourness. You can't keep a good Brett down.

The brewery can be toured and the beers enjoyed in a tasting room.

Cantillon Iris

Source: Brasserie Cantillon, Anderlecht, Brussels, Belgium

Strength: 6%

Website: www.cantillon.be

It may seem perverse to include a renowned brewer of lambic beer in this section but Cantillon has spread its wings in recent years (see next section and *300 Beers to Try Before You Die!*). The legendary Jean-Pierre Van Roy, who built the brewery's international fame, has retired and handed over control to his son, Jean. While it's not possible, let alone desirable, to change the brewing area or maturation halls in a lambic production site, Jean Van Roy has tidied up the entrance and installed a bar and visitors' reception area with plenty of seats and tables: useful when you're sampling beers and scribbling about them. Cantillon is both a brewery and a museum dedicated to the history and mystery of lambic brewing. Unless a large party is involved, when booking is essential, visitors can drop in at any time and in return for six euro can enjoy a tour of the brewery, a beer at the bar and can take bottles away with them.

Lambic and gueuze are controlled by Belgian law and also have a protective ordinance from the European Union. Essentially, to be classified as a lambic, it must be brewed with a minimum of 30 per cent wheat. Jean has introduced new beers to his range that do not adhere to the appellation and he's quite open about this. Iris is made solely with barley malt and uses 50 per cent fresh hops as well as aged versions. It takes its name from Brussels' official flower. In all respects, Iris has an aroma and palate that's unmistakably lambic, sour and musty, but with the addition of a spritzy hop character. The beer is made with the house yeast and is hopped with Saaz hops from the Czech Republic. It's aged for two years in the Cantillon oak casks and at the end of that period linen bags containing more Saaz are added to impart a fresh hop aroma.

The beer that emerges from this long process is red/gold in colour and has a nose that's both sour from the yeast and spicy from the hops at the same time. It's tart, tangy and sour in the mouth, with lemon fruit, toasted malt and spicy hops, with a long, quenching finish that's a fine blend of toasted grain, tart and sour fruit and spritzy hops. In short, it's superb.

TASTING NOTES

APPEARANCE:

AROMA:

TASTE:

OVERALL SCORE:

APPEARANCE:

AROMA:

TASTE:

OVERALL SCORE:

Dupont Bons Voeux

Source: Brasserie Dupont, Tourpes-Leuze, Belgium

Strength: 9.5%

Website: www.brasserie-dupont.com

You know Dupont is a serious brewing operation: there's a logo of a glass of beer on the wall facing the road along with a weather-beaten statue of St Arnold, the patron saint of Belgian brewing. But the brick buildings based around a cobbled courtyard clearly identify the site as a farm. It stands on a narrow road in the village of Tourpes and in the early 19th century the farmer added a small brewery known as Rimaux-Derrider. In 1920 Louis Dupont bought the site and handed it to his son to persuade him from emigrating to Canada. The brewery has been in the hands of the Dupont family ever since and they have turned it into the best-known producer of saison in Belgium.

On my visits, the brewery was in the hands of Marc Rosier, the grandson of Louis Dupont. Marc ran the business with his sisters and other family members but he has since handed over brewing duties to his nephew Olivier Dedeycker. Much of the brewing equipment dates from the 1920s and, in the style of small farm breweries, the mash tun doubles as the hop back, with the hopped wort returning to the vessel following the boil with hops in the copper. Brewing liquor comes from a spring on the site.

Dupont's main beer, simply called Saison, is the classic of the style. I featured it in *300 Beers to Try Before You Die!* but didn't add the stronger Bons Voeux because at the time it was a Christmas beer: the full title is Les Bons Voeux de la Brasserie Dupont, a seasonal greeting meaning 'the best wishes of the brewery'. It has become so popular that it's now a regular beer. It's brewed with Pilsner malt and a touch of caramalt and is hopped with East Kent Goldings and Styrian Goldings. With such a high level of alcohol, the beer is dry hopped after fermentation to prevent any cloying sweetness. The result is a beer of enormous depth and profundity, with rich silky and honeyed malt exquisitely balanced by peppery and spicy hops, with a delicious note of lemon/citrus fruit.

The Duponts use square fermenters as they feel the size and shape is fundamental to the flavour of their beers. Fermentation temperature can reach as high as 32 degrees Celsius (94 degrees Fahrenheit), which accounts for the fruity character of the beers. Primary fermentation is followed by a secondary fret and then warm conditioning for six to eight weeks at 23 degrees Celsius (73 degrees Fahrenheit). Bon Voeux, in common with all the beers, save for a Pils, is refermented in the bottle. There's an intriguing mystery at Dupont concerning the house yeast culture. Some people consider that the high fermentation temperatures and the fruity character of the beers is the result of using a culture that was once used to make red wine. Dupont keeps silent on the subject.

As well as Saison and Bons Voeux, Dupont produces several beers labelled Moinette, which means 'little monk': it's thought there was once an abbey in the area. There are also organic versions of several of the beers, and cheese is also produced. Dupont produces 6,500 hectolitres a year and beer is exported to the United States, Britain, Japan and Scandinavia.

De Halve Maan Brugse Zot Blond/Zot Dubbel

Source: Brouwerij De Halve Maan, Bruges, Belgium

Strength: 6%/7.5%

Website: www.halvemaan.be

Bruges may have magnificent medieval buildings, canals, and market squares of jaw-dropping beauty... but it has no breweries. Surely one of Europe's great trading cities in a country where beer is deeply locked into history and culture must have breweries. It had 20 or more at the start of the 20th century, but mergers and takeovers took their toll, and big brewers concentrated on Pils lager.

The last brewery in Bruges was Straffe Hendrik. It became part of the Riva group and the Straffe Hendrik brands were moved to the group's main plant in Dentergem in the 1980s. When I was invited to tour the brewery site during the Bruges beer festival weekend in February 2013 I thought I was going to view a museum. Imagine my delight when I discovered that brewing has restarted and is back in the hands of the original family owners.

The brewery, now called De Halve Maan, the Half Moon, was founded in 1856 by Henri Maes and it's his descendants, the Vanneste family, who have restored brewing at the site. The ground floor is occupied by functional enclosed 1960s vessels but the visit just gets better and better as you clamber up narrow stairs and walkways. Here are old wooden brewing vessels with, under the roof, a copper cool ship, an open vessel where beer used to ferment at ambient temperature.

De Halve Maan has won the right to brew two Straffe Hendrik beers, Tripel (9%) and Quadrupel (11%). It's good to see them back but the main point of interest lies in the two house beers designed by the Vanneste family, using their treasured recipes. Zot is a Flemish word meaning fool and the beers take their name from an ancient Bruges legend. It seems the city had more than its fair share of mentally ill people in the 15th century and the citizens lobbied

the Austrian emperor Maximilian to build an asylum that would be called the Fools' House. The emperor waved a dismissive hand and declared: 'Just close the city walls – Bruges is full of fools'.

The fools have had the last laugh. Blond has met with great acclaim and won a gold award in the World Beer Cup in the U.S. It's brewed with pale and Munich malts and hopped with Czech Saaz and Styrian Goldings. It has a pale bronze colour with a big spicy hop aroma balanced by cracker-like grain and a strong hint of butterscotch. Citrus fruit builds in the mouth, balanced by rich honeyed malt and increasing hop bitterness, followed by a dry finish with tart fruit, ripe grain and bitter, spicy hops.

Amber and chocolate malts are added to pale and Munich for the Dubbel. It has a deep russet colour with spicy hops and toasted malt on the nose with notes of burnt dark fruit. The palate is packed with vinous fruit, roasted grain, caramel and bitter hops, while the complex finish is dry and hoppy, overlain with roasted malt and fruit.

The brewery at 26 Walplein has a shop, bar and restaurant. Tours can be booked using the website above. I enjoyed the tour guide's sharp wit and her aside that 'in Belgium, lager beer is for children'.

> ❛ *The fools have had the last laugh. Blond has met with great acclaim and won a gold award in the World Beer Cup in the U.S.* ❜

TASTING NOTES

APPEARANCE:

AROMA:

TASTE:

OVERALL SCORE:

TASTING NOTES

APPEARANCE:

AROMA:

TASTE:

OVERALL SCORE:

St Austell Cardinal Syn/Bad Habit

Source: St Austell Brewery Company, St Austell, Cornwall, England

Strength: 8%/8.5%

Website: www.staustellbrewery.co.uk

St Austell, the large family-owned brewery, has spread its wings and, as we shall see in the Bock section, has even moved in to lager production. Head brewer Roger Ryman shares with Stuart Howe, his opposite number at Sharp's brewery (see p254) a great interest in Belgian beer and in 2013 added two Cornish equivalents of Dubbel and Tripel strong ales, brewed with the addition of fruits and spice.

Cardinal Syn is made with Pilsner malt, crystal and black malts and brewing sugar. The copper hops are Hersbrucker, Perle and Styrian Goldings, with coriander added to the boil, and the beer is dry hopped with Dana from Slovenia. The yeast culture comes from a Trappist monastic brewery. The deep russet/brown ale has a big vinous/port wine aroma with strong hints of old leather books, liquorice, rich chocolate, espresso coffee, woody/leafy hops, fresh tobacco and a whiff of coriander. Sweet dark malt is first in the mouth with liquorice, dry chocolate, vinous fruit, peppery hops and spice. Rich dark fruit, toasted and roasted grain, chocolate, coffee and spicy hops linger on the long finish with continuing notes of coriander.

Bad Habit is brewed with Pilsner malt, wheat malt, malted oats and brewing sugar. The hops are Citra and Dana, and coriander, dried orange peel and Grains of Paradise are added during the boil. The same Trappist yeast culture is also used. The hazy bronze beer has a big orange Muscat nose with honey malt, gentle peppery hops and powerful notes of spice and fruit. There's a massive hit of tart fruit and spices in the mouth, with honeyed malt and peppery hops. The long bittersweet finish offers creamy malt, orange fruit, tangy spices and assertive peppery hops.

> *There's a massive hit of tart fruit and spices in the mouth, with honeyed malt and peppery hops.*

Sint Bernardus Grottenbier

Source: Brouwerij St Bernard, Watou, Belgium

Strength: 6.5%

Website: www.sintbernardus.be

Grottenbier stands as a memorial to Pierre Celis, the renowned Belgian brewer who restored the fortunes of spiced wheat beer with Hoegaarden (see *300 Beers to Try Before You Die!*). Pierre brewed in the United States for several years, which brought him to the attention of a much bigger audience of beer lovers. He returned to Belgium and his home in Hoegaarden where he had time to rekindle his interest in a type of beer he had tinkered with in the 1980s. The beer, Grottenbier, came to fruition before Pierre died in 2011, aged 86. Such was his fame that newspapers all over the world ran obituaries: I was delighted when the *Guardian* in Britain published a substantial piece by me.

The name Grottenbier means grotto or cave beer. It was Pierre's dream to produce a beer using the méthode champenoise that results in sparkling wine as a result of a second fermentation in the bottle. He chose caves in the valley of the Jeker river, which flows into the Meuse or Maas. The entrance to the caves is in the village of Kanne, which is in Belgium but close to Maastricht in the Netherlands. The limestone caves are enormous and visitors can drive cars in. They are the result of extracting stone for building material and the excavations have unearthed fossils from several millennia ago, including dinosaur bones. In the manner of Dom Perignon with champagne in France, Pierre stored 5,000 bottles of his Grottenbier in a cellar in the caves where the temperature is a constant 12 degrees Celsius (53-54 degrees Fahrenheit) and there is a high moisture level of 95 per cent. He was keen to see how the temperature and the moisture would create different flavours to the drier conditions of a refrigerated brewery cellar. The bottles are held in racks known as riddlers or pupitres, where they can be tilted and turned every day to encourage the yeast to slowly collect in the necks. Pierre decided not to go the whole hog and freeze the yeast and then remove the icy plug as is the case with Champagne. The result is a beer that still contains yeast, making it the most profound version of bottle-conditioned beer.

The beer was first brewed by Affligem but has since moved to Watou. Frustratingly, Sint Bernardus says the recipe is secret: the brewery has not entirely broken its links with the Trappist tradition. But we do know that Pierre used some exotic spices – it would not be a Celis beer without some spice! For Hoegaarden, he used coriander and orange peel, but that's not to say they are present in Grottenbier. The hazy chestnut-coloured beer throws a deep collar of foam with glacé cherries on the nose, toasted malt, powerful hints of butterscotch and nose-tingling peppery hops. It's surprisingly dry in the mouth, with herbal, spicy hops balancing the richness of the grain, with continuing notes of candied fruit and butterscotch. The finish begins with a bittersweet note but becomes dry: along the way toasted grain melds with rich fruit and toffee but spicy hops have the last word. It's a rewarding and intensely satisfying beer that's a fitting tribute to a magnificent brewer.

TASTING NOTES

APPEARANCE:

AROMA:

TASTE:

OVERALL SCORE:

TASTING NOTES

APPEARANCE:

AROMA:

TASTE:

OVERALL SCORE:

Sharp's Quadrupel Ale

Source: Sharp's Brewery, Rock, Cornwall, England
Strength: 10%
Website: www.sharpsbrewery.co.uk

As I reported in the Old Ales section with Sharp's Massive, brewer Stuart Howe has a great love of Belgian beer, and that is reflected in this offering. Both the name and the method of fermentation and ageing are in keeping with the finest traditions of brewing in Belgium. Four yeast strains are used to reach both the high level of alcohol and to develop aroma, flavour and character during maturation and bottle conditioning. Stuart combines pale, crystal and chocolate malts, and hops the beer with Aurora, Centennial and Hallertauer varieties. Following fermentation, the beer lies for a month on a deep bed of Simcoe hops at -1 degrees Celsius. The fourth yeast strain is added at the time of bottling.

Stuart Howe says the beer will continue to develop over a period of 10 years. As it's a vintage beer in a special group called Connoisseurs' Choice it will be interesting to compare one year's brew with the next and to see how ageing alters the profile. The 2012 vintage sampled for this book has a Burgundy colour with a suitably vinous aroma with roasted grain, dry chocolate, peppery hops and a cinnamon spice note. There's a vinous/port wine note on the palate with developing hop bitterness, spices and chocolate. Chocolate and spice build in the long finish with toasted grain, sweet fruit and peppery, grassy hop note.

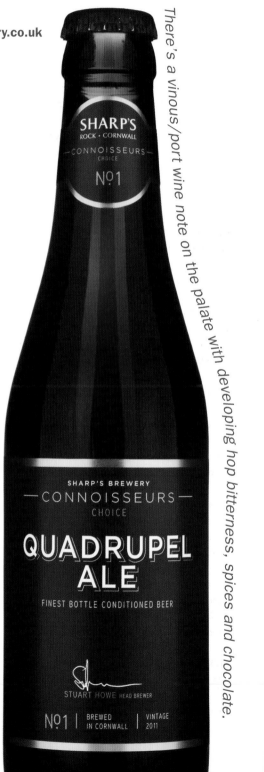

There's a vinous/port wine note on the palate with developing hop bitterness, spices and chocolate.

Silly Saison de Silly

Source: Brasserie de Silly, Silly, Belgium

Strength: 5%

Website: www.silly-beer.com

Silly is a perfectly sensible name, with both the village and the brewery based alongside the River Sille in Hainaut province, but as the Saison is widely exported the name does catch the attention in English-speaking countries. In common with Dupont, the brewery, with its cobbled yards and low-slung buildings, started life as a farm. As both barley and hops are grown in the area, it seemed sensible for farmer Nicholas Meynsbrughen to add a small brewery in 1850. Following World War Two, the family decided to stop farming and concentrate on brewing. They added several local cafes and in 1975 bought a brewery in the neighbouring village of Enghien, adding the acclaimed Double Enghien Blonde to the portfolio (see *300 Beers to Try Before You Die!*).

The brewhouse is small and cramped and, in the style known as 'artisanal', the mash tun doubles as the filtration vessel following the boil with hops in the copper. Saison is brewed with French malt and Belgian darker caramalt and is hopped with English Challenger and German Hallertauer varieties. Fermentation lasts for 15 days and the beer is then matured in tanks for a further two weeks. Saison is the result of blending young and older versions of the beer. The brewery has bowed to pressure from aficionados who thought it was going against the grain – if not downright silly – to filter the blended beer and it's now reseeded with yeast and bottle conditioned. The copper-coloured beer is notably fruity and vinous on the nose and palate with a good underpinning of roasted malt and spicy hops. The finish is bittersweet with ripe fruit, toasted malt and bitter and spicy hops.

The brewery has a small museum with many fascinating artefacts, including a delivery truck with a large bottle on the roof. The beers can be enjoyed, along with local cuisine, in the restaurant and bar La Titien Bassilly, where I played a version of bar billiards in which the mushroom stools that guard the holes in the British version are replaced by Champagne corks. That's what you call style.

The finish is bittersweet with ripe fruit, toasted malt and bitter and spicy hops.

TASTING NOTES

APPEARANCE:

AROMA:

TASTE:

OVERALL SCORE:

TASTING NOTES

APPEARANCE:

AROMA:

TASTE:

OVERALL SCORE:

Verhaeghe Duchesse de Bourgogne

Source: Brouwerij Verhaeghe, Vichte, Belgium

Strength: 6.2%

Website: www.brouwerijverhaeghe.be

More history in a glass. The Verhaeghe family started brewing on a farm and production moved to the present site in 1880. The family refused to make beer for the occupying German troops during World War One and paid a heavy price, with their copper vessels dismantled and confiscated. The brewery was overhauled in the 1960s and a new generation of the family has improved the product range and marketing. But they have not tampered with ancient oak vessels where some of the beers, including Duchesse, come to fruition.

There are strong similarities with such 'sour red' beers as Rodenbach and even a nod in the direction of lambic brewing, but the Verhaeghe beers deserve to be recognised in their own right as a singular contribution to beer making. Duchesse is named in honour of Marie, daughter of Charles the Bold, the Duke of Burgundy. To emphasise the tangled history of the region, despite her Burgundian title, she was born in Bruges in 1457 and, against her family's wishes, married Archduke Maximilian of Austria instead of the French Dauphin, which heightened tensions in Europe. But her enlightened rule in the Netherlands made her a hero of the Flemish people and she was buried in Bruges.

The beer that carries her name is a blend of two beers. One is aged in oak vessels for 18 months where it picks up some sourness from natural bacteria and wild yeasts locked in the wood. It's then blended with a younger, eight-month-old version. The beer is made with a blend of pale malt, wheat malt and roasted grain. In the manner of lambic, only aged hops are used for their anti-bacterial character, rather than for bitterness. The ruby red beer has a sour note on the nose with vinous fruit, roasted grain and a light hop note. Chocolate makes an appearance in the mouth with rich, silky malt, port wine fruitiness and light peppery hop notes. The finish is sweet to start, with chocolate and creamy malt but ends dry with tart fruit and a hint of hop. It's a superb and memorable beer, a fitting end to this section.

> ❝ The Verhaeghe beers deserve to be recognised in their own right as a singular contribution to beer making. ❞

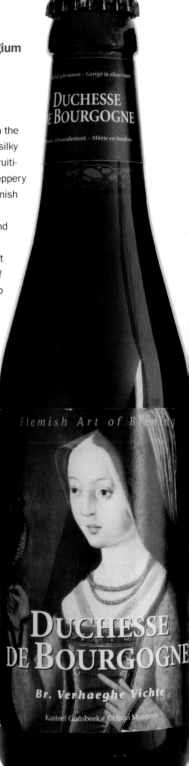

Lambic & Gueuze

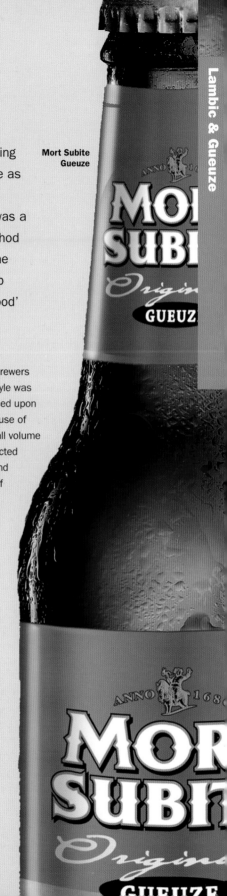

Mort Subite
Gueuze

Lambic and gueuze beers enable us to reach out and touch the origins of brewing some 5000 years ago. Beer makers in Egypt and Mesopotamia watched in awe as the sugary liquid they had made was magically turned into a stimulating and palatable drink by the action of wild yeasts in the atmosphere. Yeast to them was a type of froth. They learnt to keep it and reuse it for further brews. It was a method that prevailed until modern times, when the invention of the microscope and the work of Louis Pasteur revealed the true workings of yeast and the need to keep bacteria at bay. Until then, English brewers referred to yeasty froth as 'Godisgood' and stepped back to allow the Almighty to finish their work.

Brewers today carefully nurture and protect their yeast cultures, with the exception of a small number in the Payottenland region of Belgium where they still make beer by a method known as spontaneous or 'wild' fermentation. It's a method that is endlessly fascinating and creates drinks that, with their vinous and sour aromas and flavours, should be as acceptable to wine and cider lovers as beer connoisseurs.

The beer is as old as history, locked into the slow and ruminative way of life of the hamlets and villages of the Low Countries where farmers would garner grains and fruits from the fields and allow natural fermentation to turn sugars into alcohol. If the method is old, so too are the terms used to describe it. Nobody is certain of the origin of the term lambic. Does it come from the village of Lembeek, which had a brewers' guild in the 15th century and a shrine to the patron saint of lambic brewing, Saint Veronus? Or is it the result of Spanish rule in the Netherlands in the 16th and 17th century and the adoption of the word alembic, meaning a distillery? And then there is gueuze, the name given to blended lambics, some aged, some young. The beer gushes and foams when served, bringing to mind the action of a geyser.

In the 20th century lambic seemed a style destined for the history books, overtaken in popularity by Pils lager and ale. But the dogged determination of a handful of passionate brewers in Payottenland to continue to make the style was taken up by foreign beer writers who chanced upon lambic as they discovered the rich storehouse of brewing in Belgium. Lambic remains a small volume product but its future seems secure, protected by both Belgian and European Union law and ordinance that also stipulate the method of production and the ingredients that can be used. Lambic is designated as a type of wheat beer in which 30 per cent of the mash must be composed of unmalted wheat. The grain gives a tart and spicy note to the beer while its companion, barley malt, is exceptionally pale, often made with Pilsner malt. The grains are mixed in a conventional mash tun and the resulting wort is boiled for a lengthy three hours in a copper with hops. The hop level is high but the plants are around four years old and have lost much of their aroma and bitterness. Brewers use them specifically for their preservative quality as bitterness would not marry well with the characteristics created by wheat and wild yeasts. This is especially true with the versions of lambic that are infused with such fruits as cherries and raspberries.

Lambic beers are matured in oak casks

It's the stages following the copper boil that mark out lambic beer from any other style. The hopped wort is pumped to the attic in the brewery and it's beneath the roof that alcohol starts to be made. The renowned veteran brewer Jacques De Keersmaeker, who was born in his family's brewery, describes the inoculation in the cool ship as 'the signature event in the creation of lambic, unique in beer making'. The hopped wort is run into the shallow open cool ship, made either of copper or stainless steel, and begins to cool. Louvred windows are left open and during the night wild yeasts enter and attack the sugars in the wort. To encourage the yeasts, brewers even remove tiles from their roofs.

The wild yeast strain present in the Senne Valley and Payottenland is known as *Brettanomyces*. Research at the brewing faculty of Leuven University has identified two main strains, *bruxellensis* and *lambicus*. But the total number of strains – from the atmosphere, brewery cellars and inside the oak casks where the beer is aged – number as many as 35. Conventional beer is fermented with one or two strains.

Lambic brewing does not take place during the summer, late spring or early autumn as the temperature is too high, which affects the balance of yeasts in the atmosphere and can attract strains that wouldn't be sympathetic to beer-making. Once fermentation is under way in the cool ship, the beer is transferred to large oak casks in cool, dark maturation halls. The yeasts already active in the beer are joined by microflora in the wood. Together they create a head on top of the liquid that's similar to the *flor* in sherry casks that helps prevent oxidation.

The casks are sourced from port and sherry makers in Portugal and Spain, as well as wine and Cognac producers in France. The beer will remain in cask for several years, during which time it will darken and develop an aroma known to brewers as 'horse blanket' from the action of the yeasts. Depending on the age of the beer in cask, a cheesy note from the hops will disappear and the beer will become sour and winey, with a pronounced Sherry character.

Straight lambic, tart and cidery, is usually served on draught. The most popular form of the beer is gueuze – sometimes spelt gueze – a blend of young and aged lambics served from bottles with corks and cradles in the manner of Champagne. The young lambic creates a further fermentation in the bottle and the beer is foaming and spritzy. The skill of the blender is to marry young and old in the best quantities, usually 60 per cent young. The bottles are laid down in cellars for between six and 18 months. Neither straight lambic nor bottled gueuze are high in alcohol, at least not by Belgian standards, and are usually between 4.5 and 6%, though some Oude Gueuze can be stronger.

The versions of lambic that cause most interest and raised eyebrows are those to which fruit has been added. The two main fruits used are cherry and raspberry. They increase fermentability and, far from adding sweetness, add tartness to the finished beer. Cherries, often the Scharbeek variety that grows in Brussels, are picked late when the fermentable sugars are concentrated, a similar practice to the 'noble rot' grapes used to make certain wines such as Sauternes. As soon as the fruit is harvested, it's added to the casks in the maturation halls. The sugars in the fruit and the young beer create a fresh fermentation. Tannins on the skins add to the dryness of the finished beer while even the pips in the cherries are attacked by the yeasts and contribute an almond-like note. A cherry lambic is known as *Kriek*, the Flemish word for the fruit: the French *cerise* is never used. On the other hand, raspberry lambic is known by both Flemish and French words: *frambozen* and *framboise*.

Most of the main producers of lambic and gueuze featured in *300 Beers to Try Before You Die!* In this section I've selected a few further examples from those producers and some new beers produced by an existing practitioner. I include only lambic and gueuze brewers, not blenders who buy in beer and age it.

Cantillon Mamouche/Zwanze

Source: Brasserie Cantillon, Anderlecht, Brussels, Belgium

Strength: 6%/8%

Website: www.cantillon.be

We've encountered Cantillon in the previous section, but the brewery takes pride of place in this section as one of the torchbearers for lambic beer. The brewery dates from 1900, but Jean-Pierre Van Roy, who built its reputation and retired after a lifetime's devotion to lambic, married into the Cantillon family and took charge in 1978. He is a fierce critic of bigger commercial brewers who produce what he calls 'industrial gueuze' and who speed up production and use syrups rather than whole fruit in their versions of *kriek* and *framboise*. What he thinks of such aberrations as 'peppermint gueuze' cannot be printed here. He turned Cantillon into the Museum of Gueuze, open every day, and which attracts large numbers of visitors who marvel at the halls of oak casks where lambic quietly matures.

Jean-Pierre's son, Jean Van Roy, has built on his father's legacy with several new beers. Mamouche is a lambic made with the addition of fresh elderflowers. It has a bronze colour and an earthy elderflower and sour aroma. The beer is extremely sour in the mouth, with elderflower, yeast and the lightest of hop notes. The finish is long, dry, sour and fruity, with a continuing powerful note of elderflower and a salty, iodine note.

Zwanze is an annual vintage produced by Jean to celebrate Zwanze Day. The word is almost impossible to translate and comes from a dialect expression in Brussels that stands for drivel or nonsense. There are specialist artists and comedians who perform in the dialect and tell outlandish stories. Jean's vintage varies from year to year. When I last visited the brewery he presented me with a sample of Zwanze Zoll that was the result of collaboration with a renowned

French sommelier Olivier Le Masson. Le Masson makes wine in the Loire Valley using organic grapes, which suits Cantillon as all production is now based on organic materials. For the beer, Pineau d'Aunis grapes from the Loire were added to the lambic, which was then aged for two years.

The beer that emerged from the oak casks in the brewery had a bright ruby colour, a sweet grape and lambic sourness on the nose and an intensely sour palate balanced by tart fruit. The finish has a challenging sour dry note but is balanced by a late burst of fruity grapes. The following year, Jean made a rhubarb lambic for Zwanze Day, which he said had a wonderfully delicate flavour.

Jean Van Roy has built on his father's legacy

Lindemans Cuvée René Gueuze/Kriek

Source: Brouwerij Lindemans, Vlezenbeek, Belgium
Strength: 5.5%/6%
Website: www.lindemans.be

Lindemans is a brewery that went down the route of crude commercialism and then returned to the path of righteousness. In the 1980s it aped the methods of Belle-Vue, the biggest producer of lambic in Belgium and now owned by global giant AB InBev, which makes large volumes of heavily-sweetened versions of the style. Lindemans was put under pressure from importers in the United States to make sweetened lambic and gueuze that would suit the American palate but in the 1990s the family decided to return to true lambic production. This was the result of further, reverse pressure from the U.S. where attitudes to lambic had changed and drinkers were demanding the real thing. The result was Cuvée René, named after René Lindemans, who represented the sixth generation of the family to run the brewery. René has been bought out by Dirk and Geert Lindemans of the seventh generation and they have spearheaded the drive back to authenticity.

In common with many breweries in the Brabant region, the enterprise started out as a farm early in the 19th century where beer was made. Eventually, farming stopped and all the effort went into making beer.

In order to cope with demand, a new brewhouse was installed in 1991, enabling production to increase to 60,000 hectolitres a year: it's second only in size to Belle-Vue. The attractive domed copper vessels came from a closed brewery in the German Saarland and, unusually for a lambic brewery, are based on the traditional German system of mash mixer, lauter tun and boiling copper. Lindemans also installed a second cool ship in a separate building: the worts from both cooling vessels are blended prior to fermentation. Increasing demand led the family to buy 20 new 100-hectolitre oak casks from France in 2006.

The Gueuze has a big lemon/citrus aroma and palate, the signature of the brewery's style. It's tart, sour and fruity in the mouth with just a faint hint of hops. The finish is quenching and tart, with a Sherry-like fruit note. The Kriek is the result of adding cherries to a lambic that is between six and eight months old. The fruit, both Belgian and Danish cherries, is steeped in the beer for six months. The finished beer has a luscious dry, tart cherry aroma and palate, with a woody/leafy balance and the expected sourness from yeast activity. It finishes dry, tart, sour and fruity.

in the 1990s the family decided to return to true lambic production.

TASTING NOTES

APPEARANCE:

AROMA:

TASTE:

OVERALL SCORE:

TASTING NOTES

APPEARANCE:

AROMA:

TASTE:

OVERALL SCORE:

Mort Subite Gueuze/Kriek

Source: Brouwerij Mort Subite, Kobbegem, Belgium

Strength: 4.5%

Website: www.mort-subite.be

Mort Subite means Sudden Death, a daunting name for beer. It's derived from a bar in Brussels that started life as La Cour Royal but changed its name due to the fame of a game of dice played there by lawyers, staff of the National Bank and journalists from the newspaper *La Libre Belgique*. If one of them was called back to the office the players would terminate the game by Sudden Death. You can enjoy the brewery's beers there at 7 Rue Montagne aux Herbes Potagères and also admire the fine Art Nouveau surroundings.

The brewery to the north-west of Brussels has ancient roots. The Van Der Hasselt family brewed on the site since 1604 and retained a connection until the 20th century. But for five generations the brewery was run by the De Keersmaeker family, a Belgian dynasty that includes barons and other members of the nobility, and has been involved in the arts and politics as well as beer making. The brewery carried the family name until 2005, when it was overtaken by the fame of Mort Subite. Jacques De Keersmaeker worked in the family business until he became managing director of Belle-Vue. When I met him there, he sat me down and gave me a lucid and scholarly description of all aspects of lambic brewing that has informed my writing on the subject ever since: see my lengthy article in *The Taste of Beer* (Weidenfeld & Nicolson, 1998).

In the 1930s, when the future of lambic brewing was in doubt, the De Keersmaekers designed a new brewhouse that could produce Pils lager and ale as well. Fortunately lambic production continued and is now the only style, though primary fermentation is achieved by pumping oxygen into an enclosed vessel rather than an open cool ship. Ageing, however, takes place in wooden casks – *pipes* and *foudres* – from the wine, Calvados and port industries. The beer stays in the casks for two years, sometimes longer.

The fact that lambic brewing has continued at Mort Subite is remarkable when you consider the dizzy round of takeovers it has suffered over the years. It was bought by the large national group Alken-Maes, which was taken over by Kronenbourg, which in turn was acquired by the British group Scottish & Newcastle. S&N was then swallowed by Heineken. Along the way, the De Keersmaeker family gave up the ghost and handed over the brewery to Heineken's managers. Fortunately the Dutch giant, unlike some other global brewers, understands there's growing interest in small volume artisan beers as well as mass-marketed lagers. As a result Mort Subite has been encouraged to improve its product line and make truly traditional lambic as well as sweetened versions.

Gueuze has a pale bronze colour beneath a heavy collar of foam. It's sour, yeasty and nutty on the nose with a freshly baked bread grain note. The malt develops a honey note in the mouth, with some acidity and tart fruit. The finish is bittersweet with honeyed malt balancing tart fruit and a now fading sourness.

Kriek is made with the addition of Gorsem and Kallares cherries. The beer has a bright ruby-red colour with tart fruit and lambic sourness on the nose, a bittersweet palate in which tart fruit is balanced by a yeasty sourness, and a lingering tart, tangy, bittersweet finish with a final quenching acidity.

> **"** *there's growing interest in small volume artisan beers as well as mass-marketed lagers. As a result Mort Subite has been encouraged to improve its product line* **"**

TASTING NOTES

APPEARANCE:

AROMA:

TASTE:

OVERALL SCORE:

Timmermans Oude Gueuze

Source: Timmermans-Anthony Martin NV

Strength: 5.5%

Website: anthonymartin.be

Lambic breweries tend to be dusty to avoid disturbing the natural micro-flora in the atmosphere but Timmermans is a remarkably spick-and-span site. It stands in a suburb of Brussels and is surrounded by smart houses: I doubt they would get permission to open a brewery there today but perhaps Nimbyism (Not in My Backyard) doesn't exist in Itterbeek. Timmermans is second only to Cantillon as a visitor centre, attracting around 50,000 a year: tours must be booked (02 569 03 57) and must constitute a party of at least 15 or more. The brewing operation is fiercely traditional, with mash tun, direct-flame copper, a large cool ship in the attic and halls packed with oak *pipes* and *foudres* from the port industry: cask are sent to Portugal for repairs.

The brewery dates from the early 19th century. It was founded by the Timmermans family and then run by their near relatives, the Van Cutsems, who are still involved in the brewery though they no longer own it. In the 1990s Timmermans was bought by the major John Martin drinks group and is now managed by a member of the family, Anthony Martin. Martin buys and distributes beer from many sources within Belgium but Timmermans is its only working brewery and fortunately Anthony Martin is passionate about lambic.

For some years Timmermans lost its lustre by focusing on artificially sweetened lambic and gueuze, including canned versions labelled Timms. Then in 2009 it returned to the true lambic fold with an Oude Gueuze that stunned lovers of the style. It has a sour aroma and palate with a leafy/cedarwood note and tart orange fruit, followed by a long and complex finish with an interplay of acidity from the orange fruit, sourness from the yeast and a continuing woody note. Oude Gueuze and other beers from within the Martin's group can be enjoyed at a bar in the visitor area. Try the Bourgogne de Flandres, a blend of lambic and ale.

You can also sample the beers at the Café Becasse (the Woodcock) at 11 Rue Tabora, off the Grand-Place in central Brussels.

> ❝ *The brewing operation is fiercely traditional, with mash tun, direct-flame copper, a large cool ship in the attic and halls packed with oak pipes* ❞

French Beers

France is rightly revered as a great wine-making country and as a result beer tends to be overlooked or treated as a simple summer refresher. Yet the country has a long history of brewing, enshrined in the word *brasserie*. Its modern usage indicates a bar or simple restaurant but it stands for brewery, recalling a time when many bars either had breweries attached or specialised in local beers. Beer drinking has always been widespread in France and is growing, especially among younger people. And in the far north, as in neighbouring Belgium, beer lovers have discovered a rich brewing tradition. There is obvious cross-fertilisation between French-speaking Wallonia in Belgium and the Nord-Pas de Calais region of France that includes such historic areas as Artois, Flanders and Picardy.

Castelain Jade

Beer is the natural drink in an area that is flat, damp and windswept, and with a sturdy agriculture that produces grain and hops, rather than the grapes of the warm south. The people, often with Flemish names in towns and villages rooted in the history of Flanders, drink beer, cook with beer and celebrate it with March and Christmas beers, along with an annual beer festival in Douai. Farm labourers were once paid in kind with beer and potatoes, a practice that would be frowned on today, but beer remains the perfect companion for the hearty stews, sausage, vegetable and fish dishes of the region.

Brewing suffered in the 20th century as a result of two world wars that saw copper vessels removed by invading German armies, followed by the winding down, from the 1960s, of the large mining industry in the Lille area. The Castelain brewery near Lens used to depict a cheery coal miner on their labels but he has become a ghostly figure. Brewing started to revive in France as greater interest was shown in the Pas de Calais, its history, culture, food and drink. The rich storehouse of beers in Belgium helped show there was a strong link to brewing styles south of the nominal border. There was certainly a powerful connection between the *saisons* of Wallonia and the *bières de garde* of France. Both are warm-fermented ales, produced originally by farmers for workers and families, using the grains and hops from the fields. They come in blond, amber, brown and russet versions, and offer rich malt, and spicy and gentle hop character.

French beers featured strongly in *300 Beers to Try Before You Die!*, but in the few years between that book and this, French brewing has changed rapidly. Younger and more cosmopolitan brewers are influenced by American and British styles as well as Belgian. As a result consumers are now offered a wider choice, including French interpretations of Stout and India Pale Ale. Brewing is no longer confined to the north, with mash tuns and coppers now fired further south. And there are even brewers from Britain either brewing British ales or adapting French ones. But to prove that France is not unduly influenced by foreign styles, there's a beer that is quintessentially French, made with the addition of Cognac. *Vive la différence*!

Fleurac La Triple

Bellerose Bière Blonde Extra/Abbatiale Triple

Source: Brasseries des Sources, Saint-Amand-les-Eaux, Nord, France

Strength: 6.5% /7%

Website: www.brasseriedestamand.fr

This is a brewery with a short but turbulent history. It was founded in 1987 by such luminaries of the French screen as Gérard Depardieu, Claude Berri and Miou-Miou, who came to the area to film Emile Zola's novel *Germinal* about a bitter strike in the coal mines in the 1860s. The film was shot in Valenciennes and the actors developed an attachment to the area and its traditional beer. As a result they founded the Brasserie des Amis Réunis, the Reunited Friends Brewery, which concentrated on the *bière de garde* style. When the company ran into financial difficulties, it was reformed as the Amand brewery. This too faced problems and was rescued in 2005 by Jean-Luc Butez, who has run it on a sound footing as Brasseries des Sources and produces 10,000 hectolitres a year. 'Sources' suggests the plant has its own spring water supply, which adds a touch of romance to a brewery based in a former slaughterhouse.

Bellerose is a described as a cross between an IPA and a *bière de garde* but is rather more of the latter than the former. The brewery says it recalls the 1950s when French beers were of great quality and good thirst-quenchers. It has won three medals for quality in its short life, including 'best ale' category in the 2011 International Beer Challenge and the Medaille d'Or (gold medal) in the 2012 competition for agricultural products run by the French Ministry of Agriculture and Food. It's brewed with pale malt and three hops, which – frustratingly – the brewery refuses to name. It has rich perfumy malt on the nose, with strong hints of nougat and honey, along with citrus fruit from the hops. The palate is quenching, with creamy malt, tart fruit and peppery hops, followed by a creamy and honey malt finish, with a late burst of peppery hop bitterness and a lingering note of citrus fruit.

Abbatiale Triple pays homage to the long defunct abbey of St Amand. The beer enjoys a triple fermentation, including in the bottle, and is copper coloured with an enormous fluffy head of foam, rich vinous fruit on the nose with powerful notes of toasted grain, tobacco, spices and herbal hops. The bittersweet palate has a developing spicy hop character balanced by buttery malt and tart fruit. Creamy/buttery malt is to the fore in the finish with spicy hops and tart fruit.

Le Brewery Norman Gold/Conquerant/Harold's Revenge

Source: Le Brewery, Joué du Bois, Normandy, France

Strength: 4.9%/5.5%/7%

Website: www.le-brewery.com

I met Steve Skews at a very English event, a harvest supper at Warminster Maltings in Wiltshire to celebrate the autumn gathering of barley that would be turned into malt for brewing. Steve told me he was making beer in Normandy where he was producing English-style ales and sourced the finest Maris Otter malt from Warminster. He brought with him samples of his beer and I went clanking home with some unexpected treats.

Steve and Jane Skews were teachers in Peterborough who yearned to live in rural France. The only small problem was how they could earn a living while enjoying the good life. Steve had brewed at home since the age of 14 and he was a keen drinker of cask beer. He decided on an adventure: to brew English ale for French people in a region better known for cider than beer. It was a risky project, but Steve and Jane knew they could underpin it with the support of the large number of British visitors to Normandy. In 2001 they launched Le Brewery in their attractive stone farm house, using brewing kit from the closed Gale's brewery in Hampshire. They have added a shop, provide brewery tours and have won a number of awards for their beer. Their success has led to their running two pubs in the area, Secret Knight and Famous Knight that serve cask-conditioned ale by handpumps. And the whole enterprise is based on gently poking fun at Gallic pomposity with beers that have a Norman Invasion theme.

Steve has added to the quality and flavour of his beers by developing his own hop orchard next to the farm where he grows Cascade, Challenger and Fuggles. The bottled versions of the beer come in the obligatory French style with corks and cradles, and are refermented in bottle.

TASTING NOTES

APPEARANCE:

AROMA:

TASTE:

OVERALL SCORE:

Norman Gold is brewed with Maris Otter pale malt with caramalt and wheat malt and is hopped with Cascade, Challenger and Styrian Goldings varieties. It has a pale bronze colour and a luscious aroma of biscuit malt, tart citrus fruit and spicy, woody and grassy hops.

Conqueror is an amber/red beer with a big spicy and floral hop note from Steve's own Challengers plus Styrian Goldings. The grains are Maris Otter pale malt, roast barley, crystal malt, wheat malt and pale chocolate malt. The grains deliver a toasted and roasted character to the beer, with notes of chocolate, vinous fruit and spicy and leafy hops. The finish is long and quenching, packed with rich toasted malt, chocolate, tart fruit and leafy and woody hop resins.

Harold's Revenge is a big auburn beer, with warming alcohol, creamy malt, chocolate, citrus fruit and peppery hops on the nose, followed by a palate dominated by tart fruit, peppery hops, chocolate and honeyed malt. The finish is long and complex, starting bittersweet but becoming dry, with creamy, honeyed malt, chocolate, peppery and grassy hops, and intense citrus fruit notes.

TASTING NOTES

APPEARANCE:

AROMA:

TASTE:

OVERALL SCORE:

Their success has led to their running two pubs in the area, Secret Knight and Famous Knight that serve cask-conditioned ale by handpumps.

Castelain Jade

Source: Brasserie Castelain, Bénifontaine, near Lens, Pas de Calais, France

Strength: 4.5%

Website: www.chti.com

Castelain, as the website address shows, is best known for its *bières de garde* sold under the name of Ch'ti. This is a Picardy dialect word, a corruption of *c'est toi*, difficult to translate but meaning roughly 'it suits you'. It has passed in to general usage throughout France to identify people from the far north of the country. In common with many small breweries in the region, the brewery started life on a farm in 1926 and was bought by the Castelain family in the 1960s. It's been run by Yves and Annick since the 1970s and they have energetically grown the business, which now produces an impressive 45,000 hectolitres a year: in 1978, when Yves and Annick took over, production was just 3,000 hectolitres a year. In the early days it concentrated on weak beer for thirsty miners but the industry disappeared: the brewery's origins and the links with miners can be seen in a small museum on the site.

Yves Castelain built the brewery's reputation with Ch'ti Blonde (see *300 Beers to Try Before You Die!*) which accounts for 60 per cent of annual production but he has added to the range. He's also developed the production side, with a new bottling hall and, in 2008, modern fermenting vessels. The brewhouse remains firmly traditional, with attractive copper mashing and boiling vessels in tiled surrounds. The vessels are visible from the road called Rue Pasteur. Yves may venerate the great French scientist who helped unravel the mysteries of fermentation and bacteria in wine and beer, but the brewer steadfastly refuses to pasteurise his products. Brewing liquor comes from a well on the site.

Jade was the first organic beer brewed in France and has been awarded all the necessary certificates from the bio organisations.

Yves Castelain brews Jade with Pilsner Bio malt and Malt Coloré Bio, with two German hops, Spalter Select and Perle Bio. The pale gold beer has a luscious aroma of fresh-bread malt, a hint of citrus fruit and spicy, herbal hops. Honeyed malt, tart fruit and spicy hops dominate the palate, followed by a long and lingering finish that has a superb and quenching balance of juicy malt, tart fruit and herbal hops.

Jade, in common with all the Castelain beers, is made slowly and with passion. Primary fermentation takes eight days and this is followed by the crucial *la garde* – cold conditioning for a minimum of six weeks, which permits natural carbonation to take place.

TASTING NOTES

APPEARANCE:

AROMA:

TASTE:

OVERALL SCORE:

La Choulette Blonde/La d'Artagnan

Source: Brasserie la Choulette, Hordain, Nord, France

Strength: 7.5%/8.5%

Website: www.lachoulette.com

La Choulette is one of the most respected producers of *Bière de Garde* and the owners, Martine and Alain Dhaussy, have a great passion for the culture of the region, down to naming their brewery after a local sport, *la crosse en plain*, in which a wooden ball, *la choulette*, is bashed across open land with clubs: the game inspired the French-Canadian sport lacrosse. There's a vivid description of the game in Zola's *Germinal* and clubs and balls are on display in the brewery's visitor area.

The brewery is a Flanders classic, with attractive copper vessels set in tiled surrounds. It was originally known as the Bourgeois-Lecerf Brewery, founded in 1885 and whose owners made the disastrous decision after World War Two to convert to lager production. The owners found to their cost that the big Pils brewers such as Kronenbourg in the Strasbourg region could undercut them at every move, and tie bars and restaurants with cheap loans and other inducements.

Alain Dhaussy bought the redundant plant in 1977 and restored its fortunes with Ambrée, launched in 1981 (see *300 Beers to Try Before You Die!*). He has built on that success with other interpretations of *bières de garde*, including some that pay homage to the French Revolution, including Sans Culottes and Brassin Robespierre.

All the beers are conditioned in the brewery for a minimum of a month then rough filtered with sufficient yeast to continue to mature in bottles that are corked and cradled. Blonde is brewed with pale malt from both spring and winter barleys from the Nord-Pas de Calais and is hopped with Brewers Gold, Goldings and Magnum varieties. It has a rich toasted malt, pear-like fruit and peppery hops aroma, followed by a full palate of rich malt, peppery hops and sweet fruit. The finish is long and complex, juicy malt melding with bitter hop resins and sweet fruit.

La D'Artagnan celebrates the hero of Alexandre Dumas' chronicles of the adventures of the *Three Musketeers*. D'Artagnan was based on a real life Comte D'Artagnan who was born in Gascony in the 17th century but served his country in battles in Artois, Flanders and Hainaut. He was made governor of Lille by Louis XIV and remains a heroic figure in French Flanders. The beer in his name has the same malt and hops make-up as Blonde but as a result of its higher strength has a pronounced creamy and biscuit malt aroma and palate, with rich bittersweet fruit and a powerful underpinning of peppery and woody hops. The finish is complex and lingering, toasted malt combining with ripe fruit and tangy and bitter hop resins.

> ❛ *He has built on that success with other interpretations of bières de garde, including some that pay homage to the French Revolution, including Sans Culottes and Brassin Robespierre.* ❜

Craig Allan Cuvée d'Oscar

Source: Craig Allan, Méry-la-Bataille, Picardy, France
Strength: 7.5%
Website: www.craigallan.fr

This is a beer brewed by a Scot, using a brewery in Belgium and selling it in France, in the heart of the *bière de garde* region of French Flanders. Craig Allan learned his brewing skills at the department of brewing and distilling at the Heriot-Watt University in Edinburgh and then worked in a number of Scottish small craft breweries. He says he found Britain too conservative where beer is concerned (you should go home more often, Craig) and he moved to France.

Craig works closely with a specialist pub in Lille called La Capsule, where beer is matched with food. He plans to open his own brewery in the Lille area but at present his beers are brewed by Proef in Belgium. Proef was founded in 1996 and specialises in producing beer for customers who give the brewing team ideas or full recipes. Many of the Danish Mikkeller beers are produced at Proef. Cuvée d'Oscar is named after Craig's baby son and comes in an attractive 37.5cl bottle complete with cork and wire cradle. It's brewed with pale malt, wheat malt, Munich and chocolate malts and Special B aroma malt. Only one hop is used, Nelson Sauvin from New Zealand, which is used in both the copper and for dry hopping before the beer is packaged. Units of bitterness are 26. The beer is fermented with a Bavarian wheat culture.

It has a deep russet colour with a big chocolate and cafè crème aroma along with woody/leafy hops, hints of liquorice and vinous fruits. Dry chocolate and coffee build in the mouth with growing hop bitterness, dark fruit and toasted grain. The finish has some rich malt sweetness, balanced by dry chocolate, vinous fruit and fading hop notes. It's finally dry.

Craig has achieved considerable acclaim in France. His beer is now sold at several top restaurants in Paris, including L'Ami Jean, L'Arpège and Chamarrée Montmartre, where chefs carefully match beer with food. It brings a modern twist to the Auld Alliance between Scotland and France.

Dry chocolate and coffee build in the mouth with growing hop bitterness

TASTING NOTES

APPEARANCE:

AROMA:

TASTE:

OVERALL SCORE:

TASTING NOTES
APPEARANCE:

AROMA:

TASTE:

OVERALL SCORE:

TASTING NOTES
APPEARANCE:

AROMA:

TASTE:

OVERALL SCORE:

Fleurac Amerindienne/La Triple

Source: Brasserie de Fleurac, Auvergne, France
Strength: 5%/8%
Website: www.brasserie-fleurac.com

This brewery is a long way from the beery influence of the Pas de Calais. It's in the Auvergne, where the major city is Lyon. But the beer influence comes from the north. Virginie De Bodt and Grégoire Murer are Belgian and Grég served an internship at La Binchoise brewery in his home country (see Belgian Ales section). The couple moved to central France in 2005 and spent three years planning a brewery and experimenting with recipes in their kitchen. Finally in 2008 they opened the brewery, based in an old barn.

Grég brews in a slow and meticulous manner in order to draw the best flavours of malt and hops from his beers. They are unpasteurised, unfiltered and refermented in bottle. Following one week's primary fermentation, the beers are conditioned in a cool area for two weeks. They then undergo what French wine makers call *chaptalisation*: sugar is added to encourage a strong secondary fermentation in a warm area. The beers are finally cold conditioned for a second time for a few days before they are released.

Amerindienne will come as a shock to even the most experienced drinker of bitter IPA-style beers. It has 120 units of bitterness: 40 would be considered high by most conventional brewers. Grég says the bitterness levels are 'theoretical not scientific' and could be more or less than 120. The label shows a Native American Indian, which is a novel spin on India Pale Ale. It's labelled a 'Simple Blonde IPA' and carries the tag '*avec vrais houblons du Far West*' – with true hops from the Far West. The varieties used are Ahtanum, Centennial and Warrior: Grég says it's the Warrior hops that give the big bitterness boost to the beer and they are added late in the copper boil. Pale malt has an addition of a tiny amount of special malt called Aroma 100, used to give colour

and a greater malt flavour to balance the extreme bitterness. The pale bronze beer has a big fruit jelly aroma of oranges and lemon, with spicy hop resins and a freshly-baked bread note from the malt. Intensely bitter hops take over in the mouth, with powerful notes of iodine and quinine, balanced by tart citrus fruit and juicy malt. The long bitter and hoppy finish has continuing iodine/quinine notes along with tangy citrus fruit and light biscuit malt.

La Triple is a beer with a different heritage, Grég's homage to the strong golden ales of his native Belgium – with Westmalle Tripel as the benchmark. It's brewed with pale malt and a touch of Special B aromatic malt and the hops are Slovenian Perle and Belgian Brewers Gold. The beer has a more approachable bitterness in the 40s and an entrancing gold colour, a fluffy head of foam and a big tangerine fruit and spicy hop nose, with a cookie malt character. Spicy hops and tart fruit dominate the palate with a solid underpinning of honeyed malt. The finish is long, with spicy and herbal hops, a continuing tangerine fruit note and honeyed malt.

Thiriez Étoile du Nord

Source: Brasserie Thiriez, Esquelbecq, Nord, France

Strength: 5.5%

Website: www.brasseriethiriez.com

Daniel Thiriez has brought brewing back to life in the village of Esquelbecq, 20 miles from Dunkirk. The farmhouse brewery of Poidevin closed in 1945 and Daniel moved on to the site and launched his brewery in 1997. His success can be gauged by the fact that he expanded into other buildings on the farm in 2001 and installed a new brewhouse in 2006, complete with four additional fermenting vessels. The complex now offers a café and bed and breakfast accommodation.

Étoile du Nord – Star of the North – was the result of collaboration between Daniel and John Davidson, who ran the Swale Brewery in Kent and supplied Daniel with Kentish hops. Swale is now the Whitstable Brewery and Daniel has moved on, using different hop varieties, Brewers Gold and Bramling Cross. Just one malt, Pilsner, is used in the exceptionally pale beer. It's a true *bière de garde*, kept in *la garde* storage area for a minimum of two weeks and then refermented in the bottle. It has a hazy bronze colour with a fruity gooseberry note from the hops on the nose along with creamy malt and leafy/woody hop resins. Rich creamy malt builds in the mouth with tart fruit and leafy hops. The finish is long with juicy malt, woody hop resins and tart gooseberry fruit.

TASTING NOTES

APPEARANCE:

AROMA:

TASTE:

OVERALL SCORE:

TASTING NOTES

APPEARANCE:

AROMA:

TASTE:

OVERALL SCORE:

XO Bière au Cognac

Source: Brasserie des Gabariers, Cognac, Charente, France

Strength: 8%

Website: www.xobeer.com

The brewery has the ideal location for a beer infused with Cognac, standing on the banks of the Charente River in the world-famous distilling town. The beer was the idea of Didier Berthelot who owned a drinks company, Angoulême Beverages, and who was a witness to the remarkable turnaround in the fortunes of Cognac in the 21st century. For decades Cognac played second fiddle to Scotch whisky on the world stage but it acquired radical chic when it was taken up by young rappers in the United States, who spearheaded a global revival of the drink.

Didier was also keenly aware of the growing interest in craft beer, including in France, and decided to ignore the old adage that you should never mix the grape and the grain. He launched XO in Angoulême but to give it greater

authenticity moved production to the heart of Cognac. He makes other beers but the success of XO prompted the change of name for the website. It's exported widely, to the United States, Canada, Mexico and Scandinavia. Brewer Pascal Mounier says he used just Pilsner malt in the beer with Hallertau Mittelfrüh and Northdown hops. Cognac makes up 2.5% of the finished liquid. XO is the designation given to an aged Cognac, usually around 20 years old.

The beer has a bronze colour, a heavy collar of foam and a rich creamy malt aroma with massive vinous fruit, smoky hints and floral hops. The palate is fruity with roasted grain, woody/oaky notes and gentle hops. The finish is bittersweet with ripe fruit, creamy/buttery malt and a light hint of hops. XO, of course, should be sipped and savoured from a brandy balloon.

> *XO, of course, should be sipped and savoured from a brandy balloon.*

Alt, Amber & Kölsch

Schlafly Kölsch

To the casual drinker, Germany is famous for its lager beer. It comes as something of a shock to discover that the country has an ale tradition as well. In Bavaria, as we've seen, a substantial proportion of the beer brewed is wheat beer, which is a member of the ale family. The same holds true further north, with the Alt beers of Düsseldorf and Kölsch in Cologne. Both are ales, though visitors to Cologne could be forgiven for thinking the pale Kölsch beers, served cold, are members of the lager fraternity.

Alt means old and describes a beer made by warm fermentation before the arrival of lager on a commercial scale in the 19th century. Alt is a copper-coloured beer and it has an affinity with the Mild ales of England and the *bières de garde* and saisons of France and Belgium. Düsseldorf, close to the border with Belgium, once had a large mining industry and Alt, comparatively low in strength, was designed to quench the thirsts of workers who spent long hours underground digging for black gold. In spite of the decline of heavy industry in the region, Alt beer has become more popular, especially among younger drinkers. Popularity has its downside though: when I first visited Diebels brewery in Issum, just outside Düsseldorf, it was a proud and independent family-owned company and also the biggest producer by far of Altbier. But the company is now part of global giant AB InBev and produces Pils as well as its traditional style.

The best way to enjoy Altbier is to walk through the charming cobbled streets of central Düsseldorf where several pubs have small house breweries dedicated to the style. They include Im Füschen, the Little Fox, where wooden casks of beer are delivered by a dumb waiter and replaced at great speed as soon as one cask is drained. As with Belgian Trappist beers, it's difficult to talk of an Altbier style, as they vary in colour from pale bronze to deep copper. Fermentation can be in open or closed vessels and mashing can be either infusion or decoction (see Glossary). Whatever methods are used, brewers are looking for a rich malt aroma and flavour, underscored by gentle but firm hop

Schüssel brewpub, Düsseldorf

character. The beers are stored for around a month before being released: a period known as lagering, which can also come as something of a learning curve to visitors.

Kölsch gets its name from the German for Cologne, Köln. It's been an important trading city in the Rhineland since Roman times and Köln is reference to its colonial past. Beer is deeply rooted in the city's history. It was controlled by the church for centuries and when religious power waned brewing passed to small commercial producers, many of them based in taverns. Today, Cologne is in a time warp. At a time when brewing is dominated by giant global corporations that concentrate on poor imitations of Pilsner, Cologne has maintained its tradition of warm-fermented ale. There are still a dozen or more small breweries based in taverns or commercial buildings producing a beer style that is protected with the German version of a French appellation. In the 1960s, the Cologne brewers took steps to protect their tradition. The move was prompted by a twin attack, from the rapid spread of Pils lager and the appearance of beers labelled Kölsch in other parts of Germany. In 1985, after years of negotiations between the Cologne Association of Brewers and the government, the Kölsch Convention was signed. It's printed on parchment and states that the style is unique to Cologne and can only be brewed there and in a handful of other carefully-chosen towns and cities, including Bonn. The convention bears the signatures and seals of all the brewers of Kölsch, and it's proudly and jealously guarded.

In common with Altbier, Kölsch was first brewed to refresh agricultural and factory workers. Today it has found favour with the younger generation and new breweries have appeared to cope with the demand. A modern interpretation, which is now paler than in previous years, will be around 5% alcohol, will have a firm malty body, soft on the palate from the local water, and will have gentle perfumy hop notes. Extreme bitterness is avoided and most versions will have bitterness units in the high 20s. Hops from the Hallertau are the preferred varieties. Most, but not all, versions are brewed with a proportion of wheat, which helps give the finished beer its pale colour and creamy flavour. Unfiltered versions

Küppers Kölsch

are called Wiess, the local spelling of Weiss, meaning wheat. The beers are sold in large beer gardens in good weather, many overlooking the Rhine, and in beer halls known colloquially as the Schwemme or swimming pool. Waiters in traditional blue uniforms with leather aprons are all called *Kobes*, a diminutive of Jacob, on the curious assumption – also the case in Düsseldorf – that all barmen are called Jacob. They should form a common front with Scots barmen known as Jimmy.

There are no restrictions on brewing Alt and Kölsch in the United States, where there is growing interest in the styles as a result of the German ancestry of many Americans. Alt is often called Amber in the U.S. though drinkers are beginning to get to grips with a beer style from Cologne that's pronounced 'curlsch'.

Crazy Mountain Amber Ale

Source: Crazy Mountain Brewing Company, Edwards, Colorado, USA

Strength: 5.2%

Website: www.crazymountainbrewery.com

Kevin Selvy hails from Colorado and when he met his future partner Melisa over a beer in San Francisco they hatched a plan to move to the Rockies and build their own brewery. They are based in Vail Valley, famous as a ski resort, and Crazy Mountain is a simple translation from the Mexican Loco Mountain. They opened their brewery in 2010 with Amber Ale, which was an immediate success and remains their leading brand. A $4 million expansion scheme has boosted production to 25,000 barrels a year. The Selvys have established powerful roots in the local community and one per cent of the price of each beer sold goes to help local good causes, such as protecting the environment, helping youth projects and campaigns to fight cancer.

> *Their take on German Alt is brewed with pale, caramalt and roasted malt and is hopped with 'a ridiculous and obscene amount of hops'*

Their take on German Alt is brewed with pale, caramalt and roasted malt and is hopped with 'a ridiculous and obscene amount of hops', according to Kevin. The varieties are Cascade and Centennial, which create 25 units of bitterness. The beer has a pale copper colour with a nutty aroma and a strong chocolate note, along with roasted grain and spicy hops. Chocolate dominates the palate but there are strong notes of dark, chewy and nutty malt, and a growing spicy and bitter hop character. The finish is smooth, bittersweet, with chocolate, rich malt and tangy hops.

The brewery has a tap room for visitors and, continuing the German theme, there's also a seasonal Kölsch.

Küppers Kölsch

Source: Küppers Kölsch Brauerei, Cologne, North Rhine-Westphalia, Germany

Strength: 4.8%

Website: none

Küppers brewery was founded in 1890 to brew lager, but it changed course in the 1960s to take advantage of the demand for Kölsch, and has been so successful that it's become the biggest producer of the style. It has now been swallowed by the Oetker group, a giant German company that, under the reassuring name of Dr Oetker, makes everything from baking powder to pizzas and yoghurt, and runs hotels. It has snapped up a number breweries in recent years, including the major plants in Dortmund and the revered Jever Pilsner brewery in Friesland (see *300 Beers to Try Before You Die!*), as well as several other Kölsch producers.

Fortunately ownership by Oetker has not led to any diminution in the quality of Küppers beer.

The beer is brewed with Pilsner malt and around 25 per cent wheat. Hops come from the Bavarian Hallertau. A decoction mash is used and the beer is cold conditioned for several weeks. It emerges with a fresh-bread and creamy malt aroma with a fine grassy 'noble hop' character and a gentle hint of fruit. The beer is creamy in the mouth with light citrus fruit and a good balance of grassy/floral hops. The finish is bittersweet, with creamy/honeyed malt, tart fruit and gently bitter hops. There's an unfiltered Wiess version.

Schlafly Kölsch

Source: Saint Louis Brewery, St Louis, Missouri, USA

Strength: 4.8%

Website: schlafly.com

Tom Schlafly calls his brewery 'The biggest locally-owned independent in St Louis', a gentle dig at Anheuser-Busch's original Budweiser plant, now part of the global giant AB InBev, headquartered in Belgium. To date, Tom hasn't received a lawyer's letter, but AB InBev has bigger fish to fry, including the unending trademark dispute with Czech Budweiser.

Tom's wife is Ulrike, who comes from Cologne and introduced her husband to Kölsch and a relationship with the Gaffel brewery that now supplies yeast to create a true Kölsch character to the St Louis brew.

The Schlaflys opened their brewery, the Tap Room, in 1991, the first brewpub in St Louis since Prohibition. Success led to a second site, the Bottleworks, in the Maplewood district in 2010. This is now the main brewery and is open to visitors. Tom and his team produce some 50 regular and seasonal beers. Kölsch is one of the mainstays and won a gold medal in the 2010 World Beer Cup for Best German-style Kölsch. It's brewed with two-row pale malt, wheat malt, Munich malt and carapils. The hops are Hallertauer Tradition and Perle, which create 25 units of bitterness and, as mentioned above, the yeast is a pure Kölsch culture.

The beer is as pale as a Pils and throws a heavy collar of foam due to a period of cold conditioning. It has a true perfumy Kölsch nose, with floral hops and a fresh-bread and honeyed malt, along with a hint of lemon fruit. The palate is a fine balance of bitter, grassy hop resins, juicy malt and tart fruit, followed by a bittersweet finish, with honeyed malt and lemon fruit overshadowing the hops. It's a fine interpretation of the style.

Schlüssel Alt

Source: Hausbraureri Zum Schlüssel, Düsseldorf, North Rhine-Westphalia, Germany

Strength: 5%

Website: www.zumschluessel.de

Schlüssel means the Keys and its name comes from the time when the keys to the city gates were kept in local pubs. The brewpub is one of the classic producers of Altbier, in the Old Town and on Bolker-strasse, the birthplace of the poet Heinrich Heine. The pub dates from 1850 and since 1936 it's been in the hands of the Gatzweiler family. The building was bombed during World War Two and was rebuilt in the 1950s. It's bright and airy, with a tiled floor, long tables for diners and attractive copper brewing kettles on view through a window at the rear.

The beer is brewed with Pils malt and Munich malt, with hops from the Hallertau. It has a woody/grassy hop aroma with vinous fruit, a hint of chocolate and toasted malt followed by a bittersweet palate dominated by rich toasted malt, vinous fruit, chocolate and grassy hops. The finish is dry, ending with a good, firm grassy hop note but balanced by rich malt, dark fruit and a continuing hint of chocolate. In common with all Altbiers, it's served in small glasses and one local standing at the bar told me: 'After the fifth one, you start to taste it'. He was doing his best to prove the point.

TASTING NOTES

APPEARANCE:

AROMA:

TASTE:

OVERALL SCORE:

The Schlüssel brewpub

TASTING NOTES

APPEARANCE:

AROMA:

TASTE:

OVERALL SCORE:

Tyranena Headless Man Amber Ale

Source: Tyranena Brewing Company, Lake Mills, Wisconsin, USA

Strength: 5.2%

Website: tyranena.com

Rob Larson founded his brewery in an area, between Madison and Milwaukee, that was once home to a tribe that created a series of stone structures and effigies on the edge of a lake the ancients called Tyranena. Two of the effigies remain on the floor of Rock Lake, one of a headless man, the second of a turtle. In the world of the ancient tribe, the turtle helped the headless man find his way to the afterlife.

Rob brews his Amber Ale with two-row pale malt, aromatic malt and caramalt. The hops are Liberty, Perle and Tettnanger, which create 25 units

of bitterness. The brewery, in the finest tradition of the style, says the beer enjoys a 'cold lagering process', which means it's cold conditioned for several weeks before release but it's firmly in the ale camp. The pale copper beer has a pungent floral and herbal hop aroma with a rich, slightly toasted malt balance and a hint of berry fruits. There's a dry, toasted malt note on the palate, balanced by spicy and resinous hops, gentle bitterness and a hint of sultana fruit. The finish is dry with light hop bitterness, a hint of spice, toasted malt and dark fruit.

Pale Lagers

A battle is on for the future of lager beer. It's the world's dominant beer style. In many countries it's the only beer style, one with deep, historic roots: although the production of pale and golden lagers blossomed in the 19th century as a result of the Industrial Revolution, the conditioning of beer at low temperatures goes back many centuries. In central Europe brewers, including monks, solved the problem of keeping beer cool and free from bacteria and wild yeasts by storing it in cold mountain caves or brewery cellars packed with ice. The place where beer was conditioned was called the *lager keller*, from the German word *lager* meaning storage place. Once refrigeration and ice machines replaced ice that was cut laboriously from rivers and lakes, production of lager beer became possible on a vastly increased scale.

Increased production of lager didn't mean cutting corners. For lager beer to offer rich aromas and flavours of malt and hops, it had to be conditioned for lengthy periods in order that yeast could continue to turn remaining malt sugars into alcohol and for the beer to mature. The 90 days enjoyed by Czech Budweiser Budvar was once the norm for the style.

But the world of lager brewing has changed out of all recognition in recent years. Beers such as the American version of Budweiser, Carling, Carlsberg, Foster's, Heineken and Stella Artois are now global beers. The extent of the 'globalisation' of these brands is typified by the case of Foster's. It's hard, if not impossible, to find the beer on tap in its country of origin. In spite of witty TV commercials featuring men with broad Aussie accents, Foster's is now an export brand brewed under licence in such famous Australian cities as Manchester.

Globalisation has changed the way in which these beers are brewed. Lager has become an exceptionally pale, heavily carbonated and over-chilled beer, brewed as fast as possible to maximise income. The global brands no longer deserve the name of lager as they are not brewed or aged in the traditional manner. I've visited breweries in Finland, Poland and Russia owned by Carlsberg and Heineken and found that the beers have a total production time of 21 days. That period covers mashing, boiling and fermentation. Ask how long the beer is lagered and brewers, or more likely people from the marketing departments, look puzzled. It's an alien concept. These so-called lagers are produced as quickly as warm-fermented ales. It's now the industry norm.

The only argument I have heard in defence of the modern method came from the head brewer at the Velké Popovice brewery in the Czech Republic, which makes Kozel beers. Following the end of the communist period, the brewery was bought by the giant American-South African conglomerate, SABMiller. The head brewer told me he had cut the lagering time for his beers from 60 to 30 days: 'After 30 days there's no more work for the yeast to do,' he said. At least it can be said that his beers still get a month in the cellar. The counter argument, from master brewers whose work I revere, say that if you use the finest raw materials, the longer you store the beer, the better it will get. On the other hand, if a brewer blends substantial amounts of rice or corn with malted barley it's unlikely the beer will improve with long ageing or any ageing at all.

Should there be a Campaign for Real Lager? The large numbers of countries producing it make that an impossible task. What I offer here are some of the genuine lager beers still brewed by people who are determined to allow their products to mature and improve with love and care. A few of the beers listed in this section are now owned or part-owned by global producers. Let's hope their accountants and marketing departments don't step in and put profit before integrity.

Amber Žywe

Source: Browar Amber, Bielkówko, Poland

Strength: 6.2%

Website: www.browar-amber.pl

Poland deserves greater recognition as a major beer-producing country. It's third behind Germany and Britain in terms of production and it has a distinctive tradition of brewing Baltic Porters (see *300 Beers to Try Before You Die!*) as well lager beers. The tradition was hidden from view behind the Iron Curtain and the end of communism has seen a rush by global brewers to snap up large swathes of the industry. There are 70 breweries in Poland but 85 per cent of production is now in the hands of Carlsberg, Heineken and SABMiller. Fortunately, a young generation of beer lovers are seeking flavour in their beer and a number of new breweries have opened to meet the demand.

Amber Brewery is in Pomerania, the Baltic region divided between Germany and Poland. The main cities are Gdansk and Szczecin, better known by their old German names of Danzig and Stettin. For many centuries the region was under complete German control and a majority of the people were German speakers who insisted that beer should adhere to the German *Reinheitsgebot* or Purity Law. Amber is in the Moraine Hills

area where there's a brewing tradition stretching back to the 16th century, when beer was stored in caves to ripen.

The brewery is family owned and was launched in 1994. It quickly achieved a cult following, especially among students in Gdansk. It produces 250,000 hectolitres a year and emphasises that its beers are brewed using only malted barley, hops, yeast and water. *Žywe* means 'live': this does not mean it's bottle-fermented but it's unfiltered and unpasteurised, and enjoys a slow, unhurried ripening in the cellar. It has won awards from the Polish branch of the Slow Food movement, which is meticulous about production methods.

The beer is brewed with pale malt and with hops from the Lublin region. Lublin hops are highly regarded and are similar in style to Czech Saaz. Žywe has a hazy gold/bronze colour with spicy and grassy hops on the nose with toasted malt and a touch of vanilla. The toasted malt notes dominate the palate but grassy and floral hops along with vanilla provide balance. The vanilla note builds in the finish but is complemented by rich biscuit malt and spicy hop resins.

Bucanero Cristal/Cubanero

Source: Cervecaria Bucanero, Holguin, Cuba

Strength: 4.9%/5.4%

Website: www.cerveceriabucanero.com

People who visit Cuba frequently say they were surprised by the quality of the beer. It's not all rum and Coca-Cola on the island. It has a long brewing tradition and, despite acute problems of obtaining essential raw materials, continues to produce good products. While several breweries on the island predate the Castro regime, Bucanero was built in the 1980s using German technology. As a result, Cuban brewers talk of the influence of the *Reinheitsgebot* and the leading German brand Beck's is now a major import.

In 1997, Bucanero entered into a joint venture with Labatts of Canada with the aim of exporting Cuban beer for much-needed hard currency. The choice of Labatts was the result of a long relationship between the two countries. Because of the embargo placed on Cuba by the United States, malt and hops, which are not grown on the island, are flown from Canada to Havana. This includes ingredients sourced in Europe. There's irony in the fact that Labatts was taken over by global brewer InBev, which is now AB InBev. The stake in Bucanero has been maintained. The world's biggest brewing group is run by Brazilians (Ambev) and Belgians (InBev) and it's fortunate that the ultra conservative Busch family in the U.S. is not involved in running a brewery in a communist country.

Old habits die hard. As I found when I first visited Czechoslovakia in the 1980s, brewing in Cuba is treated like a state secret and I have been unable to garner any information about ingredients or lagering time, save that some Cuban sugar is used in Cubanero. My taste buds tell me the beers are well made, probably with a decoction mashing system, and are matured for a lengthy period, emerging with a clean and quenching character.

Cristal is the biggest-selling beer on the island. It has a pale gold colour and a rich toasted malt aroma with spicy hops and a hint of lemon fruit. Juicy malt, a touch of citrus and gentle hop resins fill the mouth. Spicy hop resins make more impact in the finish, which ends dry with continuing notes of honeyed malt and light but persistent lemon tartness.

Cubanero is sold as Bucanero in Latin America but for trademark reasons becomes Cubanero elsewhere, retaining the image of a Caribbean pirate on the label. *Fuerte* means strong and the pale bronze beer has a big toasted malt nose with woody and floral hops and a hint of peach fruit. The palate is filled with juicy malt, soft, sweet fruit and leafy hop resins, followed by a long finish packed with fruit, toasted malt and gentle leafy hops.

TASTING NOTES

APPEARANCE:

AROMA:

TASTE:

OVERALL SCORE:

TASTING NOTES

APPEARANCE:

AROMA:

TASTE:

OVERALL SCORE:

TASTING NOTES

APPEARANCE:

AROMA:

TASTE:

OVERALL SCORE:

Budvar Yeast Beer

Source: Budějovický Pivovar, České Budějovice, Czech Republic

Strength: 4%

Website: www.budvar.cz

The 'Battle of the Budweisers' is so well known, and was told in detail in *300 Beers to Try Before You Die!*, that a short summary will suffice here. Budvar's home town was known for centuries by the German name of Budweis – the current name means 'Czech Budweis'. As a result of the quality of malt, hops and water in the area, it became a major brewing town in medieval times and by the 15th century had no fewer than 44 breweries. Beers from Budweis were known generically as Budweiser, just as Pilsner beers come from Pilsen. Budvar is a contraction of Budějovický Pivovar, meaning the Budweis Brewery. It was founded by Czech speakers in 1895 to counter the power of the local Budweiser Bürgerbräu, the Citizens' Brewery run by German speakers.

Twenty years before Budvar opened, two German emigrants named Anheuser and Busch had launched a brewery in St Louis, Missouri and, among other beers, produced one called Budweiser – based on the reputation of the name among German speakers in the United States. At the end of the 19th century, Budvar attempted to export its beer to the U.S. with the result that for more than a century Anheuser-Busch and the Czechs have been embroiled in endless legal disputes over which company has the right to the trademark. The American brewery is now part of AB InBev, the world's biggest brewer, and the trademark dispute rumbles on with no sign of resolution.

Budvar remains a state-owned company and the Czech government has made it clear that the brewery will not be privatised while there's any risk of a takeover by AB InBev. It has complete freedom to develop its business and its brands, and it's introduced

> *The style recalls the early days of commercial lager brewing in the 19th century, before filtration and pasteurisation robbed beer of some its flavour.*

several new beers in recent years, including Yeast Beer and Budvar Dark (see next section). It brews 1,600,000 hectolitres a year and sells throughout the world, though it's known in some markets as 'Czechvar' as a result of the trademark dispute.

The management are dedicated to the finest traditions of lager brewing. The magnificent brewing hall has copper vessels where a double decoction system (see Glossary) is used to extract the sugars from the malt. Whole hops from the Žatec region are used in whole flower form. This is now rare in the Czech brewing industry where most companies use pelletised hops, but Budvar's brewers believe whole hops deliver the finest and most delicate aromas and flavours. Water, low in minerals, comes from a deep, natural underground lake.

Following primary fermentation, the beers rest for 90 days in the cellar where they enjoy a slow second fermentation. It's one of the joys of the brewing world to tour the cellars and to be given samples of beer from the lager tanks at one, two and three months of age and to see how the beer has slowly matured, purged itself of unwanted, rough alcohols and finally emerges with a soft, silky malt character balanced by a gentle grassy and floral hop notes.

Yeast Beer has been available in the Czech Republic in small volumes for many years but production was stepped up early in this century and it was launched in Britain in 2009. The aim was to promote a beer brewed as naturally as possible that would appeal to drinkers who avoid mass-market beer brands. As Budvar enjoys healthy sales in Britain, the brewery thought Yeast Beer would be enjoyed there by real ale drinkers who also appreciate good lager. The beer was first called Kräusen Beer, an inelegant title using a German word unknown to most drinkers. It was soon changed. The style recalls the early days of commercial lager brewing in the 19th century, before filtration

It has a fine aroma of lightly toasted malt, grassy and spicy hop notes and a hint of vanilla

and pasteurisation robbed beer of some its flavour. Beers were allowed to clarify themselves naturally during the long lagering period. Budvar didn't install a pasteurising unit until the 1920s and today its beers are only pasteurised for export, not for domestic sales. With Yeast Beer it has gone the extra mile and not filtered the beer. As a result of the 90-day ageing process, this leaves only a faint haze in the finished beer.

It's brewed with pale malt from Moravian barley and Žatec hops: the hops create 20 units of bitterness. At the end of the lagering period, a small amount of *kräusen* is added: this is the term given to partially fermented wort or sugary extract. The presence of kräusen creates a further fermentation in the keg when the beer is packaged. Unlike casks that contain real ale, which are vented to allow excess carbon dioxide to escape, a keg is a sealed container. The brewers have to measure the level of kräusen with great skill to avoid the kegs exploding as fermentation takes place.

Yeast Beer has to settle in the pub or bar for seven days before it can be served and then has to be consumed within seven days. It has a fine aroma of lightly toasted malt, grassy and spicy hop notes and a hint of vanilla. Juicy malt and spicy hops combine in the mouth while the lingering finish is bittersweet, with good malt and hop notes and the continuing vanilla note.

Cusqueña

Source: Unión de Cervecarías Peruvanas Backus & Johnson, Cuzco, Peru

Strength: 4%

Website: www.cusquena.com.pe

Cusqueña brewery is now part of an enterprise owned by SABMiller that includes several breweries scattered throughout Peru. The Backus & Johnson names come from a brewery founded in 1879 and registered on the London Stock Exchange. It remained a British company until 1954. In 1996 four breweries, including Backus & Johnson, merged to form the Union of Peruvian Breweries, and the group was joined in 2000 by Cusqueña. The company was formed in 1908 by Ernesto Gunther and was first known as the Cervercería Alemana, the German brewery. It used – and continues to use – German technology to produce its lager beers and draws on fine mountain water, low in minerals, from the Andes. The beer, influenced by European-style lager and Pilsner, carries the tag line 'Gold of the Incas', which stretches history and credulity. But we do know that the Incas brewed a type of beer, with fermentation allegedly started by the pure saliva of young virgins.

Cusqueña prefers to use a cold-fermenting yeast culture brought from Europe – young virgins being less readily available – along with Saaz hops from the Czech Republic. Pale barley malt is augmented by a touch of caramalt and a decoction mashing system is used. The beer enjoys a minimum of 30 days in the lager cellar. The golden beer has an enticing aroma of toasted malt with spicy, floral and woody Saaz hops and a touch of lemon jelly. Leafy hop resins and biscuit malt dominate the palate with light citrus fruit notes. The finish has spicy hop resins, toasted malt and tangy fruit.

> ❝ *The beer, influenced by European-style lager and Pilsner, carries the tag line 'Gold of the Incas',* ❞

Konrad 12°/14°

Source: Pivovar Liberec-Vratislavice, Czech Republic
Strength: 5.2%/6%
Website: www.hols.cz

Konrad is a brewery that came back from the dead. In May 1998, the big Liberec-Vratislavice brewery near the border with Germany, which had survived Nazi occupation and then 50 years of state ownership under communism, was summarily closed down and its 300 workers sacked. The brewery was one of the biggest in the Czech Republic. It was once larger than Pilsner Urquell and in 1989, when communism collapsed, it was producing 400,000 hectolitres a year (244,000 barrels). But Liberec-Vratislavice had become a shareholders' company and the British brewer Bass bought up all the shares. It merged the brewery with its major Czech acquisition, Prague Breweries, which includes the major Staropramen plant.

The Liberec brewery had been selling large amounts of beer to the Tesco supermarket group in Britain but Bass withdrew the beer and replaced it with Staropramen. When Bass closed the Liberec plant anything metal that could easily be removed was thrown out. The brewing vessels were sold to a local scrap metal dealer, but fortunately they were still in place when a local businessman, Jaroslav Martinec, arrived on the scene with a plan to revive the brewery.

Martinec owns a manufacturing company called Hols. He had no experience of brewing but loved beer, Vratislav beer in particular. He was able to mortgage the brewery buildings from Bass and bought the brewing equipment from the scrap merchant. He hired a small workforce and brought back brewmaster Petr Hostaš, who had been working in the local glass industry.

The brewery reopened in 2000. Martinec deliberately chose the date of 25 May, when Bass had closed the site, and renamed the company Konrad after the brewery's first brewmaster in the 19th century. He was not allowed to use the Vratislav trademark, which was owned by Bass and later transferred to AB InBev when the global giant bought the Czech breweries owned by the British group.

The brewery was founded in 1872 by businessmen in Liberec who had made their fortunes from the textile, glass and jewellery industries in the town. The site included maltings, still in use today, and the emphasis was on the new style of golden lager that had been introduced in Pilsen. The beer range today includes 11, 12, 14 and 16 degree beers – the Czech method of measurement – ranging from 4.8 to 7%. According to strength, the beers are lagered for between 40 and 90 days. Malt comes from Moravia with hops from the Žatec region.

Konrad 12° is pale gold and has toasted malt, woody and grassy hops and a touch of vanilla on the nose, followed by fine palate of juicy malt, leafy hops and a continuing vanilla note. The finish is quenching, with a good balance of lightly toasted malt, grassy hop resins and a light vanilla note. The 14° degree beer is a similar colour but with a pronounced fresh-bread malt note on the aroma, a touch of lemon/citrus fruit and herbal hops. Tart fruit builds in the mouth but is well balance by biscuit malt and woody and herbal hops. The finish is rich and malty, with citrus lemon and leafy hops.

TASTING NOTES
APPEARANCE:

AROMA:

TASTE:

OVERALL SCORE:

TASTING NOTES
APPEARANCE:

AROMA:

TASTE:

OVERALL SCORE:

Krušovice Imperial

Source: Královský Pivovar Krušovice, Krušovice, Czech Republic

Strength: 5%

Website: www.krusovice.cz

This is an ancient brewery with royal connections: the name means the Royal Brewery of Krušovice. It was founded in 1581 and was bought by Emperor Rudolf II two years later and remained in the hands of members of the Habsburg family for several centuries. When I first visited in the 1980s, the entrance was fronted by an old wooden lagering cask bearing the colourful image of a cavalier, emphasing a royal connection that had escaped the attention of the communist regime. The bottling hall was staffed by North Koreans: I doubt they are there now.

The brewery converted to lager production following the success of the first golden beer from Pilsen in the mid-19th century. After a period of state ownership during the communist period, it was privatised and was bought by Heineken in 2007. The Dutch giant has to date grasped the fact that Czechs not only drink a lot of beer – hence the acquisition – but take quality and traditional brewing methods seriously and it has not attempted to speed up production and cut lagering times.

The brewery sources pure water from the surrounding wooded hills and makes use of malted barley from Moravia and hops from the Žatec region. Imperial is pale bronze in colour with toasted malt and caramel on the aroma, balanced by spicy and herbal hops. Rich toasted malt and caramel dominate the palate but there's a solid underpinning of piny hops. The finish is bittersweet to start, with malt and caramel to the fore, but woody/leafy hops kick in to make a dry and bitter end.

Rich toasted malt and caramel dominate the palate but there's a solid underpinning of piny hops.

WEST St Mungo

Source: WEST Brewery, Glasgow, Scotland
Strength: 4.9%
Website: www.westbeer.com

WEST is a phenomenon: a Bavarian beer hall and brewery in Glasgow, sharing the city with Tennent's, the giant Scottish lager brewery that accounts for 60 per cent of all the beer consumed in the country. The key difference is that WEST is owned by a Bavarian, Petra Wetzel, and she brews her beers according to the German *Reinheitsgebot*. Tennent's would make no such claim for their beers but it inspired Petra and her father to open their beer hall. Herbert Wetzel is a successful German businessman who was visiting Petra in Glasgow, where she had studied for a law degree. He called for a glass of Tennent's when they were eating in the Ubiquitous Chip restaurant, took one sip, winced, and said: 'Is this what they call beer here?'

The result was a £1 million investment by Herbert in 2006 in part of the old Templeton carpet factory at Glasgow Green. This 19th-century architectural masterpiece was based on the Doge's Palace in Venice: its opulence was designed to meet the opposition of snooty dwellers in the city's West End to a factory in their presence.

One wing of the building is now home to a large beer hall and restaurant, with a brewery, open to view, which produces 250,000 litres of beer a year. The brewing equipment is Ger-man and is based on the mash mixer, lauter tun and copper whirlpool system. Following primary fermentation, St Mungo and other lager beers are cold conditioned for several weeks: the brewery also makes Bavarian wheat beer. The success of WEST has led to Petra, who now has a staff of 40, building a new brewery and centre of excellence at Port Dundas, with £1.85 million in funding from the Scottish government. She will supply bars and restaurants throughout Scotland and beyond.

St Mungo, named after the patron saint of Glasgow, is a Munich Helles or pale lager in style. It's brewed with malts from Bamberg in Franconia – Pilsner, Munich and carapils – and the hops are Bavarian Hersbrucker, Perle and Spalt, which create 28 units of bitterness. It matures for a minimum of three weeks. It's quite dark for the style, with a burnished bronze colour and an aroma of freshly-baked wholemeal bread, piny hops resins and a strong hint of vanilla. Hop bitterness grows in the mouth and the hops also continue to deliver a woody/piny and spicy note. Rich malt and vanilla continue to build and lead into a long finish that ends dry and hoppy. By Scottish standards, this is a challenging and rewarding beer that reaches out to a younger and appreciative audience.

TASTING NOTES

APPEARANCE:

AROMA:

TASTE:

OVERALL SCORE:

TASTING NOTES

APPEARANCE:

AROMA:

TASTE:

OVERALL SCORE:

Windhoek Lager

Source: Namibia Breweries, Windhoek, Namibia

Strength: 4%

Website: www.namibiabreweries.com

If a positive word can be found for the colonial period of the 19th and 20th centuries, it can be said that it did leave some countries with a tradition of good beer. To the south, drinkers have to make do with the remarkably bland offerings of South African Breweries but in neighbouring Namibia a major brewery proves just how good lager beer can be. The reason is that Namibia was once a German protectorate and settlers brought a beer culture with them, one that was underscored by the new technologies of the industrial revolution that made cold fermentation possible in even the harshest climate.

In a world dominated by global brewers, the Namibian company remains mainly in the hands of its founding families. Carl List and Hermann Ohlthaver arrived in the region in 1920 and were overwhelmed by the stark beauty of the country but appalled by the heat. They needed cold beer and as they were bankers they had the resources to buy four struggling breweries and merge them into a new company called South West Breweries. It remained with that name until Namibia gained independence in 1990.

The German legacy means that today the company can claim to the be only brewery in the whole of Africa that brews to the *Reinheitsgebot*. It makes Windhoek and other beers, including a Bock, only with malt, hops, yeast and water and imports essential raw materials from Germany, including hops from the Hallertau. While the brewery has been modernised in recent years, with stainless steel vessels replacing copper, production is based on decoction mashing, lauter tun filtrations and a lengthy period of cold conditioning following primary fermentation.

The pale gold beer has a ravishing aroma of toasted malt, spicy, leafy and woody hops with a touch of lemon fruit. Hop bitterness builds in the mouth, complementing juicy malt and light citrus fruit. The finish is spicy and bitter from the hops, but they are balanced by biscuit malt and lemon fruit.

Namibia brews 2.2 million hectolitres of beer and year and exports to 23 countries. It has even broken into the South African market, where SAB accounts for 98 per cent of beer production, and offers some relief to drinkers there.

Dark Lagers

The term Dark Lager comes as a shock to drinkers used to being bombarded with massive promotions for golden lagers produced by international companies. But dark lager beer predates the arrival of golden lager by several centuries. Cold storage of beer in central Europe dates back to the time when brewing was dominated by the church and, until new technology in the 19th century made the production of pale malt possible on a large scale, lager beers were dark. This was the result of malt being kilned or roasted over fires fuelled by wood. The result was dark brown malt and dark brown or black beer.

Even when golden lager from Pilsen took the world by storm in the middle of the 19th century, many brewers continued to make dark lager. This was especially true in conservative Bavaria where golden lager did not overtake sales of dark or Dunkel beer until well into the 20th century. Then, in common with dark Mild in England, the Dunkel style went into rapid decline, overwhelmed by the increasing popularity of the golden version of lager. It took the efforts of one remarkable man to restore the fortunes of dark lager. He is Crown Prince Luitpold of Kaltenberg, whose story is told in *300 Beers to Try Before You Die!* He's an unlikely brewer, a member of the Bavarian royal family that lost power at the end of World War One. When the prince inherited the family's castle at Kaltenberg, near Munich, in the 1970s he had to earn a living. As befits a family that was responsible in the 16th century for the *Reinheitsgebot* or Purity Law for beer, the castle included a brewery where beer had been made for centuries to refresh both royalty and their workforce. In spite of opposition from the Munich brewers, who won't allow the prince to take part in the annual Oktoberfest as he brews just outside the city, he has concentrated on Dunkel and built sales throughout Bavaria and beyond. The result has been that several other breweries in Germany have added Dunkel to their portfolios.

Over the border in the Czech Republic, dark lager never entirely went away, despite the dominance of Pilsner and golden versions of lager. During the long period of state control under communism, brewing was deeply conservative: little changed and breweries went on making dark lager as part of their entrenched routine. The return of the open market and the arrival of large foreign breweries have led to a concentration on pale lager but the Budweiser Budvar Brewery has restored the style with both élan and success in both its home nation and abroad.

Alhambra Negra

Source: Cervezas Alhambra, Alhambra, Andalusia, Spain

Strength: 5.4%

Website: www.cervezasalhambra.es

It may be due to the large number of Germans who holiday in Spain that this brewery produces a dark lager. And it's also a reflection of the interest from younger drinkers seeking an alternative to the pale lagers that are the norm in Spain. The country has a long brewing heritage that astonished the Romans where they were marching north. In the 16th century, the Emperor of Spain and the Holy Roman Empire, Charles V, who was born in Ghent in the Netherlands, had a great love of beer. 'The daughter of the grain is superior to the blood of the grape', he famously said and he encouraged German and Flemish people in his court to open breweries in Spain.

Andalusia, in the deep south of Spain, is now officially designated a 'semi-autonomous region' that helps underline its fierce independence and its determination to stake out a distinctive culture where food and drink are concerned. Even though the brewery has, since 2006, been part of the large national Mahou-San Miguel group, it continues to brew and develop its own distinctive range of beers.

The brewery was founded in 1925 by two industrialists, Carlos Bouvard and Antonio Knorr, in an area famed for its Moorish past and stunning architecture. The dark Negra is brewed with pale malt and roasted barley, with hops sourced from Germany. It throws a deep collar of barley white foam, followed by an aroma of espresso coffee, burnt fruit and roasted grain, with a good balance of peppery hops. Creamy smooth malt dominates the palate but there are solid contributions from coffee, dark fruit and leafy hops. The finish is dry, with silky smooth malt, dark fruits, coffee and gentle hop resins.

Budweiser Budvar Dark

Source: Budějovický Pivovar, České Budějovice, Czech Republic
Strength: 4.8%
Website: www.budvar.cz

TASTING NOTES

APPEARANCE:

AROMA:

TASTE:

OVERALL SCORE:

Budvar's dark lager was the result of long and passionate debates in the brewery. Head brewer Josef Tolar was against the idea, which had been presented by his deputy Ales Dvorak as a way of developing a new and distinctively different beer to the brewery's golden lager. Josef said it would give the company an old-fashioned image but, in a long journey to Prague with chief executive Jírí Boček, he was persuaded to experiment with the new beer. A few years later, when I sat down with Josef in the beer hall attached to the brewery his choice of beer was Dark. He may have lost the argument but he had learned to enjoy the end product of the debate.

It went on sale in 2004 and it has become popular not only in the Czech Republic but in Britain, too. Its British launch was at CAMRA's Great British Beer Festival in London. I was working in the press office and lost count of the number of people who asked if I'd tried the new Budvar beer. I replied, somewhat testily, that I thought the festival was supposed to be a showcase for cask beer, not lager. But modern beer drinkers are an eclectic bunch and by the time I got down to the main hall at the festival the few kegs of Budvar Dark had been drained dry. When I finally got the chance to drink the beer, I was bowled over by its richness and quality.

In Britain, Budvar found that a number of drinkers had taken to mixing Budvar Original and Dark, recalling the old tradition of 'a pint of mixed', which used to mean Mild and Bitter. Budvar responded by developing a new delivery system and bar font that draws equal amounts of both beers from their kegs and then mixes them at the point of dispense.

Budvar Dark enjoys the same 90-day cold-conditioning as Original and Yeast Beer. It's brewed with pale malt, Munich, caramel and roasted malts and hopped with Žatec varieties that create 22 units of bitterness. It has a rich aroma of roasted grain, bitter chocolate and coffee, with roast, chocolate, coffee and spicy hops in the mouth. The finish is long and lingering, with good spicy hops balancing the richness of dark grain, coffee and chocolate.

After some 50 years with the brewery, Josef Tolar has retired but still takes selected groups on a tour of his beloved brewery, ending with a glass of Dark in the beer hall.

> *modern beer drinkers are an eclectic bunch and by the time I got down to the main hall at the festival the few kegs of Budvar Dark had been drained dry.*

Kaiserdom Dark Lager

Source: **Kaiserdom Privat Brauereri,**

Bamberg, Germany

Strength: **4.7%**

Website: **kaiserdom.de**

Kaiserdom, as we have seen in the Pilsner section, is the biggest brewery in the endlessly fascinating town of Bamberg in Franconia, Upper Bavaria, famous for its Rauch or smoked beers, as well as medieval and Baroque buildings.

Influenced by both the Dunkel beers of the south and the dark lagers just over the border in the Czech Republic – Prague is a short journey these days now there's no Cold War wall to separate the two countries – Kaiserdom promotes its Schwarzbier with some gusto. As, under the strict terms of the German Purity Law or *Reinheitsgebot* only malted grains are permitted in German beers, Dark is brewed with pale, Munich and caramalt , and hopped with Aurora and Magnum varieties. It has 22 units of bitterness. The beer has a mocha/black colour with a superb aroma of freshly baked dark bread, creamy coffee, dry chocolate and floral hop resins. Coffee and chocolate dominate the palate with roasted grain and developing hop bitterness. The finish is bittersweet, with creamy malt, chocolate, coffee and a lingering spicy hop note. This is a classic of the style.

Krušovice Cerně

Source: **Královský Pivovar Krušovice, Krušovice, Czech Republic**

Strength: **3.8%**

Website: **www.krusovice.cz**

We've already encountered Krušovice in the previous section. The royal brewery has maintained a tradition of brewing dark lager that predates the Pilsen revolution, and is enjoying the revival of the style in the Czech Republic. It's brewed with pale malt, Munich, caramalt and a touch of roasted grain, with hops sourced from the Žatec region, and it enjoys a slow conditioning in the lager cellar.

The brown/black beer has a rye bread note on the nose with raisin fruit and woody/grassy hops. Sweet liquorice makes an appearance on the palate, with creamy malt, burnt fruit and grassy hops. The finish is smooth, creamy, with roasted grain, dark fruit, liquorice and leafy and spicy hops.

The royal brewery has maintained a tradition of brewing dark lager that predates the Pilsen revolution

Sprecher Black Bavarian

Source: Sprecher Brewery, Milwaukee, Wisconsin, USA

Strength: 5.8%

Website: www.sprecherbrewery.com

Randal Sprecher has helped breathe beer life back in to Milwaukee. The city was once the powerhouse of American brewing, due in no small measure to the large number of citizens of German descent. In the late 19th and early 20th centuries, Milwaukee had more than 80 breweries but first Prohibition and then a mad scramble of mergers and takeovers reduced it to just one large producer, Miller. Miller is now part of SABMiller, registered in London, but is known in the U.S. as Miller Coors, following a cosy deal with former archrival Coors to distribute their beers.

Sprecher is one of a handful of craft breweries in the city dedicated to traditional beer. Randal's German antecedents are clear from his name and his former job was working as a brewery surpervisor at Pabst, a now-defunct brewery of German origin. Randal's first small brewery opened in 1985 in the Walker's Point district but after a decade it had outgrown the facility and he moved to a former elevator car factory in Glendale. The brewery is now a major draw for beer lovers in the area, with a Munich-style beer garden, a shop and brewery tours.

Black Bavarian is aged for eight weeks and has a complex malt makeup of two-row pale, black patent, caramel and chocolate malts. The hop varieties are Cascade, Chinook, Mount Hood and Tettnanger, which create 32 units of bitterness. The beer has a rich and enticing aroma of coffee and chocolate, with roasted grain, dark fruits and spicy hops. There are smoky notes on the palate from the dark grains, with more rich chocolate, coffee, burnt fruit and spicy hops. The hops prop up the long, complex finish, packed with creamy malt, smoked notes, coffee, chocolate and dark berry fruits.

TASTING NOTES

APPEARANCE:

AROMA:

TASTE:

OVERALL SCORE:

Wolverine Dark Lager

Source: Wolverine State Brewing Company, Ann Arbor, Michigan, USA

Strength: 5%

Website: wolverinebeer.com

Matt Roy and Trevor Thrall hatched up their plans for a brewery when they were stuck in a car in a snowstorm back in the 1970s. They had plenty of beer on board but nothing from Michigan. They decided that if they wanted good Michigan beer, they would have to brew it themselves. Michigan State Brewing Co was launched in 1975 and Premium Lager was an instant success. Matt and Trevor, against the craft brewing trend, decided to concentrate on lager rather than ale and have a portfolio of 15, including a cheekily named India Pale Lager.

The beers were contract brewed until they could fund their own brewery, which opened in 2010. Oliver Roberts, an experienced brewer from Ann Arbor, joined and within two years sales had doubled. This success was helped by the indefatigable E T Crowe, the sales manager, who blogs as the Beer Wench (www.a2beerwench.com). The brewery has a Tap Room where visitors can enjoy the beers and buy merchandise.

Dark Lager is brewed with American two-row and six-row pale malts, flaked maize, brown syrup, crystal malt, black malt and dark roasted wheat malt. American Saaz hops are used for bitterness in the kettle and as a late hop. The beer is dark ruby in colour and has a big aroma of roasted grain, vinous fruit and espresso coffee. Spicy hops make an appearance on the palate, with tart fruit, roasted grain and bitter coffee. The finish is smooth, creamy, with silky malt, smooth coffee, gentle dark fruits and a lingering spicy hop note.

Bocks

Bock is a strong lager, a beer to celebrate with: there are Maibocks to greet the spring, extra strong Doppelbocks to get you through Lent, with similar Stark (strong) beers brewed for a Munich festival in early March. Bavarians claim that Bock is a speciality unique to their region but its origins lie in the north, in the city of Einbeck in Lower Saxony. The entrance to Einbeck has a sign announcing 'Beer City' (see *300 Beers to Try Before You Die!*) and the brewery there labels all its products as *Ur-Bock*, meaning Original Bock.

Einbeck was a member of the Hanseatic League, a group of merchants' guilds and trading cities that operated between the 13th and 17th centuries along the coasts of northern Europe, stretching from the Baltic to the North Sea. Einbeck's major contribution to the league was beer, the quality of which had gained great renown, especially when supplies were sent to sustain Martin Luther, the Augustinian monk who was put on trial in Worms in 1521 for attacking the excesses of the Papal court in Rome.

The people of Munich were first acquainted with Einbeck beer in the 17th century when the Duke of Brunswick in Lower Saxony married a daughter of the Bavarian nobility. The duke brought his master brewer with him to make beer to accompany the celebrations. It was called, in the German fashion, *Einbecker*, meaning 'of Einbeck'. In the Bavarian dialect this became *Oanbocker* and by the 18th century the Munich Hofbräuhaus – the Royal Court Brewery – was making an Oanbock beer. Over time the name was shortened to *Bock*, which means billy goat in German (similar to the English buck). Ever since, brewers of Bock beer have used the symbol of a billy goat on their labels to denote strength and virility.

Bock has grown beyond its German borders and there are now examples of the style in the U.S., England and the Netherlands, though some Dutch interpretations are warm-fermented ales rather than lagers.

TASTING NOTES

APPEARANCE:

AROMA:

TASTE:

OVERALL SCORE:

Amber Koźlak

Source: Brouwar Amber,
Bielkówko, Poland
Strength: 6.5%
Website: www.browar-amber.pl

In keeping with the style, Koźlak is the Polish for goat and the beast adorns the hand-embossed bottles. We have encountered the Polish independent brewery in the Pale Lagers section. Their Bock is launched every September at the annual Bielkowsich food and drink fair in the town. This mirrors the launch of strong beers brewed in March, stored until the autumn and broached at the world-famous Munich Oktoberfest. Amber makes no secret of its reverence for the Bavarian style and the traditions that surround it. It says its Bock is aged for a 'lengthy period'. It doesn't reveal the precise time but if it follows the Munich method it could be as long as six months.

Koźlak is brewed with pale and caramalts and is generously hopped with varieties from the Lublin region. The beer that emerges from the lager cellar is unfiltered and has a heavy collar of foam, a hazy ruby colour and a superb Bavarian-style aroma of fresh bread, cobnuts, burnt fruit, caramel and leafy hop resins. The palate is rich and warming, with nutty malt to the fore but with good contributions from nuts, dark fruit and woody hops. The finish is bittersweet to start but ends dry with rich malt, sultana fruit and spicy hops. It's an impressive contribution to the genre.

Brinkley's Maibock

Source: Free State Brewing Company, Lawrence, Kansas, USA

Strength: 4.4%

Website: www.freestatebrewing.com

This is a beer and a brewery with some history. The brewery was founded in 1989 by Chuck Magerl whose grandfather ended up in Leavenworth Prison for brewing during Prohibition in the 1920s. Unabashed, Chuck has named his Maibock after Doc Brinkley, a notorious Kansan character. Brinkley was a 'snake oil salesman' who sold dodgy medicines, stood twice and unsuccessfully for the governorship of the state and made and lost a fortune.

The Free State brewery takes its name from the fact that Kansas entered the union as an opponent of slavery. Chuck Magerl's company was the first legal brewery there for 100 years and has built a fine reputation for a range of beers that include ales, Stouts, wheat beers and lagers. Maibock, launched every spring, is the brewery's most popular beer, accounting for 75% of its annual production. The label carries the image of a billy goat, a link not only to Bavarian Bocks but

to the unfortunate history of Doc Brinkley, one of whose 'medicines' was a virility pill for men that contained delicate parts of a goat's anatomy. The parts, Chuck is anxious to stress, are not included in his beer.

It's brewed with Pilsner malt, Cara-hell and Munich malts and is hopped with Nugget and Hersbrucker varieties. The units of bitterness are 30. It has a pale bronze colour, with a perfumy aroma that combines honeyed malt with floral and peppery hops and a powerful hint of berry fruits. The spritzy palate offers smooth malt, spicy hops and tart fruits, followed by a finish that ends dry and hoppy but with good contributions from juicy malt and tangy fruit. And not a trace of goat.

TASTING NOTES

APPEARANCE:

AROMA:

TASTE:

OVERALL SCORE:

TASTING NOTES

APPEARANCE:

AROMA:

TASTE:

OVERALL SCORE:

IJbok

Source: Brouwerij 't IJ, Amsterdam, Netherlands

Strength: 6.5%

Website: www.brouwerijhetij.nl

The 't IJ brewery revived small craft brewing in the Netherlands and it did so with humour and style. In a country dominated by Heineken and Grolsch – with the latter being part of SABMiller since 2008 – choice has been in short supply for Dutch beer drinkers. It started to change in 1984 when songwriter Kaspar Peterson opened the 't IJ brewpub in Amsterdam and created such demand for his beers that other craft brewers sprang up to emulate his success.

The pub has a superb location. It's based in an old bathhouse, but – being the Netherlands – has an impressive windmill standing behind it. The IJ is the name of the waterway on which Amsterdam's harbour stands and the pronunciation of the word – 'ay' – is almost identical to the Dutch word for egg. With the exception of IJbok, which naturally has a goat on the label, the 't IJ beer labels show an ostrich with an egg. In the background there's a windmill in a desert, indicating that Amsterdam was a beer desert until Kaspar arrived on the scene. The beers include Natte (wet), Zatte (drunk), Mij (mosquito) and Vlo (flea). All the beers are made with natural ingredients and no additives, and are neither filtered nor pasteurised.

IJbok is brewed with Pils, Munich, caramalt and roast malt and the hops are Hallertauer Tradition and Northern Brewer. In common with several other Dutch bocks or boks, it's a warm-fermented version of the style, an ale rather than a lager. The tiny, cramped brewery doesn't, in any case, have the space or facilities for lager production. The beer is bright ruby/red with a big waft of herbal hops on the nose, spicy malt reminiscent of Easter hot cross buns, and a hint of chocolate. Chocolate builds in the mouth, balancing spicy malt and herbal hops. The finish is rich, rewarding, refreshing, packed with rich malt, chocolate and woody hops.

If you visit Amsterdam don't miss the opportunity to try the beers and the stimulating atmosphere at the pub: 7 Funenkade, 1018 AL Amsterdam. Opening hours are limited: 2-8pm every day: 020 622 8325.

St Austell Cornish Bock

Source: St Austell Brewery Company, St Austell, Cornwall, England
Strength: 6.5%
Website: www.staustellbrewery.co.uk

St Austell brewery has moved fast in recent years to present a new and modern image to the world. The family-owned company, with a large estate of pubs in Cornwall, had rested on the laurels of its Bitters and strong Bitters but urgently needed new brands to appeal to both connoisseurs and younger drinkers. Encouraged by managing director James Staughton, a young and dynamic member of the ruling family, head brewer Roger Ryman has overhauled the brewery's beer list and developed such new brands as the best-selling Tribute, Proper Job (see IPA section) and even Belgian-style strong ales. He has been given the investment to install a small lager plant where the beers include his Cornish Bock, complete with the essential billy goat on the label and a back label that faithfully records the history of the style from its origins in Einbeck.

Cornish Bock is brewed with Pilsner malt, flaked maize, carapils and crystal malts and is hopped with Hersbucker and Perle varieties from Bavaria and Saaz from the Czech Republic. It has 23 units of bitterness and is lagered for a month. It emerges from the cold room with an inviting bronze colour and a leafy and peppery hop note on the aroma, with fresh cookie malt and a hint of sultana fruit. Rich, sweet and biscuit malt takes over in the mouth but with light fruit and peppery hops providing balance. The finish is bittersweet with rich malt and woody hops in perfect balance, and a continuing note of gentle fruit. In spite of the strength, it's wonderfully refreshing.

TASTING NOTES

APPEARANCE:

AROMA:

TASTE:

OVERALL SCORE:

TASTING NOTES

APPEARANCE:

AROMA:

TASTE:

OVERALL SCORE:

Shiner Bock

Source: Spoetzl Brewery, Shiner, Texas, USA

Strength: 4.4%

Website: www.shiner.com

This is more than a beer: it encapsulates American history, immigration, Prohibition and a determination to brew good lager in spite of all the odds against it. The brewery was founded in 1909 by Czechs and Germans who had settled in the town of Shiner. It was a ramshackle affair and in 1914 the owners, who ran the company as a kind of co-operative, hired a German, Kosmos Spoetzl, to oversee brewing. He was determined to impose the brewing traditions of his native Bavaria in order to produce quality lager beers for the immigrant community. Bock was launched in 1913 and its success prompted Spoetzl to buy out the owners and take control of the company. It's been in his family's hands ever since.

The brewery survived the long years of Prohibition by making ice and 'near beer'. Spoetzl managed to avoid the mergers and takeovers in the American brewing industry that followed the end of Prohibition and led to the rise of giants such as Anheuser-Busch, Coors and Miller. Spoetzl survived and thrived. In 1973, Bock became a regular rather than a seasonal beer and the company stressed its Bavarian roots with such additional beers as Helles pale lager and Hefeweisse wheat beer. In 1995, a new brewhouse was built, production has doubled since then and the company stages an annual Bock-toberfest to celebrate its beers.

Shiner Bock has a modest strength by Bavarian standards, but this is the result of Texan law that restricts the manufacture and sale of strong beer. It's brewed with pale and Munich malts and is hopped with English First Gold and Nugget hops. It has a modest 13 units of bitterness but, by American standards, has a reasonable 30 days in the lager cellar before it's released. The pale bronze beer has a big juicy and toasted malt aroma with a hint of citrus fruit and gentle spicy hop resins. Toasted malt, light fruit and spicy hops fill the mouth, with a finish that starts bittersweet with rich juicy malt dominating but ends dry and quenching with the aid of light fruit and hop notes.

Gruit & Speciality Beers

There is so much emphasis on the role of hops in beer, with enormous interest in the aromas and flavours each variety imparts, that we are apt to forget the hop plant is a comparative newcomer to the brewing process. It wasn't until the 15th and 16th centuries that the use of the hop became widespread in brewing. Before that time, brewers used a variety of other plants, herbs and spices to balance malt and in attempt to keep beer free from infection. The mixture of ingredients was known as *gruut*, *grut* or *gruit* in various Germanic languages and it was a mixture fuelled by religious and political controversies.

Gruut brewery

Sharp's Spiced Red

The use of gruit was controlled by the Roman Catholic Church, which made a substantial income from the sales of the mixture and the taxes imposed on it. In Cologne, for example, the archbishop had cornered the gruit market through a law called the *Grutrecht* and he attempted to ban the use of hops. There were similar attempts to outlaw hops in other European countries, in Russia and in the British Isles. The use of hops was forbidden in Norwich, even though many Flemish weavers had settled there and brought a taste for hopped beer with them. In 1519, the use of the 'wicked and pernicious weed, hops' was prohibited in Shrewsbury. The use of gruit was so much in evidence in Britain that it was used as a form of exchange and a coin, the groat, emphasised its importance. The terms 'groats' in the plural is still used and means milled grain that's used to make porridge.

The Reformation was the hop's best friend. When Martin Luther attacked the Papacy in 1517 and was excommunicated for his sins, he helped break the power of the church over the ingredients permitted in brewing. But while the hop plant broke free and its use spread, gruit was slow to disappear. Writing in 1588, Jacob Theodor von Bergzabern noted that while hops were now used in the copper 'the English sometimes add to the brewed beer, to make it more pleasant, sugar, cinnamon, cloves and other good spices in a small bag. The Flemish mix it with honey or sugar and precious spices and so make a drink like claret or hippocras [spiced wine]. Others mix in hops, sugar and syrup, which not only makes beer pleasant to drink but also gives it a fine brown colour.' He added that 'Flemings and Netherlanders' had discovered that adding laurel, ivy or Dutch myrtle strengthened beer, preserved it and stopped it from going sour.

It was not until the rise of commercial brewing in the 18th and 19th centuries and a more scientific appreciation of the role of yeast, bacteria and fermentation that gruit fell out of use. The development of both India Pale Ale in England and commercial lager brewing in central Europe led to a better understanding of how the hop plant kept beer in good condition and free from infection. In recent years there has been some interest among brewers in returning to the limited use of herbs and spices. Nethergate's Umbel Magna, which uses coriander and bog myrtle, and Fraoch Heather Ale in Scotland both featured in *300 Beers to Try Before You Die!*, but both use hops as well. It has taken the dedication and research of one woman in Ghent at the Gruut pub and brewery to return to the sole use of herbs and spices. At the same time, a growing number of brewers have added to the pleasure and complexity of beer by adding such ingredients as honey, coffee, chocolate and fruit.

TASTING NOTES

APPEARANCE:

AROMA:

TASTE:

OVERALL SCORE:

Bourganel Bière au Nougat

Source: Brasserie Bourganel, Val-les-Bains, Ardèche, France

Strength: 5%

Website: www.bieres-bourganel.com

The Ardèche, the French say, is where the south begins. The architecture has a distinctive Mediterranean feel, with whitewashed and red-roofed houses, and the countryside is ravishing. Its mountainous vastness allowed the Resistance to hide and strike swiftly during World War Two. The region is famous for its special confectionery, nougat, made with sugar, egg whites and nuts.

Christian Bourganel has a passion for beer and he wanted to bring it to a wine-making region with little local brewing activity. He worked with the French Institute of Brewing and Malting in Nancy to create his recipes and in 1997 launched his first beers, brewed for him by Castelain near Lens in the far north of the country. In 2000 he opened his own plant in Val-les-Bains, an old spa town in the nature park of Monts d'Ardèche.

The spacious buildings look like an old French railway station and house a modern stainless steel brewhouse, which can make both ale and lager, with a shop and facilities for tasting and buying beer. As a result of the success of his first beers, Christian installed bigger equipment in 2004 and his business took off two years later with the launch of Bière au Nougat. It's brewed with pale malt, using French-grown barley, with hop pellets from the German Hallertau, and pure mountain water from the region, plus the local confectionery. Christian uses nougat made with the addition of almonds.

The combination works remarkably well. The pale gold beer has a big creamy and nutty aroma but in the mouth peppery hops make an appearance alongside juicy malt and big nougat and almonds notes. The finish starts creamy and nutty but peppery hops build and prevent the beer from becoming cloying. It finally ends surprisingly dry, with good hop notes, as the rich nougat character fades.

It finally ends surprisingly dry, with good hop notes, as the rich nougat character fades.

Flying Dog Kujo Imperial Coffee Stout

Source: Flying Dog Brewery, Frederick, Maryland, USA

Strength: 8.9%

Website: flyingdogales.com

Flying Dog doesn't do things by half. It makes big, bold and brassy beers and its Coffee Stout is up close and personal, booming with freshly roasted coffee flavours. We have encountered the brewery in the IPA section and told the story of how founder George Stranahan teamed up with writer Hunter S Thompson and, through Thompson, got British artist Ralph Steadman to design striking labels for the beers.

The stout is a powerful ale brewed with pale, chocolate, black, roast and Cara Munich malts. It's hopped with English Goldings and Northern Brewer varieties that create a resounding 40 units of bitterness. The coffee is a special roast from the Black Dog Coffee Company in West Virginia: brewery and coffee dogs clearly hunt in packs. The jet-black beer has a nostril-widening aroma of coffee beans, smoky grain, peppery hops and vanilla notes. Fruit notes – raspberries and blackcurrants – break through in the mouth to balance the rich coffee character. Creamy malt dominates the finish as the coffee notes diminish but spicy hops make more of an impact, with continuing contributions from vanilla and soft fruit.

> *Flying Dog doesn't do things by half. It makes big, bold and brassy beers and its Coffee Stout is up close and personal*

TASTING NOTES

APPEARANCE:

Dark no head

3

AROMA:

Chocolate burnt light coffee

3

TASTE:

Dry smooth chocolate long after taste

3

OVERALL SCORE:

9

TASTING NOTES

APPEARANCE:

AROMA:

TASTE:

OVERALL SCORE:

Gruut White/Blond/Amber/Bruin

Source: Gruut Gentse Stadsbrouwerij, Ghent, Belgium

Strength: 5%/5.5%/6.6%/8%

Website: www.gruut.be

Annick De Splenter has beer in her blood. Her father, Ivan, ran Liefmans brewery in Oudenaarde for several years and she is a trained brewer, a graduate of Ghent School of Brewing. She has researched gruit beers in depth and opened her brewpub in 2009 to make and sell beers made solely with herbs and spices. The pub is in a former textile factory and inside it's open-plan, with the small brewery on view to the right. There's a long bar and a main room that's like a large, comfortable sitting room, with deep leather sofas and tables. A large mural on the wall is reminiscent of the cover of the Beatles' Sgt Pepper album, depicting artists and writers and other notables from Ghent.

Annick keeps her recipes secret. Gruut is the newest brewery in Flanders, she is exporting beer to the Netherlands, Italy, Spain and the United States, and she doesn't want people jumping on her unique bandwagon by attempting to replicate her beers. She will admit to using pepper, ginger, aniseed and even peanuts, among other ingredients, but won't be drawn on which are used in particular brews. She produces 5,000 hectolitres a year. The beers are unfiltered and unpasteurised, with the 'botanicals' added during the copper boil.

White, following the naming style of the Low Countries bière blanche/witte beers, is

TASTING NOTES

APPEARANCE:

AROMA:

TASTE:

OVERALL SCORE:

a wheat beer. It has a turbid, extremely pale colour and a big hit of ginger on the aroma with a sweet, perfumy malt note. It has a tart, ginger palate with hints of orange and creamy malt. Ginger notes and orange fruit continue in to the finish.

Blond, in contrast to White, is crystal clear and has a pale gold colour. It has a spicy and peppery nose with biscuit malt. The palate is dry, with pepper, spices and tart fruit balancing juicy malt, followed by a long, quenching finish that has a hint of coriander.

Annick describes her Amber as 'old English ale' and she uses roasted malt alongside pale malt. It lives up to its name with a bright amber colour followed by a nutty, floral nose with powerful hints of aniseed and fresh tobacco – the latter coming from malt and fermentation, not the use of real tobacco. It has a bittersweet palate with blood orange fruit, spices and biscuit malt. The finish is long, with nutty malt, a late burst of pepper and aniseed.

The only secret Annick let out of the bag was that she adds crushed peanuts at the end of the production of her strong Bruin: instead of dry hopping, dry peanutting! The beer has a big oatmeal aroma with roasted peanuts and pepper notes. Sweet malt, spices, blood orange fruit and smooth peanuts fill the mouth followed by a long, dry finish with warming alcohol, tart fruit, spices, rich roasted grain and further peanut hints.

I have been to Gruut twice and tasted and enjoyed the beers. I found them to be marvellously tasty and refreshing and, above all, 'beery'. To my surprise, I didn't miss hops and I marvelled at the thought that this was how beers may have tasted several centuries ago. Since my last visit, Annick has added an abbey beer, 9% Inferno.

Gruut can be visited at 10 Grote Huidevelter-shoek in Ghent and opens Monday to Saturday: see website for details of opening hours, brewery tours and beer-and-food matching.

TASTING NOTES

APPEARANCE:

AROMA:

TASTE:

OVERALL SCORE:

TASTING NOTES

APPEARANCE:

AROMA:

TASTE:

OVERALL SCORE:

TASTING NOTES

APPEARANCE:

AROMA:

TASTE:

OVERALL SCORE:

Hop Back Taiphoon

Source: Hop Back Brewery, Downton, Salisbury, England
Strength: 4.2%
Website: www.hopback.co.uk

John Gilbert, the founder of Hop Back Brewery, also takes a keen interest in food and cooking, and he has designed a beer that is the perfect companion for Asian cuisine. Hop Back is one of the longest-running British small artisan breweries, founded by John in 1987, and which built its success with Summer Lightning (see *300 Beers to Try Before You Die!*), one of the country's first golden ales, and one which has won many awards at CAMRA beer festivals and other events.

Hop Back has come a long way since John installed a tiny brewery in the cellar of the Wyndham Arms in Salisbury. He moved to an industrial estate outside the cathedral city, and installed a 20-barrel plant. He owns 10 pubs and supplies more than 500 other outlets.

Taiphoon was launched in 1999 and is available in both cask and bottled-conditioned formats. It's brewed with Maris Otter pale malt, wheat malt and flaked maize. A complex hop recipe includes Goldings, Pioneer, Saaz and Tettnang hops. The special character of the beer comes from the addition of a generous amount of lemongrass and coriander. The pale gold beer has a honeyed malt nose with spicy and leafy hop resins and a distinctive aroma of coriander and lemon. Peppery and woody hops build in the mouth, with creamy and honeyed malt and the continuing powerful notes of coriander and lemon, which all continue in to the long, assertive and dry finish that ends on a big spicy hop note. Hold the fizzy lager, this is the perfect companion to rich Bangladeshi, Indian and Thai dishes.

Peppery and woody hops build in the mouth, with creamy and honeyed malt

Little Valley Ginger Pale Ale

Source: Little Valley Brewery, Hebden Bridge, West Yorkshire, England

Strength: 4%

Website: www.littlevalleybrewery.co.uk

For a little brewery, Little Valley has big ideas. We have already comes across its Python IPA and its work in developing beer for the monks of Ampleforth Abbey. But Wim van der Spek and Sue Cooper have other arrows in their brewing quiver. They stay true to their organic beliefs with Ginger Pale Ale, brewed with organic and Fairtrade malts, hops and ginger, with water drawn from the surrounding Pennine hills. The recipe is composed of pale, crystal and cara malts, with Cascade and Pacific Gem hops, plus Fairtrade ginger and sugar. The beer is certified by the relevant organic and Fairtrade organisations and is available in both cask and bottle-conditioned forms.

It's ginger beer with a difference, a long way removed from the ginger pop of my childhood. It's exceptionally pale in spite of the use of crystal and cara malts. There's a big hit of ginger on the nose with a hint of lemon, too, and a cookie malt note and light hop resins. Ginger fills the mouth and warms the chest – it would make a great cold cure – and spicy hops starts to build alongside the rich biscuit malt. Ginger lingers in the finish and the beer finally becomes dry with a late burst of bitter hops.

TASTING NOTES

APPEARANCE:

AROMA:

TASTE:

OVERALL SCORE:

Sharp's Spiced Red/Honey Spice

Source: Sharp's Brewery, Rock, Cornwall, England

Strength: 9%/10%

Website: sharpsbrewery.co.uk

TASTING NOTES

APPEARANCE:

AROMA:

TASTE:

OVERALL SCORE:

The takeover of Sharp's by Molson Coors in 2011 has not curbed the bubbling enthusiasm of head brewer Stuart Howe. As we have seen with his Quadrupel, Stuart has a great love and passion for Belgian beers and he shares that commitment with drinkers with two more contributions to his Connoisseurs' Choice range of bottle-conditioned ales. Both will improve with long ageing in a cool cellar.

For Honey Spice, Stuart uses pale malt, Cornish honey and candy sugar. Hops are Czech Saaz and Styrian Goldings from Slovenia, with ground

Spiced Red is a radically different beer. It's brewed with Cassata best pale ale malt, with rye crystal and roasted barley.

coriander seeds and dried citrus peel added during the copper boil. The yeast culture comes from a Belgian Trappist brewery – in the traditions of the order, Stuart's lips are sealed about which monastery he works with – which ferments the beer until it's dry and tart. The pale gold beer has an enormously complex aroma: a big hit of honey with biscuit malt, spicy hops and a fruit note reminiscent of that ancient confectionery, orange and lemon slices, and a hint of coriander. Honey coats the tongue but is not cloying, balanced by tart fruit, juicy malt and spice notes from coriander and hops. The finish starts sweet but lingers long into a quenching, fruity finish with honey, citrus, spices and bitter hop resins.

Spiced Red is a radically different beer. It's brewed with Cassata best pale ale malt, with rye crystal and roasted barley. The single hop variety is Hallertauer Perle and coriander is added to the boil. Stuart says the 'very fruity' yeast strain comes from Ireland. A further addition of coriander is added prior to bottling. The glowing red beer has rye bread, a 'wine gums' fruit note, tingling hop resins and coriander on the nose, with rich rye and roasted grain, and fruit building on the palate, balanced by spice notes from hops and coriander. The finish starts bittersweet but ends dry and spicy, coriander coming to the fore, but with roast grain and light hop resins.

❝ The takeover of Sharp's by Molson Coors in 2011 has not curbed the bubbling enthusiasm of head brewer Stuart Howe ❞

TASTING NOTES

APPEARANCE:

AROMA:

TASTE:

OVERALL SCORE:

TASTING NOTES

APPEARANCE:

AROMA:

TASTE:

OVERALL SCORE:

Shipyard Smashed Pumpkin

Source: **Shipyard Brewing Company, Portland, Maine, USA**

Strength: **9%**

Website: **www.shipyard.com**

Alan Pugsley is a British brewer who has been at the cutting edge of the American craft brewing movement since the early 1990s. In his native country he trained at the Ringwood Brewery in Hampshire under the tutelage of Peter Austin, honoured as the father of British micro-brewing. When Alan moved to the U.S. he took two vital elements of brewing with him: a sample of Ringwood's fruity yeast culture and an agreement to brew Ringwood's award-winning Old Thumper strong bitter under licence in New England.

His brewery is based in the harbour town of Portland and close to the home of the poet Henry Wadsworth Longfellow. Alan brews a wide portfolio of beers, including a fine IPA and Longfellow Winter Ale, both of which featured in *300 Beers to Try Before You Die!* His Smashed Pumpkin recalls the early days of brewing in New England when settlers from Old England used squashes to make a type of beer until they could develop their own supplies of malt and hops. As well as pumpkin pulp, Alan uses pale ale malt, wheat malt and Light Munich malt. The hops come from the Bavarian Hallertau with American Willamette. He says the natural tannins in the pumpkin blend well with spicy hops.

The beer is straw coloured and the aroma is heavy with pumpkin but there's a good balance of floral and spicy hops. In spite of the strength, the palate is quite delicate, with pumpkin, sweet malt and light floral hops. The finish is a skilful balance of fruit, malt and hops, with pumpkin lingering on the back of the tongue.

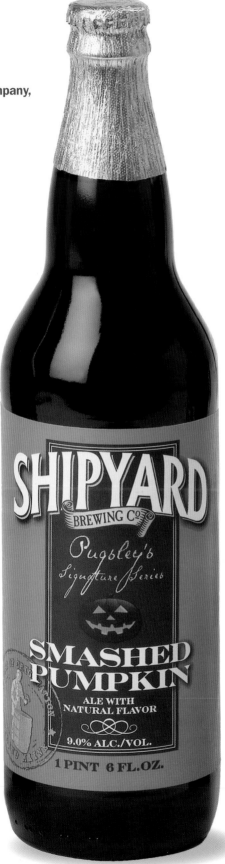

Danish Gypsy Beers

The Mikkeller Brewery in Denmark is a phenomenon. In a few years it has taken the world by storm and forced many brewers to rethink their attitude to beer, its tastes and the ingredients used to make it. Mikkel Borg Bjersø taught maths and physics in Copenhagen and brewed beer in his kitchen in his spare time. As his interest grew, he was determined to challenge the perception of beer in a country dominated by lagers from one company, Carlsberg/Tuborg. He wanted to take drinkers on an 'intense taste adventure' and he began to experiment with ingredients and storing beer in unconventional containers. He set up Mikkeller in 2006 and such has been his success that today he exports to 40 countries, supplies beer to top restaurants and organises an annual Copenhagen Beer Celebration that draws vast crowds.

All this has been achieved without owning a brewery. Mikkeller is known as a gypsy, phantom or cuckoo brewery, using other people's equipment to make their beers. There are other examples of the practice in the U.S. and in Britain but nobody else brews on Mikkeller's scale. In eight years, the company has brewed 600 beers and the numbers go on rising. Mikkel travels the world to brew in collaboration with other brewers in Belgium, Norway, Russia, the U.S. and Britain, to name just a few countries. Many of his beers are made at the Proef brewery in Belgium that was set up specifically for brewers without equipment, home brewers that wish to develop their skills, and restaurant and bar owners who want to fashion their own products to match with food.

Mikkel is not content with brewing conventional beer. He infuses his beers with a dazzling variety of ingredients that would make most other brewers – including even Annick De Splenter at Gruut (see p308) – breathless with wonder. He uses avocados, chillies, beans, syrups, flour made for tortillas and other breads, and ground coffee beans. Some of the beers are aged in wooden casks drawn from the whisky and wine trades and bottled versions are often refermented with fresh yeast. The beers are frequently supplied to top restaurants in order that chefs can match them with their dishes. The restaurants include Noma in Copenhagen, named the world's best restaurant three years running. The beers are available in specialist bars in many countries, including the BrewDog chain in Britain.

The list of beers is enormous and includes many single-hop IPAs, but few are regulars. Following a discussion with Mikkel I am listing four beers that – cross his heart – he says are regular brews. Look out for them and other beers in the portfolio and prepare for a wholly new taste experience. Please note: brewery tours are not available as there's no brewery but the beers can be sampled in a bar attached to the offices at 20 Vesterbrogade and a new bar, Mikkeller & Friends, at 35 Stefansgade, Copenhagen.

Mikkeller bar, Copenhagen

Mikkeller Milk Stout/Mexas Ranger/Invasion Farmhouse IPA/Sally's Field

Source: Mikkeller ApS, Copenhagen, Denmark

Strength: 6%/6.6%/8%/8.5%

Website: mikkeller.dk

Milk Stout, by Mikkeller standards, is a conventional beer, but a strong interpretation of a now rare style. The term 'milk' comes from the use of lactose or milk sugar, a by-product of cheese making. There's no actual milk in the beer but lactose does contain carbohydrates and calories that add a distinctive creamy quality to the finished beer as it cannot be fermented by brewers' yeast. By far the best-known example of milk stout is the English Mackeson, which once rivalled Guinness in popularity but is now owned by AB InBev, which treats it as a sideline, if not an irritant. Mikkeller's version is twice as strong as Mackeson, which means it has far more pronounced aromas and flavours. It's brewed at Proef in Belgium and the recipe is comprised of Maris Otter pale malt, flaked oats, pale chocolate and chocolate malts with lactose, which is added during the copper boil with American hop varieties Amarillo, Cascade and Columbus. The beer is a dessert in its own right, with a massive hit of chocolate and cream on the nose, with roasted grain and spicy/woody hop resins. Creamy malt and chocolate build in the mouth, balanced by bitter and spicy hops. The finish is long, with chocolate and cream dominating, but ending with dry roasted grain and spicy hop notes.

Mexas Ranger, also brewed at Proef, is a hymn of praise to Mexican plants, herbs, spices and cuisine. The conventional ingredients are Maris Otter pale malt, with chocolate malt, roasted barley, cara crystal malt, brown malt and smoked malt. The hops are Centennial, Columbus and Saaz. Then come the additions to the copper boil. They are avocado leaves, black torte beans, epazote (a herbal leaf similar to anise or fennel) maize (used in pozole stew), masa harina (used to make tortillas), Mexican grated chocolate, horchata syrup, and four different chillies. The beer has an enormous aroma of tart, medicinal spices, chocolate, smoked grain and nose-tingling chillies. Spices build in the mouth, the heat of the chillies tempered by smoky grain with hops making a walk-on role. The finish is long and challenging, chillies offering heat along with the alcohol, with contributions from smoked grain, chocolate and tangy/leafy hop resins.

Invasion Farmhouse IPA is just one of Mikkel's many interpretations of the style. It's brewed at the Anchorage Brewery in Alaska, proving how far Mikkel will travel for his beery collaborations. But then IPA is a well-travelled style. This version is made with two pale malts, Pilsner and Maris Otter, cara Munich and Munich malts and flaked maize. The hops are all American varieties, Cascade, Centennial, Columbus and Simcoe. The first Burton-brewed IPAs were fermented in wood and then travelled in wood to India. Mikkel's version picks up on this by ferment-ing in wooden *foudres* from the French wine industry. He adds *Brettanomyces*, the 'wild yeast' used to make Belgian lambic beer. The finished beer has wood, smoke and sour fruit on the aroma and rich toasted malt and leafy hop resins. Sour fruit dominates the palate along with major contributions from smoke and oak, rich toasted malt and leafy hops. The finish is long and deep, ending hoppy and bitter but with sour fruit, wood notes and toasted malt along the way.

I don't know whether the great American actor Sally Field, twice an Oscar winner and whose work ranges from *Smokey and the Bandit* to Steven Spielberg's 2012 Oscar-winning *Lincoln*, knows a Belgian-style ale has been brewed in her name but we can raise a glass in her honour. The beer is brewed at Proef and is aged for six months in Chardonnay casks. It's made with Pilsner malt and white sugar and hopped with Czech Saaz and Styrian Goldings. The golden Tripel-style beer has a grape and mango aroma with develop-ing hints of banana and candy sugar, and oak notes from the wood. The fruit builds in the mouth with peppery and spicy notes from the hops and a strong toasted malt character. The finish has enormous length, with continuing notes of grapes, mango and banana, oak, pep-pery hops and toasted malt.

> ❝ *Mikkel Borg Bjersø taught maths and physics in Copenhagen and brewed beer in his kitchen in his spare time* ❞

TASTING NOTES

APPEARANCE:

AROMA:

TASTE:

OVERALL SCORE:

TASTING NOTES

APPEARANCE:

AROMA:

TASTE:

OVERALL SCORE:

Glossary

ABV (Alcohol by Volume): international method for measuring and declaring for tax purposes the strength of beer. In the US, a system known as Alcohol by Weight is used: 5% ABV is 4% ABW. Many American brewers now also declare the strength of beer in ABV.

Abbey beer: commercial beers – produced principally in Belgium – that may be brewed under licence from monasteries, though some have no monastic links whatsoever. Not to be confused with Trappist beers (qv). Abbey beers are labelled Abbaye (French) or Abdij (Flemish).

Adjuncts: cereals and sugars added to beer, often as a cheap substitute, but sometimes used by brewers for special flavours. Producers of mass-market lagers may often dilute the barley mash with corn [maize] or rice. On the other hand, Belgian brewers use candy sugar for palate, while British brewers often use caramel and invert sugar. Adjuncts are not permitted in Germany where the Reinheitsgebot (qv) allows only malted grain.

Ale: the world's oldest beer style, produced by warm or top fermentation. The term covers such styles as (in Britain, Ireland and the US) mild, bitter, porter, stout, old ale and barley wine, and in the Low Countries, Abbey and Trappist ales, and some types of Bock, or Bok.

Alpha acid: the natural acid in the cone of the hop plant that gives bitterness to beer. Some international brewers use only 'high alpha' or 'super alpha' hops that give a high level of bitterness but little aroma.

Alt & Amber: an 'old' style of warm-fermented beer from the Dusseldorf region of Germany, often known as Amber in the US.

Aroma: the 'nose' of a beer that gives an indication of the malty, hoppy and possibly fruity characteristics to be found in the mouth.

Attenuation: If a beer is 'fully attenuated', most or all of the malt sugars will have turned to alcohol. In some styles, such as English mild or Dortmunder Export, some malt sugars are left in the beer for fullness of palate and some sweetness. Such beers are not 'brewed out' or fully attenuated.

Barley: the preferred grain used by all brewers as the main ingredient in beer and source of fermentable sugar.

Beer: generic term for an alcoholic drink made from grain. It includes ale, lager and Belgian lambic/gueuze.

Bière de Garde: French 'keeping beer', a style associated with French Flanders, first brewed by farmer/brewers in spring and stored to refresh their labourers during the summer months, but now produced all year round.

Bitter: A draught English pale ale that may range in colour from gold through amber to copper. The name indicates a generous amount of hop bitterness.

Blond/blonde: term used in mainland Europe to indicate a light-coloured beer. The term is often used when a brewery produces brown and pale versions of the same or similar beers, as in the case of Leffe Blonde and Brune.

Bock: German term for a strong beer, which can be pale or dark, usually stored or lagered for several months. The term is associated with the 'liquid bread' beers brewed by monks to sustain them during Lent. In the Netherlands, the term is sometimes spelt Bok, and beers there may be warm fermented.

Bottle conditioned/bottle fermented: a beer bottled with live yeast that allows the beer to mature, gain condition ('sparkle') and extra alcohol in its glass container.

Brettanomyces: Wild yeasts in the atmosphere in the Senne Valley region of Belgium that start the fermentation of Lambic beer (qv).

Brew-pub: a pub that brews beer on the premises.

Brune: a brown beer. See blond.

Burtonise/Burtonisation: addition of such salts as gypsum and magnesium to replicate the hard brewing waters found in Burton-on-Trent.

Campaign for Real Ale (CAMRA): Beer drinkers' organisation founded in 1971 to protect cask-conditioned beer – dubbed 'real ale'.

Carbon dioxide (CO_2): a gas naturally produced by fermentation. When beers are said to be 'naturally conditioned', as in cask-conditioned ale or bottle-conditioned beer, the gas is natural. When beers are filtered in the brewery, CO_2 may added either in the brewery or as part of the dispense system in a bar or pub. This can make beer too gassy.

Cask ale: also known as cask beer or real ale. A draught beer that undergoes a secondary fermentation in the cask in the pub cellar, reaching maturity as a result of natural processes. The style is mainly confined to Britain.

Condition: the level of carbon dioxide (CO_2) present in beer, which gives beer its sparkle.

Copper: vessel used to boil the sugary wort (qv) with hops. Traditionally made of copper but more often today of stainless steel. Known as a brew kettle in the US.

Gruut brewery in Belgium uses the medieval method of flavouring beer with gruit instead of hops

Decoction mashing: a system used mainly in lager brewing, in which portions of the mash are removed from the mashing vessel, heated to a higher temperature and then returned to the first vessel. Improves enzymic activity and the conversion of starch to sugar.

Doppelbock (double bock): extra strong type of Bock, usually around 7.5% ABV or more, but not – despite the name – twice the strength of an ordinary Bock.

Draught: beer served from a bulk container and drawn to the bar. Spelt 'draft' in the US.

Dry hopping: the addition of a small amount of hops to a cask of beer to improve bitterness and aroma. Usually associated with cask-conditioned beer in Britain.

Dubbel: Flemish word for double, first coined by the Westmalle Trappist brewery, to indicate a strong dark ale of around 6.5% ABV.

Dunkel: German for 'dark', indicating a lager beer in which colour is derived from well-roasted malts.

EBC: European Brewing Convention. A scale that measures the colour of a finished beer. A Pilsner may have 6-8 units, an English pale ale 20-40, porters and stouts 150-300 or more.

Enkel: Dutch word for single, used to indicate a beer of modest strength, as in La Trappe Enkel.

Esters: Flavour compounds produced by the action of yeast turning sugars into alcohol and carbon dioxide (CO_2). Esters are often similar to fruits, and fruitiness is associated with members of the ale family.

Fermentation: turning malt sugars into alcohol and carbon dioxide (CO_2) by the action of yeast. Ale is made by warm fermentation, lager by cold fermentation. These are often called top and bottom fermentation but the terms are misleading, as yeast works at all levels of the liquid.

Fining: Clarifying beer with the addition of finings, usually isinglass made from fish bladders. Caragheen [Irish Moss] can also be used and is preferred by vegetarians and vegans.

Finish: the aftertaste of a beer; the impression left at the back of the tongue and the throat.

Grand Cru: a term given to the finest beer of a brewery, one thought to typify the house style. Often used by Belgian brewers.

Grist: brewers' term for the milled grains to be used in a brew. The term comes from the word 'grind' and is still used in the expression 'all grist to the mill'.

Gruit: medieval method of adding a blend of herbs and spices to beer.

Gueuze: see Lambic.

Hefe: German for yeast. Beers 'mit hefe' are naturally conditioned and not filtered. Usually applies to wheat beers.

Helles: German for light, indicating a pale beer, either lager or wheat beer.

Hops: climbing plant with cones containing acids, resins and tannins that gives aroma and bitterness to beer, and helps prevent bacterial infection.

IBUs (also known as EBUs): International or European Units of Bitterness. A measure of the acids in hops that create bitterness in beer. Some extremely bland international lagers have around 10-15 IBUs whereas Pilsner Urquell has 40. An English mild ale will have IBUs in the low 20s, a pale ale or IPA will start at around 40 and can rise as high as 75 or 80.

Infusion: method of mashing beer, mainly associated with British ale brewing. The grain is left to soak with pure hot water in a mash tun at a constant temperature; enzymes in the malt convert starch to sugar.

IPA: short for India Pale Ale, the first pale beer in the world, associated with Burton-on-Trent in the English Midlands in the 19th century. First brewed for soldiers and civil servants based in India, it spawned pale ale and bitter in England, and even inspired the first lager brewers of Austria and Germany.

Kölsch: Golden ale brewed in Cologne and protected by a special ordinance.

Kräusen: The addition of some partially fermented wort (qv) to beer in the lager cellar to encourage a strong secondary fermentation.

Lager: from the German meaning store or storage place, similar to the English word larder. Following primary fermentation, beer is 'cold conditioned' in tanks where the temperature is held just above freezing. As the yeast settles at the bottom of the tanks, a slow secondary fermentation takes place, carbonation increases, and a clean, quenching, spritzy beer results, usually lacking the fruity esters associated with ale.

Lambic: Belgian beer made by 'spontaneous fermentation', using wild yeasts in the atmosphere. True lambics are confined to the area of the Senne Valley centred on Brussels. A blended lambic, using young and aged beers, is known as gueuze. When cherries or raspberries are added, the beers are known as kriek and framboise, or frambozen.

Lauter: vessel used to run off and filter the wort from the grain after mashing. The word comes from the German for clarify, and the vessels were once associated with lager or wheat beer brewing. But many ale brewers with modern equipment now employ lauter tuns, as the mash tun (qv) can be used to start a new brew once the mash has been pumped to the lauter.

Liquor: Brewers' term for the pure water used in the mashing and boiling process.

Maibock: in Germany, a strong, usually pale, lager brewed to herald the arrival of spring.

Malt: grain – usually barley – that has been partially germinated, dried and cured or toasted in a kiln. The grain contains starches that will be converted by natural enzymes into fermentable sugar during the mashing period in the brewery. The colour of malt is determined by the degree of heat in the kiln. All beers are made primarily from pale malt, which has the highest level of natural enzymes. Colour and flavour are derived from darker malts, such as amber, brown or chocolate.

Märzen: Traditional Bavarian lager brewed in March and stored until the autumn, when it is tapped at the Oktoberfest.

Mash: the mixture of malted grain and pure hot water, the first stage of the brewing process, when sugars are extracted from the malt. Mashing can be either by decoction or infusion (qv).

Mash tun: vessel in which malted grain is mixed with 'liquor' to start the brewing process.

Microbrewery: a small brewery with a small staff, often just a couple of people, brewing batches of beer for local distribution. 'Micros' in Britain and the US have been at the forefront of innovation in brewing in the past 20–30 years. Many micros have recreated old beer styles and designed new ones. In the US, micros may be big by European standards, but are considered small when compared to giant American producers.

Mouth-feel: the sensation that beer and its constituent parts – malt, hops and fruity esters – make in the mouth. The tongue is a highly sensitive organ and can detect sweetness, sourness, saltiness and bitterness as the beer passes over it.

Oktoberfest beers: medium-strength lager beer brewed in Munich for consumption at the famous autumn beer festival.

Original Gravity (OG): system once used in Britain for measuring the level of 'fermentable material' – malt, other grains and sugars – in a beer. Tax was levied on the OG until the system was replaced by Alcohol By Volume (ABV – qv). However, many brewers still list the OG and the ABV of their beers.

Parti-gyle: making more than one beer from a brew with the addition of brewing liquor to water the wort (qv) down to the required strengths.

Pasteurisation: heating process developed by Louis Pasteur that kills bacteria and stabilises the beer. It can be done quickly by flash pasteurisation as the beer passes through a pipe or more slowly by tunnel pasteurisation when the beer comes into contact with heat. If pasteurisation is clumsy, the beer can take on unpleasant cardboard or cabbage-like aromas and flavours. Many brewers now prefer to sterile filter beer. One leading opponent of pasteurisation was Pasteur himself, who developed the method to protect wine, and said beer was too delicate to withstand it.

Pilsner/Pilsener/Pils: originally a golden, hoppy lager brewed in the city of Pilsen in Bohemia, now part of the Czech Republic. A true Pilsner is usually around 4.5–5% ABV. In Germany, many brewers either spell the word Pilsener or shorten it to Pils, to avoid any suggestion their beers come from Pilsen. In the Czech Republic, Pilsner is an 'appellation': only beers from Pilsen can use the term.

Porter: a brown (later black) beer first brewed in London early in the 18th century. Called 'entire butt' by brewers, it acquired the name of porter due to its popularity with street-market porters. The success of porter created the modern commercial brewing industry in England and later in Ireland. The strongest porters were known as stout (qv).

Priming: the addition of priming sugar to encourage a strong secondary fermentation.

Quadrupel: a Belgian beer of exceptional strength but rarely four times as strong as other beers.

Racking: running beer from a conditioning tank into a cask or keg.

Rauch beer: speciality beer brewed in Bamberg, Franconia, Germany, where malt is kilned over wood fires that give a smoky aroma and palate.

Real Ale: term coined by CAMRA (qv) in Britain to denote a beer that is neither filtered nor pasteurised, which undergoes a secondary fermentation in its container and is not served by applied gas pressure.

Reinheitsgebot: The Bavarian 'Pure Beer Law' dating from 1516 that lays down that only malted barley and/or wheat, hops, yeast and water can be used in brewing. Cheaper cereals, such as corn or rice, and sugar are not permitted. The law now covers the whole of Germany, but export beers may not necessarily adhere to it.

Shilling: 19th-century Scottish designation for ales that indicated the gross price payable on each barrel, ranging from 60 Shilling to 90 Shilling and sometimes higher.

Sparge: to rinse the grain after mashing to flush out any remaining malt sugars (from the French *esperger*, meaning to sprinkle).

Stout: Once a generic English term for the strongest or 'stoutest' beer produced in a brewery. With the rise of porter (qv) in the 18th century, strong porters were known as stout porters. Over time, the term was shortened to just stout, indicating a strong, jet-black beer, made with highly roasted malts and roasted barley, and generously hopped. The style is most closely associated today with Ireland.

Trappist: beers of the ale family made in breweries controlled by Trappist monks in Belgium, the Netherlands and France. Trappist beers carry the 'Authentic Trappist Product' logo that differentiates them from commercially-brewed beers.

Tripel: strong, usually pale beer, associated with the Westmalle Trappist brewery in Belgium, but now widely used throughout the Low Countries.

Tun: a large vessel once used to store beer. The term today is confined to the mash tun, the vessel in which malt and water are blended at the start of the brewing process (qv).

Vienna Red: term for the first successful commercial lager beer brewed in Austria in the 19th century. It was a halfway house between the dark lagers of Munich and the golden lagers of Bohemia. Vienna Red inspired the Munich Märzen beers (qv).

Wheat beer: known as weizen (wheat) or weiss (white) in Germany, blanche in French or wit in Dutch and Flemish. Beer made from a blend of wheat and barley malt. Wheat beers are members of the ale family and may be unfiltered and cloudy, or filtered bright.

Wort: the sweet, sugary extract produced by mashing malt and water. Wort is boiled with hops, then cooled prior to fermentation.

Yeast: a natural fungus that attacks sweet liquids such as wort, turning malt sugars into alcohol and carbon dioxide (CO_2). Brewers' yeasts are either warm or top fermenting cultures for ale brewing, or cold or bottom fermenting cultures for lager brewing. Belgian lambic brewers (qv) use wild Brettanomyces yeasts (qv) from the atmosphere.

Trappist beers are marked by the Trappist logo

Brewery museums

National Brewery Centre, Burton on Trent, England

Brewery museums offer the chance to tour historic breweries, and explore more about the history and national culture of beer and brewing, as well as the agriculture and supporting industries that play a key part in our enjoyment of beer. Below are a selection of the best. In addition, many breweries – both large and small – have visitor centres where you can see the brewery, sample and buy the products and, increasingly, dine on menus especially tailored to match the brewery's beers. There are too many brewery visitor centres to list, but details are given on individual brewery websites.

Great Britain:
The Hop Farm, Paddock Wood, Kent www.thehopfarm.co.uk
National Brewery Centre, Burton on Trent www.nationalbrewerycentre.co.uk
Marston's Brewery, Burton on Trent www.marstonsbeercompany.co.uk

Australia:
Cascade Brewery, Hobart, Tasmania www.cascadebreweryco.com.au
Castlemaine Perkins, Brisbane, Queensland lionco.com

Austria:
Stiegl's Brauwelt, Salzburg www.stiegl.at

Belgium:
Brewery Museum, Grand' Place, Brussels www.belgianbrewers.be

Cantillon Brewery & Museum, Anderlecht, Brussels www.cantillon.be
Schaerbeek Museum of Belgian Beer www.brusselsmuseums.be

Czech Republic:
Brewery Museum, Pilsen www.prazdrojvisit.cz
Budweiser Budvar Brewery Museum, Ceské Budějovice www.budweiserbudvar.cz
Prague Beer Museum www.praguebeermuseum.com
Temple of Hops & Beer, Žatec www.beertemple.cz

Denmark:
Carlsberg Brewery Museum, Copenhagen www.visitcarlsberg.com

Estonia:
A Le Coq Beer Museum, Tartu www.alecoq.ee

France:
European Beer Museum, Stenay, Lorraine www.soleildegaume.be

Germany:
Bavarian Brewery Museum, Kulmbach www.kulmbacher-moenchshof.de
Beer & Oktoberfest Museum. Munich www.bier-und-oktoberfest-museum.de
Deutsches Brauereimuseum, Munich www.muenchner-stadtmuseum.de
Dortmund Brewing Museum www.brauereimuseum.dortmund.de

Ireland:
Guinness Storehouse, Dublin www.guinness-storehouse.com

Lithuania:
Svyturys Brewery, Klaipeda www.svyturys.lt

Netherlands:
De Boom National Beer Museum, Alkmaar www.biermuseum.nl
Heineken Experience, Amsterdam www.heinekenexperience.com

Norway:
Mack Brewery, Tromso, Norway www.mack.no

Poland:
Brewery Museum, Zywiec www.muzeumbrowaru.pl
Tyskie Brewing Museum, Tychy www.tyskiebrowarium.pl

Spain:
The Beer Museum Zaragozana, Zaragoza www.facebook.com/fabricalazaragozana

Ukraine:
Lvivske Museum of Beer & Brewing, Lviv www.lvivbeermuseum.com

United States:
Boston Brew Tour, Boston, Massachusetts bostonbrewtours.com
Milwaukee Beer Museum, Milwaukee, Wisconsin milwaukeebeermuseum.org
National Brewery Museum, Potosi, Wisconsin www.potosibrewery.com
Yuengling Brewery, Pottsville, Pennsylvania www.yuenglingbrewery.com

Hop farm family park, Kent, England

Online beer retailers

As both beer and online retailing have blossomed over the past decade or so, a range of specialist beer retailers have sprung up around the world, selling both domestic and foreign beers – usually in bottle, but some also have casks, kegs or polypins available. These are some of the better-stocked ones. In addition, the number of specialist physical beer shops has also grown in recent years. A list of beer shops can be found at www.insidebeer.com

UK:
Ales by Mail, Essex
www.alesbymail.co.uk
Alesela, Glasgow
www.alesela.co.uk
Beautiful Beers, Suffolk
www.beautifulbeers.co.uk
The Beer Boutique, London
www.thebeerboutique.co.uk
The Beer Club of Britain, Norfolk
www.beerclubofbritain.co.uk
Beers of Europe, Norfolk
www.beersofeurope.co.uk
Beer Hawk, North Yorkshire
www.beerhawk.co.uk
Beer Here, Norfolk
www.beerhere.co.uk
Beer Ritz, North Yorkshire
www.beerritz.co.uk
Beer Merchants, Kent
www.beermerchants.com
Belgian Beer Company, Staffs
www.thebelgianbeercompany.com
Belgique, London
www.belgique.co.uk
Best of British Beer, Cheshire
www.bestofbritishbeer.co.uk
Classic Ales, West Midlands
www.classicales.co.uk
Craft Beer Store, Glasgow
www.craftbeerstore.co.uk
Flipping Good Beer Shop, Notts
theflippinggoodbeer-shop.co.uk
My Brewery Tap, Surrey
www.mybrewerytap.com
Noble Green Wines, London
www.noblegreenwines.co.uk
The Real Ale Company
www.therealalecompany.co.uk
The Real Ale Shop, Norfolk
www.therealaleshop.co.uk
realale.com, London
www.realale.com
Slurp, London *www.slurp.co.uk*

North America:
99 Bottles, Washington
www.99bottles.net
Argonaut Liquor, Colorado
www.argonautliquor.com
Beer Boxx *www.beerboxx.com*
Beer on the Wall, California
www.beeronthewall.com
Beer Liquors
www.beerliquors.com
Bier Kraft, New York
www.bierkraft.com
Beer Ship, Washington
www.beership.com
Binny's Beverave Depot, Illinois
www.binnys.com
Bottle Trek, Oregon
www.bottletrek.com
Brewforia, Idahio
www.brewforia.com
Firefly, British Columbia, Canada
www.fireflyfinewinesandales.com
France 44, Minnesota
www.france44.com
Gary's Wine, New Jersey
www.garyswine.com
Half Time Beverage, New York
www.halftimebeverage.com
Hi-Time Wine Cellars, California
www.hitimewine.net
Holiday Wine Cellar, California
www.holidaywinecellar.com
Lets Pour, Washington
www.letspour.com

Liquor Mart, Colorado
www.liquormart.com
Merwin Liquors, Minnesota
www.shopmerwins.com
Shoppers Vineyard, New Jersey
shoppersvineyard.com
Total Wine, Maryland
www.totalwine.com
Vendome Store, California
vendomestore.com
Vintage Cellar, Virginia
www.vintagecellar.com

Australian & New Zealand:
Beer Boys, Australia
beerboys.com.au
Beer Cartel, Australia
www.beercartel.com.au
The Beer Cellar, New Zealand
www.beercellar.co.nz
Beer Direct, New Zealand
www.beerdirect.co.nz
The Beer Store, Australia
www.aclandcellars.com.au
Boozzee, New Zealand
boozee.co.nz
Cult Beer Store, New Zealand
www.cultbeerstore.co.nz
Dan Murphy's, Australia
danmurphys.com.au
Glengarry Wine, New Zealand
www.giengarrywines.co.nz
The Good Wine Co, New Zealand
www.thegoodwine.co.nz
Herne Bay Cellars, New Zealand
www.hernebaycellars.co.nz
International Beer Shop, Australia *www.internationalbeershop.com.au*
Liquor King, New Zealand
www.lk.co.nz
The Mill Liquor, New Zealand
www.themill.co.nz
Purvis Beer, Australia

www.purvisbeer.com.au
Wine List Australia, Australia
www.winelistaustralia.com.au
World of Beers, Australia
www.worldofbeers.com.au

Europe:
Ales in France, France
www.alesinfrance.com
Au Nom de la Biere, France
www.aunomdelabiere.fr
Beer City, Belgium
www.beer-city.be
Beer Planet, Belgium
www.beerplanet.eu
Beer Shop, Belgium
www.beershop.be
Bier Shop, Germany
www.biershop.bierpost.com
Bier&Zo, Netherlands
www.bierenzo.nl
Biershop Bayern, Germany
www.biershop-bayern.de
Cervezas Online, Spain
www.cervezasonline.com
Drink Store, Ireland
www.drinkstore.ie
EstuCerveza, Spain
www.estucerveza.com
Excellence Biere, France
www.excellence-biere.com
Mein Biershop, Germany
www.mein-biershop.de
MyBier.at, Austria *www.mybier.atxs*
Molloys, Ireland *www.molloys.ie*
Pivni Shop, Czech Republic
www.pivnishop.cz
Portale Birra, Italy
www.portalebirra.it
Saveur Biere, France
www.saveur-biere.com
Speciaal Bier Pakket, Netherlands *www.speciaalbierpakket.nl*

Index

By beer name

- [ ] Emerson's Pilsner (New Zealand) 65
- [ ] Emerson's Weizenbock (New Zealand) 221
- [ ] Engelszell Gregorius (Austria) 234
- [ ] Epic Armageddon IPA (New Zealand) 35
- [ ] Erdinger Pikantus Weizenbock (Germany) 220
- [ ] Erdinger Weissbier (Germany) 220

- [ ] Fire Island Red Wagon IPA (USA) 36
- [ ] Firestone Walker's Reserve Porter (USA) 165
- [ ] Flensburger Pilsener (Germany) 66
- [ ] Fleurac Amerindienne (France) 272
- [ ] Fleurac La Triple (France) 272
- [ ] Florida Beer Swamp Ape IPA (USA) 37
- [ ] Flying Dog Imperial IPA (USA) 38
- [ ] Flying Dog Kujo Imperial Coffee Stout (USA) 305
- [ ] Fordham Tavern Ale (USA) 99
- [ ] Franciscan Well Purgatory (Ireland) 235
- [ ] Franciscan Well Rebel Red (Ireland) 215
- [ ] Franciscan Well Shandon Stout (Ireland) 166
- [ ] Freedom Pilsner (England) 67
- [ ] Fuller's 1845 (England) 144
- [ ] Fuller's Bengal Lancer (England) 39
- [ ] Fuller's Old Burton Extra (England) 176

- [ ] Gambrinus (Czech Republic) 68
- [ ] Grainstore Rutland Panther (England) 79
- [ ] Green Jack Trawlerboys Best Bitter (England) 122
- [ ] Greene King Hen's Tooth (England) 133
- [ ] Greene King IPA Reserve (England) 40
- [ ] Growler Augustinian Ale (England) 235
- [ ] Gruut Amber (Belgium) 306
- [ ] Gruut Blond (Belgium) 306
- [ ] Gruut Bruin (Belgium) 306
- [ ] Gruut White (Belgium) 306

- [ ] De Halve Maan Brugse Zot Blond (Belgium) 251
- [ ] De Halve Maan Brugse Zot Dubbel (Belgium) 251
- [ ] Hargreaves Hill Extra Special Bitter (Australia) 134
- [ ] Harveys Elizabethan Ale (England) 145
- [ ] Hawkshead Bitter (England) 107
- [ ] Hawkshead Lakeland Gold (England) 185
- [ ] Hepworth Prospect (England) 185
- [ ] Hesket Newmarket Catbells Pale Ale (England) 134
- [ ] Highland Dark Munro (Scotland) 204
- [ ] Highland Scapa Special (Scotland) 204
- [ ] Hobson's Mild (England) 80
- [ ] Hogs Back A Over T (England) 146
- [ ] Hogs Back TEA (England) 123
- [ ] Holden's Golden Glow (England) 186
- [ ] Holgate ESB (Australia) 135
- [ ] Holgate Hopinator (Australia) 41
- [ ] Hop Back Entire Stout (England) 167
- [ ] Hop Back Taiphoon (England) 309
- [ ] Hopshackle Double Momentum (England) 42
- [ ] Hopshackle Imperial Stout (England) 168

- [ ] Hopshackle Restoration (England) 147
- [ ] Houblon Chouffe Dobbelen IPA Tripel (Belgium) 41

- [ ] IJbok (Netherlands) 300
- [ ] Inveralmond Lia Fail (Scotland) 205
- [ ] Invercargill Pitch Black Stout (New Zealand) 169
- [ ] Ironbridge Gold (England) 187
- [ ] Itchen Valley Pure Gold (England) 188

- [ ] James Squire Jack of Spades Porter (Australia) 170

- [ ] Kaiserdom Dark Lager Germany 294
- [ ] Kaiserdom Hefe-Weissbier (Germany) 222
- [ ] Kaiserdom Pilsener (Germany) 69
- [ ] Kaltenberg Weissbier Dunkel (Germany) 222
- [ ] Kaltenberg Weissbier Hell (Germany) 222
- [ ] Kelburn Cart Blanche (Scotland) 206
- [ ] Kelham Island Pride of Sheffield (England) 108
- [ ] The Kernel India Pale Ale (England) 44
- [ ] Konrad 12° (Czech Republic) 287
- [ ] Konrad 14° (Czech Republic) 287
- [ ] Krombacher Weizen (Germany) 223
- [ ] Krušovice Cerně (Czech Republic) 294
- [ ] Krušovice Imperial (Czech Republic) 288
- [ ] Küppers Kölsch (Germany) 277

- [ ] Lagonda IPA (England) 45
- [ ] Liefmans Goudenband (Belgium) 81
- [ ] Lindeboom Pilsener (Netherlands) 69
- [ ] Lindemans Cuvée René Gueuze (Belgium) 260
- [ ] Lindemans Cuvée René Kriek (Belgium) 260
- [ ] Little Creatures Bright Ale (Australia) 189
- [ ] Little Creatures Stimulus IPA (Australia) 46
- [ ] Little Valley Ginger Pale Ale (England) 309
- [ ] Little Valley Hebden's Wheat (England) 224
- [ ] Little Valley Python IPA (England) 47

- [ ] Maredsous Blonde (Belgium) 236
- [ ] Matilda Bay Bohemian Pilsner (Australia) 70
- [ ] McMullen's Country Bitter (England) 124
- [ ] Mighty Oak Maldon Gold (England) 190
- [ ] Mikkeller Invasion Farmhouse IPA (Denmark) 314
- [ ] Mikkeller Mexas Ranger (Denmark) 314
- [ ] Mikkeller Milk Stout (Denmark) 314
- [ ] Mikkeller Sally's Field (Denmark) 314
- [ ] Moles Mole Catcher (England) 136
- [ ] Mont des Cats Bière Trappiste (France) 237
- [ ] Mort Subite Gueuze (Belgium) 262
- [ ] Mort Subite Kriek (Belgium) 262
- [ ] Murray's Icon 2IPA (Australia) 48

- [ ] Nøgne ø Brown Ale (Norway) 83
- [ ] Nøgne ø Imperial Brown Ale (Norway) 83
- [ ] North Cotswold Monarch IPA (England) 49

Index

By country

- [ ] Kaiserdom Hefe-Weissbier (Germany) 222
- [ ] Kaiserdom Pilsener (Germany) 69
- [ ] Kaltenberg Weissbier Dunkel (Germany) 222
- [ ] Kaltenberg Weissbier Hell (Germany) 222
- [ ] Krombacher Weizen (Germany) 223
- [ ] Küppers Kölsch (Germany) 277
- [ ] Schlüssel Alt (Germany) 279
- [ ] Schneider Weisse Tap 4 (Germany) 226
- [ ] Schneider Weisse Tap 5 (Germany) 226
- [ ] Veltins Pilsener (Germany) 72

- [ ] Einstôk Icelandic Pale Ale (Iceland) 98
- [ ] Einstök Icelandic Toasted Porter (Iceland) 161

- [ ] Dungarvan Copper Coast (Ireland) 213
- [ ] Dungarvan Helvic Gold (Ireland) 183
- [ ] Eight Degrees Sunburnt Irish Red (Ireland) 214
- [ ] Franciscan Well Purgatory (Ireland) 235
- [ ] Franciscan Well Rebel Red (Ireland) 215
- [ ] Franciscan Well Shandon Stout (Ireland) 166
- [ ] O'Hara's Irish Red (Ireland) 216
- [ ] O'Hara's Irish Stout (Ireland) 172
- [ ] Porterhouse An Brain Blásta (Ireland) 148
- [ ] Porterhouse Hop Head (Ireland) 100
- [ ] Porterhouse Plain Porter (Ireland) 173
- [ ] Porterhouse Red (Ireland) 216

- [ ] Il Chiostro Scottish Ale (Italy) 203

- [ ] Windhoek Lager (Namibia) 290

- [ ] IJbok (Netherlands) 300
- [ ] Lindeboom Pilsener (Netherlands) 69

- [ ] 8Wired Hopwired (New Zealand) 92
- [ ] Croucher Pilsner (New Zealand) 64
- [ ] Emerson's Bookbinder Bitter (New Zealand) 106
- [ ] Emerson's Pilsner (New Zealand) 65
- [ ] Emerson's Weizenbock (New Zealand) 221
- [ ] Epic Armageddon IPA (New Zealand) 35
- [ ] Invercargill Pitch Black Stout (New Zealand) 169
- [ ] Three Boys Wheat (New Zealand) 228

- [ ] Nøgne ø Brown Ale (Norway) 83
- [ ] Nøgne ø Imperial Brown Ale (Norway) 83

- [ ] Cusqueña (Peru) 286

- [ ] Amber Kožlak (Poland) 298
- [ ] Amber Żywe (Poland) 282

- [ ] Black Isle Hibernator Organic Oatmeal Stout (Scotland) 200
- [ ] Cairngorm Black Gold (Scotland) 202
- [ ] Highland Dark Munro (Scotland) 204
- [ ] Highland Scapa Special (Scotland) 204

- [ ] Inveralmond Lia Fail (Scotland) 205
- [ ] Kelburn Cart Blanche (Scotland) 206
- [ ] Orkney Skull Splitter (Scotland) 207
- [ ] Renaissance Stonecutter (Scotland) 208
- [ ] Stewart Brewing 80/- (Scotland) 209
- [ ] Stewart Brewing Edinburgh Gold (Scotland) 209
- [ ] Stewart Brewing Edinburgh No 3 (Scotland) 209
- [ ] Sulwath Black Galloway (Scotland) 210
- [ ] WEST St Mungo (Scotland) 289

- [ ] Alhambra Negra (Spain) 292

- [ ] 16 Mile Old Court Ale (USA) 130
- [ ] Samuel Adams Irish Red (USA) 212
- [ ] Samuel Adams Latitude 48 IPA (USA) 29
- [ ] Samuel Adams Noble Pils (USA) 63
- [ ] Ballast Point Wahoo Wheat Beer (USA) 219
- [ ] Bayou Teche La 31 Bière Pâle (USA) 94
- [ ] Berkshire Brewing Steel Rail Extra Pale Ale (USA) 95
- [ ] Brinkley's Maibock (USA) 299
- [ ] Brooklyn East India Pale Ale (USA) 30
- [ ] Cigar City Maduro Brown Ale (USA) 77
- [ ] Cigar City Marshal Zhukov's Imperial Stout (USA) 159
- [ ] Crazy Mountain Amber Ale (USA) 277
- [ ] Deschutes Hop Henge Experimental IPA (USA) 33
- [ ] Devil Dog Imperial IPA (USA) 34
- [ ] Fire Island Red Wagon IPA (USA) 36
- [ ] Firestone Walker's Reserve Porter (USA) 165
- [ ] Florida Beer Swamp Ape IPA (USA) 37
- [ ] Flying Dog Imperial IPA (USA) 38
- [ ] Flying Dog Kujo Imperial Coffee Stout (USA) 305
- [ ] Fordham Tavern Ale (USA) 99
- [ ] Odell 5 Barrel Pale Ale (USA) 100
- [ ] Odell Myrcenary (USA) 49
- [ ] Rogue Brutal IPA (USA) 53
- [ ] Schlafly Kölsch (USA) 278
- [ ] Sebago Frye's Leap IPA (USA) 55
- [ ] Shiner Bock (USA) 302
- [ ] Shipyard Smashed Pumpkin (USA) 312
- [ ] Sierra Nevada Torpedo Extra IPA (USA) 57
- [ ] Sprecher Black Bavarian (USA) 295
- [ ] The Bruery Saison de Lente (USA) 248
- [ ] Tyranena Headless Man Amber Ale (USA) 280
- [ ] Uinta Hop Notch IPA (USA) 59
- [ ] Wolverine Dark Lager (USA) 296
- [ ] Wynkoop Silverback Pale Ale (USA) 102

- [ ] Bryncelyn Holly Hop (Wales) 104
- [ ] Otley O-Garden (Wales) 225
- [ ] Otley O1 (Wales) 190

Books for Beer Lovers

CAMRA Books, the publishing arm of the Campaign for Real Ale, is the leading publisher of books on beer and pubs. Key titles include:

300 Beers to Try Before You Die!
Roger Protz

300 beers from around the world, handpicked by award-winning journalist, author and broadcaster Roger Protz to try before you die! A comprehensive portfolio of top beers from the smallest microbreweries in the United States to family-run British breweries and the world's largest brands. This book is indispensible for both beer novices and aficionados alike. The companion volume to *300 More Beers to Try Before You Die!*

£14.99 ISBN 978-1-85249-273-1

Good Bottled Beer Guide
Jeff Evans

A pocket-sized guide for discerning drinkers looking to buy bottled real ales and enjoy a fresh glass of their favourite beers at home. The 8th edition of the *Good Bottled Beer Guide* is completely revised, updated and redesigned to showcase the very best bottled British real ales now being produced, and detail where they can be bought. Everything you need to know about bottled beers; tasting notes, ingredients, brewery details, and a glossary to help the reader understand more about them.

£12.99 ISBN 978-1-85249-309-7

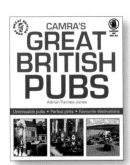

Great British Pubs
Adrian Tierney-Jones

Great British Pubs is a celebration of the British pub. This fully illustrated book presents the pub as an ultimate destination – featuring pubs everyone should seek out and make a visit to. It recommends a selection of the very best pubs in various different categories, as chosen by leading beer writer Adrian Tierney-Jones. Every kind of pub is represented, with full-colour photography helping to showcase a host of excellent pubs from the seaside to the city and from the historic to the ultra-modern.

£14.99 ISBN 978-1-85249-265-6

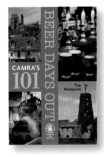

101 Beer Days Out
Tim Hampson

101 Beer Days Out is the perfect handbook for the beer tourist wanting to explore beer and brewing culture in their local area and around the UK. From historic city pubs to beer festivals; idyllic country pub walks to rail ale trails – Britain has beer and brewing experiences to rival any in the world. *101 Beer Days Out* brings together for the first time the best of these experiences – perfect for any beer tourist.

£12.99 ISBN 978-1-85249-288-5

London's Best Beer, Pubs & Bars
Des de Moor

London's Best Beer, Pubs & Bars is the essential guide to beer drinking in London. This practical book is packed with detailed maps and easy-to-use listings to help you find the best places to enjoy perfect pints in the capital. Laid out by area, find the best pubs serving the best British and international beers wherever you are. Features tell you more about London's rich history of brewing and the city's vibrant modern brewing scene, where well-known brands rub shoulders with tiny microbreweries.

£12.99 ISBN 978-1-85249-262-5

CAMRA's Book of Beer Knowledge
Jeff Evans

This absorbing, pocket-sized book is packed with beer facts, feats, records, stats and anecdotes so you'll never be lost for words at the pub again. More than 200 entries cover the serious, the silly and the downright bizarre from the world of beer. Inside this pint-sized compendium you'll find everything from the biggest brewer in the world to the beers with the daftest names. A quick skim before a night out and you'll always have enough beery wisdom to impress your friends.

£7.99 ISBN 978-1-85249-292-2

London Pub Walks
Bob Steel

CAMRA's pocket-sized walking guide to London is back. This fantastic second edition is packed with fully updated walks, new pubs and a new selection of routes that take full advantage of London's public transport network. With 30 walks around more than 190 pubs, *London Pub Walks* enables you to explore the entire city while never being far from a decent pint. Full-colour maps and easy-to-follow instructions make this the perfect companion for anyone intent on discovering the best of London.

£9.99 ISBN 978-1-85249-310-3

Britain's Best Real Heritage Pubs
Geoff Brandwood

CAMRA's definitive guide to over 260 pubs throughout the UK which have interiors of real historic significance – some of them stretching back a century or more. It is the first time ever that these pubs have been collected into a single volume. Illustrated with high quality photography, the guide's extensive listings are the product of years of surveying and research by CAMRA volunteers dedicated to preserving and protecting our rich pub heritage.

£9.99 ISBN 978-1-85249-304-2

BOOKS

Order these and other CAMRA books online at *www.camra.org.uk/books*, ask at your local bookstore, or contact: CAMRA, 230 Hatfield Road, St Albans, AL1 4LW. Telephone 01727 867201

A Campaign of Two Halves

Campaigning for Pub Goers & Beer Drinkers

CAMRA, the Campaign for Real Ale, is an independent not-for-profit, volunteer-led consumer group. We campaign tirelessly for good-quality real ale and pubs, as well as lobbying government to champion drinkers' rights and promote local pubs as centres of community life. As a CAMRA member you will have the opportunity to campaign to save pubs under threat of closure, for pubs to be free to serve a range of real ales at affordable prices and for a fair rate of tax on beer.

Enjoying Real Ale & Pubs

CAMRA has over 150,000 members from all ages and backgrounds, brought together by a common belief in the issues that CAMRA deals with and their love of good quality British beer. From just £23 a year – that's less than a pint a month – you can join CAMRA and enjoy the following benefits:

Subscription to *What's Brewing*, our monthly colour newspaper, and Beer, our quarterly magazine, informing you about beer and pub news and detailing events and beer festivals around the country.

Free or reduced entry to over 160 national, regional and local beer festivals.

Money off many of our publications including the *Good Beer Guide*, the *Good Bottled Beer Guide* and *CAMRA's Great British Pubs*.

Access to a members-only section of our national website, **www.camra.org.uk**, which gives up-to-the-minute news stories and includes a special offer section with regular features.

Special discounts with numerous partner organisations and money off real ale in your participating local pubs as part of our Pubs Discount Scheme.

Visit **www.camra.org.uk/joinus** for CAMRA membership information.

Do you feel passionately about your pint?
Then why not join CAMRA

Just fill in the application form (or a photocopy of it) and the Direct Debit form on the next page to receive three months' membership FREE!*

If you wish to join but do not want to pay by Direct Debit, please fill in the application form below and send a cheque, payable to CAMRA, to: CAMRA, 230 Hatfield Road, St Albans, Hertfordshire, AL1 4LW. Please note than non Direct Debit payments will incur a £2 surcharge. Figures are given below.

Please tick appropriate box

	Direct Debit		**Non Direct Debit**	
Single membership (UK & EU)	£23	☐	£25	☐
Concessionary membership (under 26 or 60 and over)	£15.50	☐	£17.50	☐
Joint membership	£28	☐	£30	☐
Concessionary joint membership	£18.50	☐	£20.50	☐

Life membership information is available on request.

Title _____ Surname _____

Forename(s) _____

Address _____

_____ Postcode _____

Date of Birth _____ Email address _____

Signature _____

Partner's details (for Joint Membership)

Title _____ Surname _____

Forename(s) _____

Date of Birth _____ Email address _____

CAMRA will occasionally send you e-mails related to your membership. We will also allow your local branch access to your email.
If you would like to opt-out of contact from your local branch lease tick here ☐ (at no point will your details be released to a third party).
Find out more about CAMRA at **www.camra.org.uk** Telephone 01727 867201

*Three months free is only available the first time a member pays by DD

CAMPAIGN FOR REAL ALE

Instruction to your Bank or Building Society to pay by Direct Debit

Please fill in the form and send to: Campaign for Real Ale Ltd. 230 Hatfield Road, St. Albans, Herts. AL1 4LW

Name and full postal address of your Bank or Building Society

To The Manager _____ Bank or Building Society

Address _____

Postcode _____

Name (s) of Account Holder (s)

_____

Bank or Building Society account number

_____

Branch Sort Code

_____

Reference Number

_____

Originator's Identification Number

9	2	6	1	2	9

FOR CAMRA OFFICIAL USE ONLY
This is not part of the instruction to your **Bank or Building Society**

Membership Number _____

Name _____

Postcode _____

Instruction to your Bank or Building Society

Please pay CAMRA Direct Debits from the account detailed on this Instruction subject to the safeguards assured by the Direct Debit Guarantee. I understand that this instruction may remain with CAMRA and, if so, will be passed electronically to my Bank/Building Society

Signature(s) _____

Date _____

Banks and Building Societies may not accept Direct Debit Instructions for some types of account

---

This Guarantee should be detached and retained by the payer.

The Direct Debit Guarantee

- This Guarantee is offered by all Banks and Building Societies that take part in the Direct Debit Scheme. The efficiency and security of the Scheme is monitored and protected by your own Bank or Building Society.

- If the amounts to be paid or the payment dates change CAMRA will notify you 10 working days in advance of your account being debited or as otherwise agreed.

- If an error is made by CAMRA or your Bank or Building Society, you are guaranteed a full and immediate refund from your branch of the amount paid.

- You can cancel a Direct Debit at any time by writing to your Bank or Building Society. Please also send a copy of your letter to us.

detached and retained this section